American Protestantism and Social
Issues, 1919-1939

AMERICAN PROTESTANTISM

AND

SOCIAL ISSUES

1919-1939

By ROBERT MOATS MILLER

GREENWOOD PRESS, PUBLISHERS
WESTPORT, CONNECTICUT

Library of Congress Cataloging in Publication Data

Miller, Robert Moats.
   American Protestantism and social issues, 1919-1939.

   Reprint of the 1958 ed. published by University of
North Carolina Press, Chapel Hill.
   Bibliography: p.
   Includes index.
   1. Church and social problems--United States.
2. Protestant churches--United States. 3. United
States--Church history--20th century. I. Title.
[HN39.U6M49 1977]   261.8'3'0973   77-22031
ISBN 0-8371-9777-5

To

My Mother and Father

Introduction

THIS STUDY ATTEMPTS to sketch some of the social attitudes of American Protestantism during the decades of prosperity and depression, to note how the Protestant churches faced up to the most fundamental problems confronting American society between the First and Second World Wars.

"Social attitudes," however, is an extremely broad term and the boundaries of this investigation require closer definition. I am concerned mostly with the views of the churches on those basic, controversial issues that struck at the roots of society: civil liberties, labor, race relations, war, and the contending merits of capitalism, socialism, and communism.

This means, in the first place, that I have largely ignored dancing, card playing, tobacco, whiskey, immodest dress, and other questions to which the churches devoted considerable attention, partly because their attitudes are already known or could be surmised, and partly because these sins—if such they be—are essentially personal rather than social. Secondly, I have minimized also the views of the churches on subjects in which there is little room for conflicting opinion: prison reform, civic corruption, slum clearance, and juvenile delinquency. After all, who argues *against* clean jails, honest mayors, and tidy streets. Further, I have made no effort to assess the great work done by American Protestantism in relation to schools, hospitals, settlement houses, and missionary enterprises, important as I deem these activities to be. And lastly, problems of theology, doctrine, and organization are touched on only in so far as they shed light on the social attitudes of the churches.

This inquiry, then, does not pretend to contain the full story of American Protestantism during the twenties and thirties, but simply an appraisal of the churches' attitudes on certain ranking subjects.

If the term "social attitudes" almost defies precise definition, the same might be said of "American Protestantism." There are some 250 Protestant denominations and sects in America. Attention was limited to a few numerically powerful groups, but in some cases, such as the Unitarians, I have let influence rather than size be the determining factor. A systematic examination was made of only the following bodies: Northern Baptist Convention, Southern Baptist Convention, Methodist

Episcopal Church, Methodist Episcopal Church, South, Presbyterian Church in the United States of America (North), Presbyterian Church in the United States (South), Congregational, Congregational Christian, Protestant Episcopal, Disciples of Christ, Unitarian, United Lutheran Church in America, Evangelical Synod of North America, Reformed Church in the United States, and, after 1934, the united Evangelical and Reformed Church. From time to time other churches are mentioned, but only in a cursory fashion. In addition, an effort was made to probe the attitudes of a number of cooperative agencies, the greatest of these being, of course, the Federal Council of Churches.

It might be well to clarify a point here. In this study it is necessary to distinguish between the Universal Church, God created and divinely inspired, and the churches as human institutions finding their existence in finite society. Of necessity, our attention will be with the churches rather than the Church. The devout believe the Church to be more than a sociological grouping, a voluntary association of like-minded men and women. Rather, they know the Church is God's creation and subject only to His judgment. However, the churches—as distinct from the Church—must stand or fall in terms of their contributions to society, and as human institutions they are open to scrutiny and criticism by men.

Further, in speaking of the attitudes of the Protestant churches, it should be remembered that they are, as Frederic Stamm observed, only the lengthened shadows of their people. They are mostly democratically governed and reflect the views, wise or foolish, sane or curious, of their members—although the reflection may not be perfect. That is, evidence of a denomination's attitude might be reflected when an assembly passes a resolution or when a leading clergyman delivers a sermon or when a church editor writes an editorial or when a group of churchmen sign a petition or form an organization or when, in a few cases, a poll is taken. If there are enough resolutions, sermons, editorials, and petitions in agreement on a subject, then we can say that that is the denomination's attitude, even though the view of every member is not on record. In any event, pragmatically speaking we must make this assumption. An obvious example serves to illustrate this point. Although some—perhaps a great many—individual Methodists drink, it is nevertheless accurate to state that the Methodist Episcopal Church—as a church—is opposed to the use of intoxicants.

The following method was employed to ascertain the attitude of a denomination toward a particular social issue. To begin with, an examination was made of the literature already bearing upon the subject. This material might be in book, article, dissertation, or pamphlet form. It included general studies of American society, denominational histories, accounts of religion in the United States, articles in learned journals and in the popular press, and highly fugitive pamphlets. Additionally, unpublished studies were frequently employed. From time to time, the files of secular groups also proved helpful. For example, the American Civil Liberties Union files were essential to the chapters on civil liberties; the publications of the House Committee on Un-American Activities were helpful in determining the association of churchmen with organizations said to be Fascist or Communist dominated; the bulletins of the Sacco-Vanzetti Defense Committee were valuable for information regarding the churches in that *cause célèbre;* and the records of the Socialist party at Duke University shed some light on clerical criticism of capitalism. In short, an effort was made to first determine what was already known about the attitude of a church toward a particular social issue.

It was then necessary to examine the official minutes of the denomination's national meetings, variously termed assembly, conference, convention, synod, and the like. The frequency of these meetings ranged from annual to quadrennial. These official denominational records contain the reports and recommendations of denominational agencies to the national governing bodies, convention speeches, episcopal addresses, and official resolutions, sometimes those defeated as well as those passed.

Since these national meetings did not always faithfully mirror local sentiment, an attempt was made to probe the record at the state and local level. The two chief sources for evidence of this type were unpublished studies and the church press.

A study of the church press was vital. Some of these journals were the authorized spokesmen of a denomination; others were undenominational or privately owned. Whatever the status of a particular journal, on the whole this was an extremely important source. The religious press was consequential not only for editorial comments, but also for contributed articles, information concerning church activities in the news columns, book reviews, correspondence from subscribers, and special polls and symposiums which the papers themselves conducted. In a very real sense, what these publications left unsaid was often as important as what they said. For the purposes of this inquiry silence on a key social issue was as informative as a ringing editorial. An effort was made to examine journals published both north and south of the Mason-Dixon Line; and those of a liberal as well as of a conservative persuasion. In addition, a very large number of pamphlets published by church groups were perused.

Since a denomination is, after all, composed of individuals, it was necessary to probe the attitudes of leading churchmen. Their opinions were found in articles and sermons appearing in the church press, in

sermon collections, books written by the churchmen themselves, bi-
ographies, autobiographies, and polls. Only a handful of unpublished
papers of churchmen were examined. Future historians undoubtedly will
find this important source more readily available.

Further, churchmen of like mind frequently banded together in
societies or joined existing secular organizations. A special attempt was
made to examine the publications of these groups, and to cover all the
secondary works, published or unpublished, dealing with them.

Inasmuch as the Protestant churches are generally democratic institutions, the attitudes of a denomination's laymen could not be ignored.
The evidence here is not abundant. Polls were of some aid. Societies
of laymen, formed by liberals or conservatives, were straws in the wind.
Laymen were represented at most denominational conferences, and their
vote counted with that of their clerical brethren. The fact is, nevertheless,
the attitude of each individual Protestant layman is simply not on record.
About all the student of American Protestantism can do is to note the
gulf between pronouncement and practice, admonition and action, and
then make an intelligent guess as to how closely official utterances reflected lay sentiment.

This study rests upon the assumption, which I shall not pause to
defend, that the social attitudes of the Protestant churches are an important and integral part of modern American history. In recent years
scholars have come increasingly to this recognition. Excellent studies by
Aaron I. Abell and Henry F. May have traced the impact of urbanization
and industrialization on the churches in the years following the Civil
War. Charles H. Hopkins, Ralph H. Gabriel, Robert T. Handy,
Maurice C. Latta, James Dombrowski, and W. Adolph Visser 't Hooft
have contributed to our understanding of the rise of the Social Gospel.
The general works of William W. Sweet, Willard L. Sperry, Gaius G.
Atkins, Gerald C. Brauer, and Winfred E. Garrison, the specialized
investigations of Ray H. Abrams, Liston Pope, Walter W. Van Kirk,
Ralph L. Roy, and Norman F. Furniss, the monumental volumes of
Anson P. Stokes, and the incisive observations of Herbert W. Schneider,
Sidney E. Mead, Paul A. Carter, and Reinhold and H. Richard Niebuhr
all indicate a renewed interest in the story of religion in recent American
history, as do the studies of Charles C. Cole, Timothy L. Smith, and
John R. Bodo for the pre-Civil War period. The fact that many doctoral
candidates have labored in this vineyard reinforces this conclusion.

In these studies, however, the time period or emphasis or selection of
sources differs from the present investigation. I do not know of any
volume that examines in detailed and inclusive fashion the social attitudes
of Protestantism during the years from 1919 to 1939. Certainly most of

the familiar histories of modern America either slight or distort the role of the churches as social institutions.

A few additional observations may be in order by way of introduction. In the first place, I have endeavored to steer between what Harry Elmer Barnes has called the "sneer" approach and the "drool" approach, to present both the clear and the spotted actuality. Perhaps that "noble dream" has not been achieved. I can only say, however, that I retained few of the views on American Protestantism at the end of the research that I had held at the beginning.

Secondly, while I believe that a reasonable society must rest upon spiritual foundations, this inquiry is written from the point of view of a secular historian and not that of a theologian or churchman. I am aware of the severe limitations of such an approach.

But one must do what one can do. Brilliant interpretations, sweeping generalizations, provocative insights, burning evangelical pleas must come from pens more competent than mine. I beg theologians and churchmen to accept this essay for what it is, rather than for what they might wish it to be. It is simply an honest attempt to report the social records of several Protestant churches for a two decade period. Perhaps the evidence presented in these pages can serve as a jumping-off-point for the grand interpretations of more gifted and trained church historians. It is with humble trepidation that I trespass on an area of study already illuminated by scholars of the Faith.

The sources for a study of recent American Protestantism are abundant. Some indication of their nature is given in the bibliography. Yet so far reaching are the implications of this inquiry, so complex are the issues involved, and so voluminous is the source material, that it is impossible to present a definitive treatment within the limitations of a single volume. The fragmentary nature of this study is self-evident.

One last word concerning presentation. Limitations of space and some decent concern for readability necessitated drastic cutting. In the original draft the notes rivaled the text in length; notes were lopped from each succeeding draft until only a few now remain to support direct quotations. An unpublished version of this study of almost double the present length and containing references to approximately thirty-five hundred separate items in the notes is deposited in the Northwestern University Library.

An unconscionable number of debts were incurred in the preparation of this volume. I am grateful to those church officials who answered naïve queries, forwarded material, and permitted access to denominational files. Even deeper is my obligation to those exceedingly patient and helpful librarians in El Paso, Albuquerque, Chapel Hill, Durham,

Evanston, Chicago, Washington, New York, New Haven, Boston, Chester, and Philadelphia who cheerfully shared their written riches. To those librarians, too, of other institutions who permitted their volumes to make the trip to El Paso on loan, thanks. And it would be unseemly not to mention the librarians at Texas Western College, especially Mr. Baxter Polk and Mrs. Yvonne Greear, who with good humor arranged for the loan of many books. I would also like to acknowledge my indebtedness to the Ford Foundation for a grant under its program for assisting American university presses in the publication of works in the humanities and the social sciences.

Dr. Gray C. Boyce, Dr. Ray Allen Billington, Dr. Richard M. Brace, Dr. Franklin D. Scott, and Dr. George T. Romani, all of Northwestern University, gently introduced me to the not always gentle facts of history. Dean John L. Waller of Texas Western College and Dr. Fletcher M. Green of the University of North Carolina extended sympathy and encouragement. However, my deepest obligation is to Dr. Richard W. Leopold of Northwestern. Without him this study would not have been attempted, conducted, or completed. He has been—and I choose my words with care—a true mentor.

Carol Herter Miller served above and beyond the call of wifely duty. The dedication comes from the heart.

All errors of fact and interpretation and all barbarities of style are, unhappily, mine alone.

Contents

Introduction   vii

I. Setting the Stage   3

Part I

The Churches and the Social Order

II. The Churches Corpulent and Contented in the Twenties   17

III. A Dissenting Report of the Churches in the Twenties   31

IV. A Footnote to the Election of 1928   48

V. The Churches Move to the Left: I   63

VI. The Churches Move to the Left: II   88

VII. The Churches Move to the Left: III   100

VIII. The Conservatism of the Churches in the Thirties   113

Part II

The Churches and Civil Liberties

IX. The Churches and Lynching   131

X. Protestants and Patriots   137

XI. Parsons and Pedagogues   154

XII. The Churches and *Causes Célèbres*   169

XIII. Commissars, Clergymen, and Civil Liberties   184

Part III

The Churches and Labor

XIV. The Churches and Labor: Setting the Stage   203

XV. The Condition and Status of the Worker: I   220

XVI. The Condition and Status of the Worker: II   246

XVII. Post-War Strikes   255

XVIII. Prosperity Decade Strikes   262

XIX. Depression Decade Strikes   274

PART IV

THE CHURCHES AND RACE RELATIONS

XX. The Churches and Race Relations   291

PART V

THE CHURCHES AND WAR AND PEACE

XXI. War and Peace in a Peaceful Decade   317

XXII. War and Peace in a Warring Decade   333

XXIII. Conclusion   345

Bibliography   351

Index   371

American Protestantism and Social
Issues, 1919-1939

CHAPTER I

Setting the Stage

"What's past is prologue."—Shakespeare

I

THE STORY OF Protestantism in America is not a tale of pure souls seeking perfection in cloistered solitude; rather it concerns fallible men and women battling with the World, the Flesh, and the Devil in an environment the realities of which were all too pressing. If, as critics of America insist, saints have been strangers to the land, it is partially because Americans have been too occupied in this daily struggle to contemplate in monastic solitude the dazzling mystery of God.

This refusal to withdraw from the world stems in part from Protestantism's high regard for the active life in the service of God as preached by Calvin and Luther. In so refusing, furthermore, American Protestants made a virtue of necessity, for survival in the New World wilderness, as every pioneer from Jamestown to Willamette Valley recognized, depended on conquering Nature in continuous combat.

Because American Protestants accepted the duty—nay, the necessity—of living in the world, it does not follow that they were bound to accept the world as they found it. John Winthrop dreamed of a Wilderness Zion and Walter Rauschenbusch hoped for the earthly establishment of the Kingdom of God in history, and both the seventeenth century Puritan and the twentieth century Baptist fought the good fight in this world and (as they saw it) for the world.

If the theocratic blueprint of the one and the socialistic plan of the other were sketched this side of heaven; if colonial Massachusetts and modern America fell dismally short of divine standards; if, in short, every attempt to perfect society broke on the rocks of human pride, ignorance, and greed, it was not because Protestant churchmen were indifferent to the fate of society. The pews of American churches, as again critics rightly insist, are filled with bald-headed sinners. But in fairness to the churches it should be said (as indeed Henry Ward Beecher did say it) that the hair of these sinners had been thinned by the friction of countless sermons that had been aimed at them and then glanced off to hit the man in the pew behind. This would indicate a low sermon velocity and such was often the case. Not even the warmest friend of American Protestantism would deny that all too often clerical criticisms of sin and society have been poorly aimed, timidly delivered, and tepidly conceived. And yet, as the old village reprobate remarked, it was a mighty poor sermon that did not hit him somewhere.

It is not necessary to take the reprobate's word for it. Fifty years after the Revolution, Alexis de Tocqueville noted the great strength of the American churches. How paradoxical, he observed, that these churches, divided, splintered, shorn of state support, should exercise greater influence than the established churches of the Old World. If at the end of the colonial period churchmen reconciled themselves to disestablishment, never did they relinquish their right to speak on public issues nor did they divorce themselves from the main streams of American life.

And thus it is that historically the Protestant churches in America have been deeply concerned with the structure and functioning of society. They have been characterized by activism and participation rather than by quietism and withdrawal. In the New World the pulpit rather than the altar or monk's cell has been accorded the place of honor.

Although this inquiry is confined to only two decades of the social attitudes of American Protestantism, a sense of continuity might be gained by a very brief sketch of the position taken by the churches on public issues in earlier periods.

To begin with, the Protestant churches have not been aloof to the problem of war, and America's struggles all have knifed to the heart of these institutions which preached a gospel of peace on earth and good will toward men. It is doubtful that the Revolution, for instance, would have been successfully consummated without the support of the Protestant churches. The Congregational divines of New England, aflame with the "fierce spirit of liberty," as Burke noted, preached sermons on the evils of political tyranny, steeled the Northern colonies to the ultimate appeal to the sword, and after Lexington strengthened the American will to win. The Baptists also supported the Revolution, but it was the rugged Scotch-Irish Presbyterians who were fiercest in the contest. As John Adams observed, they were a "flame of fire." And a Western preacher opened a recruiting meeting with the prayer: "Lord God, if Thou art unwilling by divine grace to assist us, *do stand aside and let us fight it out!*"

It is true that pacifist groups such as the Quakers and Mennonites sought to follow their historic course, but many forsook their heritage to support the patriot cause. And Methodists ignored Wesley's admonitions to remain loyal to the Crown. Only the priests of the Anglican Church stood firm in the Loyalist faith, but even here deflections from England were not uncommon. One Anglican divine during the Revolution, momentarily forgetting the temper of the times, in the course of a Sunday service invoked a blessing on "our excellent King George." "O Lord," he quickly amended the prayer as the congregation stirred, "I mean George Washington!"

It is not necessary to pass judgment on either the "Loyal" Anglicans or the "patriotic" Presbyterians to make the point that American Protestantism was not indifferent to the American Revolution.

Protestant opinion was less unanimous regarding the War of 1812. New England clergymen such as Lyman Beecher and Timothy Dwight opposed "Mr. Madison's war" both as northerners and as Federalists. They objected aligning the United States with infidel France and, in any event, a successful conclusion to the war could only strengthen the hated Jeffersonians and serve as a catalyst to the rising West at the expense of the North East. On the other hand, frontier parsons, as frontier politicians, supported the struggle—Baptists, Methodists, and even such seaboard Presbyterians as the Reverend Alexander Macleod whose volume, *A Scriptural View of the Character, Causes and Ends of the Present War,* was the most significant writing from a cleric's pen to come out of the war. The great revivalist Charles G. Finney sought unsuccessfully to enlist in the navy and that Paul Bunyan of circuit riders, Peter Cartwright, served as a chaplain under Jackson and climaxed his military career by taking part in the battle of New Orleans. A Baptist preacher, David Jones, a seventy-six year old veteran of the Revolution, offered his services to the army and held that critics of the war—"confounded Tories"—should be hung. Lutheran opinion as reflected in the leader, Henry Augustus Muhlenberg, supported the administration, and Episcopal priests in the South, remembering the experiences of the Revolution, were less pro-British than the Congregational divines of New England.

Thus the attitudes of Protestant churchmen toward the War of 1812 were as inconclusive as the war itself. Most of the educated, conservative theocrats of the seaboard area and especially New England opposed the struggle as heartily as their Federalist constituents, while the western evangelists echoed the militant whoops of the "War Hawks."

Somewhat the same lines were drawn during the Mexican War, as Clayton S. Ellsworth has shown. The Congregationalists and Unitarians led by Horace Bushnell, Henry Ward Beecher, William Ellery Channing, and Theodore Parker, stubbornly refused to admit the justice of the conflict. Their sermons echoed the poems of Lowell, the writings of Emerson, and the deeds of Thoreau in believing—to quote Parker—"Americans were fighting Mexico to dismember her territory, to plunder her soil, and plant thereon the institution of slavery." Quakers shared this attitude, and Episcopalians, Lutherans, Dutch and German Reformed, and some Northern Presbyterians, Baptists, and Methodists were also critical of the war.

This critical attitude stemmed from several factors. The strongest opponents of the war, the Congregationalists and Unitarians, were concentrated in the North East and were geographically remote from the area of conflict. Further, these northern clergymen believed the war would benefit only the southern states and this in turn would mean an extension of slavery. They agreed with Lowell when he wrote

> But *my* narves it kind of o' grates
> Wen I see the overreachin'
> O' them nigger-drivin' States. . . .

Pacifists augmented the ranks of the opposition. In the decades before the Mexican War there had developed a powerful peace movement led by William Ladd and Elihu Burritt; and by 1846 there was a strong current of pacifism in American Protestantism—a current not confined simply to the smaller sects such as the Friends. Obviously pacifist churchmen could not support the war and President Polk failed to convince the near-pacifists that Mexico was the aggressor and that the United States was fighting a justified war of defense.

Although opposition to the war was strong and vocal and embraced many leading divines, it was pretty much confined to the North East; whereas sentiment in most of the South and the Old Northwest and everywhere along the frontier favored the struggle. Thus majority opinion among Methodists, Baptists, and possibly Presbyterians was pro-war; certainly this is true of the southern wings of these denominations.

In the first place, the war was popular in the geographic regions where these churches were strongest, and once again it is apparent that the clergy reflected lay sentiment. In fierce competition for men's souls, it would have taken a rare courage for a church to denounce a popular war. Secondly, did not Protestants have a divine mandate to rescue the benighted Mexican masses from the oppression of the Roman Church? Thirdly, the Mexican War was simply an incident in the westward expansion of the frontier. Was it not America's manifest destiny to extend the blessings of liberty and Protestantism to the far Pacific? Protestant churchmen had known since the days of Bradford and Winthrop that God had a special purpose for His people in America; that the unfolding of history in the New World was a chapter in the gradual realization of His will; that, indeed, the consummation of the American Dream was indivisible from the fulfillment of the Kingdom of God. Hence, the Mexican War was wholly acceptable as a stage in the progress of the world's last, best hope—America!

The tragic impact of the Civil War upon American Protestantism is known to all. Brothers in opposing entrenchments prayed to the same God to sustain their arms. Denominational chaplains ministered alike to the boys in blue and the boys in gray. Church assemblies in the North and in the South assured their respective leaders in Washington and Richmond of their loyalty and steadfastness. Indeed, ministers and bishops forsook their normal peacetime callings to fight and die on the field of battle. National denominational ties were weakened and, in the case of Methodists, Baptists, and Presbyterians, rendered asunder.

It is inconceivable that northern morale could have remained firm for four long years if the northern churches had not remained unshaken in their devotion to the Union and in their opposition to slavery. Lincoln's strength rested to no small degree on the loyalty of the churches. Even as this was so, the churches in the South gave sustaining courage to the Confederate cause, and everywhere below the Mason-Dixon line prayers were raised to deliver the South from Yankee conquest.

Thus the Protestant churches divided along sectional lines and the bitterness engendered by the Civil War is yet to be erased. And yet, the churches were not merely innocent bystanders in this tragic drama. In the decades preceding 1861 what they did and what they failed to do helped make an appeal to the sword inevitable. As Lincoln reminded all Americans in his Second Inaugural Address, "The judgments of the Lord are true and righteous altogether."

The Spanish-American War found American Protestantism virtually united in viewing the contest as a humanitarian crusade to free Cuba from Spanish oppression and from "that system of iniquity, the papacy." Indeed, as Julius W. Pratt has demonstrated, Protestant churchmen were as eager for war as any group in the country—and far more ardent than those Mammon worshippers, the businessmen! Nor were the Protestant churches reluctant to accept the fruits of the crusade: Puerto Rico, the Philippines, Guam, and, incidentally, Hawaii and Samoa. What a splendid missionary challenge these islands presented! What a golden field for Protestant evangelization! The fact that the Roman Catholic Church already had preempted the souls of many of "our little brown brothers" simply underscored the challenge. Hence the Protestant churches, with the exception of a few groups such as the Quakers and the Unitarians, spoke early and late in justification of the Spanish-American War.

Nineteen years later the United States entered the First World War and once again Protestant churchmen presented arms with the rest of the nation. As Ray Abrams has demonstrated, only a handful of pacifist clergymen challenged the justice of the war. They paid a high price for their convictions, often facing the loss of pulpit, prestige, and rank. Perhaps it was inevitable that the churches should accept the necessity of the struggle once war had been declared. But it is difficult to condone the complete identification of the American cause with the will of God made by so many ministers. Nor is it easy to justify the really venomous preachments of hate toward the "Hun" that spewed from Protestant pulpits.

It is clear that historically American Protestantism has been concerned with the issue of war. The churches refused to leave undisturbed the field of battle to Mars. Assuming the pacifist position is untenable even from the viewpoint of an absolute Christian ethic, it is nevertheless fair to say that in their attitudes toward war, the Protestant churches have reflected too faithfully their environment. Their critique of America's battles has been bounded by class and sectional lines and not by a transcendent loyalty to a supra-historical Church in the world but not of the world.

The ambivalent attitude displayed by the churches toward slavery further illustrates how deeply they have been enmeshed in the milieu of society. In the South clerical criticism of slavery was not unknown, especially in the earlier years. Clement Eaton believes that the southern ministry contributed a larger proportion of outspoken critics of slavery than any other professional group. In the opening years of the nineteenth century churchmen agreed with Jefferson that slavery was an evil which must be terminated. Clerical opinion in the South gave strong endorsement to the American Colonization Society which dreamed of colonizing freed Negroes in Liberia.

But this dream broke on the rocks of economics and, in any event, was based on the unchristian premise that blacks were unfit to live in freedom in the South. The harsh truth is that at no time were the churches strong enough to end slavery in a single southern colony or state. By 1830 they had ceased, for all real purposes, even to make the effort. And by 1860 ministers were performing yeoman service in the sanctification of human bondage. They prostituted their scholarly training to justify slavery on Biblical, historical, and biological grounds. In a very real sense, it was not the Civil War itself but the slavery issue which strained national denominational ties and severed those of the Baptists, Methodists, and Presbyterians. Accommodation to the mores of southern civilization dulled the Christian conscience. Sincere, devout, conscientious, and even charitable churchmen saw no peculiarity in their defense of the South's "peculiar institution." It may be observed without malice that this was an unconscionable rendering of things unto Caesar. To be sure, the Civil War generation inherited a problem not of its own making and, as so often in history, the sins of the fathers were passed on to the sons. True, the profits of the slave trade had fattened the purse of many a Puritan merchant. True, how to peacefully abolish slavery taxed the wisest minds and no man, North or South, knew the perfect answer. But who can deny that in their failure to peacefully end slavery the churches in the South failed in their witness, left their mission unfulfilled, and stumbled as messengers of God's redeeming mercy to the world.

Nor was the record of the northern churches unblemished. In the colonial period a few ministers, including the redoubtable Cotton Mather and the Congregational divines Samuel Hopkins and Ezra Stiles, spoke out, but the most eloquent antislavery voices were those of the despised Quakers, John Woolman and Anthony Benezet. John R. Bodo has shown that the educated, respected theocrats of the early national period—the pillars of the clerical profession—supported colonization schemes, but that they took a dim view of abolitionism. Both Lyman Beecher and Henry Ward Beecher tip-toed into the chilling controversy, and Francis Wayland spoke with considerable restraint until after 1842. William Lloyd Garrison's bitterness toward the churches is well known and he poured his wrath upon slaveholders and timid ministers with a fine impartiality. Little wonder since he found the doors of respected Boston churches closed to him while proud pulpits rang with denunciations of his work. To be sure, shortly after the Revolution many of the major denominations spoke vigorously on the slavery question, but as the nineteenth century deepened they soft-pedalled the issue in order to mollify southern members.

But the issue would not down and, on the whole, Garrison's strictures against the churches were unfair. It is impossible to conceive of the antislavery movement minus the religious element. The crusade drew its inspiration from the Christian ethic, its major leaders from the clergy, its rank and file members from Christian laymen, and its greatest organized support from the churches. It was, in short, a religious movement breathing the spirit of Jesus and wielding the muscle of organized Christianity. Subtract the martyred Lovejoy, the eloquent Channing, the fiery Parker, the saintly Weld, and the countless Christian men and women—the Tappans and the Gerrit Smiths and the Grimké sisters—subtract these figures from the antislavery crusade and little remains save the sound and fury of Garrison who, indeed, was closer to the Old Testament prophets than he himself realized.

The abolition of slavery—how terrible the cost!—did not end the race problem. If the years between Jamestown and Fort Sumter saw an element of American Protestantism slowly challenge the entrenched institution of slavery, the years between Appomattox and Versailles saw the churches almost completely mired on the muddy and rut-pocked road to racial equality. Hopkins, May, and the other historians of the rise of social Christianity devote isolated sentences, not chapters or books, to Protestantism's fight for racial justice. The story does not deserve much fuller treatment. Assuredly, the churches contributed alms to the freedmen in the South. They established schools, hospitals, and charitable institutions to succor the untrained blacks. But few were the clerical voices to challenge the racial status quo or to question the divine right superiority of the white man. As C. Vann Woodward has observed, the quest for social justice in the early twentieth century, championed so heartily by the churches, did not embrace justice for the Negro. It is one of the ironies of American history that the Progressive Era witnessed a retrogression in the area of race relations. Even as the churches advanced the Social Gospel, the lines of segregation within the denominations hardened.

Thus, the Protestant churches in America have reflected in the race question, as in the case of war, the environment in which they were nurtured. About the best that can be said—and it is not inconsiderable— is that the forces of organized Christianity wrote a period to the most monstrous evil in nineteenth century America, slavery.

Slavery and war were two important public issues confronting the churches. There were others. Examine, for instance, the antidueling campaign and the Sabbatarian movement. Sophisticated commentators have termed these causes "curious," "mossy," and "periphial." Perhaps they were. But it is salutary to remember that dueling was as baneful an evil in the early nineteenth century as lynching was in the early twentieth century, and the extinguishment of the one was as important as the banning of the other in the growth of a Christian nation. The fact that there were no lynchings in 1954 does not minimize the enormity of the 130 lynchings in 1901, anymore than the absence of dueling in 1904 softens the murder of Hamilton in 1804. In their day they were terrible abuses and in combating them the churches made a positive contribution to a more just society. As for Sabbatarianism, it was more than an effort of blue-nosed, hatchet-faced parsons to make the Lord's day dull. After all, the setting aside of one day in seven for rest and worship was a beneficent step in the history of man and beast. One wonders if American steelworkers sweating before the furnaces seven days a week as late as 1923 would have shared the historians' nonchalance concerning the sinfulness of Sunday labor.

Many other public issues in the nineteenth century passed under the judgment of the churches: prostitution, cruel and unusual prison conditions, the "snake pits" that served as asylums, convict labor, slums, child labor, the second class citizenship of women, inadequate schools, civic corruption, plutocracy, and the sweating of labor.

In the ante bellum period there existed a "benevolent empire" of leading laymen and ministers which leveled a bead on many of the ills of society. And these churchmen, as Timothy L. Smith showed, embraced orthodox revivalists in the more evangelical denominations, as well as the adherents of "enlightened" and "liberal" theology. The chief reform movements of the period were united by a series of interlocking directorates and almost without exception the leaders of one reform were in the forefront of the others. Assuredly, the contributions to these reforms made by such secular champions as Tom Paine, Robert Dale Owen, and Francis Wright were important, but without the support of the churches "Freedom's Ferment" in the "Age of the Common Man" would have been a flat thing. The impetus given by organized Christianity to the attack upon social evil in America is beyond calculation. Remove the example of Christ and the devotion of Christian ministers and laymen from the history of reform in America and progress would need be measured in inches not miles.

This is not to say that the churches realistically assessed the priority to be given the various reforms. Nor is it to say that the churches were incapable of working both sides of the street.

As the Puritan divines banished Roger Williams from Boston, so the clergy of Federalist New England denied Jefferson any hope of a heavenly haven. And if good Massachusetts spinsters, alarmed by the warnings of their ministers, quaked in their lonely beds at the thought of Jefferson's election, just so did Whig theocrats quail at the prospects of Jacksonian Democracy. Lyman Beecher consoled the businessmen of Boston that all was not lost with Jackson's election, and his son, Henry Ward, counciled the workingmen of Brooklyn in Cleveland's day (such are the mysteries of evolution) to live on bread and water. In point of fact, a rather effective case could be made for the conservatism of the churches on economic issues throughout much of the history of the United States.

Frequently in the colonial period they championed conservative, seaboard vested interests against leveling movements arising among disenfranchised urban mechanics and Western farmers. Surely the New England divines served Hamilton and his rich and well-born Federalists above and beyond the call of duty. The workingmen's associations of the Jackson era called forth much clerical criticism, and embattled Whigs found loyal allies in the pulpit as they expounded divine right property views. After the Civil War churchmen continued to denounce the legitimate protests of labor, and if the agrarian uprising of the nineties took on the aspects of a religious crusade, there were an unconscionable number of men of God in the infidel ranks of Mark Hanna and McKinley.

Further, the rich were comforted to know that they had been elected by the Almighty to manage His wealth. This doctrine of stewardship gave great encouragement to worthy charitable and philanthropic enterprises. It also gave divine sanction to a grossly inequitable distribution of the nation's wealth. The poor were admonished to accept meekly the lowly station in life Providence had assigned to them. But no matter. There would be sweet rewards in heaven and on the near side of eternity their interests would be protected and cared for, as George Baer opined, "not by the labor agitators, but by the Christian men to whom God in his infinite wisdom has given the control of the property interests of the country."

But it would be unfair to conclude this introduction on this gloomy note. As has been observed, the churches have not been indifferent to the public issues facing the American nation. Every good cause in American history has drawn its inspiration from the Christian ethic and has received backing from at least an element in the churches. Much has been made of the orgiastic nature of Protestant revivalism, but as W. W. Sweet and Charles Johnson demonstrated, the churches were the moral courts of the frontier and saved the West from barbarism. It was the churches—and often the churches alone—that stood for decency, justice, and enlightenment from Plymouth to Deadwood and from Kentucky to Texas.

As early American Protestantism faced the challenge of the New World wilderness, so later Protestantism faced the challenge of urbanization and industrialization. Hopkins, May, and Abell have shown how unprepared the churches were to meet this new crisis. By the Gilded Age they were generally middle class in composition, self-satisfied in their respectable standing, secure in their embodiment of the American Way of Life, and geared by their theology and frontier training to an individualistic piety.

However, after much stumbling they responded creditably to the challenge of modern, urbanized, industrial America. They rediscovered a social ethic capable of reckoning with the social sins of slums, sweatshops, plutocracy, and unfettered captialism's iron laws. The Social Gospel—as this response came to be called—sought to regain the fellowship of the urban masses through such institutionalized agencies as settlement houses and "Y's." It appealed to the working classes by championing reform legislation, endorsing unions, and supporting strikes, although often there was an air of *noblesse oblige* in these efforts. It exposed the plight of American's disinherited—tenement dwellers, sweated children, blackened miners, night-working women, sharecroppers, and migratory laborers. Above all, perhaps, it questioned the basic premises of laissez-faire capitalism, and a number of Social Gospel prophets believed only the Socialist road led to the Kingdom of God.

Whatever the road, the establishment of the Kingdom of God in history was a cardinal element in the Social Gospel dream. The Kingdom would come not by shattering intervention from beyond, but in evolutionary stages through an immanent God working in cooperation with "enlightened" men who followed in the steps of an historical Jesus.

This hopeful belief, drawing upon Horace Bushnell's *Christian Nurture* (1846) and Walter Rauschenbusch's *A Theology for the Social Gospel* (1917), was exploded by a searing depression bracketed by two world wars and the shadow of nuclear destruction. By mid-century many Protestant churchmen found the old social Christianity shallow, optimistic, feeble, and inadequate. As these modern realists rejected the liberal theology, so they questioned the worth and contributions of the Social Gospel movement itself.

But as this inquiry will attempt to demonstrate, it was a rich and useful legacy that was bequeathed to the Protestant churches of 1919—the year in which this study begins. Herron, Gladden, Bliss, Strong, Rauschenbusch and the other great leaders of early twentieth century social Christianity had sought answers, in their day and in their way, to the fundamental problems facing American society. They perpetuated a great and historic tradition of American Protestantism in believing in a "religion that rises every morning and works all day." In the following pages we shall see how Parker's dictum fared in the two decades, 1919-39.

Part I

The Churches and the Social Order

CHAPTER II

The Churches Corpulent and Contented in the Twenties

"And the wind shall say: Here were decent godless people:
Their only monument the asphalt road
And a thousand lost golf balls."—T. S. Eliot

I

THE DECADE FOLLOWING the First World War has been termed the "Roaring Twenties," the "Golden Twenties," the "Era of Wonderful Nonsense," the "Jazz Age," the "Flapper Age," and the "Aspirin Age." None of these appellations is entirely accurate for the period is exceedingly complicated, baffling, and paradoxical; and the historian attempting to interpret the twenties must come to his reader, like St. Denis, with his head in his hands.

Curiously, however, most commentators have agreed on a single, simple interpretation concerning the role of the churches in this decade. They have painted a picture free of subtleties and nuances. It might be said that these commentators concur that for American Protestantism the twenties were the "Age of the Babbittonian Captivity."

The usual interpretation goes something like this. The businessman was master of America and the churches, like the eunuchs of old, adorned, without seriously disturbing their master's establishment. The churches rendered unto George F. Babbitt the things that were Babbitt's, leaving precious little for the Lord. But then, according to the gospel of Barton and Babson, the Lord was a sort of glorified Rotarian anyhow. "Come weal, come woe, my status is quo" came perilously near to being written into the Apostle's Creed. Pep replaced prayer; *savoir faire* became a substitute for faith. Perhaps the churches still admonished men not to lay up treasures for heaven, but a man was considered well on the way there if he laid up a Stutz Bearcat or two in his garage. To speak less obliquely, after the First World War the churches lost their questing spirit and crusading zeal, equated the United States with the Promised Land, embraced the materialistic standards and high pressure techniques of the business community, and sunk into contented corpulency.

Now, this interpretation, prevalent though it may be, is a gross distortion of the facts. It simply does not jibe with the evidence—as this study will try to show. Unhappily, however, there is some truth in the proposition that the churches partially succumbed to the materialism of the twenties, and it is to this baneful story that the discussion now turns.

II

How can this partial deadening of social Christianity during the Prosperity Decade be explained? To begin with, it was dead among large elements of American Protestantism for the sufficient reason that it had never existed among these elements in the first place. Millions of good Christians felt the churches should concern themselves merely with prayer, hymn singing, and the preparation of individual souls for the Day of Judgment. Ministers should "stick to the gospel" and preach that "old-time religion," finding sufficient reason for their existence in getting souls into heaven rather than attempting to establish heaven here on earth. The regeneration of individuals and not the reformation of the social order was the proper function of the churches. Parsons were warned to preach only "Christ—and Him crucified." What tired and careworn men and women wanted was the promise of life everlasting and not a disquisition on the Promise of American Life. The opponents of social Christianity were not entirely confined to the more fundamentalist denominations, but there does seem to be a definite correlation in this decade between theological and economic and political conservatism; hence the courtship of the capitalist and the premillenarian was an affair of the purse as well as of the heart.

A second factor contributing to the churches' indifference to the sins of society was their prodigious interest in the sins of the individual—and the "Lost Generation" of the twenties seemed to furnish multitudinous examples in the latter category. Much of the moral indignation of the churches was expended on personal sins to the neglect of any searching analysis of the social order. They displayed a wonderful and fearful concern with whiskey, dancing, cigarettes, rising skirts and plunging necklines, "fallen" women, wife beating, Sunday baseball, lurid movies, joy riding, euchre, and Judge Ben Lindsey. A detailed examination of these matters is outside the scope of this study, but that they occupied the attention of the churches is beyond cavil.[1]

To cite a very few examples, the prohibition experiment elicited more comment in pulpit, press, and assembly than almost any other single

---

1. The editors of the *Herald and Presbyter* named the following as the most outcrying and menacing evils of the day: desecration of the Sabbath, liquor, polygamy, white slavery, gambling, child labor, dishonesty, and avarice. It is with great difficulty that one resists the temptation to discuss at length the churches' attitude toward these sins; it would be far and away the most sprightly chapter in the study. It seems unnecessary to footnote many of these items.

issue. With only a few exceptions, official American Protestantism was as dry as a powder flask. The conclusion is inescapable that many clergymen fervently believed that upon "earth's grateful sod would rest the city of our God" if only grape juice supplanted gin everywhere.

Newfangled dances were attacked with a fervor as intensive if not quite as extensive: the bunny hug, turkey-trot, hesitation, tango, texas tommy, hug-me-tight, fox-trot, shimmy-dance, sea-gull swoop, camel-walk, and skunk-waltz, as one minister listed their names. The hopes of the Dancing Masters' Association of America of winning Methodist approval for the Terpsichorean art by introducing a decorous step entitled the Wesleyan Waltz proved sanguine; Methodists were not to be duped into giving their approval even by such a flattering title. According to the Association, the partners were to follow a list of ten "don'ts." The *Nashville Christian Advocate* added one more: "Don't dance." Nor were ministers fooled by a troupe of light-footed "artists" who disguised (if such is the word) their gyrations under the claim that they were merely emulating the ancient Greeks. As the *Arkansas Methodist* opined: "No decent Greeks ever performed in *that* way." The advocates of dancing really did not have a chance, for as one church leader stated: 'We hate the dance with all the hatred possible. We detest it. We loath it. We abhor it as of the devil." In all conscience, many of the clerical descriptions of the "modern dance" were so detailed, so intimate, so lascivious, as to warrant their being banned in Boston. If, however, many of the descriptions of dancing were suspiciously sophisticated, some of the solutions for the "evil" were mildly naive, one minister arguing with impeccable logic: "If it were a law in our land that the sexes should dance alone—separately, the dance problem would be solved."

The increased use of profanity by the younger generation also shocked church leaders. The editor of a Kentucky Baptist paper expressed horror upon attending a football game between Harvard and Centre College and hearing "cultured, refined Christian women" being exposed to such cheers as "ROLL THEM IN THE SOD—YES, BY GOD" and "GIVE 'EM HELL."

Desecration of the Sabbath and irreverence for the Bible came in for much comment. One parson pictured the modern generation as singing:

> Holy Bible, flecked with spots,
> How I love thee, marred by blots;
> Word of God in thee I find,
> Each according to his mind.

The charges were rung on other sins. The General Assembly of the Presbyterian Church, U.S.A., for example, received a petition asking financial aid be withheld from all students for the ministry "who spend any portion of their income for tobacco." Hollywood was pictured as a cesspool of iniquity and movies were flayed for their immoral madness. A proposal to produce a film based upon *The Rubáiyát* of Omar Khayyám brought a cry of outrage, for there could "be no doubt that Omar was pro-alcohol."

The new styles in female clothing called forth comment that was considerably more fulsome than the styles themselves. It was charged that modern dresses, "cut with a 'C' in front and a 'V' behind," were so scanty that if the material cost five dollars a yard a woman would be fully clothed for forty-five cents. "We get our styles from New York, New York from Paris, and Paris from Hell," moaned one parson. Said another in regard to card playing: "Great guns! Think of women leaving their housework undone and their husbands to come home to a cold supper so that they might spend the day at the euchre club and bring home the booby prize." Youthful morals were another source of alarm. Great ministers such as S. Parkes Cadman, Congregational president of the Federal Council of Churches, warned girls: "As for promiscuous kissing, what decent girl wants to resemble a piece of rock salt licked by all kinds and conditions of passing cattle?"

Much of this clerical concern with personal morality was justified. The "Lost Generation's" vaunted revolt against the old standards was often puerile. The churches would have been remiss in their duty if they had not been alarmed by the growing number of bad-mannered, Freud-quoting, hipflask-toting, blasé men and women in the country. Still and all, in some cases their attention was so completely focused on these personal sins as to blind them to maladjustments in the social order. And there is at least some indication that the churches compounded for sins that they were inclined to by damning those they had no mind to.

Still a third reason for the decline of social Christianity in the twenties was the fact that the energies of the churches were sapped by the fundamentalist-modernist controversy. Churchmen devoted a prodigious amount of time and thought to this theological crisis. The criticism here is not that ministers concerned themselves with theology. In point of fact, the fundamental weakness of early twentieth century social Christianity was its neglect of theology, for the problem of faith is prior to the problem of action, and ultimately patterns of reform depend on ethical premises which in turn rest upon the bed-rock of theological beliefs. The criticism is, rather, that neither the modernists nor the fundamentalists evolved an enduring theology. Thus the controversy was a sterile thing and when the smoke cleared it was difficult to see where any positive gains had been made. It is significant that the highly important neo-orthodox theology of the thirties owed little to the fundamentalist arguments; nor did it claim a kinship with modernism. It should be said, however, that the modernists fought a battle against obscurantism that had to be fought, and to this extent deserve high praise. In any case, many a good cause was temporarily set adrift while churchmen concentrated on the prior questions of theology.

Fourthly, a growing number of once ardent advocates of social Christianity wearied of the reform fervor and grew increasingly suspicious of all this "do-goodism" and uplift. Clerical as well as some secular progressives emerged from the First World War disillusioned, cynical, and tired. Episcopal Bishop Charles Fiske confessed that he had been running so hard in the reform race his breath was gone. These puzzled and penitent parsons termed themselves social reformers who at last were undertaking the task of reforming themselves. They were sick to death of open forums, resolutions endorsing birth control or denouncing white slavery, "Y" work, welfare study groups, uplift gatherings, meddling commissions, money raising drives to build basketball courts, paid secretaries and assistant secretaries teaching kiddies to basket weave—in short, all those activities that had turned Protestantism into the "Great Society of the Outstretched Hand" and ministers into glorified social workers. And this sentiment was shared by restless parishioners. They complained that they needed guidance in their spiritual life and yet heard nothing from the pulpit but lectures on the industrial situation, prohibition, and international peace.

Then there were those churchmen who carried on the conservative social traditions of American Protestantism that harked back to the clerical defenders of McKinley, Webster, and Hamilton. Their influence may have waned during the Progressive Era, but even in the years immediately preceding 1919—in the period when the Social Gospel came of age— conservative clergymen had remained powerful. As in the case of secular conservatives, they re-grouped their ranks in the twenties and launched a counter-offensive against the social prophets.

All of these explanations for the decline of the reform fervor in American Protestantism during the twenties are subordinate to a more basic consideration: there seemed precious little in American society that required reformation. Most citizens felt they had solved the central problems of their civilization. The United States was the Promised Land of Prosperity. God had rewarded an industrious and righteous people with riches. And who (aside from the Almighty, of course) was responsible for this millennium of radios, refrigerators, and indoor plumbing? The businessman, naturally, with his efficiency, his practicality, his promotional techniques, his mastery of mass production, and, withal, his keen sense of social service.

III

The uncritical attitude of the churches toward the business community is perhaps best illustrated by the fact that the churches paid the businessman the high compliment of emulating his techniques and jargon. It was reported that a typical prayer of the twenties went something like this: "Dear Lord, we thank thee for all thy favors of recent date. Permit us to express our heartfelt gratitude. We trust that we may continue to merit your confidence, and that we shall receive more blessings from you in the future. Amen." Perhaps this prayer is apocryphal, but there are numerous authenticated instances bearing on the same point. Huckstering became an acceptable mode of getting men into heaven—or at least into the churches which would point men in a celestial direction. Ministers were admonished with the advice: "Early to bed and early to rise/ Preach the gospel and advertise."

"SELLING RELIGION—That is the only business of the Church," proclaimed Dr. Lewis S. Mudge, Stated Clerk of the Presbyterian Church, U.S.A. He then went on to say that every minister was a salesman of religion and listed five tips on how they might best vend their goods.[2] "The old idea that a minister is above stooping to commercial devices," opined another clergymen, "must disappear if the church is to grow." After all, he continued, "Ministers are salesmen with a wonderfully fine 'line' to sell to their congregations—the hopes and the blessedness of a spiritual and moral life."[3]

During the twenties theological seminaries introduced courses in church advertising. A dozen books were written on the subject. Many of the denominations established departments of publicity which adopted the most up-to-date advertising methods. One of these publicity directors proudly reported to the Northern Presbyterian General Assembly that telegraph editors of the daily newspapers were amazed at the news of Presbyterian activity humming over the wires. A convention of advertising clubs meeting in Atlantic City deemed it wise to devote a session to church advertising, the Reverend John Myskens informing the delegates that they must advertise by printer's ink and brightly illuminated signs to change the lamentable cry of "S.O.S." to "S.R.O."—standing room only. A similar convention in Philadelphia listened to a keynote address by S. Parkes Cadman, distinguished Congregationalist. Each night of the session a cabaret entertainment, including bathing beauties, was furnished the delegates, but as Frederick Lewis Allen observed, it was

2. *New Era Magazine*, Sept., 1921, p. 520.
3. *Zion's Herald*, April 11, 1923, pp. 469-70.

merely a sign that even men of high faith must have their fun. And that these advertising executives were men of high faith could not be denied. Dr. Christian F. Reisner, noted New York Methodist, informed the students of Boston University School of Theology that in associating with advertising people they would be working with "high-minded, clean-cut men, who have as their motto 'Truth.'" He further observed that many "newspapers absolutely refused 'copy' from firms that exaggerate or do not tell the exact truth."[4]

This determination of the churches to spread the gospel need not in itself indicate a growing materialism. Indeed, as institutions dedicated to the glory of Christ they could do no other. What one does find distasteful are the cheap and often vulgar appeals—sermon titles such as "The Irishmen of the Old Testament," "Christ: From Manger to Throne," "Whose Birthday Is Christmas?" and "Two In a Bed." These titles compare favorably (if this be the word) with such church promotion slogans as "Be a Sport—Come to Church," "Public Worship Increases Your Efficiency," "Business Success and Religion Go Together," and "They Come for Miles To Get It Straight."[5]

Catchy sermon titles and peppy slogans were matched by other "surefire" promotion techniques. The Reverend John T. Bailey, Methodist pastor of Georgetown, Delaware, employed pretty girls to act as ushers and take up the collection. A New York minister staged a service in which six flimsily clad young ladies, bare of foot, executed a religious dance in honor of the Virgin Mary. The best that can be said for these gimmicks is that they probably seemed somewhat more enticing to reluctant churchgoers than offers of chewing gum and hats, both examples on record. Declaimed a Denver parson: "We are giving away a $50 lid, a spiffy affair, in first-class shape, and some lady who comes to church will go away happy, a new hat on her head, and peace and thanksgiving bubbling in her heart." Undismayed by this sort of competition, another pastor sent a steam calliope down the street announcing the merits of his wares. The Reverend Duane B. Aldrich of Malden, Massachusetts, mined money from his parishioners by instructing his ushers to blow a whistle every time a dollar bill was dropped in the collection plate. His temple reverberated with 105 toots on that particular Sabbath. Then there was the minister who announced that he was going to play indoor baseball for the Lord and asked his congregation to join in the game. The rules

4. *Ibid.*, Feb. 21, 1923, p. 236.
5. The following sermon titles and slogans may not be authentic, but they are indicative: "Thanks for the Buggy Ride," "Eventually, Why Not Now?" "Three In One Oil," "His Master's Voice," "Ask Dad, He Knows," "The Flavor Lasts," "What the Devil Wants," "I'd Walk a Mile for a Sermon," "Four Out of Five Go to Hell," "A Sermon a Day Keeps the Devil Away," and "For that Sinful Feeling Go to the Corner Church."

were rather complicated. Suffice it to say that a quarter in the collection plate stood for a single, a half-dollar a two-bagger, and so forth.

Truly, the numerous money raising schemes of the twenties can only be described as diabolically clever. "Go, Grace Church, Go!" chanted the creamed chicken eaters at an Oak Park, Illinois, church promotional dinner. "Invest in Grace, with Interest," "Over the Top, the Tower," and "Prayer, Pep, and the Pocket-Book" were other edifying slogans used in this particular campaign.

If in the twenties more Americans were church members than ever before, it was not because of any widespread fear that the unchurched would go to hell. Indeed, ministers who suggested as much stood a fair chance of being told to go there themselves. Rather, it was because church membership brought wonderfully large dividends in the form of health, wealth, and, if not wisdom, peace of mind. As Eddie Guest, America's folksy troubadour, put it: "Religion pays. Get this straight, Bud—crooks and highwaymen and gangsters and rioters, and all the lowest elements of mankind, are seldom or never religious. But Presidents, and statesmen, and great lawyers and great artists, and the leaders in all the trades and professions, usually are. . . . My mother was right when she taught me to believe in God. . . . It has actually paid me in dollars and cents."[6]

A Methodist minister compared a partnership with God to one with Henry Ford, although in fairness it should be added that the parson considered the former a slightly better "arrangement." Similar comparisons were made between the dividends declared by the United States Steel Corporation and the Lord, it being made clear that the stockholder in the Almighty's corporation always enjoyed good times. Unquestionably these ministers who placed God in the company of Henry Ford and Judge Elbert Gary were conferring upon Him their highest accolade.

Church attendance, argued a prominent New York clergyman, is more beneficial to frayed nerves than a Sunday game of golf. Church membership, it was repeatedly pointed out, enabled one to rub shoulders with the keenest businessmen in town; thus the alert go-getter made both heavenly and earthly contacts on the Sabbath morn. Put a church in town and all real estate values increase, observed Roger Babson, noted Congregational layman. Eliminate from any community the churches and property of all kinds would become practically worthless, adjured a business journal. When the promoters of a new town lay out their plots, boasted a Presbyterian paper, they often offer a choice corner lot to any church that will build upon it, because they know that that lot will enhance the value of

6. *American Magazine*, Oct., 1925, p. 9. It was reported that a typical prayer of the decade went something like this: "Unless you repent, in a measure, and are saved, so to speak, you are, I am sorry to say, in danger of hell-fire and damnation, to a certain extent."

every other piece of property in town. And this theme was played upon repeatedly: the churches everywhere stand for law, order, sobriety and property. Thus, stated innumerable churchmen, invest in religion—it pays! Proof of this contention, as it was fondly and frequently pointed out, lay in the fact that the giants of American industry and politics (including Harding's cabinet!) were virtually all God-fearing men of deep religious convictions. Or so, at any rate, interviews and questionnaires revealed.

To repeat, the aim of the churches to bring the "good news" of Christ to the unchurched was laudable; one's only criticism is of the vulgar and shoddy recruiting methods sometimes employed. It came to pass that quantity rather than quality often served as the standard of a successful church. The size of a congregation rather than its devoutness, was all important. Dr. Henry Sloane Coffin, distinguished Presbyterian president of Union Theological Seminary, put it succinctly when he declared that some ministers of the large churches had ceased to be shepherds and had become ranchers.

This passion for size embraced not only congregations, but also church edifices. The famous lines of Bishop McCabe are certainly applicable to the twenties: "A new church greets the morning's flame/ Another evening's ray/ All hail the power of Jesus' name/ We're building two a day." In the decade between 1916 and 1926 the value of church property more than doubled. In the year 1921 the amount spent for new church structures was 60 million dollars; in 1926 the amount expended for the same purpose was 284 million dollars. Some of these churches were huge skyscraper cathedrals costing millions of dollars.

John D. Rockefeller, Jr., explained his great contribution to the building of Harry Emerson Fosdick's Riverside Church by saying he did not want the business world to look down on the churches. This desire to glorify God's name with magnificent temples of worship is wholly laudable. They stand as visible symbols of an unseen faith. Notwithstanding, as many commentators pointed out, the construction of these costly churches served to enmesh Protestantism even more deeply in the milieu of the existing economic order. These great buildings were often built by contributions from wealthy businessmen. They were maintained by these same individuals. A pastor less fearless than the great Baptist leader Fosdick might easily have succumbed to the often unvoiced pressure that these commitments made inevitable.

But more than that, a multi-million dollar church was in fact, if not in theory, a multi-million dollar business. Some of these churches had plants costing over a million dollars, budgets as high as a quarter million, and possessed real estate valued at fifteen million. Like the modern university president, the metropolitan pastor often subordinated scholar-ship and saintliness to administrative details. The investment of funds, the meeting of monumental budgets, the payment of huge debts, the management of cafeterias and dormitories and gymnasiums and all the other appurtenances of a large urban church gave to such a church a tremendous stake in the prevailing economic order. Hence it is not sur-prising to find the church represented as the "greatest industry in the world today, as well as the oldest."[7]   And thus, also, it is not strange to find the heroes of the Bible, and even Christ himself, transformed in the image of a modern, successful, American businessman.

Bruce Barton's *The Man Nobody Knows* was for two years—1925 and 1926—the best-selling non-fiction book in the United States. In this obviously sincere and frequently skillful biography of Jesus, Mr. Barton sought to show the close resemblance between Christianity and business. Jesus, the reader is told, was a virile, aggressive, young executive who picked up twelve men from the bottom ranks and forged them into an organization that conquered the world. He was a champion salesman and the most popular dinner guest in Jerusalem. His parables were the most forceful advertisements of all time. It is difficult to escape the conclusion that Babbitt would have felt quite comfortable with Barton's Jesus. In the same vein, the Reverend Burris Jenkins, famed Kansas City Disciples pastor, averred that if Jesus were alive today he would be a great business tycoon. "Jesus," wrote the noted Dr. Frank Crane, "is the great Master Artist in the business of getting along."[8]   The New Biography's proudest triumph, however, appeared in a serial in a New Jersey paper. Its title: "Jesus As I Knew Him."

In like manner, the Metropolitan Casualty Insurance Company of New York issued a handsomely illustrated booklet entitled, "Moses, Persuader of Men," designed to inspire the company's agents to higher achievements. According to the author, "Moses was one of the greatest salesmen and real estate promoters that ever lived." He was a "Successful Personality in one of the most magnificent selling campaigns that history ever placed upon its pages."[9]

If Jesus and the Bible heroes were made over in the image of a typical American executive it was because the businessman enjoyed phenomenal prestige in the Prosperity Decade. And from pulpit, assembly, and press there poured a fulsome stream of praise for the leaders of American fi-nance and industry. Carnegie, Rockefeller, Gary, Mellon, and, above all,

---

7. Roger W. Babson, *Religion and Business* (New York, 1920), p. 5.
8. *Christian Century*, May 21, 1925, p. 658.
9. *Harper's Monthly*, Sept., 1927, p. 438.

Ford, were extolled as shining examples of Christian stewards who in amassing their millions served God and their fellow men.

This admiration for the businessman carried over to the largely business-dominated Presidencies of Harding and Coolidge. Warren Gamaliel Harding was a kindly, handsome, likeable good fellow who led the nation back to "normalcy" after his election in 1920. He brought to the White House all the qualifications for greatness save ability and character. During his incumbency Washington was disgraced by corruption. Even cabinet members, heeding the Biblical injunction, "Go, sell thy oil," were implicated in the scandals.

Clerical estimates of Harding as President were amazingly favorable. "We take a chastened pride," said the *Western Recorder,* "in the fact, that though Baptists have only furnished the country one President, they furnished, in that one a Warren G. Harding!"[10] It was a Disciples journal, not Rupert Hughes, who felt more inclined to liken Harding to Washington than to any of his other predecessors. A Presbyterian spokesman believed he was enthroned in the Pantheon of America's great men. "His life," opined a Methodist leader, "affords another illustrious instance of the possibilities of American manhood."[11] "He associated himself with political giants, but he was outshone by none of them," cried the *Baptist.*[12] Said the *Christian Herald*: "If any man had and preached ideals for the world, President Harding was that man."[13] The Reverend William J. Hampton, after undue emphasis on the fact that the funeral flowers cost one hundred thousand dollars, predicted: "How President Harding's gracious smile would be missed! How much he desired to help folks and not hurt them! What loyalty he had for the law! What faith in God, and how he exalted the Christ!"[14] History, believed the *Continent,* will number Harding with the "good succession of strong men who have made the Presidency of the United States the noblest seat of power in Christendom."[15] Few were the religious voices that did not share in a high estimation of Harding as President.

On the surface Calvin Coolidge contrasted greatly with his predecessor. Meager figured and sour visaged, taciturn and torpid, supremely upright in his private life and definitely conscientious in his public life, he was truly a "Puritan in Babylon." And yet Coolidge like Harding failed to give America aggressive Presidential leadership. Nevertheless, he won the affection of his country, perhaps because he contrasted so greatly

10. Aug. 9, 1923, p. 12.
11. *Arkansas Methodist,* Aug. 9, 1923, p. 1.
12. Aug. 11, 1923, p. 871.
13. Sept. 8, 1923, p. 694.
14. *Zion's Herald,* Dec. 3, 1924, p. 1551.
15. Aug. 9, 1923, p. 987.

with the Roaring Twenties. In any event, from pulpit and press there flowed considerable praise of Coolidge.

Although criticism of Harding and Coolidge was very rare, when Senator Robert M. La Follette threw his hat in the ring in 1924 and ran on the Progressive Party ticket, much church opinion protested. A Methodist spokesman termed "Fighting Bob's" supporters "chronic critics" and "hyphenates . . . who have not learned what Americanism means."[16] The *United Presbyterian* held La Follette's appeal was to the circumscribed in mind and the uncircumcised of heart.

The domestic policies of Harding and Coolidge, as largely determined by such cabinet members as Secretary of the Treasury Andrew Mellon and Secretary of Commerce Herbert Hoover, were designed to please the business community. (Farmers and progressives were still strongly represented in Congress, but they were not very successful in getting their policies adopted.) Church spokesmen from Maine to California made clear their approval of the principle of more business in government and less government in business.

This reluctance to criticize the Republican administrations of the Golden Twenties was paralleled by a hesitancy to question the over-all justice of American society. The general prosperity of the people seemed self-evident to many churchmen and, as they explained, there were few radicals in the country simply because there was little to be radical about.

The "rags to riches" theme of Horatio Alger found myriad advocates among churchmen. Our national coat of arms, suggested a Presbyterian minister, should have on it a log cabin. A Methodist observer declared: "Driver or draw-back; worthy or weakling; genius or good-for-nothing—such is the choice set before every boy of average ability."[17] True, as one Congregational minister pointed out, some men still soiled their hands with money gained in the opium trade! True, as another cleric observed, poverty still dogged those who were not industrious and frugal and upright and who wasted their wealth in dissipation and drunkenness. But many churchmen agreed with the Reverend Rolfe Cobleigh when he predicted all would be well if America kept the Bible open, the flag flying, and pushed forward.

In any event, the cure for whatever ailed the United States was certainly not to tamper with the capitalist system. "Christian Socialism—A Contradiction in Terms," "Socialism Is Un-American," "The Opposition of Socialism to Christianity" were titles of articles that appeared in the church press. And when Christian groups flirted—or appeared to flirt—with socialism, the anger of conservative churchmen was unbounded.

16. *Arkansas Methodist*, Oct. 30, 1924, p. 1.
17. *Zion's Herald*, Aug. 30, 1922, p. 1095.

This is evidenced by the many charges leveled against the Federal Council of Churches. It is also seen in the almost continuous attacks upon liberal church leaders and liberal church agencies. To relate these assaults in any detail would require many pages. Suffice it to say that a large element in American Protestantism believed the churches were the conservers and not the subverters of the established order. This view is epitomized in a full-page advertisement sponsored by the Christian Education Movement. Under the picture of a huge, hairy hand clutching a sputtering black bomb there appeared the admonition that the one sure antidote for radical agitation and Bolshevik poison was an education in a Christian school.

The home of this "radical agitation" was, of course, Soviet Russia. Hundreds of church spokesmen took the measure of the Russian experiment and found it a ghastly failure in every respect. For instance, a Methodist minister spoke of the immorality of Russian youth under Communist rule, sex being rampant in the schools with multitudes of young girls leading lives of shame. When Lenin died in 1924 the *United Presbyterian* joyfully cried: "Lenin is dead. The great beast has gone down into the pit! Glory be to God!"[18] There was much more of this impassioned condemnation of Russia, but it should be noted that there existed also much analytical criticism, calmer in tone, and probably more effective, coming from liberal sources.

IV

The materialism and conservatism of the churches in the twenties is a favorite thesis of virtually all commentators on this decade. To demonstrate the *partial* validity of this thesis has been the purpose of this chapter. Elements in Protestantism adopted the techniques and jargon of the business community. More to the point is that the churches, in some cases, accepted a standard of success that was essentially materialistic. Further, some churchmen gave hearty support to the perpetuation of the status quo. Like individuals grouped before a camera, they seemed to feel that any movement would spoil the picture. In particular, the churches evidenced an unconscionable reluctance to criticize the administrations of Harding and Coolidge. Perhaps the Kingdom of God had not yet been established in the twenties, but some churchmen apparently believed the Kingdom of Gold was upon them—and that would be quite sufficient for the nonce.

It would be mistake, however, to assume smugly that the complacency and conservatism described in this chapter could only exist in the Roaring Twenties. Thoughtful Protestants will observe the deadly

18. Feb. 7, 1924, p. 8.

parallels between the post-Versailles decade and the 1950's. Churchmen continued to advertise the pragmatic merits of church attendance in terms of meeting the best people and attaining peace of mind. It was still assumed that a large congregation made a successful church and that the righteousness that exalted a nation could be measured by the statistics of conversion. Americans confidently supposed that "somebody up there liked them" and that "the Man upstairs" was a kindly Fellow who could be counted upon to extricate them from an occasional tight place. Gasconades were still made about the value of church property and the cost of new buildings. Evangelists continued to denounce personal sin and ignore social injustice, and under their pleas men went to the feet of Jesus even as they mobbed Negro school children. As in the twenties, the fifties saw liberal ministers under attack and "radicalism" in the pulpit denounced. And there abided the hope that organized religion was the surest bulwark against the tides of world revolution.

CHAPTER III

A Dissenting Report of the Churches in the Twenties

"The wicked flee when no man pursueth, but they make better time when they know someone is after them."
—Charles H. Parkhurst

I

IN THE PRECEDING chapter evidence was advanced to confirm the widespread impression that social Christianity was in feckless health in the twenties and that the churches, as the rest of America, worshiped before the "bitch goddess Success." But this generalization, valid as it may be for certain elements of Protestantism, grossly oversimplifies the picture. The announced death of social Christianity after the First World War, like that of Mark Twain, was somewhat exaggerated. Even in the Roaring Twenties the churches continued to interest themselves in social matters, and it is to this evidence that the inquiry now turns.

II

If social Christianity were in truth dead, it is a little difficult to explain the constant criticism of the churches for meddling in secular matters. Why all the alarums and excursions over a mere corpse? Individual ministers, official and unofficial church agencies, entire denominations, and even the Federal Council endured a constant barrage of invective for their alleged radicalism. This unrelenting attack by business associations, patriotic societies, and, indeed, by conservative churchmen themselves, like Hobbes' description of man in a state of nature, is a nasty and brutish story. It is, however, not a short one. And so one of many incidents must suffice by way of illustration.

In 1920 the Y.W.C.A. adopted the "Social Creed of the Churches" with its planks on industrial justice. Angered by this excursion into secular matters, the Employers' Association of Pittsburgh called upon the local branch of the "Y" to repudiate the action of its national board. Their demand refused, the businessmen then circulated a letter severely critical of the "Y," concluding that any individual who gave financial support to this organization would be subverting the established economic order. It was an effective argument; the Pittsburgh "Y's" money raising campaign of 1921 brought in scarcely one-third of the expected amount.

"May I be permitted to suggest," said Harry Emerson Fosdick, "that these gentlemen have somewhat seriously misapprehended the temper of the Christian ministry of America? I am speaking for multitudes of my brethren when I say, *'Before high God, not for sale!'* "[1] William Pierson Merrill, pastor of Brick Presbyterian Church, New York, believed that if such intimidation forced the churches to alter their policies by a "hair's breadth" it would be "spiritual treason."[2] Shailer Mathews, great dean of the University of Chicago Divinity School, warned that the churches must continue to preach the whole gospel. The Pittsburgh Ministerial Association issued a very sharp rebuke to the business group.

Methodists, rather accustomed to speaking bluntly, resented the intimidation. A half-dozen Methodist journals answered the challenge. The attack upon the Y.W.C.A., believed the *New York Christian Advocate,* was only a preliminary to a full scale onslaught against social Christianity, for these businessmen "can hardly be so unchivalrous as to wage war only upon women."[3] And of course the Methodist Federation for Social Service, gadfly of the established order, was not silent.

At least three Presbyterian papers voiced their disapproval. The *Continent* averred the action against the "Y" was "every bit as foolish as the craziest blatancy of the 'reds.' "[4] Congregational, Episcopal, and Unitarian papers all held the attack sinister and advised the churches to stand their ground. The *Christian Work* maintained a new heresy hunt was on with economics rather than theology dominating the scene, while the *Christian Century* observed that the "tired businessman" was evidently not *too* tired. The Federal Council of Churches, frequent victim itself of similar attacks, gave its support to the "Y."

Scarcely a month passed that the religious press did not carry an account of a similar act of intimidation somewhere in the United States. Sometimes the churches succumbed to the pressure, but frequently they stood fast and gave their accusers back word for word. And on occasion, too, the replies were somewhat lacking in Christian humility and restraint. For instance, a Methodist editor termed certain charges against the liberal *Christian Century* the

largest assortment of mares' nests, roorbacks, hallucinations, ghost stories, campaign rumors, back stairs gossip, pipe dreams, *d. t.* visions and general incredibilities that has been assembled in one place since Fairy Tale Freddy

1. *Social Service Bulletin,* June, 1921.   Italics original.
2. *New Era Magazine,* Aug., 1921, p. 452.
3. Feb. 10, 1921, p. 172.
4. April 28, 1921, p. 476.

made his memorable though fruitless visit to that pair of professional thau-maturgists, William J. Burns and Harry Daugherty.

About the only recent and unhappy events for which the *Christian Century* is not held primarily responsible are the Japan earthquake and the Democratic Convention of 1924. The paper is flattered scandalously, as even its warmest partisans will admit. It is credited with influence and intelligence compared with which the highest genius of Machiavelli and the Russian Secret Police are in a class with amateur night at the Posey County Library.[5]

But perhaps the most effective and succinct reply to intimidators of the pulpit was made by the Reverend George A. Martin when he reminded the businessmen of Detroit: "One and only one is our Master, even Christ."[6]

The frequency and intensity of the attacks upon the churches for meddling in secular affairs implies that social Christianity was not dead in the twenties; that it still lived was explicitly asserted in pulpit, press, and assembly. An examination of the sources of Protestant opinion in the Prosperity Decade reveals abundant statements and resolutions up-holding the Christian's duty to transform society as well as the individual. A social age beset by social sins required a social faith. The angels of heaven might rejoice over the conversion of an inveterate wife beater or gambler, but even a moral man could be crushed by an immoral society plagued by war, race hatred, and economic inequality. And further, often respectable tithers were virtuous only in their personal relationships, shunning the old immoralities but practicing such corporate sins as ex-ploiting child labor, bribing legislators, advertising miraculous powers to a shoddy product, violating safety laws, and underpaying their workers. As E. A. Ross noted twenty years earlier, the modern high-powered dealer of woe sinned with a calm countenance and a serene soul because, so long as his private life was immaculate, he could still be counted among the elect. The traditional Protestant ethic, with its emphasis on personal sins, did not impinge on his conscience. Besides, as one parson pointed out, society was making sinners faster than the churches could save them.

It is difficult to draw from among the hundreds of expressions defend-ing social Christianity, but perhaps the following illustrations catch the flavor of the argument. "How can you separate the personal gospel from the social gospel," inquired the *Northwestern Christian Advocate,* "so long as the saved sinner has to live among a lot of unsaved sinners, most of whose sins do harm to the neighbors."[7] Said Harry Emerson Fosdick, "Repress the endeavor to apply the principles of Jesus to the social order;

5. *Northwestern Christian Advocate,* March 5, 1925, pp. 219-20.
6. *Zion's Herald,* Oct. 13, 1926, p. 1293.
7. Feb. 25, 1926, p. 172

repress the agencies that seek the amelioration of human relations in industry; try to keep the economic situation static in a dynamic world; and when you have long enough represt the possibilities of orderly social progress you will get the inevitable consequence, disorderly social revolution."[8] With much the same thought, the Reverend Roy H. Beane warned, "If we confine Jesus to heaven and imprison His spirit within our churches, shall we express surprise if the common people crown Karl Marx in the street?"[9] The famous Baptist minister, James Gordon Gilkey, cried, "You are here not to see a hideously cruel social order perpetuate itself, while men say slyly that there will always be poverty, always be unemployment, always be strife and war. You are here to fight these things—fight them with the God who has always been fighting them, and who has forever been dreaming of a world redeemed at last from the horror of poverty and the agony of battle."[10] But perhaps Charles R. Brown, Congregational dean of the Yale Divinity School, caught the spirit best when, asked if he was his brother's keeper, replied by saying, "No, I am my brother's brother."[11]

The fact that American Protestantism did not completely succumb to the materialism of the twenties is further attested by the cold reception some churchmen gave to the Gospel according to Bruce Barton. His best selling biography of Jesus the efficiency expert was termed by the *Christian Register* a travesty bordering on blasphemy. The book, believed the Reverend P. B. Hall, revealed the author did not know Christ, nor Paul, nor the Holy Spirit. Referring to the biography, a Disciples leader declared it had been a long time since he had read anything as reckless or ridiculous. Barton's Jesus, opined Halford L. Luccock, noted Northern Methodist, was truly a figure nobody knew until Mr. Barton contributed him to modern fiction. Methodist and Baptist journals held the same opinion, but perhaps it was the editors of the *Christian Century* who made the most penetrating criticism. They accused Barton of moral blindness, and suggested that the ideal of service was upheld by business only because it paid. "But where is the business man," they concluded, "who is willing to listen to the gospel of Jesus when it makes demands upon him which will decrease his dividends and imperil his obvious success?"[12] The writings of Barton are almost invariably cited as proof positive of the materialism of the churches in the twenties. Is it perhaps not time that historians noted the heavy criticism of these writings coming from within Protestantism itself?

8. *Literary Digest*, June 18, 1921, p. 30.
9. *Zion's Herald*, April 23, 1930, pp. 522-23.
10. *Christian Century*, Jan. 17, 1924, p. 80.
11. Charles R. Brown, *The Gospel for Main Street* (New York, 1930), p. 24.
12. *Christian Century*, July 2, 1925, p. 852.

The portrayal of Jesus as the very model of a modern American businessman was only one aspect of religious trends that was questioned by churchmen. Jazzy advertising techniques, catchy sermon titles, peppy promotion stunts, overly-costly church buildings, go-getting good fellows in the pulpit, prodigious church programs in such fields as bowling and basketball, the equating of size with success, and the whole concept that "religion pays" came in for severe censure.

Countless were the statements made by leading ministers and religious press editors warning the churches that by uncritically accepting the materialistic standards and techniques of the business community they were in danger of losing their souls. This fact is important. Reinhold Niebuhr and Fosdick, not Henry L. Mencken and Walter Lippmann, penned the sharpest indictment of the churches. The *Christian Century* and *Zion's Herald,* not the *American Mercury* and the *New Republic,* carried the more acute criticisms of Protestantism. It is a little absurd, then, for commentators to speak without qualification of the materialism of the churches in the twenties when many ministers, including the greatest, and many church journals, including the most influential, did not embrace this materialism. That such a materialism did exist and grow is true; that it engulfed all of American Protestantism is false.

III

The Federal Council of Churches did not find American society in the twenties above criticism. A plank in the original "Social Creed of the Churches" called for a new emphasis upon the application of Christian principles to the acquisition and use of property. In 1919 and 1920 both in resolutions adopted at a special meeting in Cleveland and in the Council's statement on "The Church and Social Reconstruction" the need was emphasized for a reconstruction of society upon humane, democratic, and cooperative principles. Throughout the twenties the Council called attention to the autocracy, poverty, and materialism that still required reformation. That the Council was critical of the basic assumptions and the results of capitalism is clear; equally apparent is the fact that the Council did not embrace a doctrinaire program of reform. Thus, while calling for a just society, it withheld commitments concerning the implementation of this society. The Council believed that the Kingdom of God was far from being established in America. It did not, however, and in spite of charges to the contrary, equate socialism or any other specific program with the Kingdom.

In 1920 the Committee on the War and the Religious Outlook, an interdenominational group, published a volume on *The Church and Industrial Reconstruction.* It rang the charges on the extreme inequalities in the distribution of wealth, over-emphasis on the motive of self-interest, industrial autocracy, and the selfish spirit in the productive processes. A cooperative commonwealth was urged.

A third interdenominational group, the Interchurch World Movement, which did such important work in connection with the Steel Strike of 1919, adopted an industrial platform urging the promotion of the cooperative movement in the production and distribution of goods. It specifically warned that the church should not be committed to the present or any other political, social, or industrial order as a finality.

The social creed of the Northern Methodists, originally adopted in 1908, stood for the establishment of a society in conformity with the Golden Rule and the mind of Christ. Buttressing this statement, the Board of Bishops in 1919 declared that unselfish cooperation must replace selfish competition in the struggle for daily bread. The General Conference of 1920 implied and those of 1924 and 1928 specifically resolved that property rights possess no inherent sacredness that puts them beyond the reach of criticism, that there was an ethical difference between property for use and property for power, and that the profit motive in the acquisition and use of property must give way to the motive of service.

From time to time annual conferences pointed out the abuses that existed in America. Some of these statements, those of the New York East and Rock River (Illinois) Conferences, for example, repudiated the profit motive. And in 1927 the Michigan Conference held: "The church stands for the making of men; industry, with few exceptions, stands for the making of profits. The Christian motive and the profit motive are irreconcilable."[13]

Although the General Conferences of the Methodist Episcopal Church, regional conferences, and official boards and agencies issued comments critical of the existing order, it was the Methodist Federation for Social Service that loomed as Methodism's true gadfly in the twenties. Scarcely an issue of the Federation's *Bulletin* failed to carry some type of criticism of capitalism, either of its basic premises or of its results. Moreover, in 1922 and 1926 the Federation conducted conferences on "Christianity and the Economic Order." Leading laymen as well as ministers were in attendance. A large number of the delegates shared the conviction that a just society required the substitution of capitalism by some type of Christian socialism. The immorality of the existing economic order was not merely questioned; it was accepted as self-evident.

Northern Baptists in 1919 acknowledged that a radical change and a thoroughgoing readjustment in the social order were inevitable, and the Northern Baptist Convention of the following year resolved that "industry

13. *Information Service*, Oct. 22, 1927, p. 3.

is a social service whose ruling motive should be not the profit of the few, but the welfare of all, and that the service motive must become the dominant spirit in both the method and processes of industry."[14] Toward the end of the decade the Convention resolved that our society, "built upon the competitive and profit method and motive," made the living of the Sermon on the Mount difficult.[15] From time to time Baptist boards issued statements critical of the existing order. "The present industrial system enthrones the law of selfishness as the fundamental law," proclaimed the Division of Social Education.[16] Industry, it was argued, is merely an interest to serve society and therefore must be subjected to supervision by the state.

In a similar spirit, the Social Service Commission of the Presbyterian Church, U.S.A., reported to the 1919 General Assembly that a new and righteous social order must replace the old unjust and cruel conditions. The following Assembly reaffirmed its belief in the subordination of profit to the creative and cooperative spirit. Occasionally in the decade Presbyterians called for the substitution of the spirit of love and service for that of greed and competition.

Congregationalists in national assembly in 1919 pledged themselves to "work for a social order in which there will be none without opportunity to work and in which it will be impossible for idlers to live in luxury and for workers to live in poverty." They sought "to abolish all special economic privileges which enable some to live at the expense of others."[17] It was held also that there is no divine right to property and that the possession of property is justified only when used to serve society. In 1925 the National Council adopted its famous "Statement on Social Ideals" upholding the supremacy of the service rather than the profit motive, recognizing all ownership is a social trust, and deploring the unlimited exercise of the right of private property. In addition, the Congregational Commission on Social Relations lamented the fact that in much of modern industry the profit motive had completely subordinated the service motive.

The Bishops of the Anglican communion at the 1920 Lambeth Conference asserted the superiority of the claims of human life to those of property and of human values to those of dividends and profits. In 1922 the General Convention of the Protestant Episcopal Church reaf-

14. *Annual of the Northern Baptist Convention,* 1920, p. 266.

15. *Ibid.,* 1929, p. 106.

16. Roger Marshall Larson, "Trends in the Economic Pronouncements of the Major American Church Bodies, 1908-1948" (unpublished Ph.D. dissertation, University of California, 1950), pp. 251-52. The Southern Baptist Convention, Lutherans, and the Methodist Episcopal Church, South, while not silent on personal sins and on certain specific abuses suffered by labor, gave no indication of dissatisfaction with capitalism as a system.

17. *Minutes of the National Council of Congregational Churches,* 1919, p. 35.

firmed these principles, holding "co-operation for the common service must be substituted for the present competition for private advantage as the paramount motive and end of all industry."[18]   The official Department of Christian Social Service brought home to Episcopalians the fact that not all was perfect in the social order, but undoubtedly the most militant criticisms came from unofficial Episcopal groups.   The Church Socialist League, before its demise in the early twenties, sought the abolition of capitalism.   The Church Association for the Advancement of the Interests of Labor exposed many abuses in America, although it too did not survive the decade.   Of greater importance during these years was the Church League for Industrial Democracy.   It explicitly stood for the substitution of the motive of service for that of profit and for the method of cooperation rather than that of competition.   Throughout the twenties this group exposed the inequities in society and the paganism (as the group saw it) of the capitalist system.

In the years following the First World War, Unitarians, through their Annual Conferences, Department of Social Relations, and the Unitarian Fellowship for Social Justice, had some critical things to say about the justice of the social order.   While Unitarian demands for a more equitable distribution of wealth were buttressed by endorsement of such specific measures as a steeply graduated inheritance and income tax, they did not include the outright repudiation of capitalism.

The Disciples of Christ, particularly through their Board of Temperance and Social Welfare, spoke of the need to democratize industry. From time to time the Universalists and the United Brethren voiced similar views.   In 1919 the Reformed Church in the United States noted the great silent revolution taking place among the disinherited, and in that year the Evangelical Synod of North America resolved that human rights transcended property rights and that production should be for use rather than for profits.

IV

These denominational resolutions suggest that the critical faculties of American Protestantism were not completely moribund in the twenties. An examination of the religious press leads to the same conclusion: the spirit of the Old Testament prophets lived on even in the age of Valentino, Barton, and Coolidge.

Two journals representing the unofficial position of the Federal Council of Churches, the *Federal Council Bulletin* and *Information Service,* ranged widely and critically over the problems of American society.   Before judgment is passed on the conservatism or indifference of

18. *Journal of the General Convention of the Protestant Episcopal Church,* 1922, p. 163.

American Protestantism to social matters, an examination should be made of the files of these papers. These observations apply with even greater force to the *World Tomorrow*. Representing the viewpoint of Christian socialism, this journal was highly censorious of the existing economic and social order. Of greater moment is the position of Protestantism's most influential periodical, the *Christian Century*. Under the able and outspoken editorship of Charles Clayton Morrison, this paper scrutinized every facet of American life. Its editorials were not designed to please the complacent and contented citizen. Morrison was nothing if not bold and he counted courage a higher virtue than caution. The *Christian Century* carried on the traditions of the old progressives. Its frame of reference was not that of doctrinaire socialism but rather that of pragmatic liberalism. It did not hoist the standard of rebellion, but it did demand a society that would jibe with Christian morality. Two other undenominational papers, *Christian Herald* and *Christian Work*, may not have been as outspoken, and yet they were far from rock-ribbed in their attitudes.

It is sometimes assumed that the denominational press was concerned solely with Rum, Romanism, and Revivals. On the contrary, many of these church journals traveled widely over the problems of American society and were quite critical of what they saw. *Zion's Herald* was Methodism's most liberal publication, but the various *Christian Advocates* also lanced the festering sores on the body politic. Indeed, the *Nashville Christian Advocate* was among the most liberal church papers published below the Mason-Dixon line. Among Baptist journals, the *Baptist* in the North and the *Alabama Baptist* in the South deserve to be singled out for special mention for their critical spirit. The Presbyterian press was, on the whole, rather conservative and contented, although the *Continent* probably merits exemption from this statement, as does the *Presbyterian Advance* published in the South. The *Churchman* was the leading liberal Episcopal journal in the country and the *Congregationalist* holds that position in that denomination. The *Christian Register* and the *Christian-Evangelist*, representing Unitarian and Disciples thought, were both liberal in tone, although the latter journal tended to become more liberal as the decade deepened. The *Universalist Leader* (after 1926 the *Christian Leader*) and the *Reformed Church Messenger* were capably edited and quite liberal publications. The Lutheran press was generally conservative.

These comments on the religious press are, admittedly, very general. Limitations of space make it impossible to cite chapter and verse. And yet, these conclusions are based on an examination of almost twenty thousand issues of church journals for the years 1919-29. Having examined many periodicals representing all shades and sections of opinion, it is possible to state that while conservatism was widespread, it was balanced by considerable liberal opinion which kept alive the critical spirit of social Christianity in the Prosperity Decade.

V

"Certainly it would be true to argue," wrote the famous British historian, Harold J. Laski, "that it is the combined influence of religious institutions, including Jewish, that has dug the main abyss between the United States and the Soviet Union."[19] Other observers have arrived at similar conclusions. In fact, the unrelenting hostility of American religious groups toward godless Soviet Russia seems so absurdly obvious as to scarcely warrant comment. In the previous chapter evidence was noted to support this conclusion. Nevertheless, even during the twenties a significant minority in American Protestantism adopted what can only be termed a sympathetic attitude toward the Soviet experiment.

In the first place—and rather parenthetically—American Protestantism appeared united in the belief that food, clothing, medicine, money, and machinery should be sent to aid the Russians. The Quakers, of course, were active in this matter. And so was the Federal Council of Churches which collected relief items and appointed a special representative to aid in their distribution in Russia. Individual denominations did their part. Virtually all of the denominational journals eloquently called upon their subscribers to give freely.[20] "Just one fact stares us in the face," maintained the *Baptist*, "men and women and little children in vast numbers have not enough food to keep them alive while America has enough and to spare."[21] These evidences of sympathy for the Russian people do not, obviously, constitute an endorsement of the Soviet government. They are indicative only of the fact that the attitude of American Protestantism toward Russia was not completely dominated by fear and hate.

More to the point is the fact that occasionally churchmen and church journals found praiseworthy aspects in the Communist experiment. For instance, in 1922 the Reverend Ernest Lyman Mills, who accompanied Bishop John L. Nuelsen as the first representatives of Methodism to gain admission into Soviet Russia, presented his findings in three dispassionate and sympathetic articles in *Zion's Herald*. Bishop Nuelsen reported to the Methodist Board of Foreign Missions that there was much that was encouraging in Russia and that there seemed to be religious freedom.

Bishop Nuelsen further presuaded the Board of Bishops of the

19. Harold J. Laski, *The American Democracy* (New York, 1948), p. 29.
20. The writer has in his files editorials from twenty-two church papers calling for aid to the Russians. He did not encounter a single dissenting voice.
21. Aug. 20, 1921, p. 909.

Methodist Episcopal Church to send a deputation to the Second All-Russian Territorial Council of the Russian Orthodox Church meeting in Moscow in the spring of 1923. The deputation was halted at Paris, but Bishop Edgar Blake and Lewis O. Hartman, editor of *Zion's Herald,* continued on to Moscow, apparently in an unofficial capacity. These two gentlemen presented greetings from Methodism and proceeded to pledge aid to the Russian clerics totaling fifty thousand dollars. The repercussion in the United States was violent. The Methodist press split on the action of Blake and Hartman. The Central and New York *Christian Advocates* repudiated the friendly gesture, while the Nashville and Northwestern *Christian Advocates* and, naturally, *Zion's Herald,* endorsed the pledge. The Board of Bishops, after considerable debate, issued an equivocal statement thanking the deputation for endeavoring to fulfill a "difficult and delicate" mission and releasing it from further duties in this connection.[22]

Smarting from his experiences, Bishop Blake charged that much of the vilification of Russia was due to Roman Catholic propaganda. While admitting that the Soviet leaders were frankly atheistic, he went on to say: "There is undoubtedly a larger measure of religious tolerance in Russia than in any other country of Europe or in America, that is dominated by the Roman Catholic Church."[23] Hartman, through the editorial columns of *Zion's Herald,* repeatedly painted events in Russia in warm colors. It was his wish to counteract the "lying propaganda" about that strange land that had poisoned relationships between the United States and Russia. After all, when it comes "to the ideals of social justice and fair play, and the ultimate goal of human brotherhood, the Marxian theory has many similarities to Christian teachings." Further, "Soviet Russia constitutes the greatest social experiment in the history of the world. Never before in the life of mankind has there been an attempt on so vast a scale to equalize opportunity and to promote the genuine brotherhood of man."[24] "The Soviet regime. . . ," believed Hartman in 1926, "is essentially a struggle for human freedom, and the Communist leaders with all their mistakes are sincere, honest men working for what they conceive to be the good of humanity."[25]

Other churchmen shared the belief that there were noble aspects to the

22. So equivocal was the statement that the secular press headlined: "Recognition Given Soviet Church by U. S. Methodists" and "Methodists Not To Back Russian Living Church." Several non-Methodist papers, including the *Christian Century,* asked for contributions to meet the pledge. The *Herald and Presbyter,* on the other hand, termed this cooperation with godless Russia an example of social gospelism.

23. *Zion's Herald,* July 11, 1923, p. 897.

24. *Ibid.,* July 4, 1923, pp. 849-50.

25. *Ibid.,* Nov. 17, 1926, p. 1457.

Russian experiment.[26]   A few, such as Episcopal Bishop William Montgomery Brown (unfrocked in 1924), made no effort to conceal their conviction that Russia was riding the wave of the future.   More significant were those who tempered their enthusiasm with an awareness that the Soviets had not yet achieved utopia and who cloaked their writings in the garb of objectivity.

Harry F. Ward, Methodist iconoclast and leader of the Federation for Social Service, for example, attempted to probe beneath the hysteria (as he saw it) and report on the happenings in Russia in an objective and dispassionate fashion.   He did so in books, articles, and Federation *Bulletins*.   Inevitably, perhaps, he suffered censure by a number of Methodist groups, and for a time the authorities rejected his Sunday School lesson material.   Moreover, Ward's mildly sympathetic attitude toward Russia (unlike his white-washing in the thirties) was the cause of more hostility toward the Methodist Federation for Social Service than any other issue in the decade.   Jerome Davis and Sherwood Eddy, frequent travelers to Russia, also found a tolerable number of things to praise. They were not unaware of the darker phases, but on the whole they believed Russia had made many remarkable advances and that as an ideal communism was superior to swollen, selfish, capitalism.

Other churchmen of less liberal persuasion sought to sift the wheat from the tares regarding events in Russia.   Stanley High, then active in church work, averred that he had been permitted to travel as he pleased in the Soviet Union.   He further supposed that the people were free to criticize their government.   "It is apparent on every hand in Russia," he wrote, "that one need not live beyond the borders of the country to write the truth about it."[27]   He called upon Americans to stop anathematizing Russia and to remember that good as well as evil existed there.   A year later, in 1926, G. Bromley Oxnam, outstanding Methodist leader, returned from Russia.   He reported that in spite of the atheism of the rulers, the churches were still open and fairly well attended.   Further, every religious leader he encountered agreed that complete freedom of religious worship was allowed.   And it was another sanely liberal leader, Alva W. Taylor, Disciples churchman, who argued that the "Soviet government has as much right to its trial in the court of mankind as monarchy or republicanism."[28]   These are only a few of the really quite large number of Protestant churchmen who spoke about Russia with dispassion and sympathy.

26. Meno Lovenstein, *American Opinion of Soviet Russia* (Washington, D. C., 1941), believes the secular press gave only scant and biased coverage to Russia.   On the whole, this conclusion does not hold true for the religious press.

27. *Northwestern Christian Advocate*, April 2, 1925, p. 324.

28. *Christian Century*, Feb. 6, 1919, p. 14.

The *Christian Century* also followed events in Russia with great interest. "No more reprehensible propaganda," stated the editors in 1923, "has ever been foisted upon a public than that which was fostered by our western governments with regard to Soviet Russia."[29] With this as their thesis, the editors attempted to picture the Communist experiment free from bias. Alleged reforms in many fields were hopefully noted and Lenin's death was said to mark another chapter in the relinquishment of the dictatorship in Russia. In short, the editors believed that there was "far greater opportunity for affecting the policies of the bolsheviki from the vantage point of friendliness than as a fearful and hostile neighbor seeking refuge behind a stone wall."[30]

Several editorials and articles sympathetic in tone appeared in the *World Tomorrow*. One clerical contributor found laudable the social reforms of the experiment. And the editors chided America's "unholy desire" to make a "scapegoat of every error the Russians have made in their attempt to organize production on some other basis than that of personal profit."[31]

The Unitarian journal, *Christian Register,* is another good example of a religious paper which was far from hostile toward Russia in the twenties. Numerous contributors lauded the Communist reforms and mocked the tales of persecution and torture. Or if they were shadows to the experiment, they were the price that had to be paid The editors inclined to this position also, and they repeatedly blamed Western intransigence and hostility for Russia's own suspicious attitude—and also for the terrible famines of the early twenties. The *Churchman* occasionally devoted space to Russia. Typical was an editorial of 1921 in which biased and distorted reports were deplored, the editors calling upon America to regain its mental poise and to speak in a more measured tone. Moreover, much of the poverty in Russia was due to the Allied blockade and to the financing of the "white terror." The *Congregationalist* carried admiring stories about Russia by such writers as Anna Louise Strong and editorially deprecated accounts of terror and torture.

Many other examples from liberal church journals could be cited, but perhaps the point can better be made by noting expressions from papers that were generally conservative. "If a Socialist state is what Russia wants," shrugged the *New York Christian Advocate,* no friend of the Soviets, "it is hard to say why the American republic should say her nay. . . ."[32] "Russia is now the most colossal experimental social and political station in the world," observed the very conservative *Presbyterian*

---

29. Nov. 15, 1923, p. 1463.   30. Dec. 8, 1927, p. 1448.
31. Sept., 1921, p. 260.   32. Feb. 20, 1919, p. 227.

Banner, "and its outcome is yet to be seen."[33] And when the *Baptist* petitioned Russia to grant her people religious freedom it cautioned: "A protest in the name of religious freedom from persons who are already committed to an implacable political hostility toward the existing regime would add fuel to the fire. It would be resented as a political attack masquerading in the guise of religion. Let none but friends venture counsel."[34] Lastly, it is significant that Federal Council papers ran literally scores of items on Russia—items dispassionate and frequently friendly in tone.

VI

Finally, who were the prophets of social Christianity in the twenties? Were there any to keep alive the fervor of the pre-war years? Or had the religious progressives, like many of those of politics, become tired and given up the fight? Who now dreamed the dreams of George Washington Gladden, Josiah Strong, and Walter Rauschenbusch?

The voices of these three giants had once re-awakened in America the social implications of Christianity; they were now heard, if at all, only from beyond the grave. Dead also were many other pioneers of the Social Gospel. Those who lived on after the war followed disparate courses. George D. Herron retired to a villa in Italy. Others forsook the pulpit for militant trade unionism, as in the case of A. J. Muste, or reform politics, as witnessed by Norman Thomas, or journalism and sundry causes, as indicated by John Nevin Sayre. A few like John Haynes Holmes broke with their communions but established community churches. Many, viewing the ascendancy of conservative opinion, held their tongues out of fear. Others, like Bernard Iddings Bell, came to believe their earlier radicalism had been misguided. Since some clerical radicals had embraced pacifism during the conflict, their influence was weakened by charges of cowardice or treason and, as in the case of Episcopal Bishop Paul Jones, a loss of official status. True, some of the old pioneers of the Social Gospel lived on after 1919 unbowed and unrepentant. But year by year retirement or death thinned their ranks: Samuel Zane Batten, Lyman Abbott, Graham Taylor, Charles Stelzle, Frank Mason North, Bishop Charles Williams, and William Austin Smith.

Faced with all these facts, it would be logical to conclude, as many observers have done, that there were no exponents of social Christianity in the Prosperity Decade. However, there is some evidence to indicate otherwise.

In the first place, articles dealing with social problems—fundamental

33. Sept. 12, 1929, p. 9.
34. July 6, 1929, p. 873. In 1929 and 1930 the Northern and Southern Baptist Conventions protested religious persecutions in Russia.

problems about social change, social goals, and social strategies—were contributed in amazing number to the church press. And most of these articles were written by churchmen. Secondly, books dealing with the social implications of Christianity continued to pour from the press. Thirdly, the pulpit augmented the pen as an instrument of ministers for criticizing abuses in the existing economic and social order. Heeding the words of the great Theodore Parker, ministers continued to give the alarm when public sin appeared in the land or when a lie invaded the state. The pulpit rather than the altar had always occupied the place of honor in American Protestantism, and in the twenties the message of the American pulpit was largely social. An examination of sermon collections attests to this fact, as do the researches of several scholars.

There is additional evidence that the ministry continued to embrace men of liberal persuasion. A few parsons—R. W. Hogue, M. G. Johnson, and Herbert Bigelow, for instance—worked on behalf of La Follette in the Presidential election of 1924, as did the Methodist Federation for Social Service and the Church League for Industrial Democracy. Of greater significance is that five thousand ministers of many denominations, including those of fame, signed an open letter stating why they intended to vote for the Wisconsin leader. La Follette ran on the Progressive ticket with a platform considered shocking-pink at the time and which was, in truth, very liberal. And yet this one source alone indicated a significant minority of the Protestant clergy preferred La Follette's liberalism to the conservatism of the two major party candidates. What the percentage might be if all the clerical votes were known makes interesting speculation. It is provocative to conjecture, also, on the number of ministers who voted for Norman Thomas, the Socialist party candidate, in 1928. Although there is not enough evidence on this matter even to hazard a guess, it is probable that a number of ministers supported this Presbyterian parson turned politician.

Some of those ministers who championed social Christianity, as the news columns of the religious press revealed, lost their pulpits. But this was not an inevitable fate. In 1924 the *Christian Century* polled the Protestant clergy to discover the outstanding preachers of America. Over twenty-one thousand votes were cast to name the top twenty-five men of the cloth. About half of these twenty-five leaders could justly be ranked as champions of social Christianity, and a few of them were or later became Socialists. It is clear, then, that advanced views concerning the economic and political order were not necessarily a hinderance to gaining the respect of one's clerical colleagues.[35]

35. The list included Charles R. Brown, Henry Sloane Coffin, S. Parkes Cadman, Russell H. Conwell, Harry Emerson Fosdick, George A. Gordon, Charles W. Gilkey, Lynn Harold

Yet another indication that a liberal temper survived in the churches is the formation of the Fellowship for a Christian Social Order. First broached in the fall of 1921, the Fellowship was not formally organized until a meeting at Lake Mohonk, New York, in May, 1922. Sherwood Eddy, Kirby Page, and Reinhold Niebuhr were guiding lights, and its membership embraced a host of nationally prominent church leaders of liberal bent. Its purpose was not to propagandize for any particular social system, but rather to seek to Christianize the social relationships between man and man. The Fellowship was organized into local conferences, held retreats and summer outings, loaned books, sponsored lectureships, and generally fought the good fight until 1928 when it was absorbed by the Fellowship of Reconciliation.

The officership of another more important organization, the Federal Council of Churches, also supports the thesis that social Christianity lived on. Two of its presidents, Frank Mason North (1916-20) and Francis J. McConnell (1928-32), clearly were of liberal persuasion. Bracketed by these presidents were Robert E. Speer (1920-24) and S. Parkes Cadman (1924-28), men of more moderate social and economic views, but men who were far from reactionary. General Secretary Charles S. Macfarland and General Secretary Samuel McCrea Cavert and executive secretaries Worth M. Tippy and F. Ernest Johnson openly dissented against the temper of the twenties, and James Myers performed yeoman work for the Council in the field of industrial justice. Serving the Council also were a number of other Social Gospel leaders who gained for the Council its reputation for liberalism.

To compile and present here a list of all those churchmen who might reasonably be called exponents of social Christianity is manifestly impossible. It should be sufficient to remember that such a list would embrace a rather large number of great names.

VII

Not all, probably not even a majority, of Protestant clergymen issued a dissenting report in the twenties. In particular, and aside from the scandals,[36] there really was not much criticism of the administrations of

---

Hough, Newell Dwight Hillis, Edwin Holt Hughes, Charles E. Jefferson, Francis J. McConnell, William F. McDowell, William P. Merrill, G. Campbell Morgan, Mark A. Matthews, Joseph Fort Newton, Merton S. Rice, Frederick F. Shannon, John Timothy Stone, William A. Sunday, Robert E. Speer, George W. Truett, Ernest Fremont Tittle, and James I. Vance.

36. Jerome Davis, *Capitalism and Culture* (New York, 1935), p. 389, believes that the religious press remained discreetly silent or opposed the Senate investigators during the oil scandals of Harding's administration. The present writer has in his files almost one hundred editorials from twenty-three different church journals on the oil scandals. His evidence points to a conclusion opposite from that advanced by Davis.

Harding and Coolidge. Much of American Protestantism was indeed corpulent and contented. Yet as this chapter suggests, social Christianity continued to burn bright enough to warrant future historians in using slightly less somber hues in painting their picture of the social attitudes of American Protestantism in the Prosperity Decade.

CHAPTER IV

A Footnote to the Election of 1928

"There are too many people who think that just because
they have parishes or dioceses
It imparts infallibility to all their biases."—Ogden Nash

I

HISTORIANS are in agreement that the Presidential election of 1928 aroused the concern of American Protestantism. Many observers have expended thousands of words discussing this election. Curiously, while most investigators chide the churches for their indifference to secular affairs, in this instance condemnation is usually because the churches displayed too much rather than too little interest.*

The intense activity of the churches in the campaign can hardly be explained by any great difference between the parties. Stripped of platitudes and verbal gymnastics, the Democratic and Republican platforms stood for about the same things. The explanation of the churches' interest in the Presidential race lies rather in the character and background of the two candidates and in their attitudes toward the prohibition experiment.

Herbert Hoover and "Al" Smith (and perhaps it is indicative that the public did not refer to Hoover as "Herb") shared similar economic views, the former being less and the latter more conservative than is generally believed. Both men epitomized the Horatio Alger "rags to riches" dream which in America proved so often to be a reality. But here the similarities ended. Hoover was born close to the soil in Iowa of Quaker parents whose roots went back to colonial times. Smith was born close to the Fulton fish market in New York City of Catholic ancestors who had come to the United States from the "Old Sod." Smith smoked cigars, wore a brown derby, and spoke with an East Side accent. Hoover cut a more conservative figure, and although his prose "was suggestive of a light fog moving over a gray landscape," he at least did not call De Forest's invention the "raddio." Smith had little formal education and read little more than the newspapers. Hoover had worked his way through Stanford and had authored books and articles. Smith had made a brilliant and liberal record as governor of New York, although his

* Substantial portions of this chapter were first published as an article in *Church History*, XXV (June, 1956).

Tammany associations, real or alleged, shadowed his reputation. Hoover had served his country in many capacities, most recently as secretary of commerce in Harding's and Coolidge's administrations, but the Harding scandals left no stain upon his character. Party platforms notwithstanding, Smith was as Wet as the Pacific, while Hoover, because he referred to prohibition as "a great social and economic experiment, noble in motive and far reaching in purpose," was believed as Dry as the Sahara.

Here, then, in the character and background of the two candidates one discovers the real explanation for Protestant activity in the campaign. Smith was a Catholic, a Wet, a city slicker, a Tammanyite and of recent immigrant stock. These attributes of the Democratic candidate carried precious little appeal to the average American Protestant, particularly in the strongly Protestant sections of the rural West and South. It is impossible fully to isolate those elements in Smith's makeup and say that his Tammany connections cost him a certain percentage of the Protestant vote, his East Side accent another, and so forth. Probably in the average Protestant mind, the total picture of Smith was worse than the mere sum of the elements making up his personality.

All of this has been covered by historians and it is not the purpose of these pages to retell the story. However, certain aspects of the election deserve comment if for no other reason than that they have been misrepresented by a goodly number of commentators.

In the first place, the influence of the Ku Klux Klan in the election of 1928 has been overstated. The Klan did not lead the Protestant churches into Hoover's camp; it did not swing Protestant opinion against Smith. That would have occurred had the Klan never existed. Indeed, perhaps some Protestants refused to join the anti-Smith forces because they disliked being associated with the crudeness and vulgar intolerance of the Klan. Perhaps some liberal Protestants voted for Smith against their convictions in order to escape the charge of bigotry. The minor role of the Klan is attested by the fact that church journals, leaders, and assemblies spoke out against *both* the Klan and Smith. To attribute all—or even a significant portion—of Protestant opposition to Smith to Klan machinations is erroneous. To equate all Protestant anti-Smith sentiment to Klan propaganda is a mistake. Historians make much of the "Klan mentality" of those who weighed Smith's personal qualifications for the Presidency and found them wanting. It should hardly be necessary to issue the reminder that millions of Protestant Americans opposed Smith because of his religion or Tammany associations or Wetness who were not—never had been—members of the Klan, and who far from giving it support, actively and vocally expressed their disapproval. Thus, the influence of the Klan in shaping Protestant opinion against Smith was negligible. The sources of responsible church opinion reveal almost no support of and considerable opposition to the Klan, while these same sources disclose almost no support of and considerable opposition to Smith.

A second observation has to do with the charge that powerful clergymen, especially in the South, led their misguided flocks in an anti-Wet, anti-Catholic crusade in the election of 1928. Now, it is true that countless parsons viewed the election as pretty much a contest between the forces of light and the legions of darkness and did vigorously and unwisely labor for the defeat of Smith. But they did not coerce, dupe, or otherwise force their congregations to assume unwillingly an anti-Smith position. Such a position was already held, and in a very real sense clergymen simply shared the attitudes (or prejudices, if you will) of their people. A good many observers—Virginius Dabney, Gunnar Myrdal, Wilbur J. Cash, Harold J. Laski, and Gustavus Myers, to name only a few of the more famous—have stated that during the twenties clergymen may almost be said to have dominated the South. They then point to the election of 1928 as illustrative of this fact.

It is a poor illustration. Protestants listened to their shepherds' warnings against Smith and nodded their heads in approval. They did so not because they were cowed by their clergymen, but because what they heard agreed with convictions they had long held. When, however, Bishop James M. Cannon, Jr., Southern Methodist, and thirty other noted churchmen issued a criticism of conditions in Southern textile mills what was the reaction? These men of the cloth were brusquely—even ruthlessly—told to mind their own business. It is curious indeed to find commentators—most of them liberals—in one breath damning ministers for their overweening and baneful influence in the election of 1928 while in the next belittling as feeble and ineffectual clerical efforts to reform unjust labor or racial conditions.

This is not an attempt to justify the entrance of ministers into the 1928 campaign, but it is a suggestion that they were supported in their political activity only because most of their parishioners agreed that Smith constituted a threat to their principles. Clergymen did not so much lead, as they represented their flocks. For the clergy to have attempted to commit the churches to a policy or to use the machinery of the churches to promote a policy the churches themselves did not believe, would be a genuine case of clericalism. But it was the sentiment of a majority of American Protestants, and not merely the sentiment of the clergy, that gave strength to the anti-Smith movement.

And the heart of this sentiment—and this is the third point—was that prohibition was indeed a great and noble effort to curb a malignant evil. Smith himself, his biographers, John J. Raskob his campaign manager, most Catholic commentators, Norman Thomas, Senator George W. Norris, Harold Ickes, and many other liberals, and a number of historians, have charged that Protestant devotion to prohibition was a mask for religious bigotry, a smoke screen to hide anti-Catholic prejudice, a false issue concerning which Protestants feigned an interest which was neither sincere nor fundamental.

Applied to many Protestants this judgment probably would be fair. Certainly it could be argued with justice that in some instances the moral energy of the Protestant churches was so exclusively centered on "demon rum" as to leave little to expend on other social evils such as racial prejudice or unfair labor practices. Further, it is evident that prohibition was selected as the reform to be backed because it was a less controversial issue than, say, segregation or unionization. Many observers have suggested that prohibition laws were placed on the books in the South to keep the Negro from drinking, there being a tacit understanding that the laws would not be enforced against whites. As Will Rogers put it, "Mississippi will hold faithful and steadfast to prohibition as long as the voters can stagger to the polls." No less a figure than Reinhold Niebuhr believed the real issues in the campaign "were hid under the decent veil of loyalty to a moral ideal—prohibition."[1]

Niebuhr's greatness lies largely in his ability to cut through sham and hypocrisy. He seldom accepted appearances at their face value and hence he rarely attributed a simple motive where an unacknowledged one could be inferred. With modern psychologists he believed that individuals often act from motives hidden even from themselves.

But there are times when sophistication can be more misleading than naïveté and when the truth lies in the simple and obvious rather than in the complex and obscure. In this case it is far more likely that to millions of Protestants prohibition was truthfully an issue of transcendent importance; that when Protestants said they opposed Smith because of his Wetness, they meant precisely what they said. Prohibition was not a straw man; it was the factor that more than any other determined the vote of many Americans in the election of 1928.

This is not to be construed as a defense of the Eighteenth Amendment. It may not have caused human suffering comparable to that of the Black Death or the Thirty Years' War, as Mencken claimed, but the results of the experiment were not entirely noble.

However, the wisdom of prohibition is not the question here; its importance is. Honest men may see no moral issue involved in drinking, but if they are fair-minded also they will concede that to other equally

1. *World Tomorrow*, Dec., 1928, p. 493.

sincere men drinking is a great personal sin and social evil. The validity of this indictment of liquor is irrelevant, for in history what a people believe is often more important than the truth or falsity of that belief. Nothing is more difficult than for an individual indifferent to a certain issue to appreciate that to others it might be of transcendent importance. Protestants are unable to understand the Catholic position on certain points, but if the question of state aid to parochial schools became an outstanding issue between the two major parties, would the Catholic Church remain indifferent? To repeat, then, prohibition, wise or unwise, was a major issue in the 1928 campaign.

The importance of the prohibition question has not gone unrecognized. Hoover, naturally perhaps, in his memoirs weighed it more heavily than the religious issue, and observers friendly to prohibition have concurred. Other commentators, George Fort Milton, for example, held Rum more significant than Rome, and even Catholic laymen such as Patrick K. Callahan agreed. Both Irving Fisher, analyst for the *New York Times,* and Roy Peel and Thomas Donnelly in their study of the election rate prohibition important, although not necessarily the outstanding issue. Further, a scientific study made by William Ogburn and Neil Talbot of the vote outside the South revealed prohibition three times more influential than religion. However, almost all students of the election agree that the prosperity of the country was more important in determining the election's outcome than either prohibition or religion.

No student who has examined the sources of Protestant opinion for these years could fail to recognize the importance of prohibition. The churches did not suddenly conclude in 1927 or 1928 that drinking was an evil; they did not embrace prohibition only after Smith's nomination. These convictions were held in 1920, when imbibing first became a federal offense, continued down through the twenties, remained in the forefront even after the crash of 1929, played some influence in the election of 1932, and elevated repeal into a major indictment of Franklin Roosevelt. Nor is prohibition sentiment by any means dead in Protestant quarters today. It is only a slight exaggeration to state that from 1919 to 1939 scarcely an issue of the religious press failed to carry an editorial or article on the evils of drinking; scarcely a denominational conference failed to pass a resolution to that effect; scarcely a Protestant minister in the country— outside the ranks of the Unitarian fold and the Protestant Episcopal Church—failed to endorse prohibition; scarcely a study—published or unpublished—of recent American Protestantism neglected to comment on the anti-liquor crusade. In short, the evidence is overwhelming that to millions of Protestants, both ministers and laymen, the crusade to drive liquor from America was the greatest moral issue in their lives.

It is hardly to be expected, then, that these millions who had devoted a lifetime to fighting the liquor traffic, who saw in the Eighteenth Amendment the greatest victory over evil in all history, would remain indifferent when that victory was jeopardized. They did not!

The Methodist Episcopal Church, both North and South, viewed political action as one of the most effective instruments for the solution of social problems, and in the election of 1928 Methodism was openly committed to the defeat of Smith. Its concern with the liquor question was of long standing and, from Grant to the second Roosevelt, Methodist General Conferences emphasized the duty of Christian citizens to support political leaders who stood for temperance. In 1928 the Board of Temperance, Prohibition and Public Morals reported to the Northern Methodist General Conference that *"There should be a 'dry' plank in every party platform in 1928. . . ."* Bishop James Cannon, a guest from Southern Methodism, inquired of the Conference, as he had done in 1924, "Shall America elect a wet cocktail President?" The Conference then by specific resolution served notice on both political parties that Methodism would fight any candidate whose record and attitude were hostile to prohibition.[2]

Southern Methodists in their last quadrennial meeting before the election also called for the election of only those officials—"from revenue agent to President"—friendly to enforcement.[3] In mid-July, 1928, Bishop Cannon was elected chairman of the Anti-Smith Democrats at a conference of Drys from every Southern state held at Asheville, North Carolina. A week later three other Southern Methodist bishops—Edwin D. Mouzon, John M. Moore, and Horace M. du Bose—joined Cannon in issuing a signed statement affirming their intention to wage a militant fight against Smith on the grounds of his prohibition policy. Not all Methodists approved of taking the church into politics—Bishops Warren A. Candler and Collins Denny tried to keep Methodism out of the campaign, for example—but there is no doubt that many Methodist clergymen openly opposed Smith.[4] The reason often given for this

2. *Journal of the General Conference of the Methodist Episcopal Church*, 1928, pp. 1621, 1733, 252. For Cannon's address in 1924 see *ibid.*, 1924, p. 753.

3. *Journal of the General Conference of the Methodist Episcopal Church, South*, 1926, p. 292.

4. According to Bishop du Bose, out of 8,500 Southern Methodist preachers, only four supported Smith. Bishop Candler's biographer believes that less than a third of the Methodist ministers of Georgia agreed with Candler's non-intervention policy. A Methodist minister in Fort Worth wrote that in Texas "99% of all Baptist and Methodist churches and their preachers are out in the open against Al Smith." All authorities conclude that, whatever the exact percentage, the Methodist clergy was overwhelmingly for Hoover. It will be recalled also that Mrs. Mabel Walker Willebrant, assistant attorney general of the United States, speaking before a group of Methodist clergymen under the auspices of the Republican National Committee, urged them to advise their congregations to vote for

political activity was prohibition, and while religion was not unimportant, the charge that prohibition was merely a cloak for religious bigotry falls down.

The Methodist press, like the Methodist clergy, gave wholehearted support to Hoover, and this despite the fact that in the elections of 1920, 1924, 1932, and 1936 it remained completely neutral. Although Smith's religion was a factor, the editors were virtually unanimous in asserting that for them prohibition was the overriding issue. The *New York Christian Advocate* argued that "in pursuance of its function as a mouthpiece of Methodist opinion on the liquor traffic, as declared by the General Conference, it pledges itself to do everything in its power to make its readers understand that a vote for the Democratic presidential candidate would mean disaster to that moral reform to which the Methodist Episcopal Church has repeatedly pledged its support."[5] Even before the Democratic convention nominated Smith, the *Northwestern Christian Advocate* made clear that while it would not oppose a Dry Catholic such as Thomas J. Walsh, Senator from Montana, it would fight Smith on the single issue of prohibition. The *Nashville Christian Advocate* was much less embroiled in the election than either the New York or Northwestern editions, but in its very few editorials on the campaign prohibition was the one and the only issue deemed important.

On the other hand, *Zion's Herald* jumped into the campaign with both feet, viewing it as a moral crusade. According to the editors, the issues were "clear cut—prohibition versus the saloon, Tammany versus law and order."[6] The *Arkansas Methodist* was also extremely partisan, supporting Hoover because he was a Dry, all other issues sinking into "insignificance." Other Methodist journals that campaigned for Hoover were: *Pittsburgh Christian Advocate, Western Christian Advocate, Wesleyan Christian Advocate, Methodist Recorder, Quarterly Review,* and *Missionary Voice.*

Baptists were as fully committed to the election of Hoover as their Methodist brethren. In 1928 the Northern Baptist Convention resolved:

That this convention hereby strongly recommends to its members and urges its large constituency to support and vote for only such men for the Presidency and Vice-presidency and other high office who will unequivocally

Hoover, basing her attitude on the prohibition issue. See Rembert Gilman Smith, *Politics in a Protestant Church* (Atlanta, 1930), p. 86; Alfred M. Pierce, *Giant Against the Sky. The Life of Bishop Warren Akin Candler* (New York., 1948), pp 221-22; W. M. Rader to Allen H. Godbey, Sept. 27, 1928, Godbey *Papers.*

5. July 12, 1928, p. 868.
6. Nov. 14, 1928, pp. 1455-56.

and openly commit themselves to an honest and effective observance and enforcement of the prohibition laws of our country. . . .[7]

In 1924 the Commission on Social Service of the Southern Baptist Convention warned that "no political party can ride to the White House on a beer keg."[8] This warning was repeated in 1927, and in 1928 the Commission unmistakably described and identified Smith as an unacceptable candidate to Southern Baptists. Even more significant, the 1928 Convention adopted the following resolution:

Resolved "that by the adoption of this report we enter into a sacred covenant and solemn pledge that we will support for the office of President, or for any other office, only such men as stand for our present order of prohibition, for the faithful and efficient enforcement of all law, and for the maintenance and support of the Constitution of the United States in all its parts and with all its amendments," and that we record our fixed determination to oppose actively the nomination or the election of any candidate of the opposite type no matter by what party put forward nor on what party platform they may stand.[9]

Baptist ministers were as active, if not as well organized, as the Methodists in the campaign. Hundreds of sermons were preached and resolutions passed by local bodies in support of Hoover. Almost invariably Baptists justified their interest on the grounds of prohibition, although religion did not go undiscussed and was assuredly of great importance also.

The Baptist press was desperately interested in the outcome of the election. Significantly, in every other presidential election between 1920 and 1940 these same papers preserved a strict neutrality. The *Baptist,* official organ of the Northern Baptist Convention, believed prohibition the outstanding issue in the campaign, although it devoted as much space to Rome as to Rum. "We base our opposition to Governor Smith," editorialized the *Watchman-Examiner,* "entirely on the fact that he is and always has been the implacable foe of prohibition. The Roman Catholic papers insist on lugging in the religious question."[10] "We care nothing about the politics of Mr. Smith," read another editorial, "but we care a great deal about the war he has declared on prohibition. Let the churches everywhere fight him because there is a great moral issue at stake and because he has deliberately and defiantly taken the wrong side."[11]

7. *Annual of the Northern Baptist Convention,* 1928, p. 198. The phrase "recommends to its members" originally read "pledges its members."
8. *Annual of the Southern Baptist Convention,* 1924, p. 116.
9. *Ibid.,* 1928, p. 88.   10. Aug. 30, 1928, p. 1095.
11. Oct. 4, 1928, p. 1259.

The *Alabama Baptist,* unlike its sister journals, had very little to say concerning the election. However, on the few occasions when it did speak it maintained that prohibition and not religion was the main issue. Indeed, it was believed that had Senator Thomas Walsh, a Catholic and Dry, been the Democratic candidate rather than Smith, he would have received the support of Southern Baptists. A Kentucky paper, the *Western Recorder,* opposed Smith in literally hundreds of editorials and articles. Early in 1927 the editors flatly stated that if either party nominated a Wet candidate he would be opposed, and when it appeared that Smith might receive the Democratic nomination the editors warned: "WITH ALL POSSIBLE EMPHASIS IT NEEDS TO BE SAID AND FREQUENTLY RE-ITERATED THAT THE TROUBLE WITH MR. SMITH AS A PRESIDENTIAL CANDIDATE IS NOT RELIGIOUS BUT POLITICAL. HIS DISQUALIFICATION INHERES IN THE FACT THAT HE IS A HOPELESS AND CONFIRMED NULLIFICATIONIST."[12] Typical of some of the contributed material is the following:

Were I to support a wet candidate for President, and so announce to my family, I think I could read in the face of my wife the deep disappointment of her loyal heart, and in the bright eyes of my two boys I could see the light of filial devotion darkened into twilight because father had descended from moral heights heretofore occupied in their undoubting minds.[13]

If one is to understand the significance of the prohibition issue one must realize that writers of this sort of thing were unquestionably sincere.

The *Religious Herald,* a Virginia paper, devoted a prodigious amount of space to the election. The editor, R. H. Pitt, repeatedly stated that for him the overriding issue was prohibition, although scores of items also discussed the religious question. Pitt, a man of seventy-five, had fought the saloon for more than forty years. Prohibition brought the hope of victory and he could not—would not—see his labors smashed by the election of a Wet.

"We cannot accept Mr. Smith on several counts," said the *Baptist and Reflector,* "but our primary battle is against his prohibition and immigration policies." The *Baptist Observer* stressed the liquor question. The *Christian Index* opposed Smith on the prohibition "issue alone." "I regard the Eighteenth Amendment," said this paper's editor, "as the greatest piece of moral legislation in the history of government, and I cannot and will not stand idly by and see Governor Smith . . . destroy this part of the Constitution of my Nation which represents the prayers and labors of good men and women for the past century." "We oppose Governor Smith," averred the *Word and Way,* "because he is soaking

12. May 19, 1927, p. 11.
13. Nov. 1, 1928, p. 10.

wet and has declared in favor of the modification of the Volstead Act and the amendment of the Eighteenth Amendment." This opinion was shared by the *Southern Baptist Trumpet.* "I cannot get the consent of my conscience," stated the editor of the *Biblical Recorder,* "to vote for the outstanding leader of the liquor forces of this country. I cannot understand how those who have favored and fought for prohibition can support Governor Smith for President." Said the *Baptist Messenger:* "The campaign is primarily moral rather than political. It is a contest between the prohibition forces and the liquor traffic. . . . For this reason we are against Governor Smith. We would be against him if he were a Baptist, with his present stand on the liquor traffic." The *American Baptist* warned: "Our very civilization is at stake. As all liquorites are for Smith, why should not all prohibitionists be for Hoover?" Thus also believed the *Baptist Advance.* "The value of prohibition to the lives of children, wives, mothers and daughters," held the *Baptist New Mexican,* "is too precious for it to be cast willfully aside by any aspirant to any public office whether it be constable, policeman, congressman or President of our United States." "Not wanting prohibition destroyed or injured," admitted the editor of the *Baptist Courier,* "I am doing what I can to keep him [Smith] out of office." Other Baptist journals including the *Baptist Message,* the *Baptist and Commoner,* the *Florida Baptist Witness,* the *Baptist Record* of Mississippi and the *Baptist Record* of Iowa also campaigned for Hoover. Thus it was that at least twenty-one Baptist papers openly opposed the election of Smith, virtually all of them stating prohibition to be the outstanding issue.[14]

The Presbyterian Church, North and South, was not as fully committed to the defeat of Smith as the Methodist and Baptist denominations. Nevertheless, official Presbyterianism long had stood for total abstinence and prohibition was a cause close to its heart. So much so, indeed, that while the General Assemblies did not specifically endorse Hoover in official resolutions, many individuals, including the moderator of the General Assembly of the Presbyterian Church, U.S.A., took this step.[15] Moreover, the Presbyterian press for the only time in either the twenties or thirties openly endorsed a presidential candidate. The *Presbyterian Banner* explicitly stated that it opposed Smith, not because he was a Catholic, but because he was a Wet. The *Presbyterian Advance* took this position also, supporting Hoover because of prohibition but refusing "to believe that there would be any peril to the liberties of this country in having a man who was affiliated with the Catholic church

14. The editorial attitude of these Baptist journals for which no citations were given are all revealed in a symposium in the *Watchman-Examiner,* Oct. 25, 1928, pp. 1355-57.

15. Such noted Presbyterian leaders as Henry Sloane Coffin and Henry van Dyke publicly protested the action of the moderator.

as president."[16]   The *United Presbyterian, Moral Welfare,* and the *Presbyterian* concurred in supporting Hoover because of the prohibition issue, as did the Kentucky paper, *Christian Observer,* although the last journal devoted much less space to the election than most church papers.

The National Council of Congregational Churches resolved in 1927: "Churches of all creeds were responsible for the banishment of the saloon. This great moral achievement is now in danger. As a Christian, consider well the moral issues at stake in the coming election, and vote."[17] Congregationalists cooperated with other temperance agencies in the formulation of an appeal to the Republican and Democratic parties for candidates and platforms that would stand for the strict enforcement of the Eighteenth Amendment. The denominational journal broke its tradition of non-partisanship and openly campaigned for the election of Hoover on the prohibition issue. "The issue is a straight one," believed the editors, "as to whether this country wants a 'dry' or a 'wet' President —a man pledged to what this country has written into its Constitution, or a man pledged to its repeal."[18]

The *Christian Herald* and the *Christian Century,* powerful unde-nominational papers edited by Daniel A. Poling and Charles Clayton Morrison, in scores of instances launched an all out attack against Smith. Poling insisted that prohibition and Tammany were the chief issues, and Morrison maintained that prohibition, while not the sole issue, was the most important one. Other church journals, the *Lutheran,* the *Christian-Evangelist,* and the *Reformed Church Messenger,* for example, champi-oned Hoover, giving as their chief reason the prohibition issue. True, a few Protestant journals remained neutral,[19] and one, the *World Tomorrow,* supported Norman Thomas, but only one, the *Christian Register,* a Unitarian paper, avowedly based its opposition to Smith primarily on religious grounds.

This evidence leads to the conclusion that where there is so much smoke there must be some fire. Prohibition was not a "straw man." It was an issue of transcendent importance which more than any other determined the vote of many Protestants.

Because prohibition was a key issue in the election of 1928, it does not necessarily follow that religion was insignificant. At the time many commentators agreed with the editors of the *Catholic Union and Times* when they wrote on October 4, 1928:

16. Aug. 9, 1928, p. 5.
17. *Minutes of the National Council of Congregational Churches,* 1929, pp. 70-71, quoting the 1927 action.
18. *Congregationalist,* July 19, 1928, p. 69.
19. For example, *Christian Leader, Southern Churchman,* and *Living Church.*

Were Herbert Hoover as dry as the Sahara, as Republican as Mark Twain, but a Catholic, these dwindling, divided sects [the Protestant churches] would vote against him to a man. Were Al Smith as wet as the Niagara River, as Democratic as the electorate of Alabama, but a Protestant, these dying embers of the so-called reformation would turn out in force to put him in Washington from March 4, 1929, to March 4, 1933.[20]

The results of the election only served to confirm this opinion. A number of observers agreed with the distinguished Catholic and liberal, Dr. John A. Ryan, that "without the religious factor Governor Smith would not have been defeated."[21]

While this belief is certainly debatable, on the other hand there can be no doubt that Smith's religion served to help make him unacceptable to many Protestants. Literally hundreds of examples might be cited from the church press alone to illustrate this point. And there can be no doubt, also, that the campaign was marred by the foulest type of anti-Catholic bigotry. Apparently some Protestants agreed with Philip Guedalla that any stigma would do to beat a dogma.

The vicious and false charges made against Smith because of his Catholicism have been catalogued by several students, perhaps most ably by the liberal Catholic layman, Michael Williams, in a volume entitled *The Shadow of the Pope*. It was whispered that the Knights of Columbus was a revolutionary organization, that arsenals were buried in vaults under Catholic churches, that should Smith be elected the Pope would move to Washington, that, in short, there was a general and well-organized Catholic conspiracy to seize control of America and forcibly convert the Protestant population. Confronted with statements of this sort, not the Catholic but the Protestant must feel a sense of shame. And if opposition to Smith because of his religion rested solely on this type of propaganda nothing more need be said. The disgrace of American Protestantism would be complete.

What almost all commentators have failed to make clear, however—and this is the fourth point—is that part of the religious arguments were on a higher level than sheer bigotry. Mr. Williams, the capable Catholic analyst, concedes that some of the literature discussing religion was on a high plane of intellectual interest and value, but he insists that by "far the larger portion . . . consisted of the most obviously false, vicious, poisonously malignant, and often horrible charges against Catholicism ever fulminated against any body of men and women, the most despicable and fiendish criminals not excepted."[22] Much bigotry did indeed

20. Quoted in *Nashville Christian Advocate*, Nov. 2, 1928, p. 1380.
21. John A. Ryan, "A Catholic View of the Election," *Current History*, Vol. 29 (Dec., 1928), 378.
22. Michael Williams, *The Shadow of the Pope* (New York, 1932), p. viii.

exist, but an investigation of the established religious press and other sources of official Protestant opinion discloses also much opinion that cannot be so characterized. Or, if the reader insists that any criticism of the Roman Catholic Church is bigotry, then it was of a sophisticated sort different in degree if not in kind from that of the Klan or Senator Thomas J. Heflin. The Protestant churches did not confine their arguments to cowardly whispering campaigns; they often presented their views openly, frankly, and with candor, and the language employed was often restrained and temperate. Further, it is significant that many Protestants who opposed Smith publicly stated that Senator Thomas J. Walsh, a Catholic but a Dry, would be entirely acceptable; thus some alleged "bigots" at least exempted teetotaling Catholics from their wrath.

In April, 1927, Charles C. Marshall, a noted lawyer and a member of the Protestant Episcopal Church, wrote an open letter in the *Atlantic Monthly* in which he dispassionately raised certain questions relative to American democracy and the Roman Catholic Church, concluding that there were deep seated and serious objections to elevating a Roman Catholic to the Presidency. Marshall's doubts were based on social and political grounds, and not on the theological tenets of Catholicism. Governor Smith, not yet a Presidential candidate, replied in the following issue fully and fairly,[23] although many Protestant spokesmen observed a discrepancy between Smith's democratic answers and the official utterances and historical record of his church. As the *Reformed Church Messenger* observed, the reply was "so at variance with the history and spirit of the papal hierarchy that one cannot help rubbing his eyes in amazement. If the position taken by the popular Governor of New York is quite generally believed today by American Catholics, it is a proof of almost unbelievable progress in the thinking of our fellow-religionists of that great communion." Unhappily, the *Messenger* concluded that Mr. Smith did not and could not speak for the Catholic hierarchy, nor could one letter cancel the record and teaching of the Catholic Church.[24]

Mr. Williams' comment on the Marshall letter was very revealing. He declared: "It would be going outside the narrative purpose of this book to deal with the questions raised by Mr. Marshall. They were concerned with the most technical and recondite points of ecclesiastical and lay history, theology, and canon law."[25] Mr. Williams might have added that the "questions raised by Mr. Marshall" were not only

23. It is not entirely beside the point that several exchanges of this type between Protestant and Catholic spokesmen were held in an attempt to openly thrash out the issues, and that, unlike the even tempered statement of Governor Smith, other Catholic advocates, Father Ryan, for example, met dispassionate queries with Klan-like vituperation.

24. *Reformed Church Messenger,* May 12, 1927, p. 4.

25. *The Shadow of the Pope,* p. 171.

"technical" and "recondite," but centered on those very basic and fundamental differences between Roman Catholicism and (as Protestants believed) American democracy.

And it was these honest differences which were stressed in the recognized sources of Protestant opinion, differences so fundamental that they could not be glossed over with sentimental campaigns for "tolerance" or silenced by cries of "bigotry." In 1928, as before and after, intelligent Protestants were deeply troubled by certain aspects of Catholic political and social policy. Contrary to the impression left by most historians, these arguments as they appeared in the sources of Protestant opinion were not infrequently rather temperate in tone and scholarly in presentation. If one may generalize, the attitude expressed was that Smith's religion was a legitimate issue—not as important as prohibition—but one that must be weighed. It was not strong enough to bar a Catholic from the Presidency under any and all circumstances, but it was one of several factors mitigating against the Democratic candidate. Many Protestants, then, took the religion of the candidates into account in due proportion and in what they considered a reasonable way as constituting a part of the totality of conditions which determined their vote. Rather than cite briefly from many sources, it is perhaps sufficient to quote at length from the *Christian Century* of October 11, 1928. It is representative of the anti-Catholicism of the recognized Protestant press.

Just what kind of motive is it that actuates a Protestant to vote against a Roman Catholic for the presidency? Why does he not wish to see a Roman Catholic in the white house?

It is not because he would restrict religious freedom.

It is not because he is a religious bigot.

It is not because he does not believe in the Roman Catholic religion or does not like its ways of worship.

It is not because he disregards the constitution.

It is not because he fears that Al Smith as President will 'take orders' from the pope. Such a fear is surely groundless if for no other reason than the fact that the pope is no fool.

The anti-Catholic voter is no more a bigot than the anti-Wall Street voter, or the anti-bolshevist voter, or the anti-pacifist voter, or the anti-militarist voter or the anti-saloon voter, or the anti-Volstead voter. He is opposed to the occupancy of the white house by a Roman Catholic because he sees, or thinks he sees, a real issue between Catholicism and American institutions. It involves the exercise of just as much intelligence to discern and to define this issue as the same voter would put into his consideration of the equalization fee, or water power, or the tariff, or prohibition, or any other issue. The anti-Catholic voter may hold a mistaken view, but it is not a bigoted view. Let us see how broadly intelligent a voter must be who, among other reasons, opposes Mr. Smith on the ground of his membership in the Catholic church.

The logic of his position is somewhat as follows: The increase of Catholic influence in American society threatens certain institutions which are integral to our American system. With a Roman Catholic in the white house, the influence of the Roman Catholic system will be enormously increased in American social and political life. Therefore, without interfering with the full liberty of Catholicism to extend its influence by the normal means of propaganda and growth, this voter declines to assist in its extension by helping to put its representative at the head of the government. In so declining, and in using whatever influence this voter may have to persuade others likewise to decline, he is not acting as an intolerant person, or a bigot, but as an intelligent and faithful American citizen.

II

The observations advanced in this chapter are intended only as a footnote to the election of 1928. After reading these pages, many individuals might find themselves repeating Mr. Dooley's observation: "I know histhry isn't thrue, Hinnissy, because it ain't like what I see ivery day in Halstead street." However, until further documentation is presented, it seems fair to conclude that the Klan did not play a crucial role in the election; that clergymen did not force their congregations into the anti-Smith camp; that prohibition was not a straw man; and that not all of the religious arguments were on the level of sheer bigotry.

CHAPTER V

The Churches Move to the Left: I

"The thing to do is to get a man at first to value social justice as a thing which the Enemy [God] demands, and then work him on to the stage at which he values Christianity because it may produce social justice."—Advice of Screwtape, the Devil's assistant, in The Screwtape Letters by C. S. Lewis

I

IT IS TOO EARLY to assess the impact of the Great Depression upon American Protestantism, but that the thirties were years of stress and strain for the churches, as for all of society, cannot be doubted. As securities cascaded in the 1929 crash of the Great Bull Market, the hopes of numerous clergymen were raised. A people shorn of their material wealth, it was felt, most certainly would turn to God. They did not. Bad times did not enhance the "Gospel of Good News." Outwardly the churches suffered along with the rest of the nation. Memberships dropped, budgets were slashed, benevolent and missionary enterprises set adrift, ministers fired, and chapels closed. All this can be demonstrated statistically. That the churches proved relatively more stable than most business enterprises was of small comfort to those who confidently predicted a religious revival in the years of the locust.

There were other results for Protestantism that cannot be measured statistically. In theology, liberalism gave way before the crashing ascendancy of neo-orthodoxy. Liberalism had served its day courageously, but many churchmen believed it too feeble, too humanistic, too rationalistic, too utopian, too sweetly optimistic to withstand the shocks of total depression and total war. Barth, Brunner, and Kierkegaard in Europe had earlier re-asserted divine transcendence, but the America of the twenties considered itself much too near an approximation of the Kingdom of Heaven to heed warnings of apocalyptic judgment. Then came the crash with its tragic wake of bread lines, Hoovervilles, hunger riots, Okies, and unutterable despair. Then came also the breakdown of peace in Asia and Europe—Manchuria, Ethiopia, China, Spain, Czechoslovakia, and Poland. Shivered by those demoniac events, American Protestantism turned to a "theology of crisis." Neo-Protestantism—to use still a third name to describe the movement—was realistic, finding faith beyond humanity and beyond history. It was pessimistic, holding man a sinner in the grip of tenacious evil and placing the Cross once again at the heart of Christianity. It was God-centered, believing redemption came not through man's efforts but through God's grace. It was apocalyptic, knowing the Kingdom would never be achieved on earth but only at the end of history. And it was church centered, maintaining the church must always be at tension with the world.

Curiously, while Protestant theologians in the thirties emphasized the sinfulness of man and the transcendence of God, while they clung to salvation by faith rather than works, while they stressed individual redemption rather than the transformation of society, and while they rejected the possibility of achieving the Kingdom in history, they did not, unlike many European crisis theologians, withdraw from the world. The American Protestant churches, like the great spokesman of neo-orthodoxy, Reinhold Niebuhr, went to the Right in theology and to the Left in politics. Thus, it is misleading to speak of the "death of the Social Gospel" in the thirties. The optimistic social Christianity of an earlier more hopeful age may have passed on, but the interest of the churches in the problems of society intensified rather than slackened in the Depression Decade. And it is to the evidence of this fact that the discussion now turns.

II

"Among all the trades, occupations, and professions in this country," wrote Kirby Page in 1934, "few can produce as high a percentage of Socialists as can the ministry."[1] A year later Winfred Garrison, the distinguished Disciples historian, noted that the pronouncements of the major denominations all revealed a body of opinion critical of the existing order, and which demanded a radical program of reconstruction. Going further, Paul Hutchinson, then managing editor of the *Christian Century,* averred that literally hundreds of church bodies declared that religion demands a society purged of the profit motive. Reinhold Niebuhr advanced the belief in 1934 that the American churches probably contained more Left wing political opinion than any of the other religious institutions in the entire world. In 1931 the *Christian Register* said editorially: "No one who studies the religious press steadily and carefully can doubt that American Protestantism has gone over in its sympathy to the Russian experiment and the basic idea of the Russian philosophy. . . . These ministers, true to the traditions of the prophets, are aware of the moral evil beneath our economic and social order, and are satisfied that Russia's fundamental principle of a non-profit making and cooperative commonwealth is true to the teachings of Jesus and square with the pretensions

1. *World Tomorrow,* May 10, 1934, p. 219.

and professions of all the churches. . . . But when the keen-minded parson compares our economic individualism and its rampant competition now exhibiting its basic fallacy in a broken occidental civilization, he sees that what Russia is seeking is something infinitely better for the masses of mankind, and not for Russia only. . . . All the world wants honesty, justice, and a decent living for every decent human being. At the present writing, it looks like Russia to the informed Protestant minister. If we may estimate what is going on in the composite mind of the parsons who have spent the past three summers in that strange new land, we should say that, from the economic standpoint, they prefer it, all in all, to what we have in America."[2]

III

It is a curious fact that of the individual denominations, Methodism planted its flag ahead—or to the Left—of the general line held by American Protestantism. Steeped in a pietistic and individualistic tradition, Methodism might well have been expected to champion a "hands off" policy in regard to social matters. But Wesley's followers possessed a warm evangelical fervor (Wesley, after all, had a "heart-warming" rather than a "head-clearing" experience at Aldersgate), freedom of individual witness which left them unembarrassed by theological quarrels, efficient administrative organization, and a puritan conscience that concentrated increasingly on social as well as personal morals. Further, the leaders of Methodism's liberal wing were an unusually able and persuasive lot.

After witnessing the toll exacted by a year of depression, the bishops of the Methodist Episcopal Church made public their conviction that there is something fundamentally wrong "with a social system that, in the midst of plenteous abundance, dooms untold numbers of our people to unbearable poverty and distress through no apparent fault of their own."[3] Two years later in their Episcopal Address to the General Conference the bishops again sounded a call to take up arms against the sea of troubles surrounding the nation. The industrial practices of the past decade were specifically blamed for the appalling paradox of bursting granaries and starving people, banks bulging with money and ghastly poverty, idle machinery and idle men, mountains of coal and people freezing. They warned that the Kingdom of God could not be built upon the poverty of the many and the absurd and cruel wealth of the few. The alternatives that faced America were social reconstruction or revolution.

Taking its cue from the Episcopal Address, the Conference pro-

2. Oct. 8, 1931, pp. 772-73.
3. *New York Christian Advocate*, Dec. 11, 1930, p. 1527.

ceeded to adopt resolutions terming the depression a "rebuke and spur" to the Christian churches, noting the poverty that existed in the midst of plenty, and calling for the replacement of "our present policy of unplanned competitive industrialism with a planned industrial economy, which aims definitely at economic security for all." This meant the fullest possible cooperative control and ownership of industry and of the natural resources on which industry rested. Finally, the Conference adopted a report which termed the industrial order "unchristian, unethical and anti-social, because it is largely based on the profit motive, which is a direct appeal to selfishness."[4]

These statements caused considerable consternation among conservative Methodists, and, as will be noted, plans were laid to forestall any similar "nonsense" at the next quadrennium. In the opinion of most liberal Methodists, the conservatives were successful. The 1936 Conference was characterized as a smashing defeat for the liberal wing. This impression is not entirely accurate. While the meeting did represent a retreat from the advanced position of 1932, it did not repudiate social Christianity. The Conference again reviewed the terrible suffering caused by the depression, listing fourteen specific evils in American economic life ranging from unemployment through inequality of income to tenant farming. Solutions were suggested including demi-socialism, co-operatives, and enlightened capitalism, but whatever the answer the delegates pledged themselves to work within the democratic form and ideal and to resist both the totalitarianism of communism and of fascism. Thus, the 1936 Conference retreated from near-socialism, but it was hardly pushed back as far as the conservative trenches.

In the meantime, regional Methodist conferences felt constrained to say a few things about the economic order. In many instances, no doubt, these reports and resolutions were hurried through without any particular debate, and represented nothing more than a pleasant concession by the majority to the ego of a few young idealists fresh from hearing a lecture by a Niebuhr, Ward, or Page.

The New York East Conference, embracing some of the greatest names in Methodism, repeatedly took an advanced position on social matters. And the chairman of its social service commission, Ralph W. Sockman, hardly can be dismissed as a young cub. The Conference's description of the depression read like something out of Dante. The profit motive was damned as the supreme paganism of the day. Most of the delegates believed capitalism must be brought under some form of social control, and to some this meant socialism. "The twenty-five

4. *Journal of the General Conference of the Methodist Episcopal Church,* 1932, pp. 652-55.

months of strenuous effort under the New Deal," said the Conference in 1935, "to reform the system has only proved that it is beyond reform. The conviction grows, therefore, that capitalism must be discarded and a planned Christian economy established. . . . The tenderness with which the sacred cow of private profits has been protected, while suffering has been indescribably inhuman, indicts both the intelligence and character of our nation."[5] Every meeting of the decade had something to say along these lines.

The Pittsburgh Conference was almost equally outspoken, and repeatedly in the thirties pleas were made for increased control of the tools of production and social ownership of the natural resources of the land. The Methodists of the Rock River Conference (Chicago and vicinity) succeeded in making the solid citizens of the North Shore believe that Methodism had gone Socialist. This was not quite justified, as the Conference never formally gave its adherence to the social ownership of resources and production. But it did repeatedly denounce the competitive system and the profit motive. Equally severe were the pronouncements of the Newark and Detroit annual conferences, both bodies repeatedly stating that there could be no justice within a system based on profits and competition.

The New York East, Pittsburgh, Rock River, Newark, and Detroit annual conferences all achieved a certain notoriety for their radical utterances. Truth to tell, however, their stand was no further to the Left than those of many another Methodist group.

For instance, the New England Annual Conference of 1931, after leveling a bead on the injustices of the existing order, deplored how the common need had been exploited for private profit. The New Jersey Conference suggested an extension of social ownership in fields other than schools, roads, and postal service. Missouri Methodists held the present system doomed millions to economic insecurity, and Philadelphia Methodists believed the system morally wrong. The Northern New York, Central New York, and Troy New York Methodists all termed the existing order, based upon profit and motivated by greed, productive of only billionaires and bread lines. Wyoming Methodists averred the present order stood condemned before the bar of Christian justice, and Ohio Methodists convicted it of flagrant sin. Northern Minnesota Methodists called in 1934 for the socialization of basic industries, and Methodists in Wisconsin and California termed the basic assumptions of capitalism unchristian.

These are all examples of action taken by district conferences. Liberal expressions abounded in other quarters of Methodism. Industry based

5. *New York Times*, May 14, 1935, p. 21.

upon the profit motive is doomed, agreed a meeting of Methodist preachers in Pennsylvania in 1931. A year earlier laymen and ministers met in Evanston, Illinois, under the sponsorship of the Methodist Federation for Social Service, to discuss the economic order. Not a few believed that socialism was the only road out. In 1932 in Milwaukee the Methodist Youth Association believed the social order inherently unchristian since its standard of value was materialistic and selfish. A Methodist group in California did not feel compelled to condemn the order, for it already stood indicted in the light of its stupendous failures. In 1931, 350 ministers, laymen, and educators of Methodism met in Delaware, Ohio, and proposed numerous reforms including the extension of social control to all key industries and natural monopolies. The following year, thirty-five directors of Methodist religious education pointed to the essential bankruptcy of the capitalist regime.

The National Council of Methodist Youth held its first meeting in 1934 in Evanston, Illinois. Delegates from forty-three states gathered to solve the world's problems. As the Council's historian observed, "Here were no decadent dilettanti twirling between listless fingers cigarets and the slender stems of cocktail glasses. Here was flaming youth, to be sure, but a youth aflame with love for Christ, having caught the contagion of courage." The delegates heard addresses by Kirby Page and others in which capitalism was decried root and branch and socialism lavishly praised. They then proceeded to adopt the inevitable resolutions. The New Deal was chided for its pusillanimity, and the Council declared: "We endorse socialism, as being at present, the most workable political expression of Christian social ideals. Essentially socialism, as we define it, is the theory of government based on the principles of public ownership and democratic control of natural resources, public utilities, and all basic and essential industries for public use instead of for private profit."[6] The following meeting of the Council repeated its criticism of capitalism and its praise of socialism.

In 1934 decision cards were circulated among Methodism's lads and lasses bearing the pledge: "I surrender my life to Christ. I renounce the Capitalistic system based on economic individualism and the profit motive and give myself to the building of an economic order based on co-operation and unselfishness. . . . I believe that the possession of wealth is unbecoming a Christian."[7]

It was precisely this sort of thing that caused a group of conservative Methodist laymen to form an organization designed to check the spread

6. Miron A. Morrill, ed., *Methodist Youth Council* (Chicago, 1934), pp. 1, 178.
7. Theodore Graebner, *The Business Man and the Church: An Economic Study* (Clinton, South Carolina, 1942), p. 10.

of radicalism in their church. Disturbed liberal Methodist laymen then proceeded to form in 1936 a Layman's Religious Movement, the avowed purpose of which was to check the counterattack and defend social Christianity. The executive committee, with one exception, hailed from the Middle West.

But the most important source of fissure in Methodism was the activity of the unofficial Methodist Federation for Social Service.[8] This group, like Wesley, took the world for its parish. Formed in 1907, the Methodist Federation for Social Service was more the creation than the creator of the incipient social consciousness arising within Methodism. Although the fathers of the movement included such great names as Bishop Herbert Welch, Frank Mason North, Elbert R. Zaring, and Worth M. Tippy, the two men who guided the destinies of the Federation in the twenties and thirties were Harry F. Ward, secretary, and Bishop Francis J. McConnell, president. To use the analogy of the Federation's historian, Ward carried the message and McConnell, with the influence of his prestige and episcopal office, cleared the way of opposition. However, Ward called the signals and he was the real force directing the Federation for over two decades. Although always maintaining an unofficial relationship to the Methodist Episcopal Church, it was looked upon, as the 1912 General Conference stated, as the executive agency to rally the forces of the church in support of social thought and reform. Bishop McConnell described its purpose in more homely terms: that of raising disturbing questions—ahead of time.

During the complacent twenties the Federation served as the conscience of Northern Methodism, stubbornly refusing to concede that in America there were no conditions about which to be conscience stricken. Then came the depression. Although not blind to the depths of the economic collapse, for several years the Federation appeared content with the reformation rather than the complete destruction of capitalism. A spontaneous and unofficial Call to Action Conference held in Chicago in April, 1932, saw the Federation tack sharply to the Left. In that year also Ward returned from Russia greatly impressed between the success (as he believed) of the Soviet experiment and the decadence of Western capitalism. Besides, the Federation was in desperate financial straits and since, in the first place, the present order was to blame and, secondly, if the group was to go under it might as well be with flags flying, the Federation launched an all-out attack on capitalism in November, 1932.

It was an honest break. The Federation did not think, or speak, or

8. In 1948 the group took the name Methodist Federation for Social Action. The 1952 General Conference of the Methodist Church voted to request the organization to drop the name "Methodist" from its title. In the summer of 1953 its offices were removed from the Methodist headquarters in New York.

write with moderation. Like William Lloyd Garrison, it did not equivocate, excuse, retreat a single inch, and it was heard! Its chief organ was
renamed the *Social Questions Bulletin*. There appeared upon the masthead, with the approval of the membership, this statement of principles:
"An organization which seeks to abolish the profit system and to develop
the classless society based upon the obligation of mutual service."[9]

At this time a series of pocket-size *Crisis Leaflets* were published.
They enjoyed wide distribution. The gist of all these leaflets, printed in
three sets of six each, was the replacement of capitalism by socialism.
The *Bulletin* beat upon the same theme. Every issue for fifteen con-
secutive months was devoted to an analysis of the New Deal, and while
specific measures received the Federation's condescending approval,
Roosevelt was generally held to be leading the nation down the road to
domestic fascism and foreign war. Both results were the fruits of
capitalism. And hence the New Deal, in attempting to revitalize capitalism, was dangerous as well as useless.

Believing as it did that capitalism was doomed and fearing as it did
fascism, the decision of the Federation to affiliate with the American
League Against War and Fascism hardly comes as a surprise. And it is
important to make clear that not only did individual Federation members
join the League (Ward served as secretary), but that the Federation itself
voted to so act. Affiliation was not taken hastily. The executive committee first discussed the matter fully, and then the Regional Conferences
voted their approval. The action cost the Federation heavily in membership.

Such a result was inevitable considering the fact that the American
League Against War and Fascism was widely and probably truthfully
considered a Communist front organization. Ward always denied this
charge, although it is a little difficult to see how Communist membership
in the League would have made any difference to him. Fascism was already upon the nation, he believed, and if it was to be blocked a union
of all forces that have declared themselves against the profit motive was
imperative. It was rather common knowledge that the Communists had
so declared themselves.

As a matter of fact, Ward saw few demoniac elements in communism.
As shall be noted, his views on Soviet Russia were blurred by ethical
astigmatism. He believed the Soviet experiment was the world's last,
best hope. He denied before a congressional committee that Stalin was

---

9. From time to time in the decade this masthead statement was slightly changed.
There is a good study of the Federation: Milton John Huber, "A History of the Methodist
Federation for Social Action" (unpublished Ph.D. dissertation, Boston University, 1949).
However, the present writer made an independent investigation of Federation sources and
his conclusions are not always shared by Mr. Huber.

a dictator, and he followed the vagaries of the party line, even defending the Moscow-Berlin pact and flip-flopping from a "stop the Fascists" attitude to a "stay out of the imperialist's war" position in the fall of 1939. One of the saddest statements in recent history was Ward's attack on Fred Beal. Beal, it will be remembered, led the Gastonia textile strike, was arrested, skipped bail, fled to Russia, became disillusioned and returned to the United States to enter prison. When he described the Soviet government as reactionary and ruthless, Ward replied that Beal either completely misunderstood or deliberately falsified what he saw. There can be no doubt that the Methodist Federation for Social Service swung far Left of center in the thirties.

All of the references thus far have been to Northern Methodism. They found a pale reflection in the Methodist Episcopal Church, South. The General Conference of 1930 called for a more Christian social order, but did not hint at socialism. In 1932 the Board of Temperance and Social Service reported that the nation stood at the parting of the ways. The proper road to follow was neither the present capitalistic system, which had proved inadequate, nor communism, but the middle road of Christ's. The Episcopal Address of 1934 held Christianity neither endorsed nor condemned any economic system, but rather stood for justice regardless of the particular program. The General Conference then proceeded to adopt the revised "Social Creed of the Churches" which suggested the end of the profit motive and social planning and control in the economic processes. An adopted report at the next quadrennium reviewed the suffering in the country and concluded that "an economic system which produces the results which we see all about us is subject to the most serious investigation in the light of Christian ideals. One of our most serious needs is to deal with our economic order in terms of the Christian standards before those who are desperate—deal with it in terms of desperation."[10]

The Council on a Christian Social Order, an unofficial voluntary organization within the Methodist Episcopal Church, South, saw even more clearly the need for the reformation of the social order. Its members were pledged to work toward the discovery of the full social meaning of the gospel and toward its application to society. While not as militant as the Methodist Federation for Social Service, the Council did seek greater economic democracy in the South, especially in relation to farm tenancy.

The editors of the Methodist press bore witness to the general liberalism of that denomination. But here, as always in regard to American

10. *Journal of the General Conference of the Methodist Episcopal Church, South*, 1938, pp. 220-21.

Protestantism, it is impossible to speak in unqualified terms. The *Arkansas Methodist,* for instance, certainly did not embrace collectivist ideas. Indeed, it would be inaccurate even to describe this journal as friendly to the New Deal. And yet the editorials did take a discernible swing to the Left after 1929. At first reluctant to admit the severity of the depression, by early 1931 the editors were demanding that the federal government take immediate action to remedy matters. And shortly after Roosevelt took office, his program was termed the finest in the history of the Republic. As the New Deal continued on its erratic and pragmatic way, this paper suffered serious misgivings. It gave its blessing, however, to a number of specific measures. Interestingly, the diplomatic recognition of Russia in 1933 was hailed as a distinct triumph.

The *Nashville Christian Advocate,* general organ of the Methodist Episcopal Church, South, emerged in the Depression Decade as a lusty critic of traditional, unfettered capitalism. The breakdown of the economy undoubtedly was a determining factor in this leftward movement, but perhaps of equal significance was the fact that in July, 1932 William P. King assumed editorship of the journal. His editorials were among the sanest to appear in the church press. His position was that of a New Deal liberal, to the Left of center, perhaps, but not on the lunatic fringe. Of course, he was accused by readers of socialistic preachments and of desiring to "swap the Stars and Stripes for the red flag of Bolshevism." The former charge has some justification; the latter none. King did not believe in the abolition of private property, but he did favor the public ownership of the natural and primary sources of wealth such as electricity, mines, and oil. He did not rant about destroying the profit motive, but he insisted that profits be shared. And this, he maintained, could only be achieved through a larger measure of social control through governmental regulation. Hence, the New Deal was viewed favorably.

Among Northern Methodist journals, *Zion's Herald* won a reputation for bold liberalism. Its editor, "an elderly gentleman possessed of radical ideas," according to a report of the House Committee on Un-American Activities, was Lewis O. Hartman.[11] Hartman was a Christian Socialist and a grand crusader for social justice. This did not prevent him from becoming—in his last years—a Methodist bishop. As *Zion's Herald* admitted, the stock market crash gave a great impetus to socialism in America. Businessmen, in their greed and selfishness, made a fundamental transformation of the economic order inevitable. No mere tinkering would suffice. The profit motive and cut-throat competition were as wicked as hell itself. Laissez-faire capitalism was at bay. It would and

11. *Report of the House Committee on Un-American Activities,* 79th Congress, 2nd session, p. 31.

should be replaced. The New Deal was viewed favorably; indeed the chief criticism of Roosevelt was that he did not go fast or far enough. Interestingly, *Zion's Herald* in the thirties was much more fully aware of the brutal elements in the Russian experiment than it had been in the twenties.

The Northwestern and New York *Christian Advocates* followed a middle of the road policy, the former being mildly liberal and the latter mildly conservative. However, both were critical of the abuses of capitalism and both from time to time endorsed New Deal measures. These papers favored the diplomatic recognition of Russia.[12]

Baptists were generally less outspoken in their utterances than their Methodist brethren. This is not to say, however, that they invariably assumed a conservative position. In 1930 the Northern Baptist Convention resolved that the present organization of economic life tended to occasion unemployment. Every effort to find a cure was urged, and this position was repeated the following year. In 1932 the Convention called for the establishment of a cooperative commonwealth which would place human rights over property rights. Further, the government "must fully exercise its sovereign right to own, control and administer property; to control private business, to coordinate economic activities, to inquire what wealth the citizen possesses, how he got it, and what he does with it."[13] The 1933 Convention repined the exploitation of personality which persisted in sweatshops, coal fields, and in many industrial centers where precedence was given to profits rather than human personality.

In 1934 Northern Baptists looked toward a more Christian social order where poverty and excessive wealth would be eliminated by the establishment of a cooperative commonwealth and where the service motive would supplant the profit motive. The following year the Convention heard the first report of the newly created Commission on Christian Social Action. This document ranged critically over the injustices of society. The *Christian Century* termed the report remarkable for depth of insight, courage of declaration, and wisdom of presentation. The strength of the report lay in its exposure of existing conditions, for although it called for "fundamental" changes, it did not draft a socialistic blueprint of the perfect society. The 1937 Convention requested the replacement of ruthless competition by helpful cooperation, and this sentiment was repeated in 1939 with the warning that it was folly to have passed through a terrible depression only to return to former conditions.

12. Dan B. Brummitt, editor of the Northwestern edition, voted for Norman Thomas in 1932. Further, Halford Luccock, contributing editor to both journals, was a Socialist. His editorials were about the most trenchant to appear in the church press.

13. *Annual of the Northern Baptist Convention*, 1932, p. 97.

These Convention utterances, coupled with the action of some local Baptist groups and with the work of the Rauschenbusch Fellowship of Baptists, placed a liberal stamp upon the social attitudes of Northern Baptists. They believed in the reconstruction of capitalism, but they did not advance a doctrinaire program of socialism. Their position was, in brief, a little Left of center.

It is impossible to speak in these terms regarding Southern Baptists. To be sure, the reports of the Commission on Social Service spoke of the distress caused by the depression and of the need for greater economic justice. A few resolutions importuned a more equitable distribution of wealth. A few liberals such as Edwin M. Poteat, Jr., stirred the Convention with calls to social justice. And it is true that several state conventions, particularly that of Georgia, praised the New Deal and requested greater governmental regulation of economic activity. But on the whole Southern Baptists appeared reasonably content with the prevailing economic order. There was little vigorous criticism of capitalism and no official endorsement of socialism: the Southern soil—whether watered by Baptist immersion or non-Baptist sprinkling—did not nourish collectivist notions.

Among Baptist journals, the *Baptist* was probably the most liberal. During the years from 1929 to 1933 (it ceased publication in 1933), its editors were U. M. McGuire, a member of the Socialist party, and then Robert A. Ashworth. The dark early years of the depression witnessed some candid and blunt writing. President Hoover was termed the Chevalier Bayard of plutocracy. His administration was warned that it did not need cheer leaders to tell the people that prosperity was just around the corner. A confidence game got the country into its mess, but would not get it out. The only agency capable of affording adequate relief was the federal government. Although the editors indicated that Russia should be recognized, they noted the gulf between theory and practice in the Soviet Union.

The *Alabama Baptist* far outstripped other Southern Baptist journals in the severity of its criticisms of capitalism. The editor, L. L. Gwaltney, repeatedly warned that the existing order must either purge itself of its abuses or be replaced by some type of socialism. The old order is doomed. Change is inevitable. Will it be peaceful and moderate or violent and extreme? The New Deal seemed to provide the answer. The recognition of Russia was hailed, but Gwaltney was quite aware of its totalitarian aspects.

An examination of three other Baptist journals revealed no comparable spirit. The *Religious Herald* was close to center, but both the *Western Recorder* and the *Watchman-Examiner* were distinctly conservative.

True, a few general criticisms were leveled at injustices and a few New Deal acts were endorsed, but they were exceptions proving the rule. As might be expected, communism was severely handled and none of these papers approved the recognition of Russia.

Northern Presbyterians swung moderately to the Left in the thirties. The 1931 General Assembly made some general pronouncements concerning the need to combat unemployment, and a committee was appointed to study the social problems facing America. In 1932 this committee held and the Assembly concurred that human values must take precedence over all others and that no system economically wrong could be ethically right. "The present economic distress is not a mere incident in the history of our industrialism. It is an indicment of our whole economic system. . . . We face the necessity of some modification of our present system in favor of a fairer division of the products of capital and labor. . . . Nothing is more obvious than that the present economic order is now on probation and its continued existence and justification must be found not in the wealth produced or the power gained, but in its contribution to social service and social justice."[14] A host of liberal reforms were then urged, including the subordination of the profit motive and greater social planning and control.

The 1933 General Assembly insisted that "no economic emergency justifies human oppression; that if the right to live interferes with profits, profits must necessarily give way to that right. Christians have a mandate from the Christian conscience to question an economic order where the only answer to our industrial problems is charity drives, bread lines, and apple vendors. As Christians we need to affirm that if the present order will not and cannot adapt itself to the social conscience, based on Christian ideals, then it must give way to some more just and righteous social order that will answer our problems."[15] This again meant subordination of the profit motive and greater social control and planning.

The 1934 General Assembly gave approval to the following principles:

1. That new motives besides those of money-making and self-interest be developed in order that we may develop an economic system more consistent with Christian ideals.

2. That competition as the major controlling principle of our economic life be re-examined, and an attempt made to secure rational planning in our economic life.

3. That our natural resources and economic institutions be considered as existing for the public good and such plans for ownership and control be developed as will lead to the best use in the interests of all.[16]

14. *Minutes of the General Assembly of the Presbyterian Church, U.S.A.*, 1932, p. 126.
15. *Ibid.*, 1933, p. 167.
16. *Ibid.*, 1934, p. 202.

In 1935 the Assembly spoke of the economic insecurity harassing modern man, and the following year went on record as being dissatisfied with any industrial order which does not provide security for those who will work but find no opportunity and which provides no security against the involuntary want of children, widows, the aged, and the victims of an era of machinery. The 1937 Assembly regarded periodically recurring depressions, extremes of wealth and poverty, exploitation, and suffering as some of the unchristian elements in the social order. In the last year of the Depression Decade Northern Presbyterians were still speaking of shocking extremes of poverty and wealth.

The critical spirit of Northern Presbyterianism was illustrated also in the Labor Sunday Messages, mostly written by the Reverend John McDowell. The 1931 message indicates their general tone: "No society can reckon upon stability if one extreme of its population gets more than it earns and the other extreme earns more than it gets." The present order must reform itself or face death by revolution. If capitalism is to remain, it must prove its superiority not by wishes and words, but by work and wages.[17]

This moderate position was displayed by *Moral Welfare,* after 1934 entitled *Social Progress,* a journal published by the Presbyterian Board of Christian Education.[18] While critical of the existing economic order, this paper did not shy so far from the Right as to fall into the camp of the Left. Generally, the tone of this paper was that of Rooseveltian liberalism.

Presbyterians at the synod level on occasion evidenced an objurgatory attitude. The Synod of New York, for instance, had some unkind words to say about unfettered capitalism. But this mood was not confined to Eastern Presbyterians. The Indiana Synod, to cite one example, regretted the "cruel irrationality of an economic set-up where plenty pauperizes, where millions are denied the basic right to earn their bread by the sweat of their brows; where children go hungry to school amid abundant harvests, the housewife is penniless in a land which has the most of the world's gold, and men are ragged while the textile market is glutted. We are strongly convinced that a planned economic order should replace the present disorder."[19]

The social passion of Northern Presbyterianism also found expression in the small, unofficial, now defunct Presbyterian Fellowship for Social

17. *Presbyterian Banner,* Aug. 27, 1931, p. 10.

18. In 1936 the Department of Social and Industrial Relations of the Board of National Missions and the Department of Social Education of the Board of Christian Education were merged into what was called Social Education and Action, and this became a department of the Board of Christian Education.

19. *Presbyterian Advance,* Nov. 5, 1931, p. 23.

Action. The Fellowship was formed at a luncheon during the meeting of the Synod of New York at Buffalo, October 16, 1934, by a group of forty-two persons sharing the conviction that the Christian gospel must be effectively related to the pressing social and economic problems of the day. Although its membership was never very large—perhaps only a hundred or so—it included some of the most famous Protestants in the country: Ray Freeman Jenny, John C. Bennett, John Paul Jones, Edmund B. Chaffee, David W. Moody, and G. Shubert Frye. This organization was dedicated to the reformation of the social order, and for some of the officers this meant the abolition of capitalism.

It is a little difficult to find much social passion among Southern Presbyterians. From time to time the General Assembly voiced concern over unemployment and poverty, but the harshest statements of the decade did no more than mourn the poverty that existed in the midst of plenty. There was no suggestion that capitalism should be discarded. A few protests were heard at the synod level, but among Southern Presbyterians there were apparently few followers of Norman Thomas and almost none of Karl Marx.

The Presbyterian press was on the whole rather conservative. An important exception to this observation was the *Presbyterian Tribune*. Born in 1934, it rapidly attained a reputation for social justice under the editorship of Edmund B. Chaffee, a Socialist, who died in 1936. The liberal tone of the paper remained, however, under succeeding editors. The *Presbyterian Tribune* was an acute critic of traditional capitalism. Its editors sometimes thought Roosevelt was going neither fast enough nor far enough, but in general they gave the New Deal warm support. It is significant that this liberal journal took a dim view of events in Russia.

The *Presbyterian Advance,* published in Nashville, was by no means as liberal on economic matters as the *Tribune.* And yet, before its demise in 1934, it carried not a few critical comments on the system which brought the nation into the depression. And, as was not infrequently the case in the religious press of these years, Russia was looked upon somewhat like prohibition—a noble experiment.

An examination of a half-dozen other Presbyterian journals revealed a thoroughgoing conservatism. A few editorials and articles could be cited indicative of a liberal position. Occasionally New Deal acts were defended. Some of these papers favored the recognition of Russia. But, balancing exception against exception, none of these journals swung perceptibly to the Left in the thirties.

The Congregational and Christian Churches, merged in 1931, as-sumed a moderately censorious position toward the social order in the

Depression Decade. The 1931 General Council spoke of the need for a planned national economy to end the inequities of the present order. It was, however, the historic meeting at Oberlin, Ohio, in 1934, that captured the attention of the nation and caused much consternation among conservatives. Passion for social reform was at a peak. Council speakers affirmed the world's chief problem was that a few people had too much and most people too little. Four of the ten Council seminars dealt with social matters. The Council for Social Action was born. And then, in the dying hours when the Council had thinned from 764 voting delegates to less than 150, the following resolution was adopted by a vote of 130 to 17:

Whereas, we commit ourselves with hearty avowal of the faith of our fathers to walk in all God's ways known or to be made known to us, and with sincere passion, which we believe derives from our Master, to make abundant life available to all men everywhere,

Whereas, our present competitive profit-seeking economy shows itself to be increasingly self-destructive and,

Whereas, it depends for its existence upon exploitation of one group by another, creates industrial and civic strife and international war, precipitates periods of unemployment, perpetuates insecurity and all of its attendant miseries, and progressively curtails the cultural and educational opportunities of our people, thus destroying human values, moral and spiritual, and

Whereas, these flagrant social evils exist side by side with potential natural abundance, which the present economy is unable to utilize and distribute, however much good it may have done in the past and however honest and idealistic, individuals dependent upon the system may be,

Be it Resolved that:
We set ourselves to work toward:

The abolition of the system responsible for these destructive elements in our common life, by eliminating the system's incentives and habits, the legal forms which sustain it, and the moral ideals which justify it.

The inauguration of a genuinely coöperative social economy democratically planned to adjust production to consumption requirements, to modify or eliminate private ownership of the means of production or distribution wherever such ownership interferes with the social good.[20]

Now it is important to remember that less than one-fourth of the voting membership of the Council expressed themselves on the resolution. Additionally, the General Council is autonomous and can speak only for itself. Its statements are not binding upon the local congregations. Indeed, some churches, that of Wilmette, Illinois, for example, specifically disassociated themselves from the resolution, and for years conservative

20. *Minutes of the General Council of the Congregational and Christian Churches,* 1934, pp. 107-8.

Congregationalists took pains to point out the limited nature of the utterance. And yet, there it was! The official position of the General Council of Congregationalism in 1934, as expressed in a resolution passed in the same fashion that most resolutions are passed in any deliberative body, approximated that of socialism.

The two remaining Councils in the thirties scrupulously refrained from radical resolutions. The Oberlin utterance caused much strife within the ranks of Congregationalism, and throughout the rest of the decade moderates sought to bind the denomination's wounds and to heal the rift between the liberals and conservatives. Some observers have suggested that after 1934 Congregationalists retreated to a reactionary position. This is inaccurate. A chastened but still critical spirit was reflected in several utterances of the 1938 Council. Incidentally, in 1931 the General Council resolved to respectfully urge upon the government the recognition of Russia.

From time to time regional conferences, such as those of Vermont, Colorado, and the Middle Atlantic, adopted reports or resolutions of a questioning spirit. Certain it is that the official Commission on Social Relations did not lose its social passion in the years 1929-34. Note, for instance, the December 1931 issue of its bulletin, *Church and Society,* devoted to "The Industrial Crisis." Edmund B. Chaffee, a Socialist, contributed a general statement. Then Arnold Johnson, one-time Communist party member, described the situation in American coal fields. He was followed by Louis Budenz, another one-time party member, who talked about American textiles. Oswald Garrison Villard, a Socialist, proceeded to paint a dark picture of the European situation. Lastly, Miss Winifred Chappell, who voted the Communist party ticket, concluded with a glowing description of the prosperity of Russia under the Five Year Plan. The only possible conclusion that could be drawn from a reading of this bulletin was that capitalism in the Western world had broken down while communism in Russia was a resounding success. This conclusion—at best—was only half right. *Church and Society* went out of existence in 1934, but its evaluation of the early New Deal seemed to be that it was fascistic.

However, the best example of Congregational social passion in the Depression Decade is the Congregational Council for Social Action, the authorized agency established in 1934 to make the Christian gospel more effective in society through research, education, and action.

Valiant as were the efforts of the Commission on Social Relations, prophetic minded Congregationalists—especially Arthur E. Holt, Hubert C. Herring, and Dwight Bradley—became increasingly convinced that it should be lifted to the rank of a major society in the denominational structure. They struck in 1934—a year when the iron was hot. Proclaiming "New Crusades for Old," supporters of the proposed agency held preliminary caucuses and sounded out Congregational opinion in the denominational journal, *Advance*. Some who responded satirized the proposal as just another scheme to send out "secretarial locusts" to ravage the churches. In general, however, the discussion columns of *Advance* revealed a favorable response.

Accepting the "challenge thrown down to us by the times we live in," a number of influential men and women met at Oberlin in advance of the National Council to map the attack. It would take bitter fighting to get the plan accepted. The proposed agency would cost money; and if the times were ripe for social action they were also ones of financial retrenchment. But Holt, Herring, Bradley, Hugh Elmer Brown, John C. Schroeder, Carl Knudsen, Buell Gallagher, Allan Knight Chalmers, and others were not to be denied. Already Alfred W. Swan, Albert B. Coe, and Russell J. Clinchy were active as "missionaries at large" to other Council delegates, winning pledges of support for the resolution. After clearing the way with the Business Committee of the Council, the resolution to create the agency was presented to the hushed delegates in College Chapel on June 25, 1934, by Charles W. Merriam. Upon his stirring, climatic words, the Council broke into applause. Brushing aside a tear, the Lincolnesque Holt stepped forward to make the first supporting speech. Others followed. There were no dissenting speeches. Delegates who had only minutes before expressed vehement opposition were silent. And when Dr. Fred B. Goodsell arose and proclaimed that if a diversion of funds to the support of the new agency meant the loss of ten foreign missionaries the sacrifice was well worth the making, the issue was no longer in doubt. The resolution was passed by an almost unanimous vote. The Congregational Council for Social Action was born. It was born because a handful of prophetically minded men and women believed, as one of them said, that the Kingdom of God on earth included "the regeneration of so many people, so many confused, honest, lazy, wishful people like us that its achievement may once more require martyrs, who will be burned—by the press; imprisoned—by due process of law; stoned—by respectable organizations; forgotten—by those whom they serve."[21]

The position of CSA was Left of center. But how far Left is "Left?" From its inception the agency engendered distrust in conservative Congregationalists, partially because it was falsely associated with the Oberlin "profit motive" resolution, and partially because it was in truth far from

21. Cyrus Ransom Pangborn, "Free Churches and Social Change. A Critical Study of the Council for Social Action of the Congregational Christian Churches of the United States" (unpublished Ph.D. dissertation, Columbia University, 1951), p. 192. This is an excellent study.

conservative. The Council's chief historian believes the attacks upon it have been quantitatively unimpressive. Nevertheless, attacks there were, and they persisted for years. The record seems to indicate that, at least until 1940, the CSA was the sanest, least biased, and certainly least doctrinaire of almost all the church social agencies, official or unofficial. A wise rooster never tries to go through a hedge fence tail feathers first, but beak and brain first, was the sage advice of Holt. Herring also cautioned moderation, insisting that the Council avoid choosing for its staff those who had complete solutions to society's riddles. The Council avowed that it was committed neither to communism nor to socialism nor to the New Deal. It was not, in fact, committed to communism. It never related itself in any way to any of the Communist's favorite united fronts, and it never believed that Russia was riding the wave of the future. It was not, in fact, committed to socialism. Unlike many church groups, it did not indulge in advocating socialism as the only cure for capitalism's ills. However, although it may not officially have been committed to the New Deal, its complexion, as its president later admitted, was New Deal liberal. An examination of the files of *Social Action* leaves the inescapable impression that here was a liberal group—but one that was sanely, pragmatically, tolerantly liberal.

In 1939 the Council published the results of a plebiscite which gave further indication of Congregational economic opinion. "Indication" is the correct word, for a poll in which only 3 per cent of Congregationalism participated could hardly be considered conclusive. The results—for what they are worth—showed Congregationalists 4 to 1 in favor of government work relief for the unemployed; 3 to 1 for organization of consumers' cooperatives; 5 to 4 for federal support of agricultural prices and for the organization of labor into unions; 16 to 11 in favor of further extension of public ownership of electric utilities; 3 to 2 for further social control of the economic system. Protective tariffs, however, were approved by over half, reflecting perhaps the concentration of many Congregationalists in New England.

The pages of the denominational journal, the *Congregationalist* (after 1934 entitled *Advance*), are still another source reflecting Congregational opinion. The editor, William E. Gilroy, was not a radical. He believed, however, that millions of Americans lived in appalling poverty, and that America's problems could be solved only by a socialization of life that would substitute the service motive for the profit motive. This meant immediate and fundamental reforms, and these reforms must be backed by governmental coercion. Thus, Gilroy favored most of the New Deal and although he did not come out for Roosevelt in 1936, the distinguished weekly columnist, H. C. Herring, did so.

Protestant Episcopal opinion in the thirties was not radical, and yet it was somewhat to the Left of a village banker. The General Convention of 1931, for instance, reflected the time of troubles in which it met. The bishops in their Pastoral Letter drew a bleak picture of conditions during the depression, a breakdown precipitated not by any catastrophe of nature but by the failure of capitalism. Recovery must be accompanied by basic reforms, and the profit-seeking motive must give way. A committee also reported that the traditional philosophy of rugged individualism must be modified to meet the needs of a cooperative age. After all, when men starve because there is too much food, go naked because they produce too much clothing, sleep in parks because there are too many houses, even a fool can see that something is wrong. It was at this Convention also that Spencer Miller informed the delegates that capitalism had failed, and the Convention gave him a prolonged ovation.

A special meeting of the House of Bishops in 1933 brought forth this admonition: "No mere reëstablishment of an old economic order will suffice. Christ demands a new order . . . which shall substitute the motive of service for the motive of gain."[22] The following year the bishops hit upon the same theme. "That millions of the people of our country are denied the common necessities of life," they asserted, "that approximately one-third of our population is below the poverty level, that there is widespread want in a land that is abundantly productive, make evident the lamentable inadequacy of existing economic systems."[23] On several other occasions later in the decade the bishops spoke on economic conditions, but never did they specify an alternative system to capitalism, and their observations dealt with motives and ethics rather than specific details.

The official Department of Christian Social Service (after 1939 known as the Department of Christian Social Relations), with eighty-nine diocesan branches, faced up to the problems of the depression from the point of view of middle class liberalism, critical of the abuses of capitalism but not advocating its discard. The unofficial Church League for Industrial Democracy went even further.[24] "We are living in the twilight of the gods of capitalism," declared its president, Bishop Edward L. Parsons.[25]

In answer to an open invitation, a number of Episcopal priests and lay people met in the spring of 1919 in New York to consider how the

22. Quoted in *Journal of the General Convention of the Protestant Episcopal Church,* 1934, p. 80.

23. *Ibid.,* p. 46.

24. The group was originally named the Church League for Social and Industrial Democracy and today is known as the Episcopal League for Social Action.

25. Edward L. Parsons, *Christ Demands a New Order* (New York, n.d.), a pamphlet published by the CLID.

church might face up to the problems created by an "unchristian industrial and economic system." A two-day discussion followed and from these humble beginnings there emerged a militant new organization, the Church League for Industrial Democracy, conscious that "our Lord's revealed will" enjoined the passing of selfish competition and the birth of the democratization of industry and the socialization of life. Vida D. Scudder, Bishop Charles D. Williams, and the Reverend Richard W. Hogue were made the League's first chairman, president, and executive secretary. In time, CLID embraced over a thousand members, including a score of bishops of the Protestant Episcopal Church. The group's dominating figure was the courageous and controversial executive secretary, the Reverend William B. Spofford.

Spofford believed that fascism posed a grave danger to the United States and, hence, he was willing to join hands with the Communists in united front activity. He stated that he was not a Communist and had never voted for a Communist. But he saw no reason why Christians and Communists should not cooperate in the areas where they agreed. It would be a pragmatic alliance. If and when the Communists changed their anti-Fascist line, he said, he would probably part company with them. Other leaders of the CLID, Vida Scudder, for instance, agreed with Spofford that it was both possible and wise for Christians to cooperate with Communists in united front movements. It should be noted, however, that the CLID itself in national meeting overwhelmingly defeated a proposal to affiliate with the American League for Peace and Democracy. In short, the CLID was generally critical of capitalism and a few of its members won the reputation of naïveté toward communism.

Spofford also expressed his views through *The Witness,* on which he served as managing editor. Its liberalism was unmistakable. Equally certain was the critical spirit of a second Episcopal journal, the *Churchman,* edited by Guy Emery Shipler. Shipler was later to be termed the closest thing America had to the "Red Dean," and even liberals came to consider his paper as one lacking in sound judgment. On the whole, this evaluation is too extreme for the position of Shipler and the *Churchman* before 1940. This journal was liberal in the thirties, but not pro-Communist. Capitalism's debacle was vividly portrayed and New Deal measures defended, although Roosevelt was not openly endorsed in the election of 1936. The recognition of Russia was hailed as an intelligent act, but that land was not seen as a utopia.

The *Living Church,* published in Milwaukee, is generally considered to represent conservative opinion in the Protestant Episcopal Church. Its conservatism, however, was relative. To the Right of the journals edited by Spofford and Shipler, it was nevertheless far from rock-ribbed. It clearly favored governmental planning and federal coercion to curb the abuses of rampant capitalism. The editors were critical of the CLID, but the nature of this criticism should be made clear. "When the Church League . . . abandons its complacent attitude toward Communism," said the editors, "and bases its program squarely on the platform of Christian radicalism, our enthusiasm for it will increase a hundred fold."[26]

The *Southern Churchman* was rather more liberal in its attitudes, evidencing a position roughly equivalent to the New Deal. The *American Church Monthly,* on the other hand, was very conservative. Incidentally, the former favored and the latter opposed the recognition of Russia.

The Disciples of Christ supported many reforms in the interests of economic democracy. They did not, however, indulge in much discussion of the basic premises of capitalism. Nevertheless, several International Conventions spoke strongly, for America was faced with the "bitter fact that our economic system has tragically failed . . . and that cooperative effort to build an economic order that is both just and democratic is the way to permanent peace and prosperity."[27]

The Disciples journal, *Christian-Evangelist,* edited by Willard E. Shelton after 1934, was moderately liberal during the twenties, but emerged in the Depression Decade as an outstanding champion of reform. Its coverage of social issues was extremely full—matched by only a handful of other religious papers—and its frame of reference was distinctly New Dealish. Although not committed to socialism, the *Christian-Evangelist* was certain that traditional capitalism was doomed. Few if any church journals gave warmer support to Roosevelt's New Deal. After the 1936 election, the editors admonished the President that he could serve his country well only if he continued to be progressive. Although contributors found much that was commendable in the Soviet experiment, the editors, while approving recognition, realized that a dictatorship of the proletariat was still a dictatorship.

Although some individual Unitarians and some local congregations were very liberal, the American Unitarian Association itself drafted no Left wing social pronouncements. Demands for higher wages, social security, and the like were placed on record, but there were no resolutions denouncing capitalism as a system. However, in 1935 the Department of Social Relations, under the guidance of Robert C. Dexter, presented a Program of Social Action to the Association. It did not represent official Unitarian opinion. Among the planks in the program

26. Sept. 21, 1938, p. 255.
27. *Christian-Evangelist,* Nov. 11, 1937, p. 1441.

was an appeal for the end of wasteful competition and the profit motive, and for further governmental ownership of public utilities, transportation, banking, coal, and other natural resources.

This sentiment was shared by some regional groups. For instance, in 1933 the annual Unitarian conference of the State of Minnesota indicted capitalism as a "system under which the most useful occupations are paid least, the less useful more, and the useless or parasitic the most."[28]

The unofficial Unitarian Fellowship for Social Justice remained a mildly liberal agency in the thirties, content to preach the reformation of the social order rather than its destruction. It did not, unlike some other religious groups, embrace socialism as man's salvation. It regarded Stalin, like the rest of the dictators, as a bloody-handed butcher.

While most of Unitarianism remained near the center, the denominational journal, *Christian Register,* swung sharply to the Left. (In late 1932 the famous Albert C. Dieffenbach, in an alleged economy move, was replaced by a succession of editors.) Throughout much of the decade the *Christian Register* was hostile to unfettered capitalism. More than that, repeated editorials and articles maintained that some sort of governmental control and ownership of the nation's resources was essential. That is why Roosevelt was frequently chided for his temporizing, although specific New Deal measures were usually endorsed. Needless to say, however, Roosevelt fared better than his predecessor in the White House. The evidence indicates that this journal tacked toward socialism in the Depression Decade. For, as the editors believed, "Our political liberty is ghastly emptiness if thirty-five millions of us nearly starve. Our religious liberty a pious fraud if a multitude in winter lacks clothing. Our equality before the law an abstract hypocrisy and deceit if numberless of our neighbors have neither sufficient warmth nor shelter."[29] Another editorial read: "We believe the world has now come to an end disastrously in its unplanned and mainly profit-seeking economic system."[30]

Editorials and articles in the religious press praising—in varying degrees—the Soviet experiment were not uncommon, but the *Christian Register* contained more uncritical opinion of Russia than almost any other church journal. Russia, Dieffenbach believed in 1931, was a great cooperative commonwealth true to the teachings of Jesus and, from an economic standpoint, superior to the United States. Communism, argued a signed editorial in 1935, would be and should be the great ultimate unifying force of Europe. Contributed articles defended united front activity. Russia was painted as the most stupendously successful experiment in all history.

28. *Christian Register,* Oct. 26, 1933, p. 701.
29. March 3, 1932, p. 139.   30. Jan. 7, 1932, p. 6.

The Reformed Church in the United States and the Evangelical Synod of North America, united in 1934 to form the Evangelical and Reformed Church, harbored considerable liberal sentiment. The 1932 General Synod of the Reformed Church termed the present economic order unchristian and built upon greed and selfishness. Only a reconstruction of the entire system would suffice. In 1936 the General Synod of the Evangelical and Reformed Church heard a report which declared:

2. We can no longer accept as compatible with our Christian faith a social, economic, and political order which makes for materialism in practice, robs personality of its opportunities for development for the sake of others' enrichment, leads to an increasingly bitter hatred between worker and employer, intensifies divisive racial and national prejudices and ultimately drives nations into foolish and destructive wars, develops and perpetuates economic inequality with consequent political inequality without respect to function.

3. We cannot accept any industrial order which makes the pursuit of profit its dominant motive rather than the pursuit of the common good and thus permits the most irresponsible and unchristian practices in the acquisition and distribution of property.[31]

From time to time regional synods acted. In 1931 the New York district of the Evangelical Synod in annual conference reported: "We are beholding the disintegration of the capitalistic profit-system; the system of mammon which through the ages has depended on unmitigated selfishness and individualistic 'go-getting' for driving force."[32] In 1934 the Potomac Synod of the Reformed Church denounced capitalism and averred the churches must work for its destruction.

There was in addition to the official Commission on Christian Social Action of the Evangelical and Reformed Church (in turn a merger of the earlier Commission on Christianity and Social Problems and the Committee on Social Service), an unofficial group devoted to social action. It was not formed until 1938 and took the name Council for Social Reconstruction. This group was entirely voluntary and its activities were pretty much limited to occasional mimeographed bulletins and a series of conferences. The Reverends John Sommerlotte and John Bollens were, respectively, chairman and secretary. Until its demise in 1947 it worked to end the abuses of the social order.

The *Reformed Church Messenger* (in 1936 it became simply the *Messenger*), ably edited by Paul S. Leinbach, followed a middle of the road policy on economic matters. It clearly did not embrace socialism

31. *Acts and Proceedings of the General Synod of the Evangelical and Reformed Church*, 1936, pp. 251-52.
32. *Christian Century*, July 29, 1931, p. 964.

and had virtually nothing to say regarding the New Deal. Nevertheless, it left the impression of mild liberalism rather than reaction.

Lutherans, traditionally aloof from secular matters, were shaken by the depression. The 1932 Convention of the United Lutheran Church in America, the most representative and influential body of Lutheranism in the country, scored the suffering caused by the economy's breakdown. The 1936 Convention heard a report even more severely critical of existing conditions. A report of the Committee on Moral and Social Welfare deplored the gulf between the privileged and the poverty stricken. In 1938 a Board of Social Missions was established to further social action. Regional groups of Lutherans occasionally spoke strongly. Pamphlets were distributed as study guides dealing with social problems. The *Lutheran,* edited by Nathan R. Melhorn, followed a middle of the road policy. All of this is not to suggest that Lutheranism swung sharply to the Left in the depression. It did not. But at least a glimmering of social consciousness appeared.

IV

Thus far reference has been to denominational opinion. Before drawing any conclusions concerning the leftward swing of the churches in the thirties, it is first necessary to examine inter-denominational church opinion. And it is to this subject that the inquiry now turns.

CHAPTER VI

The Churches Move to the Left: II

"You have in extreme social radicalism the same thing as in fundamentalism: they have found the absolute, perfect truth and know it."—Henry Sloane Coffin

I

Inter-denominational groups and gatherings reflected a movement to the Left in the thirties. It is the purpose of this chapter to note the evidence supporting this statement.

II

The Federal Council of Churches, never smugly complacent, toughened its strictures in the thirties. It joined with other faiths in holding a Conference on the Permanent Prevention of Unemployment and in forming a nationwide Committee on Religion and Welfare Activity. April 27, 1930, was set aside as "Unemployment Sunday." Pamphlets were issued suggesting concrete ways for the churches to alleviate unemployment. It repeatedly suggested a public works program and unemployment insurance. Moreover, business was charged with being socially blind for failing to divert sufficient profits as reserves for the protection of the jobless. And if people were going hungry they should be given direct aid without it being stigmatized as "dole," and this aid should be raised by the heavy taxation of large incomes. The only real cure for unemployment was a more equitable distribution of the nation's wealth.

The New Deal program received almost unfailing support from the Federal Council for, as Council officer Cavert noted, it embodied many of the social ideals that the churches had long been championing. Others on the Council staff warmly hailed the Roosevelt program.

This benevolent attitude was also evidenced by official utterances of the Council. The executive committee time and again called for cooperation with the government in combating the depression. The Council's *Labor Sunday Message* of 1934 characterized the Roosevelt administration as one pledged to the welfare of the forgotten man, and both *Information Service* and the *Federal Council Bulletin* gave unexplicit but clearly evident backing to the New Deal.

This great cooperative agency of American Protestantism advocated reform as well as recovery. In 1933 the executive committee commanded the complete substitution of the motive of mutual helpfulness for that of private gain. "The Christian ideal," said the Council a year earlier, "calls for hearty support of a planned economic system in which maximum social values shall be sought. It demands that cooperation shall supplant competition as the fundamental method."[1] That same year the Council published a volume entitled *Our Economic Life in the Light of Christian Ideals*. It rang the charges on an economic system that produced such vast suffering, greed, unemployment, and inequality, warning that only intelligent social planning and control could save the individualistic system of ownership. The 1932 *Labor Sunday Message* argued that the concentration of wealth carried with it a dangerous concentration of power which in turn led to class conflict and violence. To suppress the symptoms of this inherent conflict while leaving the fundamental causes of it untouched was neither sound statesmanship nor Christian good will. And it is interesting to recall that the first two points in the revised "Social Creed of the Churches" requested:

1. Practical application of the Christian principle of social well-being to the acquisition and use of wealth; subordination of speculation and the profit motive to the creative and coöperative spirit.

2. Social planning and control of the credit and monetary systems and the economic processes for the common good.[2]

All of this brought down upon the Council's head denunciations from both the Right and Left. Conservatives charged it with "communism" while radicals scoffed at its bourgeois naïveté in thinking that reform could be achieved without revolution. The fact is, that while the Council did suggest economic planning, the substitution of cooperation for competition, and the end of the real abuses of the present economic system, it did not launch a crusade to wipe out private ownership in favor of some form of doctrinaire socialism. The Council stood for the reformation of society, and although it never made the blunder of calling upon Protestants to vote the New Deal ticket, the Roosevelt program did approximate the political equivalent of the Council's social ideals.

There is other evidence of inter-denominational interest in social matters. For example, sixty representatives of various Protestant communions gathered at Buck Hill, Pennsylvania, in 1931, and this group issued a call for the replacement of our present policy of unplanned, competitive individualism by a planned social economy definitely aiming

1. *Quadrennial Report of the Federal Council of Churches*, 1928-32, p. 64.
2. The complete "Creed" is printed in *ibid.*, pp. 72-73.

at the conservation of human values. A year earlier four hundred ministers meeting in Cleveland spoke strongly for a more Christian economic order. The Ohio Pastors' Convention, in 1932 and 1934, repudiated capitalism and demanded greater governmental regulation and ownership. In 1933 a group of parsons meeting in Minnesota believed capitalism was characterized by selfishness, greed, and predatory self-interest. A Commission of Christian Associations, coordinating the work of the student divisions of the Y.M.C.A. and the Y.W.C.A., issued a pamphlet in 1931 advocating a new political party to inaugurate social ownership of public utilities, natural resources, and basic industries. *Time* magazine spoke of "Christian Socialism" and the *New York Times* growled, "Socialism Favored by Religious Groups." Although the "Y's" took pains to make clear that the pamphlet did not represent an official view, they nevertheless had spoken frequently in a liberal fashion on economic matters.[3]

III

It is now time to mention the undenominational press. The *Protestant Digest* did not begin publication until December 1938. It was originally a monthly, published in Boston, and edited by Kenneth Leslie. Included on its editorial board were some of the most distinguished names in American Protestantism, men who over the next fifteen years were one by one to sever their connections with the paper. In 1944 the House Committee on Un-American Activities charged the *Protestant Digest* with being "fanatically devoted to the propagation of the Communist Party line, with only the thinnest religious veneer used in an obvious attempt to conceal this fact."[4] The charge was not entirely unjust. The opening issue urged Christians and Communists to cooperate for the common good. The December, 1939 issue twisted with the party line and defended the Berlin-Moscow pact. There seems little doubt that the *Protestant Digest* was oriented outside the pale of legitimate liberalism.

The *World Tomorrow* represented the non-Stalinist Left. During the thirties its editors included Kirby Page, Reinhold Niebuhr, Devere Allen, and Paul H. Douglas. "We affirm," said the editors in 1934, the last year of the journal's existence, "both Marxism and Christianity—Marxism because we believe in its immediate interpretation of history and its goal of a classless society, and more classical religion because its ultimate in-

3. "Dear Comrade Porter," wrote the executive secretary of the Socialist party, "News via the New York Times and the Milwaukee Leader that your conservative little Economics Commission of the Y.M.C.A. had decided to go whole-hog Socialist startles, amazes, and terrifies us. What's the world coming to? And how the blank do you think you'll get it over on the rank and file?" Clarence Senoir to Paul Porter, April 29, 1931, Socialist party files, Duke University.

4. *Report of the House Committee on Un-American Activities,* 78th Congress, 2nd session, Appendix IX, p. 1514.

sights in regard to the meaning of life and history are and will remain
valid."[5] As a journal of Christian socialism, it supported Thomas in the
1932 election. Hoover was boiled in printer's ink. Roosevelt hardly
fared better. Prior to the election of 1932 he was characterized as a
weathervane, beautiful against the sky, shining and resplendent, built of
hollow brass. Ambitious, evasive, irresolute, opportunistic were adjectives applied to the Hyde Park politician. After he took office the
World Tomorrow expected to see a constitutionally-coated Mussolini or
Hitler occupying the White House. The New Deal could not possibly
succeed because it sought only to humanize capitalism. Socialism was
the only road out. Nevertheless, not all Socialist roads lead to Moscow,
and the editors were quite aware that Communists were committed to
support the foreign policy of the Soviet Union and could not be trusted.[6]
Although originally a journal of socialism, pacifism, and Christianity,
the *World Tomorrow* increasingly stressed socialism.

The *Christian Herald,* edited by Daniel Poling, could be characterized
as a journal of restrained liberalism. It belonged in the camp neither of
socialism nor of the Liberty League. It praised some specific New Deal
measures, but there is no conclusive proof that it warmly admired
Roosevelt.

The *Christian Century,* American Protestantism's most influential
journal, continued on in the thirties to speak in a courageous and critical
voice. It was one of the very few Protestant papers to openly support
Roosevelt in the election of 1936. Truly, its chief criticism of Roosevelt
was that he was too cautious in his reforms. By 1940 the Administration's
foreign policies had so far alienated editor Morrison as to drive him into
Willkie's camp, but in domestic affairs the *Christian Century* stood with
or just to the Left of the New Deal.

IV

It is time now to turn from the undenominational press to an examination of several unofficial, inter-denominational religious groups.
The National Religion and Labor Foundation ranks among the foremost of these religious organizations devoted to social action. Although
a non-denominational, non-sectarian cooperative movement embracing
Protestants, Catholics, and Jews, its founders, leaders, and rank-and-file
members were mostly Protestants.

In the late twenties a small group of religious leaders led by Jerome
Davis talked of launching an inter-faith crusade for economic justice.
After considerable labor pains due to lost pledges and inability to agree on

5. Jan. 4, 1934, p. 7.
6. One of the editors, Anna Rochester, however, voted the Communist ticket.

a precise program, the movement was finally born in late 1932. Like most things entering the world in that bleak year, the National Religion and Labor Foundation was conceived as an adventure in faith and born with something less than a pair of shoe strings in cash. Calling for a reawakening of "flaming social righteousness," Jerome Davis, Edward L. Israel, Allan Knight Chalmers, Francis J. McConnell, John A. Lapp, and Stephen S. Wise proceeded to incorporate their organization under the laws of New York.

Its first two executive secretaries—George A. Hood and Francis A. Henson—lasted only one year each, and then Dr. Willard E. Uphaus took over the job and remained for sixteen years. His leadership was always vigorous but not always wise. Included at one time or another among the officers and members of the Foundation was just about every influential liberal in American Protestantism. The Foundation performed useful services in the field of labor relations. In time it became definitely hostile to communism.

And yet during the thirties the Foundation was quite far to the Left. A fair-minded examination of *Economic Justice,* the group's publication, leaves no other conclusion. It was not so much any single item, but the general tone—the use of Marxist jargon—that leaves this impression. Note, for instance, an editorial of June 1934 entitled "Bourgeois vs. Real Democracy":

An atitude common to middle-class liberals and, no less, to the great mass of nonpolitical American workers, is to the effect that our present bourgeois version of democracy must be defended against its enemies from the *left* as well as from the *right.* It is logical that bourgeois control of educational and other cultural agencies throughout our national history should have led us to persist in the illusion that we now have a democracy worth defending. . . . Counterposed to the current capitalistic dictatorship must be the workers' democracy, and it must be emphasized again and again to workers of whatever status that the democratic rights which they now chance to possess can be retained only by extending them *socially* as well as politically. And this means, primarily and practically, that private property rights in capital must be wiped out.

"We hold," read a Statement of Faith of December 1936, "that there can be no permanent recovery as long as the nation depends on palliative legislation inside the capitalistic system. Our vast natural resources and industrial equipment must come under social ownership and control. Production for use must take the place of production for profit. . . ."[7] It need hardly be added that the New Deal, with its petty tinkerings, was scarcely the solution to the bankruptcy of capitalism. Only socialism

7. *Economic Justice,* Dec., 1936, p. 2.

would do. The editor accused a young defender of the New Deal of being guilty of "instabilities." How terrible that the "so-called liberal intellectual all too often, with the first sign of returning capitalist vitality, snaps back into his conservative bourgeois shell."[8]

In spite of the many great non-Communist liberals associated with the Foundation, there were a few who could not be so characterized. And these few were in strategic positions. Arnold Johnson, field secretary, became the Communist party candidate for governor in Ohio in 1936 and 1940. Dr. Willard Uphaus, holding the extremely crucial job of executive secretary from almost the beginning, was not removed until 1950 after his unauthorized attendance and participation in the Warsaw Peace Conference. His judgment was not always trustworthy. Francis A. Henson, executive secretary for a year, was an admitted Marxist. Jerome Davis, the Foundation's guiding light, was fairly far to the Left. The Religion and Labor Foundation, in conclusion, in the thirties, not only represented socialism, it came perilously close to representing the Marx-Lenin position.

The Fellowship of Socialist Christians was probably the most influential of the inter-denominational religious groups concerned with social action. In 1931 a group of avowedly Socialist ministers banded together to do justice to the best insights of both historic Christianity and modern Marxism. Its membership, although never large, was distinguished: Roswell P. Barnes, John C. Bennett, Buell G. Gallagher, Francis A. Henson, Frank T. Wilson, and Reinhold Niebuhr composed the original executive committee.

"The Fellowship of Socialist Christians," read its statement of principles, "is a group who are agreed in their conviction that a Christian ethic is most adequately expressed and effectively applied in our society in socialist terms. They believe that the Christian Church should recognize the essential conflict between Christianity and the ethics of capitalistic individualism. They believe that the evolutionary optimism of current Liberal Christianity is unrealistic and that social change fundamental enough to prevent destructive social upheaval will require a combination of social intelligence and ethical vigor not yet in sight. Remedies for specific abuses are no adequate substitute for the reconstruction of our economic order so that production may be primarily for the use of all and not for the profit of the privileged." This meant that the members pledged themselves "to support the Socialist Party or such other party as may embody the purposes of socialism as the political organization

8. April, 1934, p. 1.

most nearly approximating a political expression of Christian ethics for our day."[9]

The Fellowship denied the materialism and ultimate goals of Marxism, but shared its analysis of the class struggle and the virtual inevitability of coercion. It hoped that violent revolution could be avoided, but this could be achieved only if a large number of the total community, using non-violent coercion, enlisted in the struggle for a new social order. The Fellowship thought of itself as tough-minded. Traditional Liberal Christianity overestimated the goodness in man and underestimated the tenacity of the class struggle. Pleas for good will and brotherly cooperation were hardly sufficient to halt the destruction and decay of capitalism. Virtually the only hope for mankind was a relatively bloodless revolution. Fascism was the final, logical, extension of capitalism, and the world might well be plunged into a cataclysmic struggle between fascism and socialism.

Could the New Deal prevent this clash in America? Nonsense! *Radical Religion,* the group's periodical, was almost as hostile to Roosevelt as the Hearst press—but for precisely opposite reasons. Liberals who look to Roosevelt lean on a "very frail reed." He is a messiah rather than a political leader, more renowned for "artistic juggling than for robust resolution." Roosevelt did not know where he was going. He talked in "accents similar to those of Hoover" and "no final good can come of this kind of whirligig reform."[10]

This attitude, reflecting as it did the views of the Fellowship's famous leader, Reinhold Niebuhr, appears a little strange coming from a group which prided itself on "realism." Contemptuous of old fashioned liberals for their doctrinaire beliefs, the Fellowship was equally doctrinaire in its unwillingness to concede that the New Deal might usher in just such relative social justice as the Fellowship believed could be found only in socialism and probably through violence.

The Fellowship pursued a wide and varied program. Numerous were the good causes to which it gave encouragement, financial assistance, and advice. Many of its members made personal sacrifices—indeed the Fellowship stiffly taxed the incomes of its members to insure personal commitment to the social revolution. History may yet prove its ideas correct. And yet, perhaps the Fellowship suffered from a failure of faith —a failure of faith in the common sense and the nerve of the American people. Fumbling, stumbling, contradictory, unplanned, and illogical as the New Deal was, the American people found in it a measure of social

9. *World Tomorrow,* Feb., 1932, p. 39. This is the 1932 Statement of Principles. It varied almost from year to year. Later in the decade support of a Socialist party was not required.

10. *Radical Religion,* Winter, 1936, pp. 3-4; Spring, 1938, p. 4.

justice and the promise of more. And they did so without embracing either fascism or communism and without any great violence or any intolerable loss of liberty. The ideas of Jefferson as well as of Marx still had application to twentieth-century man.

The United Christian Council for Democracy was a federation of Left wing religious groups: the Methodist Federation for Social Service, the Church League for Industrial Democracy, and the like. It was born at Columbus, Ohio, in November 1936. Edwin T. Buehrer, Herman F. Reissig, Charles Webber, Niebuhr, Ward, and Spofford were among those who issued the call to action. Eighty-five ministers and six laymen acted as mid-wives at the organization's birth. Methodists, Presbyterians, Episcopalians, Congregationalists, and Evangelicals were represented in that order of numerical strength. In time the Council also embraced Baptists, Disciples, and Unitarians. William F. Cochran, a businessman from Baltimore, was elected president. Niebuhr, almost inevitably, became chairman.

Almost inevitably, also, the Council proceeded to adopt resolutions and statements of principles rejecting the "profit-seeking economy and the capitalistic way of life" and endorsing socialism. This could and did mean different things to the somewhat disparate membership. But no matter. The Council's chief purpose was to serve as a rallying point for all the liberal and radical groups in Protestantism and to organize among the other denominations groups similar to the MFSS and the CLID. And partially due to its inspiration the Rauschenbusch Fellowship for Baptists and the Evangelical and Reformed Council for Social Reconstruction were born. In time the Council flirted with extremism, but before this fate worse than death, and before death itself, it performed useful work in the fields of civil liberties and labor relations.[11]

The Fellowship of Southern Churchmen inspires admiration. It was possibly the most prophetic of all unofficial church groups. It deserves to be judged by its deeds among the Negroes, the share-croppers, and the disinherited of the South. Unlike some advocates of social Christianity the Fellowship members practiced, often at the risk of physical danger, what were only pious pronouncements to others. It need only be added that a very few of its members were attracted to the extreme Left and that, in theory, the Fellowship was committed to socialism. Its first meeting in 1934 adopted a resolution holding the New Deal unworkable for its shortcomings were inherent in the capitalistic system. The delegates to the second conference pledged themselves to work for

11. It is tempting to trace the fate of these various agencies under discussion. Suffice it to say that with the return of prosperity many of these groups had no place to go. Committed to socialism which—at least for the nonce—seemed unrealizable in America, many of them either disbanded or swung ever leftward into the Moscow orbit.

a "genuinely cooperative social economy democratically planned to adjust production to consumption requirements, eliminate private ownership of the means of production and distribution wherever such ownership interferes with the social good."[12] And when later a statement of principles was adopted, included was the desire to supplant an economic system motivated by profit with one motivated by service.

Born during the First World War, the Fellowship of Reconciliation embraced a group of men and women who refused to participate in war or sanction military preparations. These individuals sought to demonstrate that love was an effective force for overcoming evil and transforming society into a creative fellowship. Originally a Christian protest against foreign war, the FOR gradually came to the realization that a warless world could be achieved only if poverty, injustice, exploitation, and racial hatred were first ameliorated. For many in the Fellowship, this meant the destruction of capitalism, that breeder of war and injustice. A straw poll of the membership in 1932 revealed 75 per cent for Thomas, 20 per cent for Hoover, 3 per cent for Roosevelt, and 1.6 per cent for Foster, the Communist party candidate. In 1936 a similar poll showed 50 per cent for Thomas, 30 per cent for Roosevelt, 18 per cent for Landon, 1 per cent for Lemke, and .7 per cent for Browder.

Although Socialist opinion was predominant in the early thirties, this did not prevent a rupture over internal policy which convulsed the entire Fellowship in 1933-34. The split largely hinged on whether or not the members should sanction or encourage armed force in the *class struggle*. Here was clear indication of the fact that economic issues had come to overshadow foreign war as the overriding concern of some of the Fellowship members. Here also was a classic illustration of the gulf between traditional Christian socialism and the newer Christian Marxism.

The former was optimistic, believing that love, education, appeals to men's best instincts, sweet reasonableness, or, at most, non-violent coercion would suffice to usher in a new social order. The latter was pessimistic, accepting Marx's thesis that violent class conflict was predetermined by the absolute laws of history. The beneficiaries of the status quo could not be dislodged by exhortations of kindliness and love. The entrenched possessors of economic and political power could not be reached by moral appeals. They would and did use ruthless, violent, coercion to protect their interests. How absurd, then, to insist that the disinherited should refrain from violence. Liberal Christianity by so insisting was, in fact, perpetuating an unjust social system because it was unwilling to sanction the only methods by which that system could be destroyed. Neutrality in the class struggle is not neutrality at all, for in practice it

12. *Christian Century*, Jan. 16, 1935, p. 91.

strengthens the vested interests who have only to defend what they already possess. What about those who would not personally participate in armed social conflict, but who would serve as non-combatants in the ranks of the disinherited? This position, believed Niebuhr speaking for the Christian Marxists, "represents an abortive effort to maintain personal purity while holding an organic relation to a social movement which is bound to result in some degree of violence in the day of crisis."[13]

Racked by these fundamental—if, to some observers, hypothetical—differences, the Fellowship executive committee sent a questionnaire to 6,395 members, some 996 replying. Approximately 21 per cent held to an absolute position of pacifism, insisting upon non-violent and even non-coercive methods of social change, without identifying itself with either the underprivileged or the privileged class. Another 22 per cent identified itself with the just aims of the workers but without sanctioning the use of any form of coercion. Taking these two groups together, 43 per cent of the Fellowship disavowed the use of force, violent or non-violent. Still a third group, 47 per cent, sanctioned the use of non-violent coercion. That left only about 10 per cent who accepted the Marxian position that armed force should be used in the class struggle.

Included in this last group was J. B. Matthews, whom the National Council refused to re-appoint as secretary. There followed the resignations of some sixty members, including Francis Henson, Roger Baldwin, Bradford Young, and Reinhold Niebuhr. In a sense, the Fellowship had simply reaffirmed its historic position of pacifism. If violence was unchristian in foreign wars, it was also wrong in the class struggle. Although the FOR was accused of turning reactionary and of betraying the masses, surely this is inaccurate. The disinterested observer might believe the basic principles of the group unrealistic, but it was hardly reasonable to expect it to continue in positions of leadership men who disavowed these principles.

This rift is not important because of its results on the Fellowship—membership jumped the following year—but because it illustrates the growing gulf between the old Social Gospel and the new social action patterns of the neo-orthodox group under the leadership of Reinhold Niebuhr.

The Christian Social Action Movement was organized by a group of ministers—most of them Methodists—at a "Call-to-Action" Conference in Chicago in 1932. Its purpose was to disseminate the belief that capitalism was doomed and that the economic aims of the Socialist party most nearly coincided with the principles of Christianity. As its name implies,

13. *Ibid.*, Jan. 3, 1934, p. 18.

action was to buttress mere discussion. Its members were to stay on the firing line and lead in picketing and demonstrations. They were to stimulate the spirit of protest and revolt within the breasts of impoverished men and women. Gilbert Cox served as chairman, Owen Greer as secretary, and included in its membership were Paul Hutchinson, W. B. Waltmire, J. Sitt Wilson, Clarence Craig Tucker, and James M. Yard. Although a few local branches were formed, on the whole the CSAM did not appear to exercise the influence of several other groups mentioned.

During the thirties a Socialist Ministers' Fellowship was formed, composed of "followers of Jesus engaged in full time religious work" who desired to band together to attack the capitalist system and to establish a new social order based on the principles of socialism. To join the Fellowship one had to become a "member of some political party committed to the 'principle of Socialism.'" The Fellowship's purpose was to engage actively in the class struggle by organizing the unemployed, promoting farm cooperatives, helping form labor unions, supporting strikes, lecturing, writing, and the like. W. B. Waltmire, Chicago Methodist minister, was chairman.

The group's meeting at Evanston, Illinois, June 25-28, 1934, is not without a certain educational value. A. V. Juvinall, Harry Spencer, and C. K. Richards maintained that the New Deal was fascistic. Dr. James M. Yard, formerly a Methodist chaplain at Northwestern University, averred that "the hope of the future for religion lies in socialist ministers and others who take the side of true religion in the class struggle." William Galatsky advocated communism rather than pussy-footing socialism. Carl Haessler informed the delegates that "the socialist is like a Christian Scientist when the surgeon knows a caesarean operation is necessary." Ernest Fremont Tittle expressed the contrary opinion that the new social order must be born free from violence.

Stimulated by this discussion, the group then adopted statements maintaining that many good Christians in the United States had joined the Communist party and that under communism religion might have a better opportunity to develop than under capitalism. For who did not know that capitalism, "by its brutal denial of the good things of life, either destroys belief in a good God or fosters ideas of religion on a superstitious level." However, the conference divided over the use of violence in the class struggle. The majority condoned only non-violent coercion. A minority, holding violent revolution inevitable, believed it must be supported. In any event, these men of God agreed that "there are real points of common interest and possible cooperation between Christianity and Communism."[14]

In the New York area, early in the decade, a Conference of Younger Churchmen was formed, with Niebuhr as the guiding light. It was socialistic, believing that the principles and platform of the Socialist party were most nearly consistent with the Christian social ideal. In the 1932 election a statement was issued supporting Thomas for President and at least seventy churchmen added their "amen" in the form of signatures.

V

From time to time other liberal church groups cropped up, but perhaps enough have been mentioned already to indicate that in the Depression Decade the cutting edge of Protestant idealism approached socialism.

14. All quotations from *Socialist Ministers Conference Proceedings* (n.p., n.d.), a pamphlet.

CHAPTER VII

The Churches Move to the Left: III

"I return from the left wing political movement, from radical Marxism, from passionate secular idealism, which made me condemn the church as conservative, as retarding progress, as martyring free spirits. I return to the church! Why? Because these years of experience have taught me that the church of the redeemed is the only great redeeming agency."—A. J. Muste

I

THE PURPOSE of this chapter is to indicate that in the thirties a number of individual clergymen assumed a position that approached socialism.[1] To be sure and speaking from the point of sheer numbers, the bulk of the clergy probably remained near and even to the Right of center. This will be the burden of the following chapter. To be sure, also, for many churchmen the New Deal approximated the political equivalent of the social ideals of Christianity. And yet there remained a significant minority who embraced socialism. It might be a vague sort of "Christian socialism" based on principles no more specific than "cooperation," "sharing," and "motives of love rather than of profits." It might be the socialism of the more moderate element of the Socialist party based on the non-violent establishment of a society in which the principal means of production and distribution would be owned by the state. Or it might be a revolutionary socialism close to the Marx–Lenin position. And for a few who adhered to the last position, Soviet Russia set the pattern to be followed.

II

To make the point it is necessary to review a few things that have been said already in the preceding chapters. It will be remembered that official denominational meetings at both the national and local level frequently passed resolutions which avowedly or tacitly advocated socialism. So much so, indeed, that the investigator receives the superficial

1. The number of churchmen in the thirties who embraced socialism probably totaled in the thousands. Even the grossly incomplete list assembled by the present writer is much too long to be presented here. Only a few names can be mentioned. And even this handful will not be subjected to searching analysis. The interested reader can find elsewhere extended discussions of the thinking of many of these liberal leaders. The purpose here is only to give some indication of the extent of socialistic opinion in American Protestantism without pausing to probe deeply the thought of any one man.

impression that two clergymen could not meet each other on the street without one of them banging a gavel, calling the other to order, and then introducing a resolution damning capitalism. Even assuming these utterances were the work of a minority, nevertheless such a minority did exist, and these resolutions cannot be entirely discounted.

A second reminder is that among the editors and contributing editors of the religious press there were a dozen or so who voted the Socialist ticket. Other editors, however they voted, gave clear indication that unfettered capitalism was not their cup of tea.

Thirdly, the reader recalls that many official and unofficial religious groups were committed to the establishment of a Socialist society.

However, it is now time to examine other evidences of socialistic sentiment. Early in 1934 Kirby Page, in association with a group of distinguished church leaders representing ten different Protestant denominations and the Jewish faith, sent out a questionnaire to 100,499 clergymen. Replies from 20,870 were received.[2]

When asked whether they preferred capitalism to a "coöperative commonwealth," only 5 per cent replied in the affirmative. Considering that each individual could fit his ideal society into the all-inclusive term, "coöperative commonwealth," it is surprising to find capitalism receiving the nod from even 5 per cent. The question was meaningless and might as well have been between the Kingdom of God and capitalism. However, the ministers were then asked which political system they believed would best bring about the establishment of this "coöperative commonwealth." Approximately 51 per cent answered "drastically reformed capitalism" and 28 per cent (or 5,879) selected socialism.[3] By denomination, the Socialist opinion ran in descending order: Methodist (34 per cent), Evangelical (33 per cent), Congregational (33 per cent), Reformed (32 per cent), Disciples (30 per cent), Episcopalian (24 per cent), Baptist (22 per cent), Presbyterian (19 per cent), and Lutheran (12 per cent). As might be expected, Socialist opinion ran higher in the larger urban areas, the proportion being close to 50 per cent in some cities.

From the point of view of meaningfulness, the best thing that can be said about the poll is that 87 per cent of those who replied stated their willingness to be quoted on their economic position. That is, the ballot was not secret and the great majority of ministers who favored socialism were quite prepared to have their position made public. The chief weakness of the poll, as indicated by the small proportion of Southern Baptists and Lutherans who replied (9 per cent and 14 per cent compared

2. All but 609 of the clergymen were Protestants.

3. The term socialism was defined as that "represented by the Socialist Party of America, or by a new and more inclusive socialistic alignment, in which the present Socialist Party would be included."

to the average of 21 per cent), is that those ministers who were socially minded were the very ones who took the trouble to reply and those who were conservatively inclined, as several church press editors admitted, simply deposited the questionnaires in the nearest wastebasket. But the fact still remains that close to six thousand Protestant ministers went on record as favoring socialism in the year 1934.

The following year, in answer to a similar questionnaire, 381 clergymen informed the National Religion and Labor Foundation that they would actively support the Socialist party in their communities, and 489 took the same position in regard to a farmer-labor or progressive party. In addition, some 2,172 parsons said they would advance in pulpit and press public ownership of utilities and basic industries.

Still other testimony of this trend to the Left is available. For instance, seventy New York area pastors signed an endorsement of Norman Thomas in the 1932 election. In that same election thirty-two Methodist ministers penned an appeal on behalf of the candidacy of Thomas, and numbered among these gentlemen were Frank Kingdom, Halford Luccock, Ernest Fremont Tittle, Edgar S. Brightman, Harris F. Rall, Dan B. Brummitt, James Yard, Robert J. Tucker, Paul Hutchinson, and Wade C. Barclay. A poll of one hundred Methodist ministers in Illinois revealed fourteen intended to vote the Socialist party ticket in 1932. In November 1935, forty-five religious leaders wrote President Roosevelt advising him that there could be no permanent recovery as long as the nation depended on palliative legislation within the capitalist system. Among the signers were Allan Knight Chalmers, Robert Searle, Harold E. Fey, Reinhold Niebuhr, Jerome Davis, and John Haynes Holmes. Bishop McConnell was vice-chairman and Niebuhr was treasurer of the Thomas and Maurer Committee of Ten Thousand. The League for Independent Political Action endorsed Thomas in 1932, and included in the League's leadership were Sherwood Eddy, A. J. Muste, Niebuhr, and Howard Y. Williams.

Williams was a Congregational minister who, like Thomas himself, forsook the pulpit for politics. There were others who did so also, on a temporary or permanent basis. Niebuhr ran for public office in New York City on the Socialist party ticket. U. M. McGuire, Baptist leader, Roy Burt, Methodist minister, and David Munroe Cory, Presbyterian minister, were all Socialist party candidates in various elections. J. Sitt Wilson, Methodist parson, sought a congressional seat on the Socialist party ticket, as did Herman J. Hahn, Buffalo pastor, until his expulsion from the Socialist party for advocating armed insurrection. Robert Whitaker, Baptist minister of California, ran for state office on the Socialist party ticket. The number of ministers who were Socialist party functionaries—state secretaries, district leaders, organizers—regardless of whether they were candidates for office, was quite large. Even more formidable in number were those parsons who gave the party aid and comfort of a more modest nature. "Here I am," wrote a Methodist minister of Indiana to the headquarters of the Socialist party, "with a university education, posted in economics, with graduate degrees that mean something, and not of any use except to preach a little each Sunday. I do not have money to help, but there is no reason why I could not be used in various ways, and I am willing to help even if it is merely folding circulars. I do not belong to the Socialist party, but voted for Thomas last time and intend to do so again."[4]

Just how many churchmen shared this sentiment is, of course, unknown. It is interesting to speculate on the ramifications of a letter written by a Kansas pastor to the publicity director of the Socialist party: "As minister of an economically conservative church I am forced to be a little, well, circumspect. I cannot link the church up with socialism because it is not socialist, but anything I can do in personal way I shall be glad to do."[5]

Then there were those clergymen who, throwing circumspection to the winds, resigned from the ministry to work for reform and labor organizations aside from the Socialist party.

When a liberal minister left a pastorate, however, it was not always a voluntary act. The shepherd, far from deserting his flock, was sometimes nudged out. Applicable to these men is Friar John's explanation for quitting the monastery. There were seven reasons, he said, the first being that he was thrown out.

It is difficult to pass judgments on dismissals of this nature because differences of personality, methods of expression, and degrees of liberalism or radicalism made each case an individual affair. And here, perhaps, is the time to mention a very few examples of the degrees of Left-of-center opinion.

Harry Emerson Fosdick, preaching from Riverside Church in New York, and probably the most respected minister of his generation, typifies pragmatic liberalism, critical of capitalism but just outside the edge of genuine socialism. In numerous sermons and several books, Fosdick rang the charges on the abuses of capitalism, and toward the conclusion of one sermon in which he called for the end of the competitive system, he declared: "If somebody wishes to call that socialism let him call it socialism."[6] Fosdick's famous sermon on capitalism, "The Ghost of a

4. Elmer Nicholas to Socialist party, Sept. 27, 1932, Socialist party files, Duke University.
5. John W. Sears to Socialist party, Oct. 17, 1932, Socialist party files, Duke University.
6. *Congregationalist*, Dec. 25, 1930, p. 853.

Chance," caused Congressman Hamilton Fish, Jr., chairman of the original House committee investigating "Red" activities, to classify the Baptist divine with the "pink intellectuals and sobbing socialists."[7] Interestingly, the *New York Daily Worker* scoffed at the same sermon as sentimental nonsense. And here is a perfect illustration of his basic faith in the middle way. Although rejecting unfettered capitalism, Fosdick believed the American people could achieve a more just economic order without embracing communism, which he dreaded as the very devil.

Methodist Bishop Francis J. McConnell forked slightly to the Left of the middle road followed by Fosdick. Churchman, citizen, educator, administrator, author, theologian, and reformer, McConnell was, as Lord Morley said of the earlier Roosevelt, a combination of St. Vitus and St. Paul. Responsible enough to be elected president of the Federal Council, he was none the less a rebel against the status quo, an acute critic of capitalism, and a champion of numerous reform causes. "We are all agreed," he wrote in 1933, "that the present social order has to give way to something more cooperative, not stopping short of the social ownership of the greater means of production, or a social control that comes virtually to the same end."[8] Although McConnell worked for Thomas in 1932, he can hardly be termed a genuine Socialist. His approach to social problems was relative and pragmatic. Perhaps the fairest statement is that he favored some sort of a socialized economy inaugurated without violence and without the sacrifice of democratic liberties. At one time he placed his hopes in socialism, but on the whole his faith was more in the essential goodness and rationality of all mankind. His comments on the Berlin-Moscow pact reveal that any illusions he might have had for Russia were gone by 1939.

McConnell is an example of a churchman who was distinctly Left of center but who fell short of being a doctrinaire Socialist. There were others who were out and out Socialists. Kirby Page, for example, ordained Christian minister, interpreted the social teachings of Christ in terms of non-violent socialism. He had been at it since 1915 and surely Social Gospel idealism never had a more energetic spokesman. More

7. *Christian Century,* Feb. 4, 1931, p. 185. Two decades later another congressman, Donald L. Jackson, said of another sane liberal, Bishop G. Bromley Oxnam: "Bishop Oxnam has been to the Communist front what Man O' War was to thoroughbred horse racing." Interestingly, as early as 1935 Bishop Oxnam had warned, "The united front is a dangerous gift horse." For Jackson's attack see Ralph Lord Roy, *Apostles of Discord* (Boston, 1953), p. 243 and for Oxnam's statement see *New York Christian Advocate,* Oct. 17, 1935, p. 924.

8. Francis J. McConnell, *Christianity and Coercion* (Nashville, 1933), p. 24. It is a commentary on our Alice in Wonderland world that Mr. J. B. Matthews, then a Marxist, reviewed this volume in the *Christian Century* of Dec. 6, 1933, and found it typically liberal, middle class, infantile unrealistic pap. Two decades later *Matthews* was accusing *McConnell* of being a Communist dupe.

than a score of books and hundreds of articles flowed from his facile pen as he pursued his career as free lance lecturer, journalist, political agitator, world traveler, and professional joiner. Page's socialism was evolutionary and optimistic, based more upon the Lord's Prayer than Marx. "When the Lord's Prayer is prayed with insight," he wrote, "it becomes a petition for the abolition of capitalism. . . ."[9] His criticism of capitalism was extremely severe, for which he in turn was severely criticized by capitalists. But one suspects the Communists held him in even greater contempt. His socialism was homely, simple, and idealistic. Page believed God was in His heaven and that in God's time, and with the aid of a little human non-violent coercion, a Socialist heaven would be established on earth. This is not to say, however, and speaking from a non-Socialist viewpoint, that Page could not be dogmatic. One need only recall his warning that for religious people to support the New Deal "constitutes betrayal of the basic principles of the Family of God on earth. Humanized slavery was not ethical, and reformed capitalism must be recognized as utterly unacceptable to true followers of Jesus' way of life."[10] Page was also dogmatic in his opinion of Communists. Urged to join in united front activity, Page refused because, like Patrick Henry in his attitude toward the Founding Fathers, he "smelt a rat." Communism, Page argued, was "pragmatically indefensible and morally unjustifiable."[11]

Polygonal John Haynes Holmes, a graduate of Harvard *summa cum laude,* had as one of his many objectives the socialization of America. In the opinion of conservatives his Community Church in New York deserved burial with great dispatch. As Holmes left the Unitarian fold, so he left the Socialist party—he did not much care for discipline. Nevertheless, he voted the Socialist ticket, believed in the principles of socialism, and precious few were his words of kindness for capitalism. It is curious, although by no means unique, that this tall, freedom lover should have looked upon Soviet Russia with such great admiration. Endorsing pro-Communist rallies, supporting pro-Communist organizations, Holmes illustrates the old proverb that there are none so blind who will not see. For example, did the Russian peasants loudly criticize their government? Well, bless my soul, that proves they are free! By 1938, however, he was terming the Communist party "hypocrisy incarnate" and "dishonest in every nerve and fibre of its organization."[12] And his words at the time of the Berlin-Moscow pact are eloquent: "I am sick over this business as though I saw my father drunk and my daughter on the street. And all

9. Kirby Page, *Individualism and Socialism* (New York, 1933), p. 311.
10. Kirby Page, *Living Triumphantly* (New York, 1934), p. 46.
11. *Ibid.,* p. 73.
12. *Christian Leader,* July 2, 1938, pp. 838-39.

the more, since I feel that I have deceived myself as well as been deceived."[13]

Even further removed from the vital center was such a man as Claude Williams, Presbyterian. Born in the hill country of Tennessee of very poor parents, Williams was no cocktail party comrade. He came by his radicalism honestly. He worked to organize the tenant farmers of Arkansas and as a consequence lost his pastorate, was flogged, and jailed. He was expelled from the Southern Tenant Farmers' Union when there fell from his pocket a secret report to Communist party headquarters in which it was made clear that his job was to "capture" the Union for the Communists. It was his tough luck that the president of the Union should be the one to pick up the report. No matter. As director of Commonwealth College and the People's Institute of Applied Religion he had a fine sounding board for spreading the glad tidings of Marx. In 1954 the Presbyterian Church, U.S.A., convicted him of heresy. He had said earlier, dropping the seventh veil, that the only reason he joined the ministry was to facilitate his preaching of communism, and no doubt he accepted his unfrocking with considerable *savoir faire*.

Fosdick, McConnell, Page, Holmes, Williams—these men are illustrative of the sweep of Protestant critical opinion, shading from moderate liberalism through genuine socialism to the dark edges of extreme radicalism. There was to emerge in the thirties, however, a man who cannot be pegged on this continuum. His name was Reinhold Niebuhr, minister in the Evangelical Synod of North America, who had left his pastorate in Detroit to assume a professorship at Union Theological Seminary. Impressive in appearance, a dynamic speaker and provocative writer, in pulpit, lecture hall, periodicals, books, and classroom, Niebuhr exercised a phenomenal influence on the thinking of American Protestant churchmen—and, indeed, on Europeans also.

Although he refused to honor himself with the term theologian, and although it is difficult to say that he developed a system, perhaps not since Jonathan Edwards had America produced such a stimulating commentator on Christian thought. In any case, there appeared to be an inter-relation between his social and theological thinking. Two basic ideas established the framework of Niebuhr's *Weltanschauung:* the transcendence of God and the sinfulness of man, set in dialectical terms. Both are in fundamental disagreement, he argued, with Liberal Christianity.

Man will not be saved through his own efforts, good works, and cooperation with an immanent God, but only through God's mercy and upon His initiative. The Kingdom will be achieved beyond history and not in history. Thus, liberal faith in evolutionary progress was replaced

13. Eugene Lyons, *The Red Decade* (Indianapolis, 1941), p. 355.

by an orthodox apocalypticism. Man is a child of God touched with divinity, driven to seek truth, to seek absolute values and goals. But man is also a rebel against God, branded with a fatal flaw, pride and lust for power. It is man's tragic destiny to strive for perfection that is always beyond his grasp. And such is man's pride that he always equates his own little systems—democracy, socialism, capitalism, and the rest—with the Kingdom, and to judge others for their failure to conform to them.

Because man is a sinner, also, liberals who rely on education, neighborliness, and good will to abolish race hatred, war, and economic justice are hopelessly naïve. Individuals might be reached by moralistic preaching, but never in history have groups—nations, classes, races—voluntarily relinquished a favored position. Hence, Niebuhr was greatly concerned with power and coercion. And hence his indebtedness not only to Augustine, Calvin, and Luther, but also to Freud and especially Marx.

He railed against the utopian elements in liberalism. He, of course, rejected the possibility of the Kingdom's establishment in history. Further, the inherent sinfulness of man made impossible the achievement of any society that totally eliminated hate, pride, greed, lust for power. About all that could be expected was a society in which power was fairly evenly divided, canceling out the dominance of any one group and maintaining a rough balance.

Niebuhr asserted that the demoniac elements in man's nature were far more tenacious than liberalism suspected. The whole history of the twentieth century is an ugly, eloquent testimony to man's irrational brutalities. Christ's absolute law of love is beyond man's fulfillment. Man cannot know perfection. He cannot attain salvation without divine intercession. Man has entirely too good an opinion of himself, which the brutal realities of history do not justify. All of this was a healthy and realistic antidote to liberalism's naïve optimism which fancied that if only enough schools were established, if only enough reform mayors were elected, if only enough nations renounced war, if only enough interracial conferences were held, if only enough employers "talked things over" with their employees, if only enough moralistic sermons were preached, then utopia would be here.

The publication of *Moral Man and Immoral Society* in 1932 marked the emergence of Niebuhr as America's foremost critic of the old Social Gospel. A score of articles and several books published in the twenties, however, contained the basic strictures against Social Gospel idealism upon which he was to build in the thirties. Originally his break with liberalism was primarily on socio-political grounds. Its inadequacies in the face of the steel-hard industrialism of Detroit and total depression and total war were too horribly apparent. He then, especially after 1935, verified his criticisms on theological grounds, concluding the decade with the famed Gifford Lectures at Edinburgh which were published in the early forties under the general title, *The Nature and Destiny of Man*.

Niebuhr dealt in paradoxes—the dialectical method provided the key to his thinking—and it is perhaps appropriate that his own life seems itself a paradox. The provisional pessimism of his views did not drive him to turn his back to the world. Never did a professor live less in an ivory tower.

There is so much that is valid in Niebuhr's indictment of liberalism, there are so many who proudly wear his colors, his reputation is so firmly established, his character so above reproach, that it must appear unseemly for one to mildly question some of his attitudes. Moreover, the nuances of his thought are so refined, his use of paradox so confirmed, his ability to see the best in a bad ideal and the worst in a good ideal so acute, that it is impossible not to misunderstand and oversimplify some of his attitudes.[14] The following comment relates only to his social thought— if it is possible to divorce it fom his theology—and is confined to his career before 1940; his views being greatly modified in recent years.

It is curious that a man who sought relative justice should have been so scornful of the New Deal—and this contempt continued through Roosevelt's first two terms. It is curious that America's supreme realist could have pinned his hopes on the Socialist party as late as 1940. It is curious that this acute student of history and brilliant commentator on economic systems could have denied to capitalism in the United States virtually any chance of escaping violent destruction in the final inevitable conflict between fascism (of course, Niebuhr believed, fascism was the logical conclusion to capitalism) and socialism. It is curious that this stern opponent of pacifism could have been early in the thirties a leader of a pacifist organization. It is curious that in the late thirties Niebuhr could warn against the appeasement of Hitler, while at the same time repeatedly denounce the military armament program of the Roosevelt administration. It is curious how a mind so alert to the complexities and paradoxes of human motivation could have subscribed to the simplicity and crudity of the Marxian interpretation of history. It is curious how a man whose favorite term of opprobrium for his opponents was "naïveté" could have believed that there was no relation between an individual's membership in the Communist party and his fitness to hold public office in the United States. It is curious that a man who possessed such a razor-sharp mind should minimize the exercise of reason and give

14. Charles Clayton Morrison, editor of the *Christian Century*, accused Niebuhr of "slippery" or "shifty use of language."

encouragement (without intending to do so, to be sure) to the cult of irrationality sweeping the country. It is curious that a man who spent so much time denouncing the dogmatism of liberals could himself have been so coldly dogmatic toward those who disagreed with him. Lastly, it is curious that a man whose own life was so honorable, selfless, and dedicated could have discounted so often these qualities in the history of the human race.

In commenting on Niebuhr most of the space has been devoted to questioning certain of his attitudes. This is because his positive contributions to a more realistic Christian philosophy of human nature and destiny are so generally recognized as to be axiomatic. Whether for good or ill, he stands as the supreme example of the differences between social Christianity in the Prosperity and Depression Decades. So telling was Niebuhr's attack on the Social Gospel that many observers speak of its death in the thirties. Certainly Niebuhr won a host of followers who joined with him in belaboring Liberal Christianity. It is fashionable to stress the differences between Niebuhr's realism and the idealism of the old liberals—at the expense, of course, of the latter. And yet, perhaps the differences have been over-stressed; perhaps the Social Gospel lived on! Niebuhr, whatever his views, continued to work as churchmen before him for a more Christian social order. And in so far as actual deeds are concerned, there is a real continuity between the social Christianity of the twenties and of the thirties.

Although Niebuhr called himself a Christian Marxist, he was much too independent a thinker to follow the party line and much too acute an observer not to recognize the ruthless elements in the Soviet experiment. There were, however, a few Protestant churchmen who demonstrated neither this independence nor this realism. Just how many it is impossible to say.

Earl Browder testified before a congressional committee that the Communist party had considerable success in infiltrating the ministry. In books and speeches he maintained there were clergymen who were party members. Benjamin Gitlow asserted that Communist infiltration of the Methodist Church was highly successful. Herbert Philbrick, F.B.I. undercover agent, mentioned a cell of ministers. J. Edgar Hoover warned that the party might attempt to invade the churches. One ex-Communist, Joseph Zack Kornfeder, estimated there were six hundred clergymen in the United States who were secret party members. J. B. Matthews testified that more than seven thousand Protestant ministers comprised the largest single group supporting the Communist apparatus. He claims to possess, as he undoubtedly does, a card index containing the names of 8,079 Protestant clergymen who have served the Communist cause—whatever that may mean. Daniel Bell, historian of American socialism, believes that the proportion of ministers among the "sucker lists" of Communist fronts was probably higher than any other group. Stanley High and Daniel Poling, respected Protestant leaders, John T. Flynn and Elizabeth Dilling, professional patriots, Congressman Harold Velde and Congressman Donald Jackson, newspaperman Frederick Woltman and historian Ralph Roy, all have spoken of Communist infiltration into the Protestant clergy. Indeed, there appeared in the early fifties a rash of accusations, far too numerous to mention here, to the effect that elements in the Protestant churches had been captured by Moscow.

Truth to tell, similar allegations had been leveled against the churches for decades. They had been almost always under fire for radicalism of one type or another since 1919. Most of the critics could be discounted as extreme conservatives who deemed anyone Left of William Graham Sumner a "Red." And it is rather curious that while the churches were being chastized for their radicalism, other observers maintained that these same churches were strongholds of reaction. Surely this is eloquent testimony to the sweep of the attitudes of American Protestantism: opiate of the masses and bulwark of capitalism on the one hand; inciter of unrest and tool of Moscow on the other. And yet, just as some ministers flirted with fascism, so a few flirted with communism.

It seems to the present writer that the only approach to this question of communism in the clergy is the common sense one. Were there Communist party members in the ministry? Certainly! Not a profession nor a skill in the country escaped infiltration. The party hardly would fail to send its agents into the ranks of the ministry. Were clergymen genuine fellow travelers? Of course! Writers, scientists, lawyers, actors, labor leaders, teachers, politicians, businessmen all were deceived— or deceived themselves—into believing that communism represented the solution to racial intolerance, economic injustice, and war. It was inevitable that a few clergymen, often unsophisticated politically and inclined to think the best of their fellow men, would uncritically accept communism's claim to the leadership of social justice. Did ministers view Soviet Russia as a noble experiment? Unquestionably! Confronted by the breakdown of capitalism in the United States, bombarded by pink colored accounts of the remarkable progress made by Russia in giving to each according to his needs and taking from each according to his abilities, some churchmen joined with much of America in believing the Russian experiment a resounding success.[15]

15. It might be mentioned parenthetically that several church assemblies, a score of church journals, and literally hundreds of ministers, including the most distinguished in the land, publicly favored the diplomatic recognition of Russia in 1933.

This flirtation with communism was at its height in the early thirties. The deviousness of American Communists, the purges in Russia, the brutality of Stalin, the growing evidence of racial distinctions, and finally the Berlin-Moscow pact and the subsequent invasions of Poland and Finland all served to disenchant the clergy. By the end of 1939 many of the friends of the Soviet Union began to apply the same standards of decency to Stalin as they had been applying all along to Hitler.

At one time, however, a few Protestant churchmen took a kindly attitude toward communism and the Soviet Union. On the whole, they probably represented the most idealistic elements in American Protestantism. Their motives are not questioned. They were perhaps "good" men; indeed their great passion for social justice was probably the most important factor in orientating them toward Moscow. Judgment is passed on them only in the sense that judgment is passed on, say, the members of the Ku Klux Klan: if enough Americans had followed their example it would have spelled the death of liberty in the land.

The Page poll of 1934 provides one indication of the limited appeal of communism for the clergy. Out of twenty thousand ministers, only 123 favored the establishment of communism in America.[16] Of the five thousand ministers who responded to the Religion and Labor Foundation poll of 1935, only 36 said they would actively support the Communist party. Proportionately, then, the number of churchmen who were genuine fellow travelers was very small.

And it would probably serve no useful purpose to list here the names of those clergymen who were, in the present writer's opinion, true party troopers, or who at one time in their lives joined a front organization, signed a party petition, attended a party sponsored rally, or wrote a pro-Russian article or book.[17] Many have returned to sanity and no doubt repent of their salad days coquetry. Others have been effectively exposed and repudiated by their own communions. Still others grown old in performing odd jobs for the party (literally from a Christian viewpoint), seem more harmless than heinous, and it is not difficult to imagine that they would be quickly purged should communism succeed

16. Communism was defined as that in "Soviet Russia and as represented by the Communist Party in the United States."

17. During a break in the testimony of The Reverend Jack McMichael before an open hearing of the House Committee on Un-American Activities, it occurred to the present writer that the publications of this committee might have some bearing on his research. He jotted down from memory and rather at random the names of a score of clergymen who he thought might possibly be mentioned in the publications. He then turned to the "cumulative index" of publications of the committee and found every one of the names listed. An examination of the files disclosed a prodigious number of clergymen mentioned in one connection or another. In this study not much weight was given to the fact that a minister was said to belong to an alleged Communist front organization.

in America. Suffice it to say that the record shows that within the ministry there were a few genuine fellow travelers and a considerably larger number who were not quite aware of the nature of the Communist conspiracy.

II

In a very real sense, the question of Communists in the ministry is the least important aspect of this section. After all, genuine fellow travelers could not have been very numerous and their influence could not have been too great. Much more crucial is the extent of Socialist or, to put it negatively, anti-capitalist sentiment within Protestantism. As these last three chapters show, a very large number of churchmen were extremely critical of unfettered capitalism, and a significant minority believed socialism was the road out. These attitudes were not only held by individual ministers, but they became the official—in varying degrees—position of some church groups and denominational agencies. In any event, American Protestantism did swing to the Left in the depression.

CHAPTER VIII

The Conservatism of the Churches in the Thirties

"Every man for himself and God for us all, as the
elephant said when he danced among the chickens."
—Charles Dickens' Sam Weller

I

CHURCHMEN raised their share of smoke and sparks in the Depression
Decade, but it would be inaccurate to conclude that all of American
Protestantism was aflame with radicalism. There were always enough
conservatives on hand—ministers as well as laymen—to keep the fires of
social Christianity well banked. It is the purpose of this chapter to
observe the conservative defenders in action.

II

Someone once remarked that if all the economists in the country were
laid end to end they would not reach a conclusion, and it might be observed also that if all the economic resolutions passed by the churches
were laid end to end they would not be conclusive. Asked what a
denominational social service commission could do for the common good,
one of the youngest and brightest members suggested they resign in a
body as a protest against churches passing resolutions and doing nothing
else. There is wisdom as well as wit to this advice, for it is unquestionably
true that many resolutions were far from a perfect reflection of majority
sentiment, and that they were passed as a sop to silence a minority of
gasconades, there being no real intent to translate words into deeds.

The evidence supporting such a conclusion is overwhelming. A number of noted liberal churchmen have been frank enough to make this
admission. As F. Ernest Johnson stated, some resolutions are "no more
than wishful thinking on the part of a small minority."[1]

It is only a little too strong to suggest that some so-called "radical"
groups bordered on hypocrisy. For instance, the Rock River Conference

1. F. Ernest Johnson, *Church and Society* (New York, 1935), p. 86. Resolutions,
however, should not be discounted entirely. They are an aid in shaping public opinion
and they do support liberal ministers who take an advanced position. Besides, there is
probably not an assembly in the world that mirrors perfectly the attitude of the people
it represents.

of the Methodist Episcopal Church in 1932 unanimously adopted a "socialistic" report, and then 86 per cent of the delegates proceeded to vote for Hoover. Another Methodist group, the Troy New York Conference, was noted for its "share the wealth" attitude. When, however, it was proposed to these sixty ministers that their salaries be equalized, they hastily tabled the motion for discussion the *following year*. As the sponsor of the measure ruefully remarked, it would have been a step toward socializing the Christian order, something the conference was always advocating. And as another minister observed, it took "unmitigated gall" for the churches to perpetually talk about social justice, considering the fate of supernumerated pastors, overworked and scandalously underpaid active parsons, and the abominable treatment of church janitors and other employees.

Conservatives, even more than liberals, of course, were fond of pointing out the limited nature of social pronouncements. In many cases these pronouncements were not binding upon the local congregations, and more than that, they did not even represent the majority opinion of those groups that passed them. Conservative after conservative came forward to reveal how liberal resolutions were passed. They were railroaded through without debate. They were sneaked through early or late in the sessions when only a handful of delegates were present. They were accepted by conservatives only to preserve harmony, there being a tacit understanding that they would be forgotten after the meeting adjourned. They were good-humoredly passed by conservatives to please a handful of pleasant but slightly unbalanced "do-gooders." They were, in short, about as representative as a modest Texan.

For instance, one minister reported that a sweeping social service report had been discussed, worked out, and written down in the moments between the finishing of luncheon at one-thirty and the beginning of the meeting at two. And Bishop John M. Moore tells how the Federal Council came to endorse a child labor amendment:

The resolution was introduced into the Council proceedings and referred to the Business Committee, of which I was the chairman. The committee endorsed the abolition of child labor, but refused to endorse the amendment. At the opening of the session, next morning, the matter was called up, and the committee's action was read. Very few delegates had come in. The social service secretary and the industrial secretary of the Council attacked the action of the committee. The substitute of endorsement was offered and received 27 votes and the opposition only 9. Thus the Federal Council, representing twenty-six denominations, endorsed the amendment with 27 persons voting in its favor and 360 of its 400 delegates absent. Yes, it was endorsed and how? Let all the fact be known.[2]

Incident after incident of this sort of thing could be cited, but perhaps the point has been sufficiently stressed. Although a great number of liberal and even radical resolutions were passed by the churches in the thirties, many of them must be partially discounted as an imperfect reflection of Protestant opinion.

These resolutions were an imperfect reflection for still another reason, and that is because of the gulf between the thinking of the clergy and that of the laity. A dozen famous church leaders or studies could be cited demonstrating the ominous "lag" between the social attitudes of the men in the manse and the men of the countinghouse and field. In marked contrast to other lands, the clergy in America on the whole seemed further to the Left than the laity. Not depending upon the state for support, American churchmen have been freer and more willing to criticize the state. Further, the Lutheran tradition of rendering unto Caesar the things that are Caesar's was never as powerful in America as the Calvinist heritage. Thirdly, in some church assemblies laymen were under-represented, and thus official pronouncements were more a reflection of the opinion of the ministers than that of their congregations. Above all, ministers probably found the ethical imperatives of the Bible more compelling, than did most laymen. And this perhaps explains why laymen so frequently protested the actions of their "pink" parsons, and why the sheep so often disassociated themselves from the attitudes of their shepherds.[3]

While the business of discounting the liberalism of the churches is under discussion, it is not irrelevant to observe that only a relatively few of the great leaders of social Christianity were ministers with actual churches and congregations. There were exceptions to prove the rule, of course, but on the whole Protestantism's most liberal leaders were seminary professors, church press editors, episcopal officers, agency heads, and the like. Apparently it was one thing to denounce capitalism from the pedagogue's chair and quite another to preach socialism from the pulpit. "Bravely and boldly," observed a young radical, "the professors tell young seminarians to preach a realistic gospel—and wave good-bye to

2. *Presbyterian,* Jan. 14, 1937, p. 5.

3. Care should be exercised not to overstress this gulf. John Paul Williams, *Social Adjustment in Methodism* (Columbia University Contributions to Education No. 765, Teachers College, 1938), shows that there was no such gulf between the Methodists of Massachusetts and their leaders. The *Northwestern Christian Advocate,* Feb. 11, 1932, p. 139, polled twenty-five thousand Methodists, ministers, and laymen, on social issues and found the two groups in substantial agreement.

them from their bomb-proof dugouts as the young hopefuls go out to the battle."[4]

The reluctance of ministers to preach Sunday after Sunday on social problems may be a reflection on their courage, but it is also a tribute to their common sense. Even a socially conscious congregation longs to hear from the pulpit something other than a disquisition on government, economics, or sociology. Whatever the reason, the fact is that the pulpit on Sunday morning was the least likely source of radical social pronouncements.

III

There is other evidence to indicate that the churches did not shift as far or as fast to the Left as liberals hoped and conservatives feared. For one thing, some church press editors and ministers were very tardy in acknowledging the onslaught of the depression. There were important qualifications to this statement, naturally, but still a goodly number of churchmen chose to ignore the breakdown of the economy. Perhaps, it was reasoned, if the symptoms were overlooked the disease would pass away. Besides, confidence was the touchstone of prosperity and to dwell upon such unhappy facts as bank failures and unemployment destroyed that magic surety. In some church journals, as late as the fall of 1930 and even into 1931, it was almost impossible to tell that a depression existed. And in some of these journals, also, much more space was devoted to the prohibition issue than to economic problems—and this after two or three years of terrible economic distress. Apparently many Protestant churchmen adopted what might be called a Christian Scientist approach to the economic sickness of the country.

And if the admission was made that there actually was a depression, in countless pulpits, assemblies, and papers the crash was attributed to the "Providence of God'—to use the wording of the Southern Baptist Convention. "The nations that forget God," the Convention continued, "shall not prosper."[5] Poverty was just punishment for a prodigal people. The land was reaping a bitter harvest the seeds of which were sowed in the sinful twenties. If an angry God unleashed the depression, only an appeased God would lift the yoke. Hence economic recovery was dependent upon a religious revival and people were urged to attend church to save their bank accounts as well as their souls.

An expected religious revival was not the only happy aspect to the depression. As a Methodist spokesman cheerfully observed, "Most of us eat too much. It will do us good to diet and live on less food and simpler fare." Besides, things could be worse: observe the "starving

4. *Christian Century*, Aug. 4, 1937, p. 973.
5. *Annual of the Southern Baptist Convention*, 1932, p. 86-87.

Chinese."[6] The *Nashville Christian Advocate* made the pleasant reminder that since more people had jobs than did not have them, the labor situation did not appear gloomy. A Southern Presbyterian journal admonished its readers: "Many Christians today are silent and without joy, whereas God expects them to be ever joyful and happy, eager to give testimony to the power and grace of their Lord."[7] The ten million or so jobless in the country probably found little inspiration in the advice of a Baptist leader: "To kick against pricks is often a dangerous thing. Cheer up, stick to your job and hope for better days!"[8] Distaste for work and prodigality, noted a Presbyterian spokesman, will be replaced by industry and thrift, and this advance must be credited to the depression.

This theme was played upon repeatedly. Forced to tighten their belts and to do without luxuries, Americans would once again fall to their knees and give thanks for the simple necessities of plain food and rough clothing. A Methodist perceived the priceless values hidden beneath the surface of the depression, one of them being increased time to think about God. Moreover, here was a grand opportunity, as countless churchmen observed, for Christians to practice charity and extend a helping hand to their less fortunate neighbors. In any event, Americans should quit their "whining" for if the country was going broke they might as well make it a joy-ride. "Let us think and talk as bravely and cheerfully as we can," suggested the *Presbyterian Banner,* "and this will help much."[9]

Other things that would help much, in addition to cheerfulness, were sobriety, thrift, diligence, honesty, and, above all, faithfulness to God. "More religion—rather than more legislation—is the need of the hour," cried the famous Congregationalist, Roger Babson.[10] Obedience to four great duties, opined the Reverend Paul Gresham, would lead America out of the depression: love God, serve God, study God's word, and keep God's commandments. Advice similar to this—return to God and all would be well—was very widespread and is of course impossible to question. Therefore it is necessary to turn to the more concrete and worldly problem of the role to be played by the government in the recovery.

IV

It is quite clear that the economic thinking of some churchmen had not changed much since the days of President McKinley. The Reverend Harry Earl Woolever, editor of the National Methodist Press, believed a

6. *Arkansas Methodist,* Sept. 4, 1930, p. 1.
7. *Christian Observer,* May 11, 1932, p. 1.
8. *Watchman-Examiner,* Jan. 12, 1933, p. 33.
9. Nov. 12, 1931, p. 9.
10. *Nashville Christian Advocate,* Dec. 5, 1930, p. 1572.

federal program of aid to the unemployed smacked of communism. Some people, he continued, confuse Uncle Sam with Santa Claus. A number of church journals shared this fear, for, as the *Presbyterian Advance* ruminated, it led to people "being clothed from a governmental 'slop-chest' and fed from a communal trough."[11]

The apparent spread of Socialist sentiment alarmed a number of distinguished churchmen. Bishop Warren A. Candler, speaking from retirement, criticized the leftward swing of the nation. He looked to the South, with its solid tradition of conservative faith, to save America from collectivism. Bishop William Manning, famed Episcopal leader, volleyed protests against leftist tendencies within and without the churches. Methodist Bishop Edwin Holt Hughes made clear his belief in capitalism, as did another leader, Ivan Lee Holt. Dr. Christian F. Reisner led the moderates in the New York East Conference, repeatedly voicing his opposition to the socialistic utterances of that Methodist group. Dr. Guthrie Speers, famed Presbyterian, rose to the defense of capitalism. More significant is that Shailer Mathews, one of the old prophets of social Christianity, expressed doubt concerning all the talk of abolishing the profit motive.

Individual clergymen were not alone in championing capitalism. The Southern Baptist Convention in 1938, for instance, termed the American economic system the "best in the world." It went on to say: "There ought to be no room for radical Socialism and for atheistic Communism in the United States of America, and the widespread propaganda now carried on in their interest should as speedily as possible and in every way possible be prevented and counteracted. . . ."[12] In 1936 the Methodist Protestant Church censured socialism, and many regional and local denominational meetings echoed this attitude.

Much of the church press, including even moderately liberal papers, questioned the wisdom of repudiating capitalism root and branch, and this is especially true of Presbyterian, Lutheran, and Southern Baptist papers.

If socialism was a threat to American principles, how much greater was the danger from communism. Many church assemblies issued pro-nouncements condemning communism. Dozens of pulpits rang with anti-Communist denunciations, and the pages of the church press were filled with warnings. It was pointed out earlier in this study that some churchmen were a little naïve concerning Soviet Russia and the methods of communism. It is clear, however, that they represented only a minority. There is abundant evidence that much of American Protestant-

11. May 28, 1931, p. 3.
12. *Annual of the Southern Baptist Convention*, 1938, p. 104.

ism was unrelenting in its hostility to godless communism, and this attitude was not a monopoly of conservatives. Fair-minded and sane liberals, in point of fact, were probably the most effective critics of party propaganda. Thus it is a grave mistake to equate criticism of communism with conservatism.

However, as much cannot be said concerning hostility to President Roosevelt, and particularly his domestic policies. Roosevelt made mistakes. The New Deal was often unplanned, illogical, contradictory, and hastily enacted and inefficiently administered. It could be argued cogently that the whole program was harmful to the United States. The point is simply that on the whole people who called themselves liberals generally supported Roosevelt, and that on the whole people who called themselves conservatives generally opposed Roosevelt. (At times, too, of course, Socialists and Communists opposed him also.) Further, on the whole people who favored such reform legislation as federal aid to the unemployed, social security, unemployment insurance, minimum wage and maximum hour guarantees, greater regulation of business, support of farm prices, progressive taxation, extension of government into the power field, aid to organized labor, and the like, generally supported Roosevelt, and that on the whole people who opposed such legislation generally opposed the New Deal. This being true and considering the large number of "liberal" resolutions passed by church bodies and the large number of "liberal" sermons preached and the large number of "liberal" editorials and articles that appeared in the church press, it is a trifle surprising to note also the prodigious amount of opposition to Roosevelt existing within American Protestantism.

The election of 1932 is not a very good illustration of this fact—after all, Roosevelt's record and the Democratic platform gave little indication of how the New Deal would develop—but it will do for a start. Regarding the election, it should be noted in the first place that the Protestant churches were not openly committed to the victory of one man as they had been in 1928. Perhaps they had learned their lesson and perhaps it was because neither candidate was a Roman Catholic. Besides, as the *Christian Century* lamented, "So far as the presidential campaign is concerned, the question of prohibition is a washed-out issue."[13] And because the churches were not openly committed, it is difficult to speak with preciseness on their attitudes.

It is true, and negatively speaking, however, that not a single church journal examined editorially supported the Democratic candidate.[14]

13. Sept. 21, 1932, p. 1126. That is, prohibition was still dear to the hearts of the churches, but it was not possible to say, as in 1928, that the immediate fate of the Eighteenth Amendment hinged on the outcome of the election.
14. The *World Tomorrow* supported Thomas.

While Roosevelt was seldom openly attacked in the campaign, an examination of the Protestant press leaves the distinct impression that he was a distasteful candidate, the chief reason for his unacceptability being his stand on the liquor question. To repeat, the press did not call upon its readers not to vote for Roosevelt, but rarely was he presented sympathetically.

It is true, also, with the exception of the *Christian Century,* that the church press did not editorially support the Republican candidate. And yet an examination of Protestant journals leaves the distinct impression that almost all of them were favorable toward Hoover. The major complaint against him seemed to be his evasive stand on prohibition. Hoover was more frequently criticized for this fault than for his action —or lack of action—in combating the depression. How often did the reader of the church press in the depression start an editorial or article entitled "The Need of the Hour," "A Time of Crisis," "The President Must Lead," "Moral Issues in the Election," "The Stakes in the Election," "It Is Time for the President to Act," only to discover that, far from dealing with the economic crisis, it was concerned with prohibition! And how often, too, did churchmen criticize the critics of Hoover!

Almost all the sources of Protestant opinion, then, *implied* support of Hoover rather than Roosevelt in 1932.[15] Part of Protestantism was on record. The Christian Endeavor Movement, for instance, endorsed the Republican candidate, apparently reasoning that a "Damp" was preferable to a "Wet." Even such liberal churchmen as Lynn Harold Hough, Daniel L. Marsh, R. E. Diffendorfer, Bishop Fred B. Fisher, Frank Mason North, and Ralph W. Sockman voted for Hoover.

Although the churches did not enter into the campaign as they had done in 1928, although Roosevelt had said or done comparitively little to indicate his warm social philosophy, it nevertheless remains strange that so very, very few churchmen and church journals, either explicitly or implicitly, supported Roosevelt. Equally curious is the fact that Roosevelt emerged from the election a landslide victor. It would seem, in the first place, that many spokesmen of social Christianity looked to Hoover, even after four years of his leadership, as the man to implement the mind of Christ in the realm of government. And it would appear, secondly, and

15. Norman Thomas, as has been noted, also had considerable backing. But the point is that the spokesmen of American Protestantism jumped from the conservatism of Hoover to the socialism of Thomas, very few of them openly endorsing Roosevelt. It is interesting to note that Clarence True Wilson, leader of Protestant temperance forces, originally supported Thomas, not because Wilson believed in socialism, but because he considered Thomas a "Dry." After reading Thomas' "wet speeches" and examining his "wet record," Wilson made a last minute change of mind.

considering Roosevelt's overwhelming victory, that many Protestants did not heed the advice of their spokesmen.

The election of 1936 was of greater significance because by this date Protestants had witnessed Roosevelt in action for four years. The *Christian Century* was the only church paper, as disclosed in this investigation, to support his re-election. And even this endorsement was marred by the fact that letters of protest fell upon the editor's desk like "autumn leaves." As editor Morrison ruefully observed, if his mail bag could be regarded as a straw poll, Roosevelt would be swept from office. A few other papers *implied* support of Roosevelt in the election, but it is meaningful that not even such liberal journals as the *Churchman, Advance, Presbyterian Tribune, Zion's Herald,* or *Christian Register* openly called for a second term.

It might be argued with justice that it was not the function of a religious journal to campaign for any candidate. However, this argument is vitiated by the record of the church press in 1928. At that time most journals excused their open endorsement of Hoover by maintaining that an overriding issue was at stake. Apparently no such issue was at stake in 1936. This would indicate that Protestantism considered prohibition (or Smith's Catholicism) a more important question than the far-reaching reforms—for good or for ill—of the New Deal.

It is interesting also that while no church paper openly endorsed Landon, a number of them *implied* that the Republican candidate was their choice. Buttressing this indication is the fact that a poll revealed that better than a majority of all Protestants who were church members voted for Landon as against Roosevelt. The breakdown of the poll by denomination is provocative. The "enlightened" Congregationalists, for instance, who in General Council only two years earlier had embraced socialism, voted 78 per cent for Landon. The "reactionary" Baptists, for the majority of Baptists belonged to the Southern Baptist Convention, a body that wholeheartedly supported capitalism, voted 65 per cent for Roosevelt. Apparently tradition and geography were more potent in influencing the vote of Protestants than the liberalism of the pulpit.

This conclusion is supported by a study of the 1944 presidential election—actually, of course, beyond the boundaries of this inquiry. Congregationalist, Methodists, Presbyterians, Lutherans, Episcopalians, and the Reform groups cast more votes for Dewey than for Roosevelt. Only the Baptists and the Christians, of the larger Protestant denominations, gave Roosevelt more support than his opponent. The smaller Protestant sects and the unchurched, significantly, also indicated a preference for the Democratic candidate. Taking the total Protestant vote, Dewey received 37.5 per cent and Roosevelt 37.0 per cent. It is only a slight exaggeration to say that this poll shows that the more "liberal" a denomination on social matters—as indicated by pronouncements, the position of its leaders, and the attitude of its press—the more likely were its members to vote *against* Roosevelt. Conversely, the more "conservative" a denomination, the more likely were its members to vote *for* Roosevelt.

This hostility to Roosevelt and the New Deal is indicated by still another poll. In 1936, 21,606 clergymen replied to the question asked by the *Literary Digest:* "Do you *now* approve the acts and policies of the Roosevelt New Deal to date?" Some 70.22 per cent, or 15,172, replied "no."[16] Even more revealing was the fact that in only three states did the clergy give majorities favoring the Roosevelt program, and these states were Alabama, Mississippi, and South Carolina. In none of these states was the clergy noted for its advanced attitude on social matters. Again the conclusion seems to be that the churches did not translate their theoretical liberalism into political action.

There is additional evidence of hostility to the New Deal. "For the moment," wrote the perceptive churchman, John C. Bennett, in 1939, "one of the hardest facts to face is that the success of the most promising political forces in American life [the New Deal] must be in spite of the opposition of the majority of the members of the Protestant churches."[17]

Thus it was that the Southern Baptist Social Service Commission looked with grave concern on the trend of affairs in Washington. "Already we have gone a long way," the group charged, "toward a regimentation and toward a centralization of power which would rob the American people of their fundamental freedom."[18] So strongly did Alabama Baptists feel about growing governmental authority that they resolved in state convention to refuse to cooperate in the federal program of a census of religious bodies.

When E. M. Poteat, Jr., proposed that the Southern Baptist Convention establish a Social Service Bureau he was greeted with derision. This "Poteat Pimple Bureau"—as one critic termed it—was nothing more than a "South-wide smelling committee that would go around meddling with everybody and everybody's business." The critic continued: "That is what the Federal Government is now doing, with the result of an increasing discouragement and impoverishment of a large number who through thrift and self-sacrifice have amassed a living, and the passing of their hard-earned savings over to mendicants and dead-beats, who never worked when they had work and who won't work after the ad-

16. *Literary Digest,* Feb. 22, 1936, p. 8. A poll by this magazine in 1934 on the same subject revealed 13,513 clergymen in favor of the New Deal and 11,346 in opposition.
17. *Christian Century,* Feb. 8, 1939, p. 181.
18. *Annual of the Southern Baptist Convention,* 1938, p. 102.

ministrative socialistic schemes finish squandering the money of the taxpayers upon them."[19]

J. Frank Norris, noted Baptist fundamentalist, informed a large group in Carnegie Hall in 1938 that Roosevelt was a dictator under whom the American people suffered grave regimentation. J. Gresham Machen, famous Presbyterian fundamentalist, believed the New Deal could only lead to slavery under a centralized bureaucracy. A New York minister warned his congregation that aid to the unemployed was unchristian because it robbed people of their responsibility to succor the needy and of their opportunity to do so. After years of "hand-outs" from the government, mumbled other cleric, it would take additional years before the "lazy, dole-seeking laborer will again honestly 'look' for work. Thank God, there are some folks left who know that real happiness comes from earning one's own bread by the sweat of the brow."[20] Remarked a Baptist leader: "The bureaucratic regimentation of the people, and the socializing of the free industries of the United States under the New Deal is a challenge to our Baptist heritage. That which infringes on the rights and privileges of free citizens is a signal for Baptist opposition."[21] A Washington minister held that law and love was the old deal, liquor and license the New Deal. But perhaps the most unique criticism of the Roosevelt administration was expressed by a Kentucky Baptist: "Our professedly Christian civilization could find a more fitting slogan for the inspiration of its national life than the 'New Deal,' a phrasing that comes with the breath of the card table and the atmosphere of the gambler."[22]

Much more of this sort of condemnation of the New Deal could be cited, but perhaps the point already has been labored sufficiently. There existed within American Protestantism a very large element that was hostile to Roosevelt and his program.

V

Witness to the conservatism of the churches was given in attacks upon liberals of the cloth as well as upon those in government. Perhaps the word "attack" is too strong or at least carries unfair connotations. The Protestant churches are democratic institutions and conservatives had as much right as liberals to propagandize their beliefs. As has been noted, Left of center churchmen banded together in organizations, pushed through liberal resolutions in church assemblies, sought to secure strategic positions, signed petitions and lobbied to effect certain policies, and de-

19. *Western Recorder*, June 27, 1935, p. 6.
20. *Reformed Church Messenger*, Dec. 13, 1934, p. 6.
21. *Western Recorder*, Sept. 27, 1934, p. 4.
22. *Ibid.*, Oct. 25, 1934, p. 6.

nounced conservatives as subverters of the "true" American and Christian way. This being the case, it is difficult to see why conservatives should be condemned for using the same tactics. And a decent respect for fair play invites the observation that if conservatives often called honest liberals "Reds," on many occasions liberals called honest conservatives "Fascists." All things considered, conservatives absorbed as much abuse as they gave.

For example, the Church League for Industrial Democracy came in for much questioning from Episcopalians. Bishop William Manning was perhaps the most vocal critic. However, he was joined by many others including Bishop Charles Fiske and Bernard Iddings Bell. Bell was one of the founders of the group and he believed that the CLID had swung from a liberal posture to one definitely radical, including for some of its leaders like Spofford a coquetting with Communists. The fight over the CLID rocked the Episcopal press and the General Convention, especially that of 1937. And in 1937, also, a Church Laymen's Association was formed to combat the radical and unchristian influences that threatened the disintegration of the Protestant Episcopal Church. This group, under the chairmanship of Merwin K. Hart, charged that the CLID advocated the principles of Marxian socialism. Although the charge was too strong, it is not unreasonable to say that the CLID brought some criticism down upon its own head.

The accusations leveled against the CLID were child's play compared to the extent and ferocity of those made against the Methodist Federation for Social Service. William Randolph Hearst, Ralph Easley, of the National Civic Federation, and a host of other conservatives continued to snipe at the Federation as they had done in the twenties. The Reverend Rembert Gilman Smith was probably the most active critic within the ranks of Methodism itself. His pamphlet, "Methodist Reds," ran to two editions and was distributed from Maine to California. In 1936 Smith published a volume entitled *Moscow Over Methodism* which enjoyed a wide popularity, and in that year also he formed the Methodist League Against Communism, Fascism, and Unpatriotic Pacifism. The exact strength of this group is unknown, although members were claimed in ten states. In any event, the MFSS was a principal target of Smith's attacks, it being termed the "Marxist Federation for Social Strife."

Indeed, liberal Methodists were hard pressed all along the line in 1936. The social resolutions passed by the General Conference marked a retreat from the 1932 position. A purge was made of the important Board of Education. Bishop Edgar Blake was replaced by the ultra-conservative Bishop Adna Leonard as the board's head, and two young leaders, Owen Greer and Blane Kirkpatrick, avowed Socialists, failed to receive reappointment. The General Conference also pointedly emphasized the unofficial character of the Federation.

A year earlier a group of Methodist laymen met at the Union League Club in Chicago on July 29, and from this gathering there emerged the unofficial Conference of Methodist Laymen. The avowed purpose of this new organization was to check the spread of radicalism within Methodism and to reorient the pulpit along personal rather than social lines. Henry S. Henschen served as chairman and Wilbur Helm as secretary. Its principal target was the MFSS. It is an unhappy commentary on American liberalism that a flood of invective was heaped upon this conservative group only slightly less violent than that endured by the Federation itself. In this case, of course, the liberals were on the sending rather than the receiving end. Much was made of the fact that Henschen was a banker, the inference being that that profession was only slightly less reprehensible than the world's oldest. It was stated that this group represented incipient fascism and that freedom of thought was on the verge of being crushed within Methodism.

The fact seems to be that the Conference of Methodist Laymen was a conservative organization composed of men who sincerely believed in capitalism and who perhaps honestly felt it was not the function of the churches to pass upon secular matters. There is nothing baneful or surprising about this. Indeed, it would have been surprising only if the conservatives had remained silent. And so these men organized, as liberals had done earlier, to give voice to their views. What it amounted to was a struggle for power. And conservatives were as much within their rights as were liberals in their attempt to dominate their church. The Conference of Methodist Laymen was mistaken in assuming that a Socialist could not be a true Christian, but it must be remembered that the MFSS made the same assumption concerning capitalists. It is more difficult to excuse the dismissals of Blaine and Kirkpatrick, under whose leadership Methodist youth was indoctrinated with Socialist propaganda. And yet in the past liberals had secured the removal of reactionaries from strategic posts, and one has the feeling that the conservatives were doubly damned because they were successful in their counter-attack.

Many other examples could be cited of conservatives banding together to check clerical radicalism, perhaps the most sinister being the National Conference of Christian Ministers and Laymen which assembled at Asheville, North Carolina, in 1936. The word "sinister" is not too strong, because this group—as indeed several others—was tinged with anti-Semitism and other proto-Fascist elements. Just as liberalism sometimes degenerated into fellow-traveling, so conservatism occasionally sunk into fascism. Responsible conservatives had the right to criticize those with whom they disagreed, but there is no possible justification for the scurrility mouthed by certain rabid reactionaries. And as will be noted, Protestantism did not go unrepresented in the Fascist organizations spawned by the depression.

VI

Conservatives might organize to defend their views, they might openly condemn the New Deal, they might cry out against radicalism within the churches, but their most potent argument in the thirties as in the twenties was the old, old one that the churches should serve to aid individual souls into heaven and not to bring heaven here to earth. The salvation of the individual was the only charge placed upon the churches and when ministers spoke on politics or economics they were "meddling."

The debate between the proponents of social religion and personal religion raged on in the Depression Decade. Countless clergymen and laymen, in pulpit, journal, and assembly, rose to defend the latter cause. Conservatives, naturally, had a stake in preserving the status quo. Their position was essentially defensive. They had merely to hold what they already possessed. And so it was inevitable that they would emphasize personal sin to the exclusion of social sin, for the good and sufficient reason that there was little in the social order that was sinful. Silence on social matters was tantamount to neutrality, and to be neutral was tantamount to blessing the established order, for only agitation could usher in change. It is easy to conclude, therefore, that proponents of personal religion really clothed their role as defenders of the established order in the garbs of pious self-deception.

But it is not as simple as that. The minister on the picket line or busy lobbying for the Socialist party is a heroic figure. One can admire his burning zeal and flaming courage. But day after day the average parson is called upon to perform quiet deeds of mercy where an immense learning in economic theory is of little help. He must comfort the bereaved, soothe those on beds of pain, and minister to the sick in heart. He must preach Sunday after Sunday to those who seek to know the truth so that they may be free. And men who examine their own hearts honestly know that the corruption they find there is, often, due to sin that cannot be palmed off on bankers, labor-sweating employers, or greedy politicians. Honest men know also that the peace that passeth understanding comes from within and not through any economic or political reform. Christian social radicals served their God and their fellow men, but it is just possible that a young liberal fresh from a seminary sociological course would have less to say to the sick, widowed, and bondaged of sin than a quiet Bible-wise parson who had never looked within the covers of an economics textbook.

And one suspects, also, that at least some ministers concentrated on social problems because they were more simple than personal ones. Complex as were, say, the causes of the depression, they were not more baffling than the problems of the human heart. Further, social problems were so much more exciting than the needs and poignant tragedies of the individual soul. How much more important, it was reasoned, to solve the unemployment problem of fifteen million than to save one rather unimpressive little parishioner. Besides, by concentrating on social sins—invariably someone else's—the radical minister could convince himself that his own personal shortcomings were unimportant. One suspects that a few leaders of social Christianity disguised a brutal coldness in their personal relations by throwing themselves into a great crusade to save all of mankind. Who has not known a Pecksniff who professed a boundless love for suffering humanity, only to reveal a mummy-like coldness in his treatment of individuals?

VII

Conservatives remained important in American Protestantism in the Depression Decade. History may not vindicate their position—Clio rarely smiles on conservatives—but it would be unjust to conclude that these defenders of the status quo were motivated by ignoble considerations. As in the case of liberals, they fought the good fight according to their own lights. About the worst that can be said is that occasionally their lights were dim and their sights ill-focused.

Perhaps even this mild condemnation is unfair. In the fifties Billy Graham, phenomenally popular evangelist, was the frequent target for the critical barbs of socially conscious ministers. They accused him of side-stepping such explosive issues as the race question in his concentration on personal conversion. Mr. Graham's admirers pointed out, however, that the reformation of society rested upon the primary conversion of lost sinners. After all, new found worlds could not be discovered by lost souls.

Certainly it was clear by the fifties—the record of Communist Russia was as forceful as it was ugly—that no social reform was better than the men who administered it; that lofty ends could be perverted by depraved means; that individuals are more important than institutions or theories.

The truth seems to be that social and personal Christianity are not mutually exclusive, and that the Church needs evangelists as well as prophets.

Part II

The Churches and Civil Liberties

CHAPTER IX

The Churches and Lynching

"If there were a drunken orgy somewhere, I would bet ten to one a church member was not in it. . . . But if there were a lynching I would bet ten to one a church member was in it."
—Reinhold Niebuhr

I

THE INQUIRY now turns to the subject of civil liberties. In a very real sense, the following five chapters are the most important in the entire inquiry. The true greatness of America lies not alone in her automobiles and skyscrapers, her tremendous wealth and power, but also in the fact that her people are free. Unless civil liberties are upheld by the letter of the law and the spirit of her citizens, America cannot claim to be the world's last, best hope. Wendell Willkie observed that today only the strong deserve to be free. Yes, but only the free can be called great.*

II

It is fashionable among sophisticated Americans to belittle the power of the Devil, but a glance at the lynching record of the United States provides substantial proof of the Old Deluder's continued activity. Surely the churches could not remain silent in the face of this shameful record, for as Rabindranath Tagore asked of American missionaries, "So long as this goes on in your land, do you think you have any Christianity to export?"[1]

Apparently some citizens answered this query in the affirmative. In any event, missionary work flourished while dark deeds of mob violence were being perpetrated. And according to the closest students of lynching, devout Protestants were among the participants at these modern Golgothas. These authorities found an unhappy correlation between Protestantism's strength and mob violence. They further disclosed that servants of the Lord frequently encouraged or silently acquiesced in lynchings. "It is no accident," believes a distinguished Negro leader, "that in these states with the greatest number of lynchings

* Substantial portions of this chapter were first published in *The Journal of Negro History*, XLII (April, 1957).
1. *Christian Century*, April 19, 1923, p. 502. There were 528 lynchings in the United States, 1919-39.

to their discredit . . . the great majority of the church members are Protestant and of the evangelical wing of Protestantism as well."[2]

Buttressing these conclusions are the findings of students who investigated the social attitudes of Southern Baptists. They disclosed that although lynching was not defended, on occasion it was accepted without serious question and even explained away. For instance, an examination of 1,003 Southern Baptist district association meetings by Hugh A. Brimm revealed only nine references to lynching—a frequency of less than one per cent. Of greater significance is the record of 117 district association metings *held within the boundaries of which a lynching took place.* These meetings all convened from one to four months after the lynching and in approximately 60 per cent of the cases, delegates, including the pastor, from the community where the lynching occurred were present at the meeting. In 116 of the 117 associations no reference was made to the local lynching and no resolution was passed on principle.

Other examples of sunshine saints and summer parsons who remained silent when lynchings erupted in their communities could be cited. Apparently it was more discreet to preach on foreign missions and booze than call the civic conscience to account. For example, in Maryville, Missouri, a demented Negro rapist was chained to the roof of a schoolhouse. The gasoline-saturated building was then fired to the delight of a large audience of men, women, and children. According to an investigator for the Federal Council, the agreed policy of the town ministers, with one exception, was to say nothing about the tragedy. One parson preached the following Sunday on the necessity of Christians giving evidence of the grace of God in their daily living, illustrating the sermon with a story of a drunkard's conversion. Another minister appealed for funds so that the gospel might be brought to the heathen across the seas. It was not that Maryville lacked social consciousness, for a week following the lynching a petition to close the town pool halls was presented in some of the churches.

In the same year, 1931, the Federal Council investigated a second lynching, this time in Shafer, North Dakota. Again the churches were silent, the minister of the Presbyterian church explaining his refusal to cooperate in the investigation by the fact that he was too busy saving lost souls in "our gracious revival" in Watford City. The story was much the same after lynchings in Mississippi, Georgia, Texas, and elsewhere.

Several Southern journals occasionally justified lynching. So long as ignorant, vicious Negroes prowled the Southland, so long as the "unmentionable crime" was committed, so long as the courts were lax

2. Walter White, *Rope and Faggot: A Biography of Judge Lynch* (New York, 1929), p. 41.

and punishment uncertain, just so long would Southern whites continue to take the law into their own hands. In any event, legislation, and particularly federal legislation, was not the solution to lynching. Only the healing balm of time and the Christian gospel provided the answer. Intervention by Northern liberals or congressional action was deemed insulting, unconstitutional, unfair, and irresponsible—a distinct aspersion upon the people of the South. To paraphrase Damon Runyon, as much as these writers were opposed to lynching, they were not bigoted about it.

A questionnaire of 1935, answered by some five thousand ministers, revealed only 3.3 per cent had worked against lynching by preachment and writing to their congressmen in favor of a federal law. Further, 1.5 per cent said they would not do so and 1.7 per cent were in doubt.

III

Happily, the official minutes of the major denominations at their national assemblies, conventions, and conferences reveal a greater concern in lynching.[3] The Northern Presbyterians, somewhat more law abiding than their frontier Scotch-Irish forebears, took a dim view of lynching. In 1919 their General Assembly recorded itself against the "wicked and unlawful" practice. In 1922 and again in 1923 this group passed resolutions endorsing the Dyer bill making lynching a federal offense. On several instances committee reports to the Assembly urged strong action, and in 1934 an adopted resolution branded lynching as the logical result in every community that pursued a policy of humiliation and degradation toward the Negro. In every succeeding year of the decade, Northern Presbyterians endorsed federal legislation, such as the Costigan-Wagner Anti-Lynching bill, to end the "unspeakable evil."

Although Southern Presbyterians spoke less frequently, lynching did not pass unnoticed. For instance, in 1921 the Committee on Home Missions vigorously condemned mob violence, as did another committee two years later. In 1936 a severe arraignment of lynching, complete with statistics, was presented, and the following year a superb report on race relations included an attack on the evil. In 1939 the Assembly called upon its members to lead the fight against lynching.

Unlike Presbyterians, Northern Methodists met only once in every four years in General Conference. At each of these quadrennials, America's most shameful barbarism was denounced. Time and again, through

3. Frank S. Loescher, *The Protestant Church and the Negro* (New York, 1948), is frequently quoted as an authority on the official attitudes of the churches on lynching. Unfortunately, Loescher did not examine the denominational minutes and consequently his conclusions are incomplete and inaccurate. In most respects, however, this is an excellent study.

resolutions and Episcopal admonishments, Wesley's followers characterized lynching as an "unpardonable blight," a "black spot on America's soul" which the federal government must act to stamp out.

Southern Methodists in General Conference were not silent. The Episcopal Address of 1922 vigorously condemned lynching, and the adopted report of the Committee on Temperance and Social Service urged both preachers and laymen to make every effort to prevent outbreaks of mob violence and to endeavor to bring about the punishment in the courts of all who thus defy the law of both God and the land. The next quadrennium demanded equal justice for all persons regardless of race. In 1930 the Bishops prayed for justice to the Negro, while the entire Convention adopted a resolution expressing horror over a lynching in Texas. Four years later the Bishops again entreated the formation of public opinion that would make lynching unthinkable, and an adopted report condemned mob violence as subversive of all law and good government. "Lynching most frequently grows out of race prejudice," read the report, "often it relates itself to property values or personal piques and is even resorted to as a blind for a white man's guilt."[4] Finally, in 1938 the Bishops once again asked that the Negro be protected against extra-legal attacks upon his person and property.

In 1920 the Northern Baptists pledged themselves to do their utmost to wipe out lynching, a "barbaric symptom of anarchy." Two years later the Northern Baptist Convention called for effective legislation to remedy the evil. In 1926 a committee rejoiced in the decline of mob violence, and the following year an adopted report demanded the punishment of officers who failed to protect their prisoners. In 1931 the Convention again expressed its detestation of lynching, and subsequently a resolution was adopted requesting effective preventive laws.

Although Southern Baptists in local meetings hesitated to speak on lynching, this was not true of the Southern Baptist Convention. At almost every annual meeting lynching was termed "brutal" and "shameful." Baptists were urged not to rest until every vestige of the barbarity had been eradicated, and law officers were importuned to forfeit their lives rather than surrender their prisoners to a mob. At no time, however, did the Southern Baptist Convention endorse federal legislation.

In 1919 the National Council of Congregational Churches adopted a resolution asking Congress to pass a law making lynching a federal offense. The 1921 Council attacked the abuse and the following meeting accepted a resolution voicing approval of the Dyer anti-lynching bill. In 1925 Congregationalists called for the protection of the Negro, and

4. *Journal of the General Conference of the Methodist Episcopal Church, South,* 1934, pp. 329-30.

two years later they resolved to support all public officials in their protection of prisoners. The members of the 1934 General Council pledged
themselves to use their influence "to condemn and oppose the iniquitous and inexcusable crime of lynching until this disgraceful, inhuman
and barbarous practice disappears from our land."[5] Convinced that local
and state authorities could not do the job, the delegates saw the "high
necessity" of federal legislation.

Other denominations, with faith in the right as God gave them to
see the right, labored to heal the wounds of racial and class hatred by
condemning lynching. The Episcopalians, for example, voiced their
disapproval of mob violence in 1919, and in 1934 the House of Bishops
endorsed a federal anti-lynching measure. In that year the Board of
Temperance and Social Welfare of the Disciples of Christ indicted lynching, and in 1934 the International Convention of the Disciples adopted
a strong resolution against the evil. The following Convention officially
endorsed the Wagner-Van Nuys Anti-Lynching bill.

Additional evidence abounds. The Unitarians, Universalists, Church
of the Brethren, United Brethren in Christ, Reformed Church in
America, and the Evangelical and Reformed Church all called for the
elimination of brutish lynching, and, in some instances, supported
federal action.

The Federal Council of Churches consistently and courageously concerned itself with lynching. At a special session in 1919 the Council
memorialized Congress to enact a federal law for the suppression of
lynching. The Council pledged to use its authority in every way to remove from America this disgraceful evil. Under authority granted by
the quadrennial meeting of 1920, the president of the Council called
together leading white and Negro citizens at Washington, D. C., on July
12, 1921, and there was formed the Commission on the Church and Race
Relations. Among the manifold activities of this group was the distribution of thousands of pamphlets denouncing lynching. In 1928 the
Administrative Committee adopted a strong resolution against lynching,
and in that same year the Council's Commission on Race Relations
issued a summons to church people to penitence and prayer to free the
nation from the evil of mob violence. The day chosen for this observance
was February 12, known as Race Relations Sunday.

The Council acted in other ways. Scarcely an issue of the *Federal
Council Bulletin* or *Information Service* failed to carry an editorial or
article on the subject. An honor roll was kept listing the states free from
the blot and this information was given widespread distribution in both
the secular and religious press. The Council commended such organiza-

5. *Minutes of the General Council of Congregational Christian Churches,* 1934, p. 111.

tions as the Association of Southern Women Opposed to Lynching, itself a group with a strong religious orientation. Special investigators were sent to towns where lynchings took place and letters of protest were mailed to state and local officials in areas shamed by mob violence. In 1934 Dr. Samuel McCrea Cavert, general secretary of the Council, testified at a Senate hearing on the Costigan-Wagner bill. Armed with quotations damning lynching from many church groups, Dr. Cavert made a powerful plea for congressional action. Two months later the executive committee of the Council adopted a resolution calling for federal legislation to cope with the evil.

Scores of local church groups placed themselves on record. Thousands of ministers signed petitions condemning lynching and, frequently, endorsing federal action. Thousands of editorials damning lynching appeared in the church press. In a few cases on record, ministers resolutely risked their lives to hold back lynch mobs. Indeed, it becomes as plain as a pikestaff that Protestant protests against lynching were almost as thick as bald headed sinners at an Amy Semple McPherson revival.

It is fitting to conclude this chapter with a brief reference to a lynching in California defended and justified by the governor of that sunny state. Dr. Henry Darlington of the Church of the Heavenly Rest, New York, condoned the governor's inexcusable excuse (although Dr. Darlington later repented), and for this his church was picketed by Union Theological students. Whereupon a solemn deputation of ruffled vestrymen presented a demand to President Henry Sloane Coffin of Union that he expel the students. Said Dr. Coffin: "How old is your rector?" "Forty-eight," said the vestrymen. "Do you intend to ask him to resign?" "We do not," they answered. "Well," said President Coffin, "if at forty-eight he can be excused for the stupidity he exhibited, my students in their twenties might well be treated in the same way."[6]

IV

What conclusions can be drawn from this evidence? The record of the Protestant churches was spotted, but on the whole their concern with lynching was both deeper and more widespread than commonly believed. Surely it would not be unfair to say that they deserve some share of the credit for helping to expel this evil from the land.

6. Walter Russell Bowie, "Preacher," *This Ministry. The Contributions of Henry Sloane Coffin* (Reinhold Niebuhr, ed., New York, 1945), p. 65.

CHAPTER X

Protestants and Patriots

I

A DISCUSSION of the attitudes of American Protestantism toward civil liberties would be incomplete without some reference, however brief, to an organization which flaunted a vicious brand of racial and religious intolerance and flouted the Bill of Rights—the revived Ku Klux Klan. It is altogether fitting and proper to begin this review of "patriotic" organizations with the Klan, for its connection with Protestantism is notorious, and writers wishing to illustrate the extreme reaction of organized religion in America invariably present the Klan as their star witness.*

That the group stood at fundamental variance with the American Dream few objective students would deny. By 1925 perhaps as many as four or five million white, Protestant, native-born patriots were engaged in or tacitly supporting acts of intimidation, terror, and torture against their Negro, Catholic, Jewish, and foreign-born neighbors. They justified these acts on the ground that America was in dire peril and could be saved only if it remained, oddly enough, predominantly white, Protestant, and native-born. Professing to be a Christian organization and composed of Protestants, the Klan became an extremely powerful force in American life, especially in the Southwest, Middle West, and Far West. Appealing to men's patriotism and idealism, as well as to their fears, hates, and frustrations, the Klan increased rapidly in size in the early twenties. Not only did minority groups feel the sting of its displeasure, but union organizers, birth control advocates, internationalists, village reprobates, and "fallen" women as well. As these good, substantial, bed-sheeted citizens rode off in their Model T's or on their plow horses to do their nightly, patriotic, Christian business, one wonders if the more thoughtful members did not quiet their consciences with the words from the old hymn, "God moves in a mysterious way."

The connection between the Klan and the Protestant churches has

* Substantial portions of this section on the Klan were first published in *The Journal of Southern History*, XXII (August, 1956).

not proved much of a mystery to many scholars. Although the definitive history of this group has not yet been written, a number of students investigating the Klan noted a close tie-up between it and Protestantism. These writers are mostly agreed that the Klan worked hand-in-glove with the more fundamentalist denominations, that it received the open or tacit support of countless clergymen, and that many of its officers were Protestant preachers. Moreover, both the secular and church press occasionally carried news items telling of the Klan visiting a church. Scholarly opinion holding the KKK to be a malignant aspect of American Protestantism is, then, overwhelming. It would be foolish and inaccurate to maintain that such was not the case. The fact that Klan membership was open only to Protestants is in itself sufficient to establish a prima-facie case. The evidence implicating the Protestant churches in the rise of the group has been presented by so many noted authorities that it need not be reviewed here.[1]

Perhaps, however, certain points need to be emphasized, if for no other reason that that they have been rather neglected by historians. The observations that follow are less in the nature of a dissenting opinion than of a modifying report. Guilty the Protestant churches may be of supporting the Klan, but there are certain facts which serve to soften this indictment.

In the first place, it seems apparent that if Protestantism and the Klan had worked hand-in-glove, the church press would have supported this alliance, or, at least, remained judiciously silent. On some two score occasions the *Christian Century*, America's most influential Protestant journal, saw fit to mention the Klan, and in every instance the reference was unflattering. The Klan, of course, claimed to be the minister's friend, which prompted the editors to devoutly pray to be delivered from the tender mercies of such friends. Further, clergymen who supported this hate-breeding organization prostituted their sacred calling. The Klan's growing power elicited a three-page editorial warning, but the editors firmly believed the evil would pass, for, as they put it, "Klannishness Karries Its Own Cure." By the following year its strength seemed on the upsweep and the *Christian Century's* readers were reminded that the spirit of the Klan was against the very genius of Christianity, "that if it succeeds, Christianity fails, no matter what other gains may be

1. There is little statistical evidence on the extent of Klan infiltration into the ministry. However, the National Catholic Bureau of Information, during the years 1922-28, found the names of sixteen Protestant ministers among 102 Klan officials. Moreover, an incomplete list of ministers who, at various times, preached pro-Klan sermons or entertained the Klan at their churches numbered sixty-nine. Further, of the Klan's thirty-nine "national lecturers," twenty-six were Protestant ministers. See Williams, *The Shadow of the Pope*, pp. 317-18.

thought won."[2] When it appeared that the Klan's strength finally had ebbed—when each Knight removed his bed sheet for presumably the last time—the editors were filled with joy and thanksgiving (tempered with a little judicious misgiving).

Another undenominational journal, the *World Tomorrow,* gave solemn warning against the Klan, even devoting an entire issue to an exposure of the group. A third undenominational Protestant periodical, *Christian Work,* on almost a score of instances leveled blistering attacks on the Kleagles, Kludds, and Imperial Wizards. As early as 1921 the editors were calling for an investigation of the KKK by the Department of Justice, for the Klan was unchristian and undemocratic, promising only deceit, delusions, hopelessness, anarchy and cruelty. The editors believed that a "religious revival under the auspices of the Klan reminds one of the 'Christian' mob in Russia or Poland or Roumania howling for blood in the Jewish quarter, for the glory of the good Lord Christ!"[3] Further, Klansmen were said to be traitors—the greatest menace to true Americanism the country had known since the Civil War. The *Christian Herald* also found precious little Christianity in the Klan. It could only result in lawlessness and disorder, maintained the editors, for justice is pictured as having her eyes bandaged for the sake of dealing with impartiality, not with her entire face masked to escape detection. Two Federal Council periodicals, *Information Service* and *Federal Council Bulletin,* described the Klan in uncharitable terms.

Undenominational journals and the Federal Council papers, perhaps, might have been in a position to attack the Klan without fear of reprisals. Editors of denominational papers, however, were in a more vulnerable position, and surely they would not have been able to withstand the Klan's wooing if their readers had all been seduced by persuasive Klaliffs and Klaziks.

Contrary to the belief of at least one scholar, all the Methodist papers were not discreetly and shamefully quiet about the Klan. For example, the *Northwestern Christian Advocate* termed the Klan an abnormal and vicious organization. Any pastor who "refrains from denouncing an organization that plots its deeds in secret and executes its purpose cruelly and under mask, is not worthy to preach the gospel of an open-minded and clear-breasted Christ."[4] A sister publication, the *New York Christian Advocate,* said the Klan was neither Christian nor American. Ministers approached by the bed-sheeted patriots with bribes of money should cry, thy money perish with thee. The fact of the matter is, the editors

2. Nov. 20, 1924, p. 1497.
3. Jan. 31, 1925, p. 113.
4. May 24, 1922, p. 581.

considered "The K.K.K. No Per Cent American." It was a group "which hides its very face from the light of day, and pursues its ends by the method of the mask, the black hand and the poison pen."[5]

Naturally perhaps, much less space was devoted to the Klan in the *Nashville Christian Advocate.* Yet it is of interest to find both contributors and the editors damning the group. Both the *North Carolina Christian Advocate* and the *Wesleyan Christian Advocate,* published in Atlanta, warned against the Klan's machinations. Even the conservative *Arkansas Methodist,* while not always disapproving of the aims of the Klan, condemned its methods as dangerous, saying let us have none of it. Other Methodist periodicals spoke. *Zion's Herald* termed the organization pernicious, unlawful, and un-American, while both the *Western Christian Advocate* and the *Pacific Christian Advocate* warned against being duped by secret organizations that appealed to passion and prejudice.

It appears, then, that while the Methodist press might have denounced the Klan more vigorously and frequently than it did, at least nine leading papers of this denomination were not completely silent. Moreover, not a single endorsement of the Klan was found by the present writer in the Methodist press, while many of the attacks on the Klan were quite severe.

Presbyterian editors, apparently, were too good logicians to be duped by the Klan's dictum: "Let us do evil that good may come." For example, the *Presbyterian Advance,* published in Nashville, carried at least a dozen references to this society, all barbed as Scottish thistles. The Klan, so the editors maintained, was un-American, unchristian, and unnecessary. Moreover, there is always potential danger in the political activities of a secret society which had no political principles. Its aims were diametrically opposed to American ideals. To clinch matters, the editors quite wisely pointed out that the churches were having troubles enough of their own without mixing up with those of the Klan.

Another Presbyterian publication, the *Continent,* charged the Klan was merely a money-making scheme and that Protestants should everywhere "set faces like flint against the Ku Klux revival and denounce it for the devilish mischief it is."[6] The *Presbyterian Banner* believed the KKK was the "essence of mobocracy" and that its "methods strike at the very heart of what is held most dear to American principles, and by the best in American life."[7] A similar position was taken by the *Herald and Presbyter,* although this paper also condemned Roman Catholics who mobbed Klan meetings.

5. Dec. 14, 1922, p. 1565.   6. Sept. 29, 1921, p. 1085.
7. Aug. 25, 1921, pp. 3-4.

There is an old saying that true gentlemen travel only the Episcopal road to heaven. It goes without saying that few gentlemen would travel the Klan road to Americanism. Thus it is not surprising to find Protestant Episcopal journals scorning masked mobs. The Klan, snapped the editors of the *Southern Churchman,* was a menace which all thoughtful persons should combine to prevent. After all, wrote a contributor, masked organizations are an invitation to "any band of roughnecks" to punish those who incur their displeasure. The same writer also believed the Klan an insult to the democracy of the South.

Being gentlemen, the editors of *Living Church* found "incredible" the mere suggestion that an Episcopalian would be among these masked ruffians. "Real men," pontificated the editors, "engaged in honorable pursuits, do not find it necessary to disguise their features."[8] The *Churchman* held the Klan a "pernicious and cowardly breeder of class hatred" which violated "every basic principle of the religion of Jesus."[9] If it were successful, American democracy would go into discard.

Few Unitarians were Klansmen and the *Christian Register* reflects this fact, although one suspects the usually outspoken editor, C. C. Dieffenbach, of pulling his punches. Perhaps he was too busy fighting to uphold civil liberties against the onslaughts of the Boston Irish to have much sympathy with Roman Catholics. In any event, while this paper criticized the Klan, it was in somewhat weak tones. The *Universalist Leader,* however, on a dozen occasions used very trenchant tones in unmasking the Klan's pretensions.

Other religious editors spoke their piece. The *Reformed Church Messenger,* for instance, termed the Klan a source of dishonor and shame which should not be tolerated among free men. A Disciples paper issued a very strong warning against ministers joining the Klan. The *Lutheran* called it a dangerous and ill-advised scheme, "projected by a dreamer, siezed by profiteers and used by mobs." In short, the order was "utterly indefensible."[10] A Congregational journal blamed racial violence on the skulking night riders of the Ku Klux Klan.

Baptists, together with Methodists and Disciples, are generally considered to have given the Klan it strongest support. However, the official organ of the Northern Baptist Convention, the *Baptist,* did not endorse the society. For instance, in an editorial significantly entitled, "White Faces, but Red Hands," the editors warned that "in the name of liberty, humanity, Christianity and the principles of Americanism, we must denounce this order as criminal and dangerous. No com-

8. May 5, 1923, p. 5.
9. July 28, 1923, p. 7.
10. July 17, 1924, p. 13.

munist conspiracy could be more so."[11] Probably more than one subscriber could have been heard mumbling under his breath the classic words of Owen Wister's Virginian, "When you call me that, smile!" If so, the statement of the assistant editor penned six years later probably increased the incident of apoplexy among a good many people, both Baptists and gangsters. U. M. McGuire found the methods of the Klan even more ruthless and efficient than those of Chicago gunmen—and this in the era of Capone!

A second Northern Baptist paper, *Watchman-Examiner,* edited by a leading fundamentalist, Dr. Curtis Laws, was mildly critical in its evaluation of the Klan. While agreeing with the Klan that America faced a threat from certain sources, Dr. Laws hoped the Klansmen would take off their masks and make their fight in the open. And when, in 1928, the Knights unmasked, he rejoiced and hoped they would take off their night gowns too, "except when they go to bed."[12]

The situation in regard to the Southern Baptist press is difficult to evaluate. A Virginia paper, the *Religious Herald,* carried no open attack upon the Klan, but in several editorials and articles its opposition to masked bands was made clear. A second paper, the *Alabama Baptist,* did a cowboy-like job of straddling. Never vigorously condemning the Klan, never openly endorsing it, this paper followed a policy that can best be described as "neutral." This was approximately the position taken by the *Western Recorder, Word and Way,* and *Baptist Courier.* In general, it might be said that the Southern Baptist press condoned the aims but condemned the methods of the Klan. On this issue Southern Baptist editors were too discreet to make good Old Testament prophets.

Here, then, is one aspect of the record which needed emphasizing— an aspect ignored or misrepresented by most commentators on the Klan. While a considerable element of the Protestant press hedged or remained silent on the Klan issue, no evidence of complete and open support was found. Moreover, the great majority of religious editors warned their readers to shun this dangerous society. Thus, when historians speak of the alliance between the Protestant churches and the Klan, an exception must be made of the Protestant press.

A second point worthy of investigation is the attitude of the Protestant churches toward the Klan as reflected in the minutes of the various national conventions, assemblies, and councils of the major denominations. It has been noted that many resolutions were adopted against lynching and mob violence. Some of these utterances could be applied

11. April 23, 1921, p. 358.
12. Feb. 2, 1928, p. 137.

with justice to the night riding activities of the Klansmen. When, however, the investigator searches for resolutions which specifically or unmistakably refer to the Klan, he is rather poorly rewarded. Official assemblies and conventions often skirted the Klan issue in an unseemly fashion. Yet, the record is relieved here and there by an occasional courageous pronouncement denouncing the bed-sheeted band. And it may be categorically stated, furthermore, that not a single major denomination in national meeting even hinted at official endorsement of the Klan.

It has been observed that two periodicals of the Federal Council repeatedly chided the Klan. Further, in 1922 the Federal Council termed the Klan subversive of every principle of civilized government, said that it had no right to speak in the name of Protestantism, and urged the churches to exert every influence to check its spread.

The following year the National Council of Congregational Churches warned its constituency to avoid secret, masked, "patriotic" organizations such as the Klan, for they "really foster social and religious suspicion, and give opportunity for lawlessness and brutality."[13] Another resolution, in an unmistakable reference to the Klan, termed it un-American. In 1922 the Episcopal House of Bishops and House of Deputies concurred in deprecating . secret groups who in the name of patriotic Americanism capitalize on bigotry, hatred, and intolerance. These groups "who seek to array man against man, citizen against citizen, neighbor against neighbor, class against class, race against race, or creed against creed, are disloyal to the spirit and teaching of the Gospel of Christ, and to the foundation principles of the American commonwealth."[14]

In 1925 the Social Service Committee of the Northern Baptist Convention attacked Klan-like lawlessness, and two years later the Committee on Interracial Relationships mentioned the Klan by name as one of the organizations lessening human brotherhood in America. Southern Baptists also acted. The Commission on Social Service in 1922, after denouncing mob violence, urged "upon our pastors and churches the importance of not becoming allied with or giving approval and support to any movement or organization that violates or tends to violate . . . sacred and fundamental principles. Let us do nothing that will bring embarrassment to us or harm to the cause of Christ and to the government."[15] The following year the Convention adopted a report condemning the cowardly and diabolical work of masked mobs. This con-

13. *Minutes of the National Council of Congregational Churches*, 1923, p. 235.
15. *Annual of the Southern Baptist Convention*, 1922, p. 98.
14. *Journal of the General Convention of the Protestant Episcopal Church*, 1922, p. 115.

demnation was repeated in 1927, not only by the Southern Baptist Convention but also by state conventions. Neither the Northern nor Southern Presbyterians in their General Assemblies mentioned the Klan by name, although they voiced strong disapproval of mob violence in general.

Methodists hit closer to the Klan home. The Northern Episcopal Address of 1924 termed secret, masked organizations which arrogated to themselves the authority of the courts essentially un-American and a menace to society. At the same Conference, E. Stanley Jones introduced a resolution deploring Klan-like groups, and the next quadrennium again saw the Bishops striking a not-too-veiled blow at the Klan. Earlier, the Detroit Conference of this church had warned against secret organizations, and the Methodist ministers of Pittsburgh expressed emphatic disapproval of the Klan. The Social Service Commission of Southern Methodism also resolved against the demonstrations of masked and hooded men.

Admittedly these illustrations are not overly impressive, but the official record of the Protestant churches as contained in resolutions and reports at the national level was not quite as black as some students have believed.

There remains still a third point to be emphasized. Historians make much of the fact that many clergymen joined the Klan or at least gave it their support. This is true. However, this group did not include any substantial number of nationally prominent church leaders. On the other hand, a considerable number of parsons, both in obscure parishes and great city cathedrals, had both the courage and common sense to condemn this nonsensical organization.

As early as 1921, for example, the associate secretary of the Home Missions Council of the Methodist Episcopal Church, South, Rodney W. Roundy, called the Klan "dangerous," "vicious," "evil," a "leprous social disease" producing only "deceit, delusions, hopelessness, anarchy and cruelty."[16] In the same year another Southern churchman, the Reverend Walter Russell Bowie, branded the Klan an insult to orderly government which played into the hands of malicious individuals. The Reverend Ralph W. Sockman was convinced that all enlightened Protestants would repudiate, as he did, the Klan, for it was a lawless organization using evil methods. A metropolitan pastor of even greater fame, Harry Emerson Fosdick, branded the Klan an utterly un-American thing. He declared that to commit American institutions to the care of

16. *Arkansas Methodist*, Aug. 25, 1921, p. 4. The files of the American Civil Liberties Unions were especially helpful in revealing the names of churchmen who opposed the Klan.

a secret order of oath-bound Protestants, making the night its covering and tar and feathers its instruments, would be to lose those institutions. The Reverend Robert W. Searle, of national prominence, preached on "Christianity and Americanism vs. the Ku Klux Klan." The noted Disciples leader, Dr. Peter Ainslie, termed the Klan a pure fraud, and even John Roach Straton, New York's heresy-hunting Baptist, declared there was no room in the United States for the man in the mask, and that the Klan must go. In the year 1922 alone at least nineteen other New York Protestant ministers preached on the menace of the Klan.

When Methodist Bishop McConnell was interrupted while addressing a church conference in Pennsylvania by the entrance of nine hooded Knights, he declined to accept the offered envelope and unceremoniously—like a good Methodist—showed them the door. Another Methodist, Bishop William F. Anderson, said the Klan was built upon both un-christian and un-American principles, while Bishop Luther B. Wilson used exactly the same terms. The Reverend Ralph B. Urmy, Pittsburgh Methodist, remembering Christ and the money changers, drove some coin-proffering Kluxers from his temple. Bishop W. F. McMurray, Southern Methodist, perhaps remembered Samson when he punched one of his ministers in the mouth for boosting the Klan. Even in Klan-ridden Oklahoma a few ministers such as George S. Fulcher believed that in the day of the Klan's victory "there must not be within its membership a single true Christian, for when the fiery cross rises over a submissive people, the true Christian must have perished in the death struggle for liberty."[17]

Episcopal Bishop Philip Cook issued a warning, while the Reverend Lynn Harold Hough, Methodist minister and one-time president of Northwestern University, termed the Klan a witch's caldron of hatreds. A Southern Presbyterian lady, Mrs. W. C. Winsborough, superintendent of the Women's Auxiliary of the Presbyterian Church, U.S., lashed out at the Klan's secrecy, violence, and doctrine of hate. This outspoken woman was not whipped for her statements, although the Kluxers were not above a little sadistic female flogging; but it is a matter of record that ministers who denounced the Klan risked retaliation in the form of bullets, branding irons, and blunt instruments.

Other sermonists were heard from. Bishop W. P. Thirkield of New Orleans termed the Klan a menace as did Bishop Edwin Mouzon, famous Southern Methodist. Bishop Edwin Holt Hughes, Northern Methodist, termed it idiotic and its claims of Nordic superiority nonsense. "It is not Anglo-Saxon blood," said Hughes, "but the blood of Jesus Christ

17. *Presbyterian Advance*, Nov. 15, 1923, pp. 6-8.

that has made us what we are."[18]   Charles E. Jefferson, Sherwood Eddy, Ashby Jones, Edwin M. Poteat, William David Schermerhorn, Hubert Herring, Bishop Federick Leete, and the officers of the Moody Bible Institute were a few of the many other prominent church leaders who refused to commend or cooperate with the Klan.   An obscure Congregational minister in Kansas predicted the Klansmen would and should "repent in dust and ashes";[19] and other small town parsons in Kentucky and El Paso announced that the Klan had better not meddle in their affairs.

These illustrations obviously do not exonerate the Protestant churches from complicity in the Klan. They do suggest, however, that the Klan was not an instrument of Protestantism in the sense, say, that the Inquisition was of the Medieval Church.   Until documentation is produced to the contrary, it seems fair to conclude that the church press opposed the group; that official church resolutions denounced it; and that nationally prominent church leaders refused to identify themselves with the Klan.

II

Unlike the Klan, the principles of neither the Daughters of the American Revolution nor the American Legion conflicted with the American Dream, and certainly both the Daughters and the Legionnaires contributed much that was wholesome and beneficial to the nation's development.   Nevertheless, the courage of the Protestant churches is amply demonstrated by the fact that on many occasions they entered the lists and splintered lances with those two redoubtable organizations. Perhaps a clash between these two patriotic societies and the churches was inevitable considering the fact that the churches strongly crusaded against militarism and to an unwise degree endorsed pacifism, while the D.A.R. and the Legion, quite naturally, could hardly be expected to take a Ghandi-like attitude toward *all* wars.   Moreover, these patriotic groups were not particularly sensitive about the methods they used to uphold their laudable aims of Americanism, and many churchmen marveled at this Jesuitical performance.

In any event, the Daughters of the American Revolution frequently took time off from hunting up their ancestors to hunting down pacifists and sundry "radicals."   Unfortunately, as they compiled their black lists, it soon became apparent that many clergymen found themselves classified in such "subversive" company as Jane Addams, Dean Roscoe Pound, and Mary E. Woolley.   Although the company was agreeable, many churchmen took exception to the adjectives with which they were described,

18. *Christian Century*, Oct. 1, 1925, p. 1224.
19. A. B. Appleby to Allen H. Godbey, Oct. 17, 1922, Godbey *Papers*.

and, with more courage than chivalry, began to take pot-shots back at the Daughters. The clerical counterattack against this red-blooded American organization composed of blue bloods received tactical support from some of the Daughters themselves. Compiling of black lists and exposing "subversives" was all very jolly, that is, until some of the members—wives of bishops and the like—discovered their husbands on the dossiers. This, after all, was carrying patriotism a bit too far.

Thus it was that churchmen and the Daughters carried on a running skirmish throughout the late twenties and early thirties. It was brutal, modern warfare stripped of all romance or glamor. For example, one clergyman wondered if the initials D.A.R. stood for "Dear Amazon Reactionaries." He hastily added that the word "Amazon" was not entirely accurate, inasmuch as the girls were only proxy warriors, willing to sacrifice all of their husbands on the battlefield, but hardly themselves. Another churchman agreed with William Allen White that these women should be more appropriately named the Daughters of American Tories, while Bishop McConnell observed that if the good women of the D.A.R. were really daughters of a revolution, then he was through with revolutions. Even such gentlemen as Lynn Harold Hough and Harry Emerson Fosdick, in the heat of battle, momentarily lost their *savoir faire*. Hough termed the girls "Daughters of the Ku Klux Klan," and Fosdick pouted because he was not on their black list. After all, to be on the Daughters' black list was an honor; to be on their white list a disgrace.

As the fight grew fiercer Christian chivalry faced severe testing. A leading Federal Council official believed the women of the D.A.R. fit subjects for both psychological and pathological study, while Robert A. Ashworth, distinguished Baptist, proved himself a cad and a bounder when he suggested that all that ailed the girls was the fact that they were getting old. At least a score of other church leaders mocked the society's bluff and bluster, and a score of church journals belabored the fluttering activities of the girls.

These few illustrations do not do justice to this pre-Marquis of Queensberry rules joust, but it is now time to turn to a larger—if hardly as formidable—critic of liberal churchmen, the American Legion.

It is a pity that such a worthy organization as the American Legion occasionally soiled its name with a spread-eaglism unworthy of the great mass of its membership; and when Legionnaires attempted to maintain the status quo in all things (save bonuses), they occasionally took from their quiver the arrows of intimidation, suppression, and slander. Mistaken as the churches were in their determination to strip America of her military shield, naïve as they were in their approach to the abolition of war, in the clash with the Legion over civil liberties, the honors are mostly with the saints rather than the soldiers.

The Legion, for example, hardly followed an honorable course when it brought pressure to bear forcing the cancellation of speaking engagements by prominent clergymen of pacifistic and allegedly radical views. Nor was the Legion wise when, in annual convention in 1929, it slandered American Protestantism by the passage of a resolution demanding a Senate investigation of the Federal Council.

In the face of these slaps, pastors refused to turn the other cheek. Dr. Bowie, then rector of the Grace Episcopal Church, New York, declared from the pulpit that the Legion's lobby was a sinister and deadly cancer upon the body of American life. To help cushion the inevitable counterpunch, sixty noted New York clergymen issued a statement publicly associating themselves with Dr. Bowie, among the signers being Fosdick, Cadman, Cavert, Coffin, Sockman, and Bishops Stires and McConnell.

On dozens of other occasions church leaders, ministerial associations, and editors indicted the Legion for its allegedly fascistic leanings, but it remained for the *Nashville Christian Advocate* to strike the hardest blow when its editor said: "My protest against the attitude of the American Legion is that it is too much like communism, as we see it in Russia, with the suppression of the free press and free speech. I recognize that it is not very agreeable to members of the Legion to be classed as communists, but they are responsible for the resemblance. In reality they are helping to spread communism."[20]

III

The Legionnaires and the Daughters were genuine patriots who fought to uphold the principles of Americanism as, according to their own lights, they saw these principles. Certainly their attitude toward armaments was more realistic than that of the churches. On the question of civil liberties, however, their rodomontade position was less tenable. But the Depression Decade spawned a variety of home-grown psuedo-patriots whose views on Americanism were so myopic as to deserve the term fascism. Mayor Hague, czar of Jersey City, Huey P. Long, the Louisiana Kingfish, and Father Charles Coughlin, the Detroit radio priest, gathered millions of followers, while lesser tub-thumpers of hate such as Gerald L. K. Smith, William Dudley Pelley, and Gerald Winrod drummed up a baneful business among thousands. The Black Legion and the Silver Shirts, the Christian Frontists and the Christian Mobilizers, the Bundists and the fading Kluxers were only a few of the many organizations bearing out Samuel Johnson's dictum that patriotism is

20. May 10, 1935, p. 582.

the last refuge of a scoundrel. Unhappily, with the exceptions of Mayor Hague and Father Coughlin, most of those flirting with fascism were Protestants, and, in fact, Protestant ministers.

Under the benighted rule of Mayor Hague, Jersey City became one of the strongholds of fascism in America. This gentleman's activities severely exercised many Protestants, probably because these performances were so pestiferous, and possibly because Jersey City was predominantly Catholic, thus permitting Protestants to combine the business of upholding civil liberties with the pleasure of reprimanding Catholic authorities. Whatever the motivation, the Protestant press and pulpit reminded Mr. Hague of the existence of the first ten amendments to the Constitution and suggested he read them.

A dozen New Jersey ministers issued courageous declarations from the pulpit condemning the mayor or opened their churches to anti-Hague meetings. Outside of the Hague bailiwick, several score Protestant leaders voiced their protest, petitioned the United States Senate to investigate the "open defiance of constitutional guarantees" in Jersey City, and formed committees on civil liberties. Many church press editors made their position clear. The *Christian Century* tossed jibes at Jersey justice. The editors of the *Presbyterian Tribune* called upon ministers to fight Hague's hooliganism, as did those of *Advance*. When the mayor called for the establishment of a concentration camp in Alaska for all un-Americans, the *Christian Leader* deemed it fitting and proper that Hague be the first inmate. *Zion's Herald* considered Jersey City a Fascist cell in a free country, and the several editions of the *Christian Advocate* compared Hague to Hitler. The *Christian-Evangelist* gave the mayor a "Plain Talk on Americanism." The *Churchman* and the *Reformed Church Messenger* voiced their protests against high jinks in Jersey. The *Living Church* believed dictatorship a present reality in Jersey City. Even the conservative *Watchman-Examiner* made bold to wonder if Hague represented an example of political Romanism. It would be superfluous to add that all of the unofficial liberal church groups in the country looked with wonder and some trembling on the developments in Jersey City.

If Mayor Hague was a menace to liberty in one state, Father Charles E. Coughlin emerged in the thirties as a threat to all Americans. This cherubic, spectacled Roman Catholic priest began his rise to fame and fortune by denouncing Wall Street, international bankers, and capitalistic exploitation. About 1936, however, his targets became, somewhat illogically, President Roosevelt, Communists, and, above all, Jews. Despite the fact that some leading Catholics repudiated this clerical demagogue, his power continued to expand. Appealing to the fears and prejudices of the lower middle class (and to some individuals of wealth and education who should have known better), Father Coughlin banefully influenced the thinking of millions with his vicious diatribes.

All men of good will, Catholics as well as Protestants, challenged the hate-breeding slanders of the Detroit radio priest. The references to him are far too numerous to relate here, and it must suffice to say that many Protestant groups and leaders took the measure of this priest in unmeasured terms.

Far to the south of the automobile city another man—this time a Protestant—was attracting the devotion of millions of disinherited Americans. Among the rural clergy of Louisiana, particularly among the smaller sects, Huey P. Long probably enjoyed warm support. Certain it is that clerical demagogues such as the Reverend Gerald L. K. Smith allied themselves with the Kingfish.

As in the case of Father Coughlin, however, Protestant spokesman made it plain that Long was a power-mad dictator bent on extending his control over Louisiana to the entire United States. His threat was doubly great because to some extent he represented the legitimate grievances of America's disinherited. "It was impossible to understand the rise of Huey Long to power in Louisiana," believed Charles Clayton Morrison, typifying the attitude of thinking American Protestantism, "without seeing him, not as a mere political adventurer, but as a leader in the revolt of the poor against the power of the planter oligarchy which ruled the state since long before the Civil War. Equally it was impossible to understand the promise which occasionally appeared that Mr. Long might gain enormous national power without seeing that it grew out of the possible readiness of the economically insecure millions to find in him an acceptable champion and leader."[21]

IV

Jersey City's mayor, Detroit's radio priest, and Louisiana's Kingfish cast ominous shadows over the American countryside in the thirties. But shadows just as dark if not so lengthened were also cast by a host of other bravos. That Protestants comprised the leadership and membership of most of these Nazi-style groups cannot be denied.

The Black Legion was one such organization. Composed of Protestants and avowing Christian aims, in reality this secret, hooded, terror group left a trail of arson, floggings, and murder across a half-dozen mid-western states. Most spokesmen for the major Protestant denominations, however, warned against joining this anti-Semitic, anti-Negro, anti-union, anti-democracy group of bully boys. In 1936, for instance,

21. *Christian Century*, Sept. 18, 1935, p. 1167.

the Federal Council adopted a resolution saying the Black Legion's "use of the name of God Almighty in its oath is blasphemous and its description of itself as Protestant is unjustifiable and shameful."[22] Several months earlier a group of liberals, including many distinguished Protestant leaders, appealed to President Roosevelt to order a congressional investigation of the Black Legion. In addition, at least thirteen leading Protestant journals flayed the band in the strongest possible terms. Indeed, "writhing vermin" was one of the kindlier characterizations.

Another shirted organization, brighter in color although scarcely so in principles, was the Silver Shirt Legion of America. Founded the day after Hitler took power in Germany and standing for about the same things as the European dictator, the Silver Shirts developed into probably the largest, best financed and best publicized Fascist organization in the country. According to one careful student, many Protestant clergymen were prominent in the organization's leadership. The Reverend E. F. Webber was an organizer in Oklahoma. In Minneapolis and New York preachers addressed meetings. In Seattle a self-styled "former Methodist" minister proselyted for the society. A clergyman was active in organizational work in Toledo and a gentleman bearing the title "Reverend" was similarly engaged in Maine, as D. S. Strong showed.

The founder of this profitable if pernicious organization was goateed, undersized, wizened, William Dudley Pelley. Accounts vary as to Pelley's origin, but he declared himself to be the only son of a Methodist minister. In any event, he always cloaked his hate-filled fulminations with a religious mantle. His Silver Shirts called themselves Christian American patriots. In 1936, under the slogan, "For Christ and the Constitution," Pelley established the Christian Party and nominated himself for President. Moreover, both before and after his imprisonment for sedition, Pelley hob-nobbed with ministers.

The most vociferous and ubiquitous of his fellow shirters was the Reverend Gerald L. K. Smith. A tall, powerful, dynamic man, Smith was born into a pastor's family in a small Wisconsin town. Even his enemies acknowledged his charm and intelligence, and declared him to be one of the most effective speakers in America. Unfortunately, Smith used his undoubted talents to preach hatred toward all Jews, Negroes, Orientals, labor unionists, liberals, and internationalists. Aligning himself with Pelley, Long, Coughlin, and Gerald Winrod in that order, and then striking out on his own, Smith incessantly mouthed Christian doctrine to exploit his ends, twisting the gospel of love into an obscene thing.

22. *Federal Council Bulletin*, Sept., 1936, p. 15.

Kansan-born Gerald Winrod was a third influential member of the ministry of hate. Son of a saloon-keeper turned preacher, Winrod like his father found the sawdust trail more beckoning than the sawdust of the saloon floor. Husky bodied and voiced, his looks and speech combined with his unquestioned sincerity to make him an appealing figure in the eyes of rural, middle class, Protestant America. Winrod illustrates perfectly Mr. Dooley's definition of a fanatic: "a man that does what he thinks th' Lord wud do if He only knew th' facts iv th' case." During the twenties Winrod was one of fundamentalism's most vigorous champions, but in 1934 (after a visit to Nazi Germany) he shifted his attack from evolutionists to Jews and Communists. And as everyone knows (so he argued), all Jews are Communists and most Communists are Jews, and consequently Hitler, the savior of Europe from Jewish-Communist domination, was *sans peur et sans reproche.*

In attempting to assess the attitudes of American Protestantism toward Pelley, Smith, and Winrod, to say nothing of the host of other flirters with fascism, the same problem is encountered that plagues students of the Klan. All of these men were sons of Protestant clergymen. All of them claimed to be ministers of the gospel. Many of their trusted lieutenants were parsons and certainly the bulk of their followers came from the ranks of Protestantism. And lastly, the movements they led claimed the sanction of the Christian gospel. Having made these admissions, it still remains, as in the case of the Klan, to note briefly what the spokesmen for the major denominations had to say.

"Of all the ballyhoo and bunk which have appeared in the last several years," wrote a Disciples leader, "the propaganda of 'The Silver Shirts of America' takes the prize."[23] Warned Charles Clayton Morrison: "Perhaps this ought not to be laughed at. The Ku Klux Klan made a lot of trouble before it strangled itself with its own froth, and these are more troubled times than those in which that madness flourished."[24] The editors of *Zion's Herald* hoped every American would keep his shirt on and not exchange it for one of silver. "Never Swap Shirts too Far from a Laundry," cautioned another editor. "Any American who can't be patriotic until he has paid ten dollars to a gabby racketeer and put on a trick shirt couldn't save a wide place in the road from an invasion of domestic ducks."[25] When one church editor said he expected any day "to meet a super patriot coming down the street attired in the full splendor of a Red, White, and Blue shirt,"[26] another replied: "Why,

23. *Christian-Evangelist*, Dec. 21, 1933, p. 1625.
24. *Christian Century*, Aug. 16, 1933, p. 1029.
25. *Northwestern Christian Advocate*, Nov. 9, 1933, p. 1060.
26. *Christian Leader*, Aug. 4, 1934, p. 964.

bless his heart, down this way we have already seen some men dress themselves up in the Stars and Stripes who, if they had their just desserts, would be dressed in stripes only!"[27]

At least a score of church journals expressed similar sentiments, and a half-dozen church organizations were on record. Further, the Reverend L. M. Birkhead, Unitarian leader of the Friends of Democracy, requested a federal investigation of all shirted groups. And it was Birkhead who aided in the defeat of Winrod when that worthy man ran for the United States Senate in a Republican primary in Kansas.

V

In conclusion, what generalizations can be made concerning the attitudes of the Protestant churches toward certain organizations which under the guise of one hundred per cent Americanism consciously or unconsciously undermined civil liberties in the land they professed to revere? In many of these groups, Protestants comprised both the leadership and the bulk of the membership. For the most part, there the indictment ends. Official resolutions, the church press, and leading ministers manifested a concern in civil liberties that made any endorsement of these societies impossible. Time and again, from pulpit, press, and conference, Protestant leaders warned against the dangers of masked, secret, shirted, pseudo-patriotic groups which equated patriotism with conformity, Americanism with the status quo.

Ralph Lord Roy has shown in his *Apostles of Discord* that the poor in spirit, like the poor in purse, will always be with us. The forties and early fifties saw the birth and alarming growth of demi-Fascist Protestant groups. As in the earlier period, however, these ministries of hate did not go unchallenged by thoughtful Protestants. Indeed, as long as the Protestant churches remain free there always will be dark fringes on the far Right and far Left, for the price of freedom is often high.

27. *Reformed Church Messenger*, Aug. 23, 1934, p. 5.

CHAPTER XI

Parsons and Pedagogues

"This institution will be based upon the illimitable freedom of the human mind. For here we are not afraid to follow truth wherever it may lead, nor to tolerate error as long as reason is left free to combat it."—Thomas Jefferson at the founding of the University of Virginia

I

A COMPARISON of Jefferson's views on academic freedom with the views of many Americans in the twenties and thirties is enough to destroy one's faith in evolution. Certain it is that a wonderous number of attempts were launched to curtail the teaching of an equally remarkable number of subjects during the years 1919-39. In general, teachers were unwise to assume any position critical of the established order or which did not judge, as James Truslow Adams suggested, the history of the United States to be on a par with the history of the Kingdom of Heaven.

II

Although the subjects attacked and the attackers themselves varied, the greatest threat to academic freedom in the twenties came from Protestants, and, more specifically, from Protestant fundamentalists who desired to ban the teaching of the theory of evolution from both private and public schools.

It is not the purpose of this study to trace the fundamentalist-modernist controversy that rocked American Protestantism in the Prosperity Decade, save in so far as it affected freedom in the schools. This internecine struggle wrought incalculable harm to the churches, divided the major denominations, especially the Baptists, Presbyterians, and Disciples, and destroyed lifelong friendships. Above all, many were the good causes set adrift as churchmen faced anew the timeless questions of man's relationship to Nature and Nature's God.

The infallible Bible, the Virgin Birth, the substitutionary atonement, the physical resurrection of Christ, and His second coming in the flesh were cardinal tenets in the fundamentalist creed. How to adapt this creed to the findings of modern science and scholarship had long plagued thinking men. In a very real sense, the fundamentalist-modernist controversy was of long standing and did not spring full-blown into existence in the twenties. A generation earlier most enlightened clergymen had succeeded in reconciling the Age of Rocks with the Rock of Ages. However, hard on the heels of the Treaty of Versailles the fundamentalist cause, disillusioned by the war, sickened by the feckless theology of the modernists, and hungry for a faith strong enough to withstand the strange new currents of thought sweeping the world, made a desperate stand for survival.

And so it was that many Protestants, unable to bridge the gulf between a literal interpretation of an infallible Bible and a narrow and faulty concept of the theory of evolution, declared themselves to be, in the saying of the day, on the side of the angels rather than the apes. Since the story of man's origin as related to Genesis could not be reconciled with the Darwinian hypothesis of the earth's development, the latter must be false. To one fundamentalist author, it was *God or Gorilla*. As a Baltimore minister saw it, evolution taught that Adam and Eve were merely names of a couple of monkeys, and another parson averred that when he desired to visit his relatives, he did not go to the zoo. One minister placed a monkey beside him in the pulpit and asked his congregation if they saw any resemblance. Presumably they did not. The fundamentalist argued, with irrefutable logic, that if the Darwinian hypothesis were correct, and if God created man in His own image, then God must resemble an ape.

The controversy became exceedingly bitter. It was flatly stated that no man believing in evolution could enter the Kingdom of Heaven. One minister suggested that those who contended for monkey-parentage were themselves the best proof of their argument. Another maintained that all evolutionists should be vegetarians to save themselves from the savagery of cannibalism. What they really should eat is "crow," he added. Evolutionists were "spiritual cut-throats" and "be-gowned vendors of filth and lies." When informed that educated people would not agree with him, the great fundamentalist William Jennings Bryan pleasantly replied that only 2 per cent of the population were college graduates, whereas 98 per cent still had souls.

These observations (which could be duplicated a hundred-fold) were all made by Protestants, mostly ministers of the Gospel. And it is on the shoulders of Protestant leaders that much of the responsibility must be placed for this dangerous threat to academic freedom. There was, for example, J. Frank Norris, the two-gun terror of Texas, from whose belt there hung the figurative scalps of a half-dozen college professors whose dismissals he caused for teaching Darwinian theories, just as his pistols might have been notched for the unarmed man he had literally killed. There was, also, John Roach Straton, another Baptist, who divided his time between denouncing Darwinism and describing, with a rather suspicious amount of detail, New York's dens of iniquity—which included, for him, Columbia University, Union Theological Seminary, and Harry Emerson Fosdick's Riverside Church. Straton branded Fosdick a Baptist bootlegger, a Presbyterian outlaw, and the Jesse James of the theological world. He suggested that Dr. Fosdick should have "socony" emblazoned on the face of his church, so oily were his sermons. Gerald Winrod of Kansas, swinging a verbal ax, worked on evolutionists much as Carrie Nation had on saloon keepers a generation earlier, while in Minnesota William Bell Riley sought to save the frozen North from the hell-fire of evolution. E. Y. Clarke, jockeyed out of leadership of the Klan, labored to recoup his fortunes by joining the heresy hunt, and in California "Fighting Bob" Shuler gained a certain fame.

The fundamentalist crusade gained support from men of greater stature. The Presbyterian scholar, J. Gresham Machen, of brilliant mind and unsullied reputation, threw his prestige behind the movement. Dr. E. Y. Mullins, influential Southern Baptist leader, assumed a position on evolution so evasive that he certainly must have aided in the degradation of that great denomination. Capable religious editors such as Curtis Laws and Victor I. Masters whipped their readers into a frenzy of fear. Then there were misguided or intimidated public officials: Governor "Ma" Ferguson of Texas, Governor Austin Peay of Tennessee, and Judge John T. Raulston who presided over the Scopes trial with all the impartiality of a Jeffries.

But, of course, the fundamentalist movement was so fearfully strong only because it struck a responsive chord in the hearts of millions of Protestant Americans: good, honest, sincere folk who thought Protestantism needed the crutch of suppressive legislation. And the greatest of these laymen was William Jennings Bryan.[1] The Great Commoner was more than a symbol of rural, Protestant America; he *was* that America. For thirty years Bryan embodied all that was best and all that was tarnished in the southern and mid-western agrarian states.

Armed with the dangerous weapons of ignorance and sincerity and a sense of mission, the fundamentalists launched a drive to free the schools and colleges of the country from the damnable doctrine of evolution. A host of organizations were formed to carry on the fight taking such names as the World Christian Fundamentals Association, the Bryan Bible League, Winrod's Flying Defenders, the American Association of Conservative Colleges, the Bible League of North America, the Bible Cru-

---

1. The *Christian Century* believed: "Had there been no such person as William J. Bryan in American Church life at that particular moment, fundamentalism as a threatening force of disruption would never have made its appearance." June 24, 1926, p. 799.

saders of America, the Supreme Kingdom, the Defenders of the Christian Faith, the National Federal Evangelical Committee, the School-Bag Gospel League, the Metropolitan Association, the Defenders of Science vs. Speculation of California, the National Reform Association, the Religious Liberty Association, the Baptist Bible Union, the National Association for the Promotion of Holiness, the Victorious Life Testimony, and the Interdenominational Fundamentalists.

Many of these organizations published their own periodicals to disseminate their views, but a portion of the established religious press was already doing yeoman work in the interests of suppressive legislation. It was Curtis Laws, capable editor of the *Watchman-Examiner,* who, at the 1920 Northern Baptist Convention, popularized the term "fundamentalist," and this paper carried literally thousands of articles and editorials attacking Darwinian doctrine. At the time of the Scopes trial in Tennessee[2] Laws claimed the issue of academic freedom was not involved. "The whole issue is this—if the Bible cannot be taught and defended in the schools, shall a chair of science be supported which is free to sneer at the Bible? Tennessee says: 'No,' and Tennessee is wholly right."[3]

Equally vehement in his attacks was Victor I. Masters, editor of the Kentucky Baptist paper, *Western Recorder.* Hounding teachers, agitating for anti-evolution legislation, Masters, too, failed to see any issue of academic freedom involved in the Scopes trial. The *Baptist and Reflector* held that if Tennessee had no right to pass a law preventing the teaching of evolution it had no authority to pass any law regulating its public school system. Still a fourth influential Baptist paper, *Word and Way,* spoke in a similar vein.

Other religious papers aided the cause of repression. A Disciples journal indicated approval of the Tennessee anti-evolution law. A. C. Millar, editor of the *Arkansas Methodist,* covered the Scopes trial impartially. He was accused by militant fundamentalists of "wobbling" in his stand, but their fears were unfounded, for when an anti-evolution measure appeared before the Arkansas people in 1928, Mr. Millar gave the bill his blessing. Similarly, both the *Baptist Courier* and the *Christian Observer* "wobbled" in that they did not clearly speak either for or against anti-evolution legislation. Other examples of "wobbling" might be cited. It was, all in all, a trying time for church press editors. One must sympathize with the editor of the *Presbyterian* when he claimed that the Christian church attracted "the most stalwart intellects of

2. The trial of a young high school biology teacher, John Scopes, for violating a Tennessee law prohibiting the teaching of the theory of evolution has been related many times. Although interesting, important, and amusing, it would serve no useful purpose to once again describe the happenings at Dayton.

3. July 30, 1925, p. 975.

every ape [*sic*]."[4] Presumably the editor had a session with his proof-reader, and, presumably also, a few irate subscribers failed to realize that the substitution of the letter "p" for "g" was entirely inadvertent.

In order that the Christian youth of America could be educated un-corrupted by the findings of modern science, many institutions of learning were established by the fundamentalists: the Bible Institute of Los Angeles, the National Bible Institute (New York), the Toccoa Falls Institute (Georgia), the Evangelical Theological College (Texas), the Gordon School of Theology (Massachusetts), and the Philadelphia School of the Bible.

Established schools, also, were scrutinized for nefarious evolutionists. The Northern Presbyterians, after killing a resolution introduced by Bryan to bar from the use of school funds any institution teaching the evolutionary hypothesis, adopted a substitute statement which provided that presbyteries and synods should not give official approval to schools which taught a "materialistic evolutionary philosophy of life." Southern Baptists went even further. Their Convention adopted a "Statement of Faith" rejecting the evolutionary hypothesis and demanded that this "Statement" be made a test of all officers and teachers in seminaries.

Some of the Southern Baptist state conventions declared in formal pronouncements that the theory of evolution was false and should not be taught in the schools. For instance, the Kentucky Baptists in 1923 called upon the State Board to withhold funds from Baptist schools that did "not come clean on this question" of evolution. There was a little trouble when a professor in Cumberland College "gave an unsatisfactory reply," but on the whole it could be reported "that all our teachers in Kentucky are free from teaching the dogma of evolution, miscalled science."[5]

The following year the Baptist State Convention of Arkansas re-solved that no Baptist board or institution could employ anyone who believed in Darwinism. In 1925, however, with boundless tolerance, the Convention exempted janitors from this ruling. The Clear Creek Mountain Springs Baptist Assembly, with something less than intellectual clarity, petitioned the Kentucky legislature in 1925 to pass an anti-evolution law, and even in the enlightened State of Virginia a Baptist Ministers' Conference protested the teaching of evolution at the University.

Other ministerial associations and church groups acted. The situation became absurd. Although mankind had evolved beyond the burning of heretics at the stake (at least religious if not political heretics), ministers

4. Feb. 3, 1921, p. 5.
5. *Western Recorder*, July 2, 1925, p. 13.

continued to burn books containing the Darwinian hypothesis. The desperateness of the whole business is made clear when one remembers that A. L. Kundred, expert in hybridizing gladioli, was expelled from his church in Goshen, Indiana, because the elders of the church maintained that "if God Almighty had wanted the gladioli hybridized, he would have made them that way."[6]

The most pernicious technique of the fundamentalists was to obtain the cooperation of state legislatures in the passage of laws forbidding the teaching of evolution. The spectacle of clergymen and magistrates working hand-in-glove was no more pleasant in twentieth-century America than it had been in seventeenth-century New England.[7]

New England, however, passed no anti-evolution legislation, although such measures were introduced in the legislatures of Maine and New Hampshire. In Massachusetts the fulminations of two champions of orthodoxy, Jasper Massee and Arcturus Zodiac Conrad, aroused some interest in the environs of "Brimstone Corner," Boston, but the best they could do was to cause the arrest and trial of one Anthony Bimba for "exposing to contempt or ridicule the Holy Word of God" in violation of a statute of 1697. On the whole, however, New Englanders chose not to relive the days of Increase and Cotton Mather.

The middle eastern states of New York, New Jersey, Maryland, and Delaware also escaped anti-evolution legislation. Unfortunately these areas did witness some book-burnings and teacher dismissals, and in one state, Delaware, a Methodist minister caused the introduction in the legislature of a bill prohibiting from public schools the teaching of evolution. This measure, appropriately enough, was referred to the Committee on Fish, Game, and Oysters, and there it stayed.

The fundamentalists were equally unsuccessful in Ohio and Indiana. No anti-evolution bills were introduced, much less passed, in either state legislature, although in 1926 the superintendent of education in Cleveland prohibited the use of certain textbooks. The threat in other parts of the Middle West was more serious. A repressive bill was introduced in the lower house of the Missouri legislature and escaped passage by the narrow vote of 82 to 62. Ridicule played some part in the bill's defeat when one representative moved that the bill be made effective in the year 2000, in order to allow time for mature consideration, and another proposed an amendment which provided that all those convicted of violating the law be confined in the St. Louis zoo for not less than thirty days nor more than forty nights. Remarked the bill's sponsor in answer

6. *Christian Century*, Oct. 8, 1925, p. 1253.

7. The next four pages draw heavily upon Norman F. Furniss, *The Fundamentalist Controversy, 1918-1931* (New Haven, 1954) and other secondary sources.

to one of his critics, "If that bird's brain were to explode they wouldn't blow the hat off his head. May God have mercy on such ignorant men as are opposing our bill."[8]

In Kansas opposition to the Darwinian doctrine led to the burning of the Book of Knowledge and the intimidation of some teachers, but not even the pressure of Gerald Winrod and his "Flying Defenders" could force the introduction of an anti-evolution bill in the legislature. Winrod's confrere, William Bell Riley, enjoyed better luck in Minnesota when such a measure was presented to the legislature; but the opposition of liberals, including such ministers as John H. Dietrich, eventually forced the bill's defeat.

Of the other northern states between the Mississippi River and the Rocky Mountains, only in North Dakota were the fundamentalists strong enough to press the issue, and even here they failed to carry the day, for the legislature easily defeated a proposed bill.

On the West Coast the strength of the fundamentalists centered in southern California. Here "Fighting Bob" Shuler and George L. Thorpe, aided by a squadron of Winrod's "Flying Defenders" and by New York's incomparable Baptist, John Roach Straton, working through such organizations as the Bible Institute of California, Defenders of Science vs. Speculation of California, the American Anti-False Science League, and the Home-Church-State Protective Association, attempted to save California from evolutionary doctrines. Local school boards did issue suppressive rulings and the State Board of Education ordered that evolution be taught merely as a theory, but the legislature voted down an anti-evolution bill, probably because of the opposition of such liberals as the Reverends B. B. Blake and Omar Goslin, and possibly because that area provided daily proof of man's kinship with the anthropoids.[9]

Despite heroic efforts, then, fundamentalists were unsuccessful in much of the country in their attempts to outlaw the teaching of evolution through legislative action. The record in the South, however, makes less pleasant reading. There the forces of conservatism were concentrated and there the pressure was the greatest.

Happily, Virginia kept faith with Jefferson and the only bill proscribing evolution was withdrawn from the legislature without a vote. In neighboring West Virginia fundamentalist agitation was more intense, but all three bills submitted to the legislature went down in defeat. Similarly, South Carolina saw two proscriptive measures introduced but none passed. In Georgia, the name Darwin, like Sherman, became a

8. *New York Sun,* Jan. 27, 1927, clipping in files of American Civil Liberties Union (Vol. 317) in New York Public Library. Hereafter cited as ACLU in NYPL.
9. Further north, in Portland, teachers were forbidden to discuss evolution.

fighting word. Representative Pope, shocked that his daughters should have heard the rotten, damnable stuff taught in the high schools, introduced an anti-evolution bill, but both this measure and another were defeated. The legislature, however, refused an appropriation to the State Library for fear it would circulate books on evolution. In Alabama it was also a case of two bills presented, two defeated. In 1922 in Kentucky a teacher was dismissed for teaching the world was round. Obviously, if Columbus was refused a hearing in the Blue Grass state, the outlook for Darwin was desperate. And there ensued a fierce battle over evolution. Thanks to religious as well as lay liberals, the three proscriptive bills that appeared before the legislature were engaged, held, and defeated, but in the turmoil more than one couragous teacher paid for his convictions with his job.

The Oklahoma legislature deserves the dubious honor of being the first to outlaw the evolutionary hypothesis from its public schools. It did so by a free textbook bill of 1923 which barred all volumes which taught the theory of evolution instead of the Biblical theory of creation. Two later attempts to enact more sweeping and permanent anti-evolution laws were defeated, however. Florida ran Oklahoma a close second for benightedness when its legislature passed a joint resolution finding it "improper and subversive" for any instructor in a public school to teach the Darwinian or any other hypothesis that links man in blood relation to any other form of life. Two attempts to write the resolution into definite law failed of passage before the monkey-fever died in that state.

The fighting was hot in North Carolina. Church groups and ministerial associations, augmented by William Bell Riley and T. T. Martin, did their best. Thanks, however, to individuals like President Harry W. Chase of the University of North Carolina and President William L. Poteat of Wake Forest, the legislature refused to pass any anti-evolution laws.[10]

Texans fear no man, but, oddly, during the twenties they evidently shuddered at the thought of monkeys. At any rate, Governor "Ma" Ferguson, in her capacity as head of the State Textbook Commission, ordered all references to evolution deleted in school books and arranged for the purchase of only those new books that remained silent on the subject. The Texas legislature, however, refused to approve three anti-evolution bills presented to it.

Tennessee's law of 1925 was the first general and explicit prohibition against the teaching of evolution. The majority of the Tennessee people

10. However, certain local school boards forbade the teaching of evolution, and Governor Morrison knew a minor victory when in 1924 he refused to give approval to two textbooks listed by the Board of Education.

desired the law; there were few with the courage to point out its dangers, although that few included leading churchmen. In the following year in Mississippi it became unlawful, by legislative action, for any teacher in any school supported in whole or in part from state funds to teach that mankind ascended or descended from a lower order of animals. In Louisiana, although the legislature voted down an anti-evolution measure, the state superintendent of schools issued an order barring the teaching of evolution in tax-supported schools.

It remained for the state of Arkansas to act. In 1927, largely through the efforts of Dr. Hay Watson Smith, Presbyterian minister of Little Rock, the legislature refused to give approval to an anti-evolution measure. Undaunted, the fundamentalists, using the method of the initiative, secured a petition signed by twenty thousand citizens, and in the November election of 1928 the people of the state approved the referendum by a large majority. Thus the sovereign citizens of Arkansas, by direct vote, made the teaching of a scientific theory a statutory offense.

And so it was that some Protestants sought to use the state to enforce their beliefs. It was not an inspiring chapter in American history. It was, bluntly, the most sinister attack upon academic freedom during the Prosperity Decade.

It should be remembered, however, that not all Protestants joined in demanding suppressive legislation. Shakespeare was correct when he observed that the evil men do lives after them but the good is oft interred with their bones. While historians quite rightly have passed judgment on the fundamentalists, the names of those church leaders and religious press editors who fought anti-evolution laws are less frequently mentioned.

It has been noted that part of the established religious press either endorsed anti-evolution laws or hedged in an unseemly fashion. However, the bulk of the church press followed a wiser course. The *Christian Century,* for instance, threw its great prestige behind the cause of freedom in education in numerous editorials and articles. "Booming Mediaevalism in Tennessee" was its comment on the Scopes trial.[11] Another important independent publication, *Christian Work,* pointed out at the time of the Scopes case that if a state legislature could proscribe what shall be taught in biology, it could determine what should be taught in history or economics. "Could a Southern legislature," wondered the editors, "pass a law that teachers of history should teach nothing in conflict with the doctrine that Abraham Lincoln was killed by overeating?" Further, "If the higher court rules the Tennessee law constitutional, which we do not expect, we shall have to add a new amendment to the Bill of Rights and definitely enumerate freedom of teaching along

11. July 23, 1925, p. 943.

with freedom of speech, press, assembly, and petition as one of the fundamental rights of mankind."[12]

In a similar vein, in an editorial entitled "In Darkest Tennessee," the *Reformed Church Messenger* asked, "If a legislature can make the teaching of evolution a criminal offense, what is to prevent them from putting a ban on Calvinism, or infant baptism, or even on the Ten Commandments?"[13] The *Lutheran* found the Scopes trial preposterous and ludicrous and one which could settle nothing, and the *Congregationalist* made clear its opposition to suppressive legislation. At least three Protestant Episcopal papers vigorously argued against proscribing the teaching of evolution, and with respect to the Dayton trial found in favor of Scopes and against Tennessee. A Unitarian journal took a dim view of this suppressive legislation, the Tennessee law being frightfully immoral and a disgrace. The *Universalist Leader* complained that the Inquisition was coming back in the form of anti-evolution legislation and if the situation grew much worse boatloads of twentieth-century Pilgrims would be fleeing America to Europe in search of religious freedom.

The *New York Christian Advocate* warned its readers to go beyond the ballyhoo at Dayton and realize the central question was one of academic freedom. The *Northwestern Christian Advocate* repeatedly fought anti-evolution legislation. It prayed that the Tennessee law would be declared unconstitutional, and made the penetrating observation that if allowed to stand, there would be nothing to prevent Mormons or Catholics in the states they dominated from passing laws obnoxious to Protestants. A more cautious editorial on the Dayton trial was carried by the *Nashville Christian Advocate,* but the editors quite clearly, if obliquely, evidenced their opposition to suppressive legislation.

In 1925 the *Presbyterian Banner* had some harsh things to say about radical teachers, but on the whole indicated that legislation was not the answer. By 1926 its stand against anti-evolution bills was rather more vigorous, and by 1928 it was branding such legislation a shameful and ridiculous yoke upon the rights and liberties of intelligent people. A Nashville publication, the *Presbyterian Advance,* carried a vigorous condemnation of the Tennessee anti-evolution law as sectarian and unconstitutional. Moreover, warned the editors, Protestants should beware of establishing a precedent that might backfire in Mormon and Catholic controlled states. The *Continent* rejoiced at the failure of Kentucky to pass an anti-evolution measure and the Tennessee law was termed sectarian legislation which would lead to the establishment of a state

12. July 25, 1925, p. 51.
13. May 7, 1927, pp. 3-4.

religion, and once again a Protestant paper pointed out the logical results that might follow in such a state as Utah.

The official organ of the Northern Baptists, the *Baptist,* in the strongest possible terms called upon its readers to stand by historic Baptist principles and oppose anti-evolution laws. "Baptists," said the editors somewhat inaccurately, "will be the last people to invoke the arm of the temporal power to safeguard their spiritual liberties. Baptists will never invoke the temporal law to punish or discipline others or to defend themselves or their religion."[14]

Among Southern Baptist papers, R. H. Pitt, great editor of the influential *Religious Herald,* courageously opposed anti-evolution laws when fundamentalist pressure must have been overwhelming. Largely because of Pitt's influence, Virginia escaped the disgrace of such legislation. One or two other Southern Baptist journals indicated disapproval of suppressive legislation.

All in all, it is fair to say that the great majority of the Northern religious papers and roughly half of the Southern papers opposed anti-evolution legislation.

Church press editors were not alone in opposing the anti-evolution campaign. The modernist camp of American Protestantism included most of the nationally famous clergymen, and to this group goes the real credit for blocking the fundamentalist's drive to power. Harry Emerson Fosdick, acknowledged champion of the liberal faction, tells the story that at the close of his freshman year in college he awoke to the fact that he believed in evolution. After the manner of young collegians, he was greatly impressed with himself and carried the startling news to his father in a letter. With some anxiety he awaited a reply and presently the laconic comment of his father came: "Dear Harry: I believed in evolution before you were born."[15]

And, as a matter of fact, so did many educated ministers. Dr. Lewis Chrisman in his volume *The Message of the Modern Pulpit* quotes many sermons reconciling religion and evolution preached by such important figures as Charles E. Jefferson, Lynn Harold Hough, Ernest Fremont Tittle, Halford E. Luccock, Carl S. Patton, and Harris Franklin Rall. In 1923 a group of religious and lay liberals signed a statement protesting against the anti-evolution crusade. Among the church leaders in this band were Bishops William Lawrence, William Manning, Joseph Johnson, and Francis J. McConnell and President James McClure of McCormick Theological Seminary, President Henry Churchill King of Oberlin Graduate School of Theology, and Henry van Dyke. At the

14. Aug. 8, 1925, p. 821.
15. Harry Emerson Fosdick, *Adventurous Religion* (New York, 1926), p. 107.

time of the Scopes trial an advisory committee was formed to aid the American Civil Liberties Union, and it included such famous churchmen as Fred Eastman, Stanley High, Shailer Mathews, Luccock, Hutchinson, and Bishop McConnell. Indeed, Dean Mathews agreed to testify at the trial if necessary. Further, the Unitarian Laymen's League also extended aid to the young teacher, and its president traveled to Dayton. The list of famous Protestants upholding academic freedom could be extended: Gerald Birney Smith, William H. P. Faunce, John Haynes Holmes, Bishop John G. Murray, Sherwood Eddy, Cornelius Woelfkin, Bishop William Thirkield, Bishop Frederick Reese, Bishop John M. Moore, Edwin M. Poteat, Bishop Warren Candler, Richard Owenby,[16] and, by 1927, E. Y. Mullins, to name only a few.

Supported by these wise leaders, several church groups acted. For instance, in 1925 the National Council of Congregational Churches adopted a resolution opposing restrictive legislation. Two years later the Educational Association of the Methodist Episcopal Church, South, declared its disapproval of any act that would interfere with the proper teaching of scientific subjects. In Kentucky the Episcopal diocese issued a statement condemning suppressive laws, and the Baptist General Association of Virginia termed anti-evolution legislation an unholy alliance of church and state. Additionally, over a dozen leading Tennessee churchmen publicly opposed that state's proscriptive measure.

Comforting as these courageous utterances may be, American Protestantism can take little pride in the whole sorry business of anti-evolution laws. Certainly the fundamentalists were prompted by sincere motives, but just as certainly their attack on academic freedom marked an unhappy chapter in American history.

III

The record of American Protestantism regarding other aspects of academic freedom was, generally, more honorable. Clergymen, perhaps because they shared a somewhat similar position in the community, seemed to feel a spirit of kinship with the teacher and possessed a more sensitive appreciation of teaching trials than the average citizen. Loyalty oaths for teachers, textbook censorship, dismissals of allegedly radical teachers, all were coldly received by a significant and vocal element in the Protestant churches. The question of loyalty oaths may be taken as an illustration.

During the twenties and thirties over a score of states deemed it

16. Owenby, pastor of the First Methodist Church in Columbia, Tennessee, declared that state's legislators were "making monkeys of themselves at the rate of 71 to 5." Kenneth K. Bailey, "The Enactment of Tennessee's Antievolution Law," *The Journal of Southern History*, Vol. XVI (Nov., 1950), 477.

necessary for their teachers to take special oaths of loyalty. Most of these oaths were innocuous and in themselves did not imperil academic freedom. Thoughtful Americans concerned with civil liberties, however, objected to them on valid grounds. In any event, many ministers, heeding the Biblical injunction to bear ye one another's burdens, denounced these affronts to the patriotism of pedagogues.

For instance, in 1936 the executive committee of the Federal Council termed teachers' oaths degrading to the teaching profession and contrary to the free spirit of our educational institutions. In the same year the Northern Baptist Convention adopted a resolution protesting against the "coercion of public servants in matters of Christian conscience through the imposition of teachers' oaths."[17] The Disciples of Christ in International Convention also repudiated "any implication that the loyalty and patriotism of teachers . . . is of such doubtful quality that an oath of allegiance is required."[18] The American Unitarian Association formally stated its opposition to teachers' oaths on the ground that they were unnecessary and a reflection upon an honored profession.

Regional and local church groups also acted. Both the Central New York Methodists in annual conference and the Methodist New York East Conference went on record against the oaths. Earlier some 150 Methodist ministers in New York protested against the campaign of terrorism against teachers, while three hundred of Wesley's followers called for the repeal of the Ives's teachers' oath law. The Methodist preachers of Greater Boston opposed a Massachusetts measure as fascistic. "Here is exposed to open view the beating heart of Hitler and Mussolini," they stated.[19] The Methodist Federation for Social Service could be counted upon, and the National Council of Methodist Youth believed such oaths dangerous. "All denials of the right of free assembly and expression," believed the Presbyterian Synod of New York, "are straws in the wind pointing to the danger of the triumph of the dictator philosophy. In this regard, we would condemn the teachers' oaths being required by this and other states, calling upon our churches to oppose this requirement in the realization that only a freely given loyalty is worth the having."[20] The Brooklyn-Nassau Presbytery also thundered its opposition to oaths.

Congregationalists in Massachusetts, perhaps remembering the colonial history of that section, deprecated the efficacy of oaths. Another Congregational group, the Council for Social Action, maintained the laws were "fascist in purpose, and are aimed at drastic restriction of the

17. *Annual of the Northern Baptist Convention,* 1936, p. 291.
18. *Christian-Evangelist,* Oct. 29, 1936, p. 1414.
19. *Zion's Herald,* April 17, 1935, p. 365.
20. *Social Progress,* Feb., 1937, p. 26.

rights of teachers to freedom of speech."[21]   The New York Baptist Convention opposed loyalty oaths for teachers because they limited free discussion of vital social and economic issues.   The Unitarian Fellowship for Social Justice registered its opposition, and the Unitarian Ministerial Association, meeting in Cincinnati, believed these oaths did nothing to create a deeper loyalty to the Constitution, but a great deal to increase a sense of insecurity and anxiety among teachers.

Noted church leaders acted in an individual capacity.   Episcopal Bishop William Lawrence called for the repeal of a Massachusetts loyalty oath before an audience of thirteen hundred Bostonians, and Episcopal Bishop Henry Knox Sherrill termed the law a dangerous cloud on the horizon.   The Reverend John Melish expressed the hope that were he a teacher, he would have the courage to refuse to sign an oath.   "Oaths of loyalty," observed S. Parkes Cadman, perhaps one of the three or four most influential clergymen of this period, "when attached to teachers, are impertinent interference with academic freedom and a reflection upon the most serviceable and sacrificial body of public servants in the United States."[22]

Church journals also fought for a free schoolroom.   The *Christian Century* termed the Massachuestts teachers' oath a little monster of fascism promoted by psuedo-patriots bent on regimenting the American mind. The *Nashville Christian Advocate* expressed strong opposition to the oath movement.   *Zion's Herald* held the oaths outrageous and highly insulting to the teaching profession, while the *Northwestern Christian Advocate* condemned them in an editorial entitled, "Gagging the Bird of Freedom."   The *Churchman* saw in these oaths a dangerous trend toward fascism and *Living Church* issued a protest.   Both *Advance* and the *Christian-Evangelist* were on record.   "We believe the movement to demand loyalty oaths of teachers," proclaimed the *Presbyterian Tribune,* "is foreign to true American principles and inimical to the very constitution they are designed to protect."[23]

The *Alabama Baptist* equated these oaths with fascism and the *Messenger* protested this degrading of the teaching profession.   The *Christian Leader* objected "to a lot of half-wits who are reactionary to the core going to our legislatures to demand legislation . . . to root out bolshevism in colleges, churches and public schools, which really means root out liberalism of all kinds, and regiment our education and religion."[24]

Teachers' oaths marked only one of the many methods by which

21. *Social Action*, Jan. 10, 1936, p. 23.
22. *New York Christian Advocate*, Nov. 28, 1935, p. 1074.
23. July 25, 1935, p. 4.
24. March 16, 1935, p. 325.

academic freedom was threatened. However, whatever the form of the assault, whether it be textbook censorship, oaths for students, compulsory flag saluting, Hearst's exposures of "radical" teachers, or the dismissal of professors, a minority element in the churches rose to the defense.

Churchmen realized of course that both teachers and students were expected to observe certain bounds. For instance, a group of students at Union Theological Seminary, motivated by what was probably a mixture of honest idealism, adolescent bumptiousness, and Marxian fanaticism, proceeded in a fashion designed to give the authorities of any school, much less a seminary, sleepless nights. They picketed the Waldorf Astoria Hotel on behalf of underpaid hotel employees. They demonstrated before the church of the Reverend Henry Darlington for his defense of lynching. But when a red flag was affixed to the chapel spire on May Day, even such a liberal as President Henry Sloane Coffin felt compelled to firmly state: "They can't make this seminary the guinea pig for some future soviet."[25]

IV

The complete story of the attitudes of American Protestantism toward the question of academic freedom has not been told. The full record has not been presented. Several journals and ministers, with appalling clarity, made evident their disdain for freedom in the schools. Further, one doubts if church supported schools enjoyed greater freedom than secular institutions. In all truth, when one couples orthodoxy in matters religious with conformity in matters secular, perhaps the opposite is true. But enough evidence exists to warrant the tentative conclusion that although the anti-evolution crusade posed a grave threat, there was always a significant element in American Protestantism vigorously devoted to the principle of a free mind in the professor's rostrum as well as in the minister's pulpit.

25. *Christian Century*, June 13, 1934, p. 799.

CHAPTER XII

The Churches and *Causes Célèbres*

⌒⌒⌒⌒⌒⌒⌒⌒⌒⌒⌒⌒

"Verily I say unto you, Inasmuch as ye have done it unto the
least of these my brethern, ye have done it unto me."—Matt. 25:44

⌒⌒⌒⌒⌒⌒⌒⌒⌒⌒⌒⌒

I

CURIOUSLY, in the fate of a "good shoemaker and a poor fish peddler"
the paradoxical nature of the twenties is tragically illustrated. The
ordeal of Nicola Sacco and Bartolomeo Vanzetti laid bare the intolerance
and fear lurking beneath the placid surface of "normalcy," but it also
indicated that the American conscience had not been anesthetized completely by bathtub gin.

Sacco and Vanzetti were foreigners, draft dodgers, philosophical
anarchists and, for most of their lives, obscure men. Arrested in 1920,
they were tried a year later and sentenced to death for the murder of a
paymaster and his guard in South Braintree, Massachusetts. They did
not die unknown and unmarked failures, because men and women
throughout the world labored seven long years to secure their retrial.
Doubtless many of these agitators were dissidents interested less in the
innocence or guilt of the accused than in criticizing America and
American society.

Surely, however, the majority of those who pleaded for a review of the
case did so out of the belief that Sacco and Vanzetti had been convicted
because of their opinions and not their deeds, and that the perversion of
justice was too high a price to pay for the silencing of alien ideas. The
sensitivity of the American conscience kept the anarchists alive for seven
years while the case was probed and re-examined, culminating in a final,
fatal review by a commission appointed by the governor of Massachusetts
consisting of two university presidents and a jurist. On a hushed August
night in 1927 the chair claimed its victims, but not until the episode had
become a *cause célèbre* that rocked American society.

Historians do not know and probably will never know with absolute
certainty if these men were guilty, nor need the conflicting evidence be
reviewed here. Rather, the present task is to determine to what extent, if
any, the heart of American Protestantism was stirred by the fate of these
humble Italians.

Although the literature inspired by the trial is voluminous, running the gamut from poetry, plays, and novels to legal briefs and sociological treatises, the story of the churches' attitude has not yet been told. The few students who have investigated the subject found the churches relatively silent and indifferent, but the evidence advanced to support such a conclusion is fragmentary, and judgment must be suspended pending a thorough study.

Of the major denominations, only the Unitarians acted on the national level. The American Unitarian Association in 1927 memorialized the governor of Massachusetts to study the case thoroughly, so as to leave no doubt that full justice had been accorded the accused.

At the local and regional level, however, at least several church groups took cognizance of the affair. For example, the Greater Boston Federation of Churches sent an observer to the trial, and he believed the men innocent. The Methodists, unable to remain silent since camp meeting days, expressed concern in the case through resolutions passed by the New York East Conference and the New England Annual Conference, both bodies urging Governor Fuller to secure an impartial and adequate review. The Methodist Federation for Social Service also labored on behalf of the prisoners. In addition, the Greater Boston Branch of the Unitarian Ministerial Association and the Chicago Preachers' Meeting passed resolutions requesting that justice be done. The annual convention of the Episcopal diocese of Massachusetts, however, held it inexpedient to take action.

One swallow does not make a summer, and judging from the above evidence alone it would be absurd to suggest that Protestantism indicated any great concern in the fate of Sacco and Vanzetti. Notwithstanding, many clergymen, acting singly and in groups, held indiscretion to be the better part of valor and refused to remain silent in the face of what they considered injustice.

Group action was taken at several theological seminaries. Petitions were sent to Governor Fuller by 135 students and teachers at the Boston University Theological School, by 103 members of the Union Theological Seminary, and by members of the Episcopal Theological School of Cambridge and the Chicago Theological Seminary, calling for a searching review of the case. The wives of twenty-five Unitarian ministers, finding themselves in agreement with their husbands and thus confounding the traditional Unitarian attitude toward miracles, joined in petitioning Governor Fuller. The Federal Council did not intervene in the case, but its general secretary and executive secretary united with representative denominational officials in sending a telegram to Governor

Fuller urging a stay of execution and suggesting a commutation of sentence.

John Haynes Holmes, the chief religious figure in the case from beginning to end, believed the cause of Sacco and Vanzetti was the cause of justice everywhere. He performed yeoman service as a member of the Provisional Committee of the Sacco-Vanzetti National League, opening his church on the evening of the execution to eleven hundred weeping and praying people. Harry F. Ward and the beloved Presbyterian, Edmund B. Chaffee, fought the good fight for the doomed radicals.[1]

Holmes, Ward, and to a lesser extent, Chaffee, all adopted lost causes, much as they would stray dogs, regardless of pedigree. This cannot be said, however, of Willard L. Sperry, dean of the Harvard Divinity School. A man unshaken by the winds of radicalism, Dean Sperry, nevertheless, wrote a public letter in which he called for a review of the case and expressed the belief that Massachusetts institutions would be vindicated only if the radicals were given a fair trial. Similar views were expressed by another seminary official, President Henry Sloane Coffin of Union. Methodist Bishop William F. Anderson and Episcopal Bishop William Lawrence also called for a careful review of the case, although both men were later satisfied with the report of the governor's review commission. However, the Reverend George Gordon of Boston's famous Old South Church deplored Bishop Lawrence's intervention in the case.

These seminary presidents and bishops were not alone in interesting themselves in the fate of Sacco and Vanzetti. It is instructive to peruse the names of some of the other church leaders who signed petitions or sent telegrams calling for a searching review of the case. The writer will risk the charge of pedantry in the interests of persuasion by listing a few of the more famous who so acted: Charles S. Macfarland, Worth M. Tippy, Bishop L. C. Sanford, Harry Emerson Fosdick, Bishop Chauncey C. Brewster, Samuel McCrea Cavert, Sherwood Eddy, Bishop Francis J. McConnell, Bishop William Scarlett, Halford Luccock, Graham Taylor, Bishop Edward T. Helfenstein, John Howland Lathrop, John Howard Melish, Hubert C. Herring, Charles W. Gilkey, Paul Jones. In addition, the evidence indicates that at least a few ministers preached sermons on the affair. It seems, then, that some Protestant churchmen boldly faced the implications of the Sacco-Vanzetti case.

The Massachusetts affair gained considerable attention in the religious press. Naturally the very liberal *World Tomorrow* condemned the in-

1. Ward believed that "there is sufficient evidence to indicate that preachers and religious editors pleaded for humanity and justice in larger proportion than any other vocational groups outside the ranks of labor." Unfortunately, he presented no evidence to support this conclusion. *Christian Century*, Feb. 7, 1929, p. 196. Bulletins published by the various Sacco and Vanzetti defense committees were an important source of this section.

justice of the case in editorials and articles ranging throughout the entire seven years. This business was murder, a striking perversion of law destroying the last shred of faith in the integrity of America's judicial system. While less vehement, the *Christian Century* maintained that it was not Sacco and Vanzetti who were on trial, but American justice, and that the case brought little honor to the State of Massachusetts. Another independent periodical, *Christian Work,* believed the testimony on which the two men were convicted shaky, and that if Sacco and Vanzetti had been native Americans it is almost impossible that they should have been found guilty. Moreover, the editors maintained the trial was conducted in an atmosphere of suspicion and hate and, since there was reasonable doubt as to the men's guilt, a review of the case was imperative.

An organ of the Federal Council, *Information Service,* clearly indicated its sympathy with the accused and its dissatisfaction with the trial. Observed the *Christian Register:* "It would be a tragedy for Massachusetts if judicial prejudice, or political passion, or legal technicalities should withhold from these men any reasonable opportunity of clearing themselves. If they were executed for their opinions it would be worse, if that is possible, than the guilt of murder. At this stage of public opinion in Massachusetts, it is not an exaggeration to say the court of the Commonwealth is on trial."[2]

The *Churchman* felt America could ill afford to take the chance of executing innocent men because their social theories were not in accord with those of the majority, and when the chair had silenced the two radicals the editors questioned: "Is there anyone anywhere so stupid as to believe that 'now the anarchists will behave,' that foreign-born residents will become more law-abiding, and that American justice will be respected?"[3] The *Congregationalist* decried certain aspects of the case which left a stain upon the integrity of Massachusetts courts. Similarly, the editors of *Zion's Herald* were not certain of the men's innocence, but they did make it clear that the trial was not fair and that the guilt of the accused was not established beyond reasonable doubt. A second Methodist publication, the *New York Christian Advocate,* called for a re-examination of the evidence, warning that faith in American justice would be shattered should the defendants be put to death when there remained such a real question as to their guilt. A sister journal, the *Northwestern Christian Advocate,* noted the hysteria surrounding the case and believed that had Sacco and Vanzetti been ordinary citizens in an ordinary time, they almost certainly would have been acquitted. "Surely we are not yet ready," continued the editors, "in this country to

2. Nov. 4, 1926, p. 897.
3. Sept. 3, 1927, p. 7.

charge people with murder and then hang them for their nationality or their opinions."[4]   On the other hand, both the editors and the news analyst of the *Nashville Christian Advocate* felt the trial fair and the decision just.   The view was shared by at least three Presbyterian journals.

While Presbyterian editors evidenced hearts as unsweetened as their oatmeal, other editors did not strain the quality of mercy from their thoughts. The *Christian Leader,* for instance, repeatedly called for a review of the case and held the evidence shaky. Precisely the same attitude was expressed by the *Reformed Church Messenger.* "As good Americans," said the editors after reviewing the unjust aspects of the case, "we must bow to the majesty of the law; but in this case there remains in the minds of thousands *a haunting doubt.*"[5] Similarly, the *Herald of Gospel Liberty* argued that the trial was shamefully bungled. However, the editors of the *Christian-Evangelist,* while urging fairness, were forced to conclude that after so many reviews the fact of guilt was probable.

The *Baptist,* while unprepared to flatly state that the men were innocent, believed that there were grounds for grave doubt, and that prejudice against the accused for their political opinions was clearly evident. Another Northern Baptist paper, *Watchman-Examiner,* on the other hand, praised Governor Fuller for standing firm in the face of radical agitation, maintaining the defendants were only getting what they deserved. In the Southern Baptist press, Sacco and Vanzetti found themselves grouped with evolutionists, low-flying airplanes, high-flying skirts, and the bunny-hug—viz., all part of a damnable brood hatched by modernism. One Southern Baptist writer questioned whether Sacco and Vanzetti were not far more dangerous to society because they were anarchists than because they were murderers, and another maintained the "Reds" had a fair and impartial trial and were beyond question proven guilty.

Pending a closer examination of the subject, it may be concluded that at least a minority element in the churches pleaded for justice. They could hardly have done less, but considering the nature of Protestantism, and of the case itself, the showing was rather fair.

II

A case involving less intense feeling but more extended agitation centered in the trial and imprisonment of Thomas J. Mooney and Warren K. Billings. In 1916, during a San Francisco preparedness parade, a bomb exploded killing a number of people. Two radical labor

4. May 19, 1927, p. 435.   5. Sept. 1, 1927, p. 3.

leaders, Mooney and Billings, were indicted for the crime, convicted, and sent to prison to live out the remainder of their lives, Mooney's sentence being commuted from death to life imprisonment. It was not until 1939, after prolonged and ceaseless agitation, that a governor of California saw fit to pardon the men.

Again, it is not necessary to review the evidence in the case. Suffice it to say, the innocence of the California radicals seemed more certain than that of the Massachusetts anarchists, and many religious voices joined the chorus calling for the prisoners' release.

For instance, the National Church Committee on Mooney and Billings, formed in 1931 and embracing over one hundred leaders of all faiths, endeavored to secure the release of the two men, Protestantism being represented by such important figures as Bishops Benjamin Brewster, Charles K. Gilbert, Frederick Bohn Fisher, William Bell and Howard Chandler Robbins, Harry Emerson Fosdick, Fred B. Smith, Albert W. Palmer, Stanley High, Allan A. Hunter, Sherwood Eddy, John Haynes Holmes, Guy Shipler, C. C. Morrison, Paul Hutchinson, and Robbins W. Barstrow. The chairman and secretary of the committee, Bishop Francis J. McConnell and Hubert C. Herring, issued a letter inviting the churches and synagogues of the country to join in an appeal to the governor of California urging him to pardon the prisoners. The letter read in part: "It is too late for either mercy or justice to Mooney and Billings. You cannot take fourteen of the best years of a man's life and still do justice. It is not too late to retrieve some shattered remnant of self-respect of the American people."[6]

Several years later another organization was formed to work toward the same end, the Interreligious Committee for Justice for Thomas J. Mooney, with headquarters in Los Angeles. The Reverends A. A. Heist and Gross W. Alexander were chairman and secretary, and among the sixty-five clergymen on the committee were Fosdick, Gilkey, Hartman, Herring, Holmes, Hough, McConnell, Morrison, Niebuhr, Page, and Ward. This group published a pamphlet entitled *Our American Dreyfus Case: A Challenge to California Justice,* and mailed it, together with excerpts from documentary evidence, official commission reports, court decisions, letters, and other material, to all the ministers, priests, and rabbis in California, hoping thus to win the last battle in their long campaign for justice.

From time to time other committees were created, and although not confined to clerics, ministers frequently formed a portion of the membership. For example, Jerome Davis, John Nevin Sayre, and Alva W. Taylor belonged to the National Mooney-Billings Committee; Davis and

6. *Christian Century,* Feb. 25, 1931, p. 277.

Holmes to the New York Tom Mooney Committee; and the Reverends R. W. Brooks, Arthur D. Gray, William H. Jernagin, Albert T. Mollegen, and John Rustin to the Washington Tom Mooney Committee.

Judging from the above evidence, at least a few ministers stood up for what they considered a worthy cause. As in the case of Sacco and Vanzetti, however, an examination of the official minutes of the major denominations, in national meeting, disclosed little concern in the fate of California's convicted bombers, only the Congregationalists in 1928 passing a resolution dealing with the case.

It does not follow that a similar silence prevailed at the regional and local level. On the contrary, many resolutions and petitions dealing with Mooney and Billings appeared. For instance, in 1929 the New York East Conference of the Methodist Episcopal Church adopted a report pledging the group to work for the release of the men, victims of injustice. The members of the Methodist Federation for Social Service and of the Religion and Labor Foundation, consistently refusing to sell their souls for a mess of patronage, labored mightily for the men's release.

Other groups acted. The Church Federation of Los Angeles, with one dissenting vote, resolved to petition Governor Young for a full and unconditional pardon for Mooney and Billings on the ground that their continued imprisonment was a travesty on American justice. The California State Federation of Churches, in annual conference in San Francisco, adopted a resolution asking the governor for speedy action in the case. While not demanding the immediate and unconditional pardon of Mooney, the Federation pointed to facts which cast doubt on his guilt, concluding: "This case, we believe, involves the basic principles of constitutional government. If this man be not guilty of the crime for which he is suffering imprisonment, then the tragedy should be brought to a close."[7]

The California Conference of the Methodist Episcopal Church asked for the pardon of the prisoners. In Los Angeles, a city-wide inter-church movement to have the men freed was launched at a public meeting in the First Universalist Church under the leadership of the Reverend Sheldon Shepard. "If Mooney and Billings can be held in prison," warned this minister, "because of their ideas and not because of any crime committed, the rest of us are not safe."[8] In San Jose the Baptists remembered their colonial leader when the Grace Baptist Church petitioned the governor for the release of the prisoners.

Across the continent more than 90 per cent of the congregation of the First Unitarian Church of Rochester, New York, signed a similar petition

7. *Denver News,* June 7, 1929, clipping in files of ACLU (Vol. 364) in NYPL.
8. *San Francisco Call,* Sept. 20, 1929, clipping in files of ACLU (Vol. 364) in NYPL.

at the close of a sermon by the Reverend David Rhys Williams. This is not too surprising, inasmuch as Mr. Williams believed the continued imprisonment of Mooney and Billings "will prove to be not only a blot on the honor of California, but a serious menace to the free institutions of this country, an insidious blow to public confidence in law and order, and a shameful disgrace to Twentieth Century civilization."[9] Presumably a sermon preached by the Reverend Herman J. Hahn on the case was equally persuasive, for his congregation also petitioned the governor of California.

Both Williams and Hahn were plagued by what William James called the "utterly utter" type of mind, but five of America's more stable Protestant liberals—Henry Sloane Coffin, Harry Emerson Fosdick, Hubert C. Herring, Bishop Francis J. McConnell, and Howard C. Robbins —in the same year joined in a letter to the governor asking that he pardon the two men serving life sentences for a crime they did not commit. Even less restraint was evidenced in a report made by a special committee of the Fresno District Council of the Methodist Episcopal Church. The report maintained that the men should have long since been pardoned. "If the three former governors," read the communication, "were not sycophants of such subversive [i.e. vested] interests, then they were amazingly and criminally ignorant, totally unworthy of the high office entrusted to them by the people of the state. We are forced to one conclusion or another."[10] At the Southern California Annual Conference of the Methodist Episcopal Church the trial was branded a miscarriage of justice and a "frame-up."

Additional evidence of clerical interest exists. Bishop L. C. Sanford believed the State of California had committed a gross act of injustice. In like manner, Dr. Oswald W. S. McCall, pastor of First Congregational Church, Berkeley, announced: "I maintain that if the state can put an innocent man in prison and keep him there and justify the doing of the same, and refuse to be sensitive and quick in response when the prisoners are not guilty—then this doctrine and practice are more darkly sinister in their character and more terribly far-reaching in these respects than any doctrine Mooney ever stood for."[11] Hubert C. Herring averred that "Mooney rots in jail because influential people prefer the wrong victim to no victim at all."[12] Robert Whitaker wrote that to be silent in the case would be to show "indifference to lawlessness bearing the badge of respectability."[13] "I rank the Mooney case with the Dreyfus

9. *Rochester Chronicle*, Nov. 25, 1929, clipping in files of ACLU (Vol. 365) in NYPL.
10. *Our American Dreyfus Case* (Los Angeles, 1935), pp. 39-40, a pamphlet.
11. *Christian Century*, Jan. 28, 1931, p. 139.
12. *Zion's Herald*, April 17, 1929, p. 492.
13. *Christian Century*, Dec. 20, 1928, p. 1557.

case," said John Haynes Holmes, "as one of the legal horrors and iniquities of modern times."[14]

A few preachers, then, ranked with Plutarch's Macedonians as a rude and clownish people because they called a spade a spade. It is, however, the religious press that perhaps gives the truest reflection of Protestantism's attitudes. The *World Tomorrow* and the *Christian Century* repeatedly fought for the release of the prisoners. With equal clarity but less passion, the Federal Council's *Information Service* reviewed the case and plainly indicated its sympathies were with the accused. "If the Christian conscience of America," asserted the *Congregationalist*, "can lightly contemplate the continuance in prison for a single day of men thus unjustly convicted, that conscience is Christian in name only and is lacking the humanity of Jesus."[15] The case was described as a "brutal miscarriage of justice"[16] and a "vicious miscarriage of justice"[17] by Episcopal and Universalist periodicals, and "the blackest stigma against court justice in these United States" by a Unitarian paper.[18] The *Christian-Evangelist* expressed the viewpoint of many moderate people in these words: "The State of California has an ignoble record in this whole case. We make no plea for Tom Mooney's high character; we have no information about him. We make no plea for his ideas; they are irrelevant. The question is: Is this a case of a social radical railroaded to prison by perjured testimony because of his ideas? A good deal of testimony would seem to indicate it."[19]

Zion's Herald believed the very foundation of the Republic was imperiled by the situation in California, and the *Northwestern Christian Advocate* came to the defense of the prisoners. Even the *Epworth Herald*, a paper for Methodist young people, called upon its readers to right this iniquity. The *Presbyterian Advance* asserted that bad as bombing was, "it is not any worse or more futile in securing the end desired than railroading an innocent man to a life sentence in prison for the purpose of terrorizing the men associated with him."[20] Editorialized the *Presbyterian Tribune*: "No Governor of California has dared to pardon him because Tom Mooney was an active labor leader. For that he was framed, for that he has spent the years of his manhood in prison, for that he remains in prison. Tom Mooney is the American Dreyfus. He is the symbol to the world that there is class justice in America."[21] On the other hand, the *Presbyterian* held the dynamiters were enemies of

14. *Our American Dreyfus Case*, p. 43.   15. Feb. 13, 1930, p. 203.
16. *Churchman*, Nov. 1, 1938, p. 7.
17. *Christian Leader*, Aug. 8, 1931, p. 996.
18. *Christian Register*, May 7, 1931, p. 372.
19. Jan. 31, 1935, p. 145.   20. July 31, 1919, p. 5.
21. Nov. 15, 1934, p. 5.

mankind and should remain safely behind bars. The only Baptist paper, apparently, to take much interest in the case was the *Baptist,* which believed the ends of both justice and domestic tranquility would be promoted by the release of the men.

These examples do not tell the full story. It is evident that if American Protestantism had cried out in a united voice for the freedom of Mooney and Billings the step would not have been postponed over two decades. But American Protestantism is rarely, if ever, united in its attitudes, and perhaps the best that can ever be hoped for is action from a vocal minority. The evidence suggests that just such a minority did work for the release of the two Californa radicals.

III

A case involving figurative dynamite detonated in 1931 when nine Negro youngsters were accused on flimsy evidence of assaulting two white girls in a box car while the train passed through the sovereign state of Alabama. The following trial became webbed with intrigue and passion as contending individuals and groups entered the arena, championing either the two girls, about whose reputation there was little doubt, or the nine boys. In a very real sense, the case concerned more than the lives of the boys or the vindication of the girls. To many a southerner, the whole principle of white supremacy was at stake. Other individuals, in Dixie as well as the North, held that American justice appeared before the bar in Alabama and left reeling with the conviction of the youths. To the Communists, here was a splendid opportunity to win friends and influence people—at the expense of the boys' lives, if necessary. The Supreme Court in two decisions involving the case remembered that the Constitution said something about personal as well as property rights.

The Protestant churches of America felt certain features of the trial unfair. At any rate, a minority element so expressed itself. The Congregationalists in national meeting in 1934 appealed in confidence to the Christian people of Alabama to see that the Scottsboro boys received a fair and unprejudiced trial. The Northern Presbyterians in General Assembly also expressed concern on three occasions. The Race Relations Department of the Federal Council urged the citizens of Alabama to request the governor to intercede in the case, and in 1933 the executive committee of the Council issued an extremely strong statement on the trial. A year later the National Council of Methodist Youth adopted one of its more conservative resolutions when it urged Alabama to free the boys, victims of injustice. In New York both the Congregational Church Assembly and the Presbytery of that city adopted similar resolutions.

Several other church groups, official and unofficial, holding the right more precious than the peace, entered the judicial arena. The Social Education and Action Department of the Disciples backed the Negro boys, as did the Department of Social Relations of the Congregational Educational Society, the American Unitarian Association, and the Universalist General Convention. After its formation in 1934, the Congregational Council for Social Action worked on behalf of the accused, as did the Methodist Federation for Social Service, the Episcopal Church League for Industrial Democracy, the Unitarian Fellowship for Social Justice, the national board of the Y.M.C.A., and the Fellowship of Reconciliation.

In the mid-thirties a new organization was formed, the Scottsboro Defense Committee, headed by Dr. Allan Knight Chalmers, pastor of the Broadway Tabernacle in New York. Represented on this committee were such notable church figures as Bowie, Cadman, Fosdick, Herring, Holmes, Melish, Morrison, Myers, Searle, and Bishops Gilbert, Scarlett, and Robert L. Paddock. In the opinion of Walter White, noted Negro leader, Dr. Chalmers deserves more credit than any other individual for the eventual freeing of the defendants.

From time to time other church leaders interested themselves in the case. Dr. Stanley Durkee, pastor of historic old Plymouth Church, Brooklyn, held a Scottsboro Defense meeting in his house of worship. Dr. George E. Haynes, of the Federal Council, was represented on the American Scottsboro Defense Committee. In 1933, Ruby Bates, one of the two allegedly outraged girls, called upon Harry Emerson Fosdick. He advised her to tell the truth and nothing but the truth at the second trial, Miss Bates's original testimony apparently having given her conscience some trouble.

The religious press, somewhat ungallantly, preferred to believe the testimony of the boys rather than of the girls. The *Christian Century* devoted over a dozen editorials and articles to the case. The *World Tomorrow,* not unaware of Moscow's desire to capitalize on the case, said the kind of legal lynching taking place in Scottsboro had little to commend it as an alternative to the more honest kind of extra-legal violence. The *Federal Council Bulletin* maintained that the churches of America had a stake in the affair and should work for justice, while that organization's *Information Service* followed the tortuous course of the proceedings in many issues. The *Reformed Church Messenger,* the *Congregationalist,* and the *Christian Register* all considered the trial a miscarriage of justice, the last journal crying shame on a country that bestows citizenship and denies rights. A Disciples paper averred that it ill-behooved America to condemn Hitler so long as this offense to Christian civilization dragged on in Alabama.

Among Episcopal periodicals, both the *Churchman* and the *Living Church* sympathized with the accused. The editors of the *Southern Churchman* exercised considerably more restraint. They believed that the boys were innocent and that the best thought in the South was awake to their plight, but they also criticized Yankee intervention in the case. Presbyterian editors were not silent. A Nashville publication, the *Presbyterian Advance,* branded the case a gross miscarriage of justice. "Cases like this," believed the *Presbyterian Tribune,* "do more to undermine our institutions than the efforts of thousands of 'agitators.' "[22] Even the conservative *Presbyterian Banner* hailed the Supreme Court's decision to grant the boys a new trial.

Precisely the same veiw regarding the Court's decision was expressed by the *New York Christian Advocate,* while the *Northwestern Christian Advocate* hit even harder, expressing regret that the state of Alabama could not be put on trial. "It is one of the grim ironies of our so-called civilization," observed the editors, "that an American state can be so complacent over its social neglect which produces such prostitutes, and over its industrial and educational policy which produces such useless men; and yet can feel perfectly virtuous over protecting the 'honor' of its womanhood as represented in the vagrant girls, and feel wholly righteous in hanging the black boys it never thought of until they were accused."[23] Equally vigorous terms were used by the *Nashville Christian Advocate* in commenting on the case, and this in the face of indignant protests from subscribers. Lastly, it can be noted that both the *Baptist* and the *Alabama Baptist* believed the original trial a farce and applauded the Supreme Court's decision saving the boys.

Two observations seem clear in conclusion. The churches of America stand convicted for permitting a society in which such a ghastly nightmare as the Scottsboro case could become a reality. However, without the intercession of these same churches the Negro boys might have gone to the gallows.

IV

Nine Negro boys were involved in the Scottsboro case and nine white men, members of the militant labor union, the Industrial Workers of the World, were the key figures in the Centralia affair. One of the tragedies of the Red Scare following the First World War occurred in Centralia, Washington, on Armistice Day, 1919. As a result of a clash between parading American Legionnaires and frightened members of the I.W.W.,

22. April 18, 1935, p. 4.
23. Feb. 8, 1934, p. 123.

four veterans lost their lives, one Wobbley was lynched, and eight others were sentenced to long terms in Walla Walla Penitentiary. In the following chapter reference will be made to the attitude of the churches at the time of the incident; here attention will be confined to Protestant interest in the fate of the imprisoned men.

Several religious journals kept the tragedy before their readers. Further, in 1929 the National Council of Congregationalism called upon its Commission on Social Relations to study the case and report its findings. Among the Methodists, the New York East Conference resolved to work for the parole of the prisoners, and the Methodist Federation for Social Service emphatically denounced the prolonged incarceration of the I.W.W.'s. Elements also among the Presbyterians, Episcopalians, and Disciples were concerned that justice be done.

In the Northwest, effective work was performed by several church groups. The Congregational Conference of Washington and the Puget Sound Conference of the Methodist Episcopal Church initiated an inquiry into the truth, while earlier a Seattle Citizens' Committee, with the Reverend James Crowther as chairman, appealed for the parole of the prisoners. The interest aroused by these inquiries and the determination of such ministers as the Reverends Theodore K. Vogler, Hubert Dukes, Fred Shorter, and E. Raymond Atteberry to see justice done, finally led to a more thorough investigation.

In cooperation with a local committee headed by the Rt. Reverend Arthur Huston, Episcopal Bishop of Olympia, and with the support of Dr. Marvin O. Sansbury, president of the Seattle Council of Churches, the Department of Research and Education of the Federal Council of Churches, the National Catholic Welfare Conference, and the Central Conference of American Rabbis jointly conducted an exhaustive inquiry. The findings of this joint investigating committee pleased the extremists in neither camp. The Wobblies were found legally culpable for preparing to defend their hall with gunfire against a probable raid. On the other hand, the Legionnaires halted their parade before the I.W.W. hall and probably started their rush before the first shot was fired. Moreover, hysteria was rife in the community where the trial was held, the prison sentences were unreasonably long, and the Wobblies, after all, had been frequent victims of mob violence in the past and these outrages had gone unpunished. The report concluded: "The six I.W.W.'s in Walla Walla Penitentiary are paying the penalty for their part in a tragedy the guilt for which is by no means theirs alone. They alone were indicted; they alone have been punished."[24] Armed with this report, a group of churchmen, representing a committee of thirty pastors and churchmen in

24. *The Centralia Case* (n.p., 1930), p. 48, a pamphlet.

Puget Sound cities, repeatedly appeared before the Washington parole
board to plead for the release of the prisoners.

The Wobblies were finally pardoned, partially, at least, through the
intercession of the churches. This may be an insignificant example of
social action, but one suspects that at least the freed prisoners thought
otherwise.

V

A final group of men, who, in the belief of many, suffered injustice
because of harsh laws and inflamed public opinion were those political
prisoners charged with violating the wartime legislation of 1917-18.
Whatever their motives may have been for refusing to serve in the armed
forces of the United States or for criticizing America's entrance into the
war, their continued incarceration long after the cessation of hostilities
smacked of vengeance rather than vigilance. It was not until Christmas
Day, 1933, that President Roosevelt granted amnesty and restored
citizenship to the last of the offenders.

During the twenties many churchmen donned hair shirts feeling their
support of the war had been a betrayal of the ideals of Christ, and, of
course, it eased their consciences to labor for the release of men who,
the churchmen now felt, had followed a bold and Christian course during
the conflict. As early as 1919, the executive committee of the General
War-Time Commission of the Churches adopted a report asking that
amnesty be granted to imprisoned conscientious objectors. In that year
the House of Bishops of the Protestant Episcopal Church adopted a
resolution calling for executive clemency, although the House of Deputies
did not concur. The Unitarians rejected a similar resolution in 1922, but
the following year resolved in favor of amnesty.

In 1921 a letter was sent to President Harding urging the release of
the political prisoners, several pastors being among the signers. Within
two years, fifty-four bishops of the Protestant Episcopal Church, led by
Bishop Brent, had arrived at this position, the bishops of Illinois, Kansas,
and California making a special study of the question. At the March
27, 1922, meeting of the Chicago Church Federation a resolution was
unanimously passed urging the prisoners' release, and this statement was
sent to the proper officials. Similar action was taken by the Greater
Boston Federation of Churches. The Federal Council requested amnesty,
as did the Episcopal Church League for Industrial Democracy. Among
the Methodists, the Rock River, Colorado, and Puget Sound annual
conferences and the Methodist Federation for Social Service all called
for the release of the prisoners.

Petitioning parsons were rather familiar figures in the twenties, and not a few of them signed letters urging that mercy be shown the political prisoners. For instance, President Harding was called upon by eighty-one prominent churchmen to respectfully consider the release of all persons in prison for infractions of wartime laws, whose offenses were prompted by no criminal intent, but by conscientious objection to war. Some years later the American Civil Liberties Union urged President Coolidge to restore full rights of citizenship to the political prisoners, and among those who signed the request were a number of famous pastors.

Enough church press editors—at least twenty—expressed similar opinions to warrant the conclusion that in this instance, at least, churchmen preferred not to be their brother's keeper.

VI

It is difficult not to conclude that in these *causes célèbres* the Protestant churches of America played a role somewhat more gallant than is generally believed. Truth to tell, it is really quite amazing to discover how the old clichés about the reactionary nature of organized religion lose their force under close examination of specific events. If this chapter drags with details it is because all honest generalizations concerning American Protestantism must rest upon a modest inquiry into particulars.

CHAPTER XIII

Commissars, Clergymen, and Civil Liberties

"But when men have realized that time has upset many fighting faiths, they may come to believe even more than they believe the very foundations of their own conduct that the ultimate good desired is better reached by free trade in ideas—that the best test of truth is the power of the thought to get itself accepted in the competition of the market, and that truth is the only ground upon which their wishes safely can be carried out."—Justice Oliver Wendell Holmes, Jr.

I

It has been shown that a significant segment of American Protestantism favored wrapping the protective cloak of the Constitution around many diverse dissident groups and individuals, feeling that civil liberties which protected only majority opinion were no civil liberties at all. Lynching was a flagrant denial of both Christianity and democracy. The night riding activities of the Klan and Black Legion were un-American. Legislation banning the teaching of evolution violated historic principles of the separation of church and state. The Scottsboro boys deserved a fair trial. Even a Socialist of the Norman Thomas variety had the right to express his views. The issues here were clear-cut, and most liberty loving individuals, conservatives as well as liberals, could find agreement on them.

Infinitely more complicated was the question of communism. Should those who advocated the overthrow of the Constitution by force be entitled to the protection of that document? Could a man owing allegiance to a foreign power claim the guarantees of an American citizen? Should the churches defend those who accepted an interpretation of society which, if established, would spell death to organized religion? Spies and saboteurs, everyone agreed, deserved summary treatment. But what of the right of American Communists to speak, publish, assemble, run for and hold public office? Did the mere existence of the Communist party present a clear and present danger? Was the Communist conspiracy of such unprecedented evil as to warrant unprecedented precautions? In the opinion of some, the attitude of the churches toward the treatment of Communists provided an acid test of their devotion to civil liberties. To others, the issue of civil liberties was not even involved because Communists had no rights and deserved none. Truly, it was argued that for a nation to protect a group dedicated to that nation's destruction was naïve, foolish, and suicidal.

The whole issue was immensely complicated by the fact that there seemed to be no agreement as to who just exactly the "Reds" were. Card carrying members of the Communist party? Individuals who avowedly sympathized with the aims of the party and worked for its success without actually becoming members? Members of the Socialist party? Those who endorsed the non-violent establishment of a Socialist society? Old time progressives? New Dealers? Pacifists? Internationalists? Labor organizers? Advocates of child labor legislation? Friends of the Negro? Critics of the National Association of Manufacturers or of the American Legion or of the American Medical Association? Supporters of birth control? Anyone to the Left of Roosevelt or, for that matter, Hoover, Harding, or Coolidge? If the term "Red" is loosely and inaccurately used in this chapter, it is because that is exactly how the word was employed in the twenties and thirties.

II

The dawn of 1919 witnessed among Americans an almost pathological desire to return to "normalcy." This yearning for peace, not merely peace in the sense of the absence of war, but peace in the sense of security, was, as Professor Paxson observed, a symptom of nostalgia in the presence of problems whose solutions were as yet unknown. Men cried "peace, peace" when there was no peace, for surely the years 1919 and 1920 were among the most turbulent in American history. If the period following the Armistice may justly be called "normalcy," there could hardly be a stronger indictment of the nation's past. Bloody race riots, brutal lynchings, savage strikes, scandals, corruption, a resurgent Klan, growing anti-Semitism, a Senate divided over the Treaty of Versailles, and a President broken in health, all marred the American scene now that the western front was quiet. And Americans indicated their failure of nerve in still another fashion: they were hag-ridden by the spectre of communism. This was the time of the Great Red Scare.

Assuredly the Communist element was small and wholly without chance for immediate success, but they did represent a disruptive force in American life, they were a *potential* threat, and by their tub-thumping and bombings they as well as enemies magnified the threat they represented.

Besides, the average American was in no mood for any milk-and-water toleration. He had been fed a witches' brew of hate during the war and he rather liked his emotional binge—he could work off his private detestation of his mother-in-law by damning Kaiser Bill. And so it was that with the sudden coming of peace, Americans, rather than sobering up, simply transferred their hate from the "Hun" to the "Red." As President Wilson had predicted, "once lead this people into war and they'll forget there ever was such a thing as tolerance."

What ensued was not pretty. Swift and sudden raids upon private homes and upon labor as well as Communist headquarters; imprisonment incommunicado; brutal interrogations; drumhead trials; deportation. Ragged little men were sentenced to twenty years for distributing ragged little pamplets, and greater men like Gene Debs suffered imprisonment. The New York legisature refused to seat five duly elected Socialist members. Legitimate strikes were broken by damning all labor leaders as Bolsheviks. Mayor Ole Hanson of Seattle made a modest sum touring the country denouncing "Reds," and "Treat 'em Rough" Empey's solution was "S.O.S.—ship or shoot." Attorney General A. Mitchell Palmer put this motto into practice. A labor organizer was hung from a railroad bridge after castration and a man was shot for shouting, "To hell with the United States." Innocent men, women, and horses were blown to bits by bombs tossed by fanatics, for which all radicals were held responsible. All in all, the Black Sox scandal in major league baseball was one of the brighter events of the post-war period.

Unhappily, some churchmen succumbed to the hysteria. A combination of what was probably great patriotism, honest concern for American institutions, and small courage caused a considerable element in American Protestantism to cry "Down with the Reds" and "God Wills It" in one breath. As Billy Sunday, ex-baseball player who entered the Big League Sawdust Circuit, put it, "If I had my way I'd fill the jails so full of them [Reds] that their feet would stick out the windows. . . . Let them rule? We'll swim our horses in blood up to the bridles first."[1] And Dr. E. P. Hill was vigorously cheered by the Northern Presbyterian General Assembly when he flung a red May Day flag upon the floor, stomped it, crying, "That is no flag at all, it is a dirty rag, and men ought to be arrested for carrying it."[2]

Representatives of other denominations felt much the same way. Virtually all the major churches put on drives at the end of the war to fatten their membership lists and coffers, and one of the most effective—or at any rate, widespread—techniques was to present organized religion as the chief bulwark against bolshevism. Full page advertisements ap-

---

1. Robert Keith Murray, "The Great Red Scare of 1919-1920" (Ph.D. dissertation, Ohio State University, 1949), p. 143. This study was published in book form in 1955.
2. *New Era Magazine*, July, 1919, p. 358.

peared in secular and religious journals depicting Christians grappling with bomb-throwing, pistol-girded, bloody-handed, bewhiskered individuals somewhat superfluously labeled "BOLSHEVIKI."

Bishop Richard J. Cooke believed the government was too soft on the "Reds," held that no methods were too severe to destroy enemies of the country, and asked, "Shall the snake warm itself under the wings of the Constitution?"[3] Of course not, mumbled the editors of the *Reformed Church Messenger*. But why all the fuss? Simply deport the "Reds" to a lonely island in the Philippines, permitting none of them to leave. These sentiments were much too mild to suit some Baptists, who forgot, perhaps, that even the Puritans had done no more than banish Roger Williams. The *Western Recorder* supposed "Reds" as justly deserved death for spreading their poison as the convicted murderer. "Better a million perish," cried this paper, "than a nation."[4] Another Baptist spokesman warned America to keep the hinges on her doors well oiled, so as to be able to expeditiously boot out the back door all those entering the front door who proved to be un-American. The Reverend George Albert Simons, Methodist, argued that deportation was the most merciful of all penalties that could be imposed upon Bolsheviks, and the Reverend Herbert Judson White, after a "first-hand" investigation of the deportation proceedings, believed the whole business was absolutely fair. Several leading liberal church journals concurred in the severe treatment of "Reds," while a dozen conservative papers completely lost their balance. Tie a tin can to each one of the agitators and send them back to their rags and beer, demanded one editor. The terrorist should be dealt with as a "mad dog." Get bolshevism or the bolshevists will get you, maintained a contributor. Bishop Manning called upon the government to make public the names of all Americans who were seeking to implant the Soviet form of government in the United States, and a second Protestant Episcopal leader, the Reverend G. A. Carstensen, declared that "Reds" were "creatures to whom the world owed nothing but sufficient voltage to rid the earth of them."[5]

The Centralia clash between returned service men and the I.W.W.'s in Washington found both the *Christian Work* and the *Presbyterian Advance* holding the Wobblies at fault. The *Continent's* account of the affair was headlined, "Reds Murder Former Soldiers," while the *Northwestern Christian Advocate* branded the I.W.W.'s as "Iniquitous Wastrels of the World."

3. *Zion's Herald*, June 18, 1919, p. 778.
4. Sept. 2, 1920, p. 8. Compared to Lenin, said the editors, Benedict Arnold was a patriot, Nero a gentleman, and Judas Iscariat a Christian.
5. *Literary Digest*, Jan. 31, 1920, p. 37.

The bestial series of bombings of 1919 and 1920 outraged the churches, and quite rightly. Some spokesmen, however, attributed the deeds to a well-organized, nation-wide plot and blamed all radicals for what was undoubtedly the work of a minority. Back of the bomb throwers, presumed a Methodist journal, were the learned and educated. "The perfumed anarchy of the cultivated doctrinaires in these days is more dangerous than the putrid anarchy of defiant ignorance. The subtle suggestion of the apologist is often more deadly by far than the blunt and grim declarations of the open advocate."[6] The re-election to Congress of the Socialist Victor Berger of Wisconsin after he had spoken out against the American war effort caused one churchman to term it a direct defiance of the United States, another to call it a vote for Germanism and bolshevism against Americanism and democracy, and still a third to observe that "Milwaukee has been made 'famous' by several disreputable products," but Berger is even worse than beer.[7]

The evidence, then, indicates that much of American Protestantism believed that deportation and imprisonment were the safest methods to deal with alien "Reds" and home-grown radicals. Even men of liberal temper felt that those who sought to destroy the Constitution should not share in its protections, and in their fear they lumped all sizes and shapes of dissenters into the category of the dreaded Bolsheviki. America in 1919 and 1920 resembled a gigantic Salem in which some preachers, as in the days of the witches, led the hunt for the enemies of the Lord. In both seventeenth-century Massachusetts and twentieth-century America sincere men held ruthless action necessary to stamp out a great evil. There was, however, a difference: witches, whatever their abilities, never tossed bombs, and the Foreign Power to whom they owed allegiance resided in a climate somewhat warmer than Moscow.

Not all of American Protestantism, notwithstanding, succumbed to the deportation delirium. Some parsons and some church press editors remained steady while the nation trembled. As has been noted elsewhere, most of the major denominations passed strong resolutions during the period 1919-20 denouncing lynching, race riots, and mob violence in general. These utterances stand as a rebuke to the hysteria raging throughout post-war America. They must be remembered when judging the attitude of the churches in the Red Scare. In addition to these numerous condemnations of mob violence, church groups spoke out even more specifically on the treatment of "Reds."

For instance, in 1919 the National Council of Congregationalism in two resolutions deprecated the spirit of intolerance and injustice in

6. *New York Christian Advocate*, Sept. 23, 1920, p. 1265.
7. *Herald and Presbyter*, Dec. 31, 1919, p. 5.

America and affirmed: "We demand for ourselves freedom of conscience and freedom of worship; even so will we maintain that right for others in the face of private and public intolerance and we would reinstate the right of free speech in American life."[8] A year later the Social Service Committee of the Southern Baptist Convention asserted its devotion to the cause of freedom of conscience and the civil rights of minorities and recorded its firm "conviction that the rights of free speech, public assembly, and all others provided for in the Constitution of the United States should be guaranteed, and that the system of espionage and official autocracy which gained a foothold during the war should be speedily abolished."[9]

A committee of the Northern Baptist Convention deplored the " 'Red' hysteria which indiscriminately classes all foreigners as Bolshevists,"[10] noting that this loose and ill-considered classification resulted only in suspicion and resentment. The Bishops of the Methodist Episcopal Church in 1920, while deploring the anarchist and bomb thrower, also made clear their opposition to the rock-ribbed contender for special privilege who arrayed class against class. The Lusk Committee, created in 1919 by the New York Legislature to investigate the extent to which "Reds" infected American society, was officially reprimanded by the Presbytery of New York, while the Pittsburgh Presbytery passed a resolution in 1920 affirming its belief in free speech and assembly.

Of greater significance is the fact that the Federal Council of Churches used its influence to stem the tide of hysteria. At a special session in the spring of 1919 the Council requested Congress to pass legislation to protect the lives and property of aliens. Several months later the Commission on the Church and Social Service issued a statement demanding that wartime restrictions upon speech, assembly, and press be removed. The commission observed with regret the hysteria fanned by the partisan press, the mobbing of radicals, and the dangerous tendency of state and municipal officials to deny fair hearings to dissenters. In addition to this strongly worded statement, the Federal Council conducted an investigation of the deportation of radicals, concluding in its report that the deportation proceedings were cruel and unjust and that deportees needed not legal punishment, but rather social and educational treatment.

Other church groups acted. The Methodist Federation for Social Service, for instance, devoted several issues of its *Bulletin* to the Red Scare, always upholding the cause of civil liberties. The Unitarian Fellowship for Social Justice protested the harsh treatment of political prisoners,

8. *Minutes of the National Council of Congregational Churches*, 1919, p. 36.
9. *Annual of the Southern Baptist Convention*, 1920, p. 255.
10. *Annual of the Northern Baptist Convention*, 1921, pp. 220-21.

while the Fellowship of Reconciliation condemned the refusal of the New York legislature to seat five duly elected Socialists. The Church Socialist League had something to say on these matters, while another Episcopal group, the newly formed Church League for Industrial Democracy, pledged itself to work for the immediate restoration of civil liberties in America. A second newly formed but larger interdenominational organization, the Interchurch World Movement, in its reports on the steel strike of 1919, pointed out how hysteria over bolshevism made any objective evaluation of the true issue involved in the strike impossible.

Groups of prominent ministers on several occasions raised their voices in joint warning. For instance, in July, 1919, a number of New York church leaders issued a stirring plea for free speech, free discussion, fair trials, due process of law, and open-mindedness. "A common resolve to abide by our time-honored principles of free discussion and the regular processes of constitutional government," believed these ministers, "is the need of the hour. Unhappily, violence, recently employed in the name of patriotism, has been allowed to go unpunished by the authorities, and has even been praised by leaders in government and in the press."[11] Among the signers of this statement were Ralph W. Sockman, William Austin Smith, Howard C. Robbins, William P. Merrill, Harry Emerson Fosdick, Henry Sloane Coffin, Charles R. Brown, Frank Mason North, and George Alexander.

Six months later a dozen noted New York ministers publicly protested the ousting of five duly elected Socialists from the New York legislature as an intolerable infringement on representative government. Later in that same month, January 1920, over a score of religious leaders of national distinction and representing all the largest denominations, including five bishops of the Protestant Episcopal Church, one of the Methodist Episcopal Church, several church press editors, professors in theological schools, famous preachers, and secretaries of mission boards, called together by the Federal Council, issued a statement pleading that civil liberties be upheld: "We have long been saying that constitutional changes can be effected without violence in America," maintained these leaders, "because of our right to free expression of opinion by voice and ballot. We cannot now deny this American substitute for violence without directly encouraging resort to revolution."[12]

Church leaders in New York were also active in their opposition to the Lusk bills introduced at Albany for the purpose of curtailing so-called radical thought. The Reverend F. Ernest Johnson, Federal Council officer, served as secretary of a committee of citizens organized to combat

11. *Christian-Evangelist*, July 17, 1919, p. 723.
12. *Christian Register*, Feb. 5, 1920, p. 131.

the measures. A mass meeting of protest was held on April 22, 1920, in the Broadway Tabernacle, and among those endorsing the assembly were many noted clergymen: Lyman Abbott, S. Parkes Cadman, George A. Coe, Henry Sloane Coffin, Arthur C. McGiffert, Charles S. Macfarland, John Howard Melish, William Pierson Merrill, William Austin Smith, Ralph W. Sockman, Worth M. Tippy, and Charles E. Jefferson.

Here and there individual churchmen preached the need for sanity. A small group of pacifists, most of them also Socialists, had refused to support the "war to end all wars" despite intense pressure. Inasmuch as they were targets of the post-war hysteria, they could hardly join the anti-"Red" crusade. This group included such controversial figures as Bishop Paul Jones, Irwin St. John Tucker, John Nevin Sayre, Norman Thomas, Edmund B. Chaffee, John Haynes Holmes, Sidney Strong, Albert Rhys Williams, A. J. Muste, Harry F. Ward, Robert Whitaker, Floyd Hardin, Harold S. Storey, and a few—about forty—others.

But there were ministers who were not pacifists who did not believe it necessary to nullify the Bill of Rights in order to protect the rest of the Constitution. Joseph Fort Newton, on his return to the United States from a pastorate in London, found America swept by a "wild, shuddering, half-hysterical fear."[13] The courageous and colorful Percy Stickney Grant compared the voyage of the *Buford* with its cargo of deported aliens to that of the *Mayflower,* much to the discomfort of those who equated Plymouth Rock with rock-like conservatism. The rejection of Socialists in the New York legislature caused the Presbyterian preacher, S. Edward Young, to remind his congregation that, "Sink or swim, live or die, we of America have committed ourselves to the proposition that the people rule, and to reject those sent by the people is to reject the people."[14] Episcopal Bishop Arthur C. Hall wrote President Wilson, calling upon him to halt the wild activities of Attorney General Palmer. Bishop Hall pointed out that nothing could be better calculated to produce a hatred of organized government and a determination to overthrow it than the antics of the Justice Department.

Late in 1919 a Denver minister affirmed his faith in the American people, for "if a croaking radical cannot be refuted by the rest of us, then we have a bad case."[15] This sentiment was expressed by a Unitarian pastor in New York, and the influential Presbyterian, the Reverend John McDowell, urged the churches to open their doors to forums at which conflicting ideas could be openly debated. Apparently many so-called 100 per cent Americans, believed Bishop Charles Edward Wood-

13. Joseph Fort Newton, *River of Years* (Philadelphia, 1946), p. 202.
14. *New York Tribune,* Jan. 12, 1920, clipping in files of ACLU (Vol. 153) in NYPL.
15. *Reformed Church Messenger,* Dec. 11, 1919, p. 4.

cock of Kentucky, do not regard civil liberties guaranteed by the Constitution as a part of their Americanism. He continued to make the observation that if our foundations are so unstable that they cannot withstand criticism, then repressive legislation would not preserve them. The famous Baptist, Dr. Cornelius Woelfkin, informed a ministers' conference that deportations would never cure radicalism. Indeed, persecution only strengthened the cause of the wretched malcontents. Methodist Bishop Williams branded the raids of Attorney General Palmer as the foulest page in American history, and Henry Sloane Coffin deprecated the reports of the Lusk Committee. He considered the suggestion that this group investigate the churches impudent presumption.

If Emerson's dictum that a foolish consistency is the hob-goblin of little minds is correct, then church press editors were indeed large-minded individuals. For although many of them fanned the flames of hysteria, these same men and others did much to bring the nation back to sanity. The editors of the *World Tomorrow*, however, cannot be accused of inconsistency. In dozens of powerful editorials they made clear their disgust with the whole sorry business. The *Christian Century* also counseled calmness. Why were Americans so terrified of a few radicals? It appeared as if they were strangely in doubt regarding the fundamental principles of democracy, for certainly there was in operation a dragnet process as full of terror and persecution as autocratic Russia formerly employed. The refusal to seat the Socialists in New York was the last straw. Here was an exhibition of mad political stand-patism at its worst. A third undenominational paper, *Christian Work*, "wobbled" slightly. While not opposing the deportation of aliens who were "really" trying to overturn by violence American institutions, the editors did concede that the "suppression of free speech is as real a danger to our country as the activity of the Reds. We need to say again that we must be careful not to sit on the safety valve."[16] The American people must set their faces like flint that never again shall the country be stained with such "Czarish 'justice.' " And when the Lusk Committee proposed a bill to deny Socialists the suffrage, the editors cried: "Men who propose and advocate laws such as these are in reality traitors to America. The lash of public opinion should be laid across their backs until they understood what political liberty is and what America has stood for."[17]

The record of the Unitarian publication, *Christian Register*, was not innocent, but on many occasions also this paper remained steady in the storm of fear, as did the *Universalist Leader*. The *Reformed Church Messenger* believed the hysteria gripping the country was an "insufferable

16. Jan. 3, 1920, p. 6.
17. April 24, 1920, p. 508.

tyranny," and that it was folly to meet error with a bludgeon and individual lawlessness with official lawlessness. The whole baneful business
was illustrated to the satisfaction of the *Continent* when a Polish Presbyterian in Baltimore was placed under arrest and ordered deported. How
absurd to think that a Presbyterian could be a bolshevist! No man could
possibly entertain both! Here was a perfect example of the perils involved
in these wholesale arrests and deportations. The *Continent's* position
was admirably expressed in these words: "The basic theory of American
democracy calls for free play of diverse opinions in popular discussion,
and the reflective citizen who in such a time as this advises against
corking up unlawfully the ferment of ideas is not a rash adventurer but
a very old fashioned patriot."[18] Civil liberties were also frequently
upheld in the *Presbyterian Advance*. About the only time, however,
that the *United Presbyterian* modified its extreme conservatism was when
it protested against the expulsion of the New York Socialists.

The *Churchman* deplored as "imbecile twaddle" the frightened cries
of some super-patriots. It sharply rebuked the United States Senate for
busily making bolsheviks even after the market was glutted by listing as
"dangerous characters" such individuals as Jane Addams. Early in
1919 this warning was given: "Some . . . men and apparently some . . .
newspapers are not aware that most of the doctrines which are branded
as Bolshevism in America have been openly held and taught by millions
of voters in Germany, France, Italy and England for more than a
generation. Whom shall we permit to define 'agitation'? Not every
congressman eager to write his patriotism into the *Congressional
Record*."[19] Three other Episcopal journals warned against the hysteria.
"It is time we got back to sanity," maintained the *Southern Churchman*,
"and realized that there is a better way of getting rid of false ideas than
by burning down the house of liberty and in the end leaving truth more
shelterless than falsehood."[20]

On a fair number of occasions Disciples, Baptist, Lutheran, Congregational, and especially Methodist journals counseled calmness and questioned the wisdom of repressive action.

All in all, the attitude of American Protestantism during the Great
Red Scare of 1919-20 might be summed up with those words found on an
old English tombstone: "She averaged well for the community."

III

Ultra-conservatism overreached itself with the expulsion of the five
duly elected Socialists from the New York legislature, and by the end of

18. July 3, 1919, pp. 812-13.
19. June 14, 1919, p. 7.
20. Jan. 31, 1920, p. 3.

1920 the Great Red Scare had burned itself out. Most Americans, somewhat ashamed of their emotional binge, turned from hunting Communists to the more prosaic pursuits of earning a living and raising families. Although the back-to-sanity movement gained the support of enlightened Americans, hurling the epithet "Red" at one's enemies was not entirely passé during the twenties—as evolutionists, pacifists, internationalists, union organizers, opponents of the twelve-hour day, and advocates of birth control discovered to their sorrow. But it was not until the Depression Decade that the issue of communism approached the intensity of 1919-20. Wisely or unwisely, during both decades a significant minority of American Protestantism felt that even Communists deserved the protection of the very Constitution they labored to subvert.

To begin with, the threat from domestic Communists seemed very slight to some observers. "The proportion of communists to the population of the United States," believed the *Northwestern Christian Advocate* in 1927, "is about the same as the proportion of bald-headed bachelors to the entire membership of the House of Representatives."[21] A decade later this journal still believed internal communism somewhat less than a menace, the talk of millions of "Reds" being pure moonshine. A sister publication, the *Nashville Christian Advocate,* maintained in 1930 that "Communism in these United States does not seem . . . in any slightest degree a menace. The theory is utterly alien to the genius of our people. In their zeal to suppress every manifestation of it, even in a purely theoretical form, our police authorities seem . . . more likely to do harm than good."[22] In 1930 also *Zion's Herald* had this to say: "What a sad and depressing situation! The monster Communism is gnawing at the very vitals of American institutions while the poor American capitalist goes blithely on his unsuspecting way! Nonsense!"[23] The *Christian Century* in both decades deplored the widespread habit of seeing "Red" which, the editors believed, threatened to drive the last vestige of common sense from the minds of Americans. A Southern Episcopalian held in 1936: "In America it is laughable to think of Communism as a direct threat." The real menace is from those who desire to maintain unaltered the status quo. Let us meet communism not as we would slap mosquitos, but by eliminating the swamps where the pests breed.[24] We should learn to pronounce the word communism without going into apoplexy, cautioned the *Churchman* in 1927, and repeatedly in the thirties this journal said not to worry about a few "Reds" when the real danger was from fascism.

21. July 21, 1927, p. 675.   22. Aug. 8, 1930, p. 1029.
23. July 23, 1930, p. 933.
24. *Southern Churchman,* Nov. 21, 1936, pp. 3, 6.

The editors of the *Messenger* in 1937 were "unable to see how Communism represents any real danger to the American form of government at this time." They believed, however, that there was a true danger from the Right and accused certain reactionary forces, including the Roman Catholic Church, of using agitation against communism as a smoke screen to advance fascism.[25] The *Baptist* held the country was getting hysterical over the "Red" menace and warned its readers not to become "godsakers" running around in circles shouting to one another, "For God's sake do something!"[26] "The truth is," said a Disciples spokesman in 1934, "that there is little danger in this country of a communist dictatorship. But there is some danger of a fascist dictatorship."[27] Even the rather conservative *Christian Herald* carried this signed editorial in 1937:

We frequently receive letters from readers about the supposed growth of Communism in this country, or expressing alarm over the situation. The purpose of this editorial is to reassure our friends concerning that subject. That we can do in all sincerity. *There is no such thing as a Communist menace in the United States.* I state that with all possible emphasis. This country is in no more danger from Communism than from Mohammedanism.[28]

Even assuming the number of Communists in America was alarming, many church spokesmen felt suppression, intimidation, and persecution were not the proper cures. Only a handful of scores of illustrations can be given here. As the editors of the *Congregationalist* reminded, "In his judgment of the Communist the Christian must not forget that he himself is judged by the rigorous standard of the law of Christ."[29] At least three Episcopal journals regretted the "Red"-baiting activities that seemed to be sweeping the country, the *Churchman* thundering that Communists were treated "as no dog ought to be" and that the spectacle was enough "to nauseate the friends of liberty."[30] "We can effectively combat the menace of communism only by abolishing the evils of capitalism," was the succinct observation of the *Christian Leader*.[31] A signed editorial in the *Christian Register* put the matter a little more emotionally: "It will be unfortunate if, in the future, having heaped trouble into the social cauldron for many years and having fanned the flames, we now try to attract attention from the nasty odor by hoisting a red flag, shooting it down, and trampling it under our own muddy feet."[32]

As might be expected, such liberal journals as the *Christian Century*

25. Oct. 21, 1937, pp. 4-5.   26. Jan. 25, 1930, p. 123.
27. *Christian-Evangelist,* June 28, 1934, p. 834.
28. April, 1937, p. 40. Italics original.
29. April 16, 1931, pp. 500-1.   30. March 22, 1930, p. 9.
31. Aug. 1, 1931, p. 964.   32. Oct. 4, 1934, p. 595.

and *Zion's Herald* forcefully upheld the civil liberties of Communists, proceeding on the assumption that a free people will make the correct choice from among the ideas presented for their consideration. Several editions of the *Christian Advocate* shared this assumption. "Let 'em talk" was the advice of a Southern Baptist spokesman concerning Communists. After all, "it is the part of wisdom to permit all kinds and classes of people to be heard and then count on truth when placed against error and falsehood to win the day."[33] And a Southern Methodist deprecated those so devoted to Americanism that they would use Communist tactics to combat the "Reds." Further, he believed, the real danger came from the radical of the Right, who in his flight from Moscow lost his bearings and landed in Rome. As the president of the Federal Council, S. Parkes Cadman, noted in an address in which he lamented the hysteria that seemed to be sweeping the country, "Since when has it been required of free men that they should not dare to criticize their own political theories and forms of government? How comes it that the present exigencies of our boasted independence and freedom are so critical that they must not be breathed upon by the faintest breath of suggested betterment?"[34]

Several events occurred which forced the specific application of these general sentiments concerning Communists and civil liberties. For example, in 1936 Earl Browder, the candidate of the Communist party for the Presidency of the United States, was arrested and imprisoned in Terre Haute, Indiana, on the technical charge of vagrancy, and thus prevented from delivering an address. The *Christian Leader* questioned whether city officials with the "mentality of children" and "backward places like Terre Haute" could take away the fundamental liberties of the people.[35] A dozen other church papers questioned the wisdom of Terre Haute's action, and the New York Presbyterian Synod looked upon the arrest as shocking. "Free speech means nothing at all," said the New Yorkers, "unless it means freedom for those with whom the majority differs."[36]

When the city of Buffalo denied the Communist party the use of any of its large halls in which to hold a rally for Browder, seven Buffalo Protestant ministers and one Rabbi issued a statement reminding the townsmen that suppression did not suppress and that truth could only emerge through free discussion. In fact, the Reverend Herman J. Hahn offered the auditorium of his house of worship to the Communists. A decade earlier, Charles N. Lathrop, noted Episcopalian, deplored the conviction of a Communist in California. "If there had been a criminal

33. *Alabama Baptist*, Sept. 5, 1935, p. 3.
34. *New York Times*, Nov. 28, 1927, clipping in files of ACLU (Vol. 322) in NYPL.
35. Oct. 10, 1936, p. 1284.
36. *Social Progress*, Feb., 1937, p. 26.

syndicalism law in the dawn of the Christian era," he said, "St. Peter and St. Paul would have been the first men incarcerated, for they were the first communists."[37]   The dismissal in 1935 of Granville Hicks, then an avowed Communist party member, from Rensselaer Polytechnic Institute, brought editorial protests from the *Christian Register* and the *Christian Leader,* and both journals carried an article by Hicks in which he argued that although Communists would not tolerate academic freedom under the dictatorship of the proletariat, all good non-Communist liberals should none the less come to the defense of Communists when they are discriminated against.

The arrest and threatened deportation of John Strachey, well known British author and lecturer, for his communistic leanings was termed cruel and stupid by several church journals, and when three years later this peripatetic "pink" was denied admittance into the United States a few protests were heard.   Moreover, among the fifty-eight liberals who petitioned President Roosevelt to intervene personally to admit Strachey were such church notables as Bishop Edgar Blake, Endicott Peabody, Samuel Guy Inman, Ward, and Morrison.

In 1936 the members of the Brooklyn Nassau Presbytery adopted a resolution condemning Borough President George U. Harvey of Queens for barring Communists from meeting in public buildings.   The Reverend Warren E. Darnell said that it seemed totally out of order for a local official to assume the role of a Fascist dictator.   In 1935 the National Council of Methodist Youth criticized laws banning the Communist party from appearing on the ballot, and in the same year a large group of Methodist ministers resolved against any law which would exclude from the mails Communist literature.   In 1939, Fosdick, McConnell, Ashworth, Henry Leiper Smith, and John Howland Lathrop publicly protested a proposed New York bill barring Communists from public office.

In 1938 Simon W. Gerson was appointed confidential assistant to Stanley M. Issacs, borough president of Manhattan.   Gerson's known membership in the Communist party aroused a storm of public protest, and he was finally compelled to resign in 1940.   However, a group of fifteen New York liberals sent a letter to Issacs condemning the so-called witch hunt and requesting him to stand by his appointment.   After all, read the letter, "The outcry against Simon W. Gerson because of his membership in the Communist party seems to us wholly unrelated to any consideration of fitness for public office."[38]   Among the signers of

37. *San Francisco Examiner,* Aug. 29, 1922, clipping in files of ACLU (Vol. 235) in NYPL.
38. ACLU *Bulletin,* March 3, 1938.

this rather naïve statement was American Protestantism's supreme realist, Reinhold Niebuhr. Other clerical signers included the Reverend John Lathrop and the Reverend John Howard Melish. Another letter also calling for the retention of Gerson was signed by such religious leaders as Ward, Bradford Young, William B. Spofford, Lawson Willard, and Miss Helen Murray.

There were other instances of clergymen upholding the civil liberties of Communists. For example, the Reverends Orlo J. Price, David Rhys Williams, and Justin Wroe Nixon made public protest when three young Communist ladies were arrested for distributing anti-war literature in front of a Rochester armory. Helen G. Murray begged that a young Italian Communist not be deported to certain death in Italy. The Reverend Albert Buckner Coe, pastor of the Oak Park, Illinois, Congregational Church, permitted the Communist candidate for governor of Illinois to speak in a small room in his church before a senior young people's group. It was in the course of a series in which each of the political parties were represented. The local post of the American Legion and sundry other individuals were on hand to protect the young people from the "Red's" rhetoric, but, nevertheless, Dr. Coe was severely criticized. His board of trustees, however, stood by him, and the Evanston, Illinois, ministerial association expressed their appreciation for his courage in upholding the right of free speech.

When certain New York Communist publishing houses were raided in 1936 and called to show cause for their continuing publication, several church leaders including Bishop McConnell, John Haynes Holmes, and John Howard Melish protested. The arrest and trial of a group of Communists in California for violating a criminal syndicalism law brought objections from the Congregational Council for Social Action, Bishop Lawrence Wilson, and Robert Whitaker. A goodly number of church leaders found certain so-called exposés of "Reds" both amusing and slightly annoying. For instance, Mrs. Elizabeth Dilling's *The Red Network* came in for considerable criticism. Mrs. Dilling was a private citizen, but governmental action was taken when a congressional committee headed by Representative Hamilton Fish was organized in the early thirties to ferret out Communists. Several church journals found this committee "A Grand Futility" and a number of famous bishops and ministers signed a petition in 1931 terming the Fish Committee futile, expensive, and unwarranted.

A later House Committee on Un-American Activities headed originally by Representative Martin Dies was severely criticized by church leaders and journals. The *Nashville Christian Advocate* advised the committee to concentrate on Fascist activities in the United States inasmuch as

"Fascism is ten times as dangerous to our government as Communism."[39] Perhaps it was, however, *Zion's Herald* that struck the most telling blow. This journal predicted that after the Dies Committee had finished its work the next dictionary would read like this:

Communist (*Kom-u-nist*), n.
1. One who believes in our constitutional liberties of free speech, free press, and free assembly.
2. One who is devoted to world peace.
3. A child actress in motion-pictures.
4. A youth of brains and ideals.
5. A friend of labor.
6. A member of the Jewish race.
7. A liberal Roman Catholic or Episcopalian, Presbyterian or Methodist.
8. An open-minded college or university professor.
9. One who favors the Loyalist cause in Spain.
10. One who opposes Hitler or Mussolini.
11. Anyone who wears a red necktie or who possesses a piercing black eye.
12. Anyone we dislike.[40]

In 1935 the Northern Baptist Convention vowed its intention not to win over Communists by suppressing them unconstitutionally. In 1935 also 250 clergymen petitioned the Senate to refrain from passing restrictive legislation designed to curb radical ideas. In 1936 the Federal Council deplored "a sinister intolerance which brands as communistic even those constructive proposals for orderly social progress which are the best defense against communism."[41] And in 1935 Northern Presbyterians in General Assembly questioned the tendency to label all liberals as "Reds."

It would be inaccurate to suggest that all of American Protestantism labored to uphold the civil liberties of Communists. It has been noted that most of the Fascist organizations in the country which fattened on anti-"Red" tub-thumping were Protestant led and Protestant dominated. Further, several religious journals evidenced no great concern for protecting "Reds." Still and all, a significant minority in American Protestantism, although perhaps detesting Marxian principles, believed that in the United States even Communists were not beyond the pale of due process of law. A decade or so later it appeared evident that Communist infiltration into positions of responsibility and influence was not negligible. A decade or so later the fearsome character of communism was more

39. Feb. 17, 1939, pp. 194-96.   40. Aug. 31, 1938, p. 1091.
41. *Federal Council Bulletin*, Sept., 1936, p. 15.

fully revealed. Certainly some Protestants underestimated the extent and misunderstood the character of the Communist conspiracy. And yet, Bible reading Protestants remembered that he who lives by the sword dies by the sword; and some of them realized also that he who lives by the suppression of the liberties of one minority group will live to see the death of these same liberties for all groups. To treat Communists in accordance with American rather than Russian principles involves dangers, but perhaps it is one of those calculated risks that a democracy always must take.

IV

Thus far an attempt has been made to sketch the attitudes of American Protestantism toward civil liberties as they applied to certain rather specific issues. This is not the entire story. Every major denomination in national convention adopted resolutions dealing with civil liberties. Local church groups and ministerial associations from Maine to California did so also. In many instances, the wording of these statements was very strong and very eloquent. Much of the church press evidenced a concern in these matters that would have done justice to the most liberal secular journals. A host of individual churchmen not already mentioned preached sermons, signed petitions, formed committees, held meetings, and sent telegrams designed to preserve civil liberties in America. But perhaps it is unnecessary to cite additional chapter and verse. Enough evidence has been advanced, possibly, to warrant certain tentative conclusions.

The record of American Protestantism on civil liberties is not perfect. Certain churches on certain matters made an extremely poor showing. Taking this into consideration, balancing exception against exception, and remembering that some of the evidence presented represented only a small but vocal minority, it is still perhaps fair to conclude that the record of the Protestant churches on civil liberties is a proud one. In the final analysis, Protestants believed they had the most to gain by preserving a society in which a man could believe as his conscience dictated. That, after all, is the glory of their faith.

Part III

The Churches and Labor

CHAPTER XIV

The Churches and Labor: Setting the Stage

"Long-haired preachers come out every night,
Try to tell you what's wrong and what's right;
But when asked 'bout something to eat
They will answer with voices so sweet:

Chorus
You will eat, bye and bye,
In that glorious land above the sky;
Work and pray, live on hay,
You'll get pie in the sky when you die."—Joe Hill

I

THE CONDITION and status of the laborer was one of the gravest problems facing American society in the twenties and thirties, and a study of the social attitudes of recent American Protestantism must inquire to what extent, if any, the churches were occupied with circumstances in mine and mill, field and factory. It has been argued that worn bodies were no concern of the churches so long as souls were lovingly nurtured. Whatever the validity of this viewpoint, the following pages rest on the proposition that, although man may not live by bread alone, it is important that he does earn that bread. After all, it was Jesus not Marx who observed that where a man's purse is there will be his heart also. This is apt to be particularly true if the purse is either too fat or too thin, for grinding poverty like excessive wealth, and St. Francis to the contrary, provides barren soil for a flourishing spiritual life.

Before embarking on this discussion, however, a reminder or two is in order. First, any evaluation of labor in the twenties and thirties must be disassociated from the climate of opinion of the early fifties, for to properly appreciate the significance of these chapters the events must be placed in their context. During the Prosperity as well as the Depression Decade, the average laborer knew neither the high wages nor the security, the shorter hours nor the safer conditions, that were his in a later period.

Secondly, in the fifties men of good will were shocked to learn the extent to which Communists had fomented industrial unrest, deliberately provoked violence in strikes, infiltrated labor unions, and played up examples of social injustice in order to create class hatred. William Z.

Foster, Benjamin Gitlow, Fred Beal, Louis Budenz, to name only a few Communists associated with labor, have told all, and what they told, substantiated by non-Communist studies, was not pretty. Important strikes *were* Communist led. Some unions *were* to a dangerous extent infiltrated by Communists. Unrest, dissatisfaction, and violence *were* intensified by Communist agitation. These are undeniable facts. But detestation of communism must not blind one to other facts of history. It must not be assumed that brutally long hours of work, bare subsistance wages, dangerous factory and mine conditions, arbitrary dismissals, labor spies, company police, black lists, child labor, and virtual peonage existed only in Communist propaganda. It must not be assumed that American workers would have been blissfully content save for the agitation of Russian-paid agents. In short, most of the grievances of labor were real, and most of the workers' unrest would have existed had Karl Marx never lived.

The point is that one must escape the danger of present-mindedness, divorce himself from the temper of the fifties, and return to conditions as they were known by miner, steelworker, and share-cropper in the years 1919-39. Only by so doing can one properly evaluate the concern or indifference of the churches to these questions.

II

Warren S. Stone, president of the Brotherhood of Locomotive Engineers, remarked in 1924: "You want to know what labor thinks of the church. I tell you, very frankly, that labor does not think very much of the church, because the church does not think very much of labor."[1] There are two theses in this statement, both firmly grounded in scholarly as well as popular opinion.

The belief that "labor does not think very much of the church" is supported by a mass of evidence. The ancient saw about religion being the opiate of the masses has had many variants. Almost poetic in its simplicity is the comment of an old worker, "The preacher points your eyes to heaven, and then the boss picks your pocket." Similar if more long-winded statements have been made by scores of labor leaders, and sensitive clergymen were not unaware of the contempt and indifference of labor. It need hardly be added that many sociologists and historians have observed also the alienation of labor by the churches.

The second thesis in Mr. Stone's statement, that "the church does not think very much of labor," is also buttressed by abundant evidence. Historically, the Protestant churches have been middle class institutions. Students of Western civilization, notably Max Weber, Ernst Troeltsch,

1. *Zion's Herald*, April 16, 1924, p. 493.

and, more moderately, R. H. Tawney, have commented on the close relationship between Protestantism and capitalism. Perhaps even in the Age of Faith, as H. M. Robertson suggests, the keeping of good books was even more important than the keeping of the Good Book. Perhaps world commerce had destroyed Aquinas' theory of a "just price" even before the Reformation. Perhaps, as Professor Walter Webb argued, the rise of capitalism was the inevitable result of the opening of "The Great Frontier," and would have come about had Luther and Calvin never lived. Indeed, perhaps these two Reformation leaders would have deplored modern capitalism just as surely as the medieval theologians. Nevertheless, it remains significant that Protestantism and capitalism emerged as forces about the same time in history. Protestantism's individualism admirably complemented capitalism's doctrine of laissez-faire, while Puritan virtues—industry, thrift, sobriety, diligence, and honesty— were the very traits embraced by the growing commercial classes. Protestantism did tend to take man out of the hereafter and place him squarely in the here; it did emphasize the dignity of labor—of a man's "calling." No navel gazing for Protestants—nor for businessmen.

Moreover, Protestant religious dissenters and the emerging commercial classes were mated by chance. Both desired the overthrow of the established monarchies, the former wanting religious freedom (at least for themselves), the latter freedom from monarchic restrictions on their business. Thus in England, Scotland, and the Lowlands, conscience and commerce allied in common opposition to the ruling authority.

This alliance between Protestantism and capitalism established in Europe was even more firmly cemented in America. The early settlers were overwhelmingly Protestant in background, coming mostly from northern and western Europe. Although in 1790 only about one in ten Americans was a church member, by 1900 the Protestant churches, through a magnificent evangelizing effort, had brought about every fourth American into their folds. By this time the descendants of the early settlers had emerged as the owner-managerial middle class. And by this time the laboring classes were composed mostly of the newer immigrants from southern and eastern Europe who were either Catholics or churchless or —in fewer instances—Jews. This being the case, it was only natural for the Protestant churches to assume the attitudes of the great mass of their membership, and hence these attitudes were those of the middle class.

One of these middle class traits was indifference to the lower, non-farming, working classes, save to remind the worker to accept his lot with patience and fortitude for all life was part of God's larger plan, and that, in any event, the sweet rewards of heaven would compensate for the hardships of this world. And if there were hardships for the masses, they were probably the result of booze, improvidence, laziness, or, ultimately, original sin.

The churches also rationalized economic inequality with the doctrine of stewardship. According to this notion, all wealth belonged to God and the rich were merely stewards of the Almighty who acquired wealth and dispensed of it (although a little might stick to their fingers) according to the Lord's plan. This concept, no doubt, proved comforting to the rich, and many of them honestly attempted to distribute God's millions for charitable purposes. But as Carnegie and the Rockefellers discovered, after a man reaches a certain degree of affluence, it is devilishly difficult to give away the money as fast as it comes in. It is suggestive, moreover, that there are few records of the wealthy viewing the Sixteenth Amendment as an instrument for the implementation of this doctrine of stewardship.

Not only did the churches defend the gulf between the rich and the ragged, they unconsciously perpetuated this inequality by denouncing as unchristian all talk of class hatred. After all, Christ preached a gospel of love, and the workingman who expressed unlovely sentiments toward his employer was being un-Christlike. Above all, strikes and industrial violence were to be abhorred, for the only true solution to disputes was Christian charity and sweet reasonableness.

So goes the explanation for the churches' indifference to labor. The validity of this thesis has been upheld by distinguished sociologists, historians, labor leaders, and journalists, but, oddly enough, the two most detailed and penetrating studies of the churches' indifference to labor in the United States in recent years were written by ministers. Rather than quote from a number of studies on the attitudes of the churches toward labor, it may be sufficient to simply review the findings of these two ministers, Liston Pope and Arthur Edwin Shelton, who have presented the strongest cases against the churches.

Dr. Liston Pope, later dean of the Yale Divinity School, published in 1942 a study of the cotton towns of North Carolina, and especially those of Gaston County, entitled *Millhands and Preachers*.[2] Although primarily concerned with the great textile strike of 1929, in which the local churches actively sided with management, Dr. Pope's picture of conditions leading to the strike is intensely significant because it is a classic and fully documented example of the churches' indifference to labor.

"So far as evidence survives," the author concluded, "virtually no preachers in the county have made clear and definitive statements concerning child labor, the mill village system, wages and hours, or other social questions which have been agitated from time to time in wider

2. The quotations that follow are all taken from this volume.

circles." Moreover, the clergy were openly hostile to labor unions, so much so that "union organizers have consistently regarded ministers in Gaston County and in the South generally as among their worst enemies." It was not that the clergy lacked social consciousness, for they did not hesitate to denounce syphilis, pool halls, low flying airplanes, slot machines, and the "marriage of Clark Gable and Carrolle [*sic*] Lombard," but that they conceived of sin as entirely personal and mainly violations of the Ten Commandments. Pubs and brothels were obvious objects of condemnation, but not so child labor, the "stretch-out" system, or night work for women. Publicans and fornicators were sinners in the hands of an angry God, but not so employers who sweated their labor in the mills.

The Marxist would explain the ministers' complete acceptance of the prevailing economic system by the fact that the mill churches were almost totally dependent for their existence upon the good will of the mill owners. In some cases church buildings were constructed and owned by the mills. In almost every instance the mill owners contributed mightily to the maintenance of the churches and to the payment of the ministers' salaries. And if all the financial support for the churches did not come out of the pockets of the owners, part of the rest resulted from the practice of deducting church contributions from the weekly wages of each worker.

Under these circumstances, it is easy to see why a minister would hesitate before condemning rugged conditions of work. Adam was tempted by a mere apple, albeit the fruit was proffered by a woman, how tempting then for a preacher living in a company owned house, serving a pastorate in a company supported church, officered for the most part with company officials, and being paid by the company, to think kindly of that company. The fate of indiscreet ministers is beautifully illustrated in the statement of a mill executive to a well-known sociologist: "We had a young fellow from an Eastern seminary down here as pastor a few years ago, and the young fool went around saying that we helped pay the preachers' salaries in order to control them. That was a damn lie— and we got rid of him."

As usual, however, this Marxist interpretation is too simple. The fact is, mill ministers did not consider themselves tools of the owners. They did not consciously see in mill subsidies to the churches fetters binding their independence. They were silent in regard to mill conditions because they found in these conditions nothing to denounce. The managers were good, upright, Christian gentlemen who looked after their workers with fatherly care. They built clinics, playgrounds, recreation halls, and community centers for their workers. And if they built churches too, why should the ministers object? All of these uplifting things were for the welfare of the worker. Radicals might call this "paternalism," but was paternalism wrong? Was it not simply a manifestation of the Lord's injunction for the strong to aid the weak, the mighty to care for the humble, the fortunate to succor the unfortunate? If the workers sometimes labored rather long hours, their fathers had probably worked even longer in cotton, corn, or tobacco field. If women and children were sometimes employed, when in God's world had not the weaker and the younger aided in sustaining the family? If the work was hard, monotonous, and a trifle unhealthy, would a man who had hoed all day under a hot Carolina sun find it so? If the company owned houses were a little drab, they were palaces compared to the cabins in the surrounding countryside. All these things being true, why should the minister cry out against the employment of young children, women working all night, the "stretch-out" system, company owned houses and stores, wages of a few dollars a week, and the absence of industrial democracy? Why should they indeed? They did not! "At no important point did they stand in opposition to the prevailing economic arrangements or to drastic methods employed for their preservation," wrote Dr. Pope. "In no significant respect was their role productive of change in economic life. By and large, they contributed unqualified and effective sanction to their economic culture, insofar as their words and deeds make it possible to judge."

A second extremely significant study is by Arthur Edwin Shelton entitled "The Methodist Church and Industrial Workers in the Southern Soft Coal Fields."[3] Shelton's investigations, although relatively unknown, are comparable to those of Pope in the field of textiles.

Shelton found that three-fifths of the Methodist Churches in the Southern soft coal fields were owned outright by the company with the trustees appointed by the superintendent of the mine instead of elected by the Quarterly Conference of the church. Many more of the churches were deeded to "the people of the camp," which simply meant that the company had built the church and owned it indirectly. This method relieved the company of any responsibility for the church unless it went contrary to the policies of the company. Moreover, the coal companies paid directly over one-third of the budget of the average church. This

3. Arthur Edwin Shelton, "The Methodist Church and Industrial Workers in the Southern Soft Coal Fields" (unpublished Th.D. dissertation, Boston University School of Theology, 1950). Shelton's investigations were for the 1940's, but there is no indication that the situation he described was any better in the twenties or thirties. Indeed, Shelton only verified in greater detail the findings of earlier observers. His conclusions deserve special attention because he was himself a minister in the coal fields. The quotations that follow are all taken from this volume.

does not take into account pledges from the individual officials of the company living in the community, but refers to direct payment from the company itself. In addition, about 50 per cent of the average church budget was met by the check-off system. It was supposed to be a voluntary matter with the men to have their church pledge deducted from their pay at the company office, but in fact the deduction was often compulsory and contributions were made even by workers wholly indifferent to the church. The companies often owned the parsonage in which the minister lived, usually free of rent payments, and with all utilities, coal, and wood supplied. In short, the evidence shows conclusively that the churches in the coal fields often could not exist without the financial aid given them by the company. As one minister put it, "The company gives us thirty per cent of the budget, and tells us to carry on and give the people the Gospel so they will not worry the company. I guess the company thinks a Christian is less likely to strike against them."

Shelton also found that not only did the companies support the church with money, but that company officials dominated the church congregations. "It is easy to see," said the author, "that the number of the company officials in the church are out of proportion to the number of industrial workers. In fact, we might say that the average coal field church is a church of management and not of the worker."

The Methodist minister in the Southern coal fields was in an unenviable position. Certainly he was much too vulnerable to effectively criticize unfair conditions. "The very privilege of ministering to his community," Shelton believed, "is often based upon an alliance with the company. He lives in a company owned house, preaches in a company owned church, and for the most part, his very salary is dependent upon the company's approval of his presence in the community. The minister, then, is placed in the social structure of coal mining as a company representative."

It is not surprising that the typical miner was suspicious of the church and believed the minister an agent of the company. One miner put his criticism in this way: "I have to bow and scrape to the company all week, and by God, when I come to Sunday, I'll not have any damn boss telling me how to believe the Bible." Another miner expressed his contempt for ministers by saying: "Most of those fellows have their heads so far up in the clouds they don't know what a miner looks like. Let him come on into the mines and work for a living like I do, then maybe I'll listen to him preach." "I pay for my house in the camps," inquired a third, "why don't the preacher?" A fourth commented: "I ain't got no use for any man who wears a white shirt around a coal camp. He's either a damn politician or a preacher, and one's as bad as the other as far as I am concerned. They don't care what happens to me and my family as long as they get theirs."

These views of the miners were reflected in the attitude of the unions. Less than one per cent of the Methodist ministers in the coal fields were union members in an honorary sense. None were members in good standing. Not a single church was union owned. Unions contributed less than one per cent to the average church budget. Ninety per cent of the unions had an unfavorable attitude toward the church both individually and collectively. In a survey of ministers, not a single one reported a wholly favorable attitude on the part of unions toward the church. One minister remarked, "The union openly defies the church, sneers at its work, and even holds its union meetings at the same time as our worship services." Another minister reported, "The members of the union as a whole seem to feel that the church is opposed to their interests and to their God, Mr. John L. Lewis. There is a definite rift between the members of the union and the supervisory workers."

As with the Pope volume, Shelton's study provides ample evidence that often the churches do not think much of labor. If the matter ended here, it would be simple to draw an obvious and damning conclusion. The complex and contradictory nature of recent American Protestantism, however, becomes clear when one examines the position of the churches regarding the twelve-hour day in the steel industry and child labor.

Although Protestantism has always emphasized the dignity of labor, there could be precious little dignity in the life of a man who toiled twelve hours a day seven days a week, with an eighteen or twenty-four hour shift thrown in for good measure. This was the plight of perhaps one-third to one-half of the nation's steelworkers in 1919. Such a worker had a somewhat outside chance of being a good father, citizen, or, for that matter, church member. The credit for ending the long hours of work in the steel industry belongs largely to the churches of America— Jewish, Catholic, and Protestant.

The greatest industrial upheaval of the unrest-filled year, 1919, occurred in September when the steelworkers of the nation went out on strike. Their grievances were many, but none more legitimate than the long working hours. The masterly propaganda of management turned public opinion, including many church leaders, against the strikers. The real issues in the strike were ignored. It was enough to brand the leaders as "Reds." It was enough to raise the cry of "bolshevism." By January 1920, the workers, sullen, gutted, without hope, were dragging their broken-spirited bodies back to the furnaces. The strike, observed Mary Heaton Vorse, had bled to death like a living thing.

But the strike had not been entirely in vain. It resulted in one of the most significant actions ever taken by American Protestantism in the field of industrial problems. The executive committee of the Interchurch World Movement, a nobly motivated but premature and grandiose cooperative venture of American Protestantism, appointed a special Commission of Inquiry, Bishop Francis J. McConnell chairman, to make a thorough investigation of the strike. The eventual *Report on the Steel Strike of 1919* ran to nearly three hundred pages. Its findings, unlike those of a United States Senate investigating committee, were almost wholly favorable to the strikers. A more detailed discussion of this volume will be undertaken below; suffice it to say here that the abolition of the twelve-hour day and seven-day week was strongly recommended.

It is impossible to overstate the importance of this study. Tens of thousands of words were written in praise or condemnation. The good effect of the report on the steel strike is beyond calculation, believed A. J. Muste, labor leader and prophetic churchman. A member of the National Labor Relations Board held the report changed the opinion of a nation. One noted historian stated it had an extraordinary effect on public opinion, and another maintained it did much to swing public opinion to the support of labor's demand for an eight-hour day in this basic industry. The *New York Call,* a Socialist daily, believed the study marked a new era in the relations between the churches and labor in this country. *Labor* printed excerpts of the report. Senator Walsh wanted it made a public document. The liberal weekly, *Nation,* praised the report, while even the rather conservative *New York Tribune* said Steel either had to refute the charges made in the study or change its policies.

On the other hand, a volume could be written on the unfavorable reaction of the business community. *Iron Age,* a trade journal, charged that the members of the Commission of Inquiry merely sat around while hired radicals did the so-called fact finding. *Manufacturers' Record* went even further and termed the members "ecclesiastical autocrats" and "rank Socialists." The National Association of Manufacturers, the National Civic Federation, the National Founders' Association, local employers' associations, the *Wall Street Journal, Industry,* and sundry other business journals joined in the outcry.

Members of the Interchurch World Movement were subjected to vilification and slander. Detectives shadowed everybody connected with the inquiry. A spy was planted in the office of Dr. Fred B. Fisher, director of the Movement's Industrial Relations Department, to ransack his files. It was charged that Dr. Fisher was pro-German, and that his name was really spelled with a "c." When this failed, Steel accused him of being pro-Russian, of associating with radicals, and of having a strong bent toward mysticism, though what mysticism had to do with bolshevism was never explained.

The leader of the attack upon the report and the men who made it was Judge Elbert H. Gary of the United States Steel Corporation. He printed and distributed a million and a half copies of an address by the Reverend E. Victor Bigelow entitled, *Mistakes of the Interchurch Steel Report.* In this address the Reverend Mr. Bigelow discovered the Commission of Inquiry had made a goodly number of blunders, one of them being its condemnation of the twelve-hour day. "It may be that eight hours is a good standard day for reckoning a unit of toil," pontificated this toiler in the Lord's vineyard, "but this world would have empty larders and raw comforts if men didn't work more than eight hours in twenty-four. Nature is so obdurate and man's needs are so many that it is physically impossible to produce what we need in those hours."[4] Among the other mistakes of the steel report, according to Mr. Bigelow, were its blind espousal of the principle of collective bargaining (after all, a higher principle is that of freedom of contract); the Commission's offer to mediate the strike (sheer effrontery); its criticism of Judge Gary (he treated his workers handsomely); and the report's exoneration of labor unions (labor leaders were bucaneers).

However, it was not until 1923 that Steel made its most ambitious reply. It was in the form of a five hundred-page volume, *Analysis of the Interchurch World Movement Report on the Steel Strike,* written by Mr. Marshall Olds, sumptuously printed, bearing a certification of a firm of public accountants that "all citations are accurate," with a foreword by Professor Jeremiah Jenks, and retailing for $4.00. Such churchmen as Dr. Alva W. Taylor and F. Ernest Johnson found the book teeming with mutilated quotations, garbled statistics, misleading statements, and factual errors. Mr. Olds made no attempt to deny the existence of the twelve-hour day. Rather, he defended it on the grounds that farmers work long hours, steelworkers *like* to work long hours too, they are only foreigners anyhow who would waste their time away from the mills, extra hours mean higher wages, and, in any event, it was a practical impossibility for Steel to institute the eight-hour day. In short, Mr. Olds bore the suffering of the workers with remarkable Christian fortitude and resignation.

Judge Gary's efforts to nullify the effects of the Interchurch report failed. Public opinion was greatly influenced against the long day. But the report did more than that. It was instrumental in reorienting the attitude of the churches toward industrial questions, particularly regarding

4. E. Victor Bigelow, *Mistakes of the Interchurch Steel Report* (n.p., n.d.), p. 20, a pamphlet reprinting an address given before the Boston Ministers' Meeting, Nov. 22, 1920.

the strike as a weapon of labor. During the year 1919 clerical opinion seemed to view the strike as an un-American form of intimidation. After the publication of the Interchurch study, churchmen tended to reserve judgment on the merits of a particular strike, and to increasingly view strikes as a legitimate weapon of labor. At the time of the strike, it will be noted, church opinion took the statements of management at their face value, agreeing that it was unjustified and "Red" inspired. After reading the Interchurch report, many churchmen admitted they had been deceived, and vowed in the future to hear labor's side of the story. Let it again be stated that the *Report on the Steel Strike of 1919* by the Commission of Inquiry of the Interchurch World Movement was of the greatest importance not only in influencing public opinion against the twelve-hour day, but also in bringing the churches and labor closer together.

The *Christian Century,* for example, time and again praised the report and defended the Commission members from much persiflage. As late as 1923 this journal could state that the "outstanding" findings of the report stand unshaken. A second undenominational journal, *Christian Work,* devoted over two full pages to summarizing the report. As the editors reviewed the findings they appeared increasingly horrified, interspersing quotations from the report with remarks about "such cold-blooded planning for evil are [*sic*] fit to be classed with treason." The editors concluded: "Altogether the report throws such a flood of light on human conditions in the steel industry that we wish the Interchurch World Movement or some representative Church organization could study every strike thus thoroughly. The steel strike report alone helps to justify the Interchurch World Movement."[5]

The Methodist press received the report favorably. *Zion's Herald* maintained the Commission was of the highest integrity, it was the duty of the church to investigate, the report should be read by all, and the evidence was unmistakable that conditions in the steel industry were bad. The *New York Christian Advocate* informed the Steel officials to stop blathering about "Reds" and either disprove the statements of the Commission or remedy speedily the conditions laid bare in the report. If there be those who still say the churches are not friendly to the working-man, suggested the *Northwestern Christian Advocate,* it might be well to read this report which is made by some of the most representative church leaders in America. The *Social Service Bulletin* commended the report highly, and Dr. James C. Baker, writing in the *Methodist Review,* was impressed with the report's sincerity, closeness to the facts, and sanity of judgment.

5. Aug. 7, 1920, pp. 164-65.

Much the same position was taken by the *Congregationalist*. Why did not the newspapers give the facts concerning the strike? Why was the public led to believe that it was the work of "Reds?" Why did the legitimate grievances of the workers go unpublicized? "If any considerable proportion of the millions of Christian people of the country," read the editorial, "give heed to the recently issued report . . . there should arise such a loud protest against conditions revealed as would compel this most powerful industry to repent of its ways and do works fit for repentance."[6] The editors of the *Churchman* admitted that "most of us" were pretty sadly misled by the propaganda of the steel industry during the strike, concluding that the "report . . . reveals to the American public the fact that in the smoking regions of Pittsburgh a grave sin is being committed against human beings who are our brothers."[7] The weekly news commentator of the *Southern Churchman* reviewed the findings of the Commission and believed the investigation fair, full, and impartial.

Editorialized the *Presbyterian Advance*: "The fact that a number of men who would be recognized as leaders of various denominations signed such a report should make many of us less ready to accept the views of any one party to a labor controversy and less easily frightened by the cry of Bolshevism."[8] Even more blunt were the comments of a Disciples paper, *Christian-Evangelist*: "Garyism must go. The workers have a right to be heard. The report is an indictment of the old order, which must be cast out before [the] march of industrial democracy."[9] The *Reformed Church Messenger* lauded the investigating group and the *Christian Register* rejoiced that at last the churches were concerning themselves with social as well as personal moralities. The editors of the latter journal admitted that after reading the report they winced somewhat "considering what it means for us to hold a very small part of the United States Steel Corporation stocks."[10] The *Universalist Leader* inquired after reading the report: "In a democracy like ours is there room for an industrial oligarchy that refuses to recognize any right of the public or its employees to the slightest voice in determining its policies or correcting abuses? To that question a democratic Church can make only one answer."[11] The *Baptist* printed a summary of the report, and a writer in the *Lutheran* commended the Commission for its unflinching courage in exposing evil conditions. He warned, however, that while the church might expose, it should not pass judgment on industrial disputes. Lastly, the *Homiletic Review* carried a favorable review of the report.

6. Aug. 12, 1920, p. 206.
7. Aug. 21, 1920, pp. 7-8.
8. Aug. 12, 1920, p. 4.
9. Aug. 5, 1920, p. 762.
10. Aug. 5, 1920, p. 759.
11. Sept. 4, 1920, p. 818.

Of course, the religious press was not unanimous in its praise of the study. Neither the *United Presbyterian* nor the *Arkansas Methodist* nor several Southern Baptist papers mentioned it. Moreover, both the *Presbyterian Banner* and the *Continent,* while not condoning the twelve-hour day, quite definitely stated that it was not the business of the churches to pass judgment on industrial disputes, and that the investigation should not have been made by a religious group. Similarly, while the report was commended by some individual churchmen and church groups, endorsement was by no means unanimous. Still and all, there can be no doubt that the study greatly influenced public opinion against the twelve-hour day and did much to bring a closer understanding between the churches and labor.

Even before the publication of the Interchurch Report, however, a committee appointed by the Commission on the Church and Social Service of the Federal Council, headed by Dr. Edward T. Devine, made a direct appeal to Judge Gary of the United States Steel Corporation to abolish the twelve-hour day. "Whether the long day is desired by the employer in the interests of profits," said Dr. Devine, "or by the worker in the interest of wages, it is equally disastrous to the American community concerned as made up of self-governing citizens."[12]

Agitation for the abolition of the twelve-hour day continued. Churchmen and laymen, as well as President Harding, intensified their opposition to conditions in the steel industry. A ray of hope appeared when the American Iron and Steel Institute appointed a committee to study the feasiblity of instituting the eight-hour shift. The predictions of the realists were fulfilled and the hopes of the optimists shattered when, on May 25, 1923, this commission submitted a negative reply. As a Methodist minister asked, will Steel "get by" with it?

A Jewish rabbi, a Roman Catholic priest, and a Protestant minister sat in conference in the City Club, New York, one night late in May, 1923, wondering the same question. Would Steel "get by" with it? Would the industry once again postpone the abolition of a terrible evil? Rabbi Horace Wolf, chairman of the Social Justice Committee of the Central Conference of American Rabbis, Father R. A. McGowan, of the Social Action Department of the National Catholic Welfare Council, and Dr. F. Ernest Johnson, of the Federal Council of Churches, all agreed that something must be done. They referred the matter to their respective organizations, and something was done, as James Myers demonstrated.

On June 6, 1923, these great Jewish, Catholic, and Protestant organizations released to the press a long statement attacking Steel's specious

12. *Literary Digest,* April 24, 1920, p. 28.

defense of the twelve-hour day. The statement began by observing that public confidence was shattered by Steel's rejection of prompt reform. It went on to demolish point by point the arguments of Steel, and concluded with the stern warning: "The forces of organized religion in America are now warranted in declaring that this morally indefensible régime of the twelve-hour day must come to an end. A further report is due from the Iron and Steel Institute—a report of a very different tenor."[13]

The press heralded the outspoken statement of the churches. "Steel King Rebuked," "Three Religions Thunder Protest," "Churches Attack the Twelve-Hour Day," they declared. Another release from the churches followed, making public a letter from President Welborn of the Colorado Fuel and Iron Company stating the practicality and profitableness of ending the long day. On June 25 the Federal Council issued its third research bulletin which dealt—and dealt critically—with the twelve-hour day. The Council made it clear that it intended to hammer away at the evil until public opinion would force even Judge Gary and the United States Steel Corporation to pause and consider.

In the meantime the church press, like General Grant, was determined to fight it out on this issue if it took all summer—or many summers. Editorials and articles reflected the intensification of the campaign. Between the time of the steel strike and 1923 almost all of the major denominations adopted resolutions calling for better working conditions which sometimes specifically included the end of the long working day. In addition, official and unofficial denominational agencies, including the Federal Council, printed tracts and held industrial seminars looking toward the abolition of the twelve-hour abuse.

Mr. Dooley once observed that apparently the Supreme Court followed the election returns. This being the case, it was not surprising to find Judge Gary, who never quite made the highest bench of the land, succumbing to popular pressure. On July 6, 1923, Steel announced the end of the twelve-hour day. This reform was wrung from management largely because the churches of the land created a demand for change that could not be denied.

Child labor was a second blot on American economic life which challenged the conscience of the churches. It should not be necessary to cite statistics or quote case studies to prove the enormity of the grief involved in child labor; a reading of Dickens more than suffices for that purpose. Dickens, it is true, was describing conditions in England of an earlier century and from this fact Americans can take what comfort they desire. It is little enough. For in American mines and mills, fields and factories,

13. *Federal Council Bulletin*, June-July, 1923, p. 5.

wan, anemic, tottering, leaden-eyed and empty-bellied boys and girls dragged out the months and years of a supposedly carefree childhood.

The Federal Council consistently and continually fought against child labor, believing an amendment to the Constitution permitting the federal government to act the only effective solution. Both the original and the revised Social Creed of the Churches demanded the abolition of child labor. A special meeting of the Council in Cleveland in 1919 repeated this plea, and in that year the Council set aside a Child Labor Sunday, with the suggestion that a 10 per cent profits tax be placed on all goods produced by children. In 1924 the Council called for the ratification of a child labor amendment then before the country, and the Labor Sunday Message of that year urged the churches to throw their support behind the measure. Ten years later the Council repeated its endorsement of such an amendment, and thus confirmed the position taken by the Council in many earlier reports, messages, and leaflets.

Northern Presbyterians were almost as vigorous as the Federal Council in their opposition to child labor. As early as 1919 they had gone on record against the evil, and in 1920 the General Assembly called for the protection of children from exploitation. This sentiment was repeated in 1932 and 1933. The following year the Assembly rejoiced in the fact that child labor had at last been temporarily curbed by the NRA, and urged all child loving citizens to give vigorous support to the pending child labor amendment. In every succeeding year of the Depression Decade the Assembly repeated its demand for the federal government to act because local and state authorities simply had not done the job. In addition, tracts were issued in which Presbyterians were informed that child labor was the least excusable form of social waste, robbing the child of his right to childhood, denying him proper education, destroying the family, and increasing crime.

Considerably less concern in this problem was shown by Southern Presbyterians, although in 1936 a committee did ask that all children be given the opportunity to attain happiness, health, mental growth, and Christian character. The next year this same committee presented to the General Assembly a very forceful picture of the evils of child labor, concluding with an unspoken plea for federal action since it was a matter of record that state legislation, especially in the South, had not solved the problem.

Early in the twentieth century the Methodist Episcopal Church repeatedly spoke on this abuse. At the General Conference of 1920 the Bishops once again called for the end of "murderous" child labor. The next quadrennium recorded its support of a proposed child labor amendment and transmitted its views to the President and Congress. Both of the following General Conferences opposed child labor, not only because of the deleterious effects it had on the youth of the nation, but also because jobs performed by children should be released to adults. Although the Methodist Episcopal Church, South, endorsed both the original and revised Social Creed which condemned child labor, the General Conference of this church indicted the evil infrequently. In 1926 the Bishop's Address called for "proper restrictions" on child labor (whatever this may mean), and in 1934 Southern Methodists stated their opposition to the abuse. In 1939 the Methodists united and this consolidated denomination also called for the abolition of child labor.

Since its inception in 1908 the Northern Baptist Convention has flayed child labor. In both 1920 and 1921 spokesmen for the Northern Baptists spoke out against it, and in 1922 the Convention adopted a resolution calling for the removal by either federal or vigorous state action of this blot on Christian civilization. The following year the Convention again resolved against the evil and in 1924 it forwarded to the Senate an urgent request for the adoption of a child labor amendment. In the years that followed repeated resolutions were passed urging the ratification of a constitutional amendment to the end that Congress might regulate the employment of children. On several occasions in the twenties and early thirties the Southern Baptist Convention flayed child labor and even hinted approval of federal control. However, in 1938 the Convention set the matter straight: a child labor amendment would destroy ultimately all parental authority and make children wards of the government. Federal regulation would lead to what was happening in Russia and was "un-American."

From time to time other denominations expressed themselves on this issue. The Disciples of Christ, for example, took a strong stand, voicing support of a child labor amendment both in the twenties and thirties. Congregationalists and Episcopalians were not unaware of the abuses involved in child labor. Universalists and Unitarians deplored the sweating of children, the latter emphatically supporting a child labor amendment. In 1921 the General Conference of the Evangelical Synod of North America declared against child labor, and in 1925 this denomination's Commission on Christianity and Social Problems endorsed federal action. After this church joined with the Reformed Church in the United States to form the Evangelical and Reformed Church, a Joint Commission on Christian Social Action reported its opposition to the abuse. The Evangelical Church and the United Brethren in Christ spoke out, while the Reformed Church in America and the Y.W.C.A. endorsed federal action.

The religious press was not silent on the issue of child labor. The *Christian Century*, for instance, on literally scores of occasions expressed itself unequivocally. A second undenominational paper, the *Christian Herald*, supported federal legislation. One contributor observed that "A Few Religious Sniffs Won't Wipe Out This Blot," and the editors branded the arguments against the child labor amendment so remarkable that they could hardly be understood by sane persons. At least eight Presbyterian papers opposed child labor and endorsed federal control, although at least two others balked at the prospects of federal regulation. With the exception of the *Arkansas Methodist*, the Methodist press gave its approval to a child labor amendment—or so, at least, the record of six Methodist journals revealed. One Methodist editor, tongue-in-cheek, suggested some "effective" arguments overlooked by opponents of child labor legislation: David slaying Goliath; the infant Hercules strangling serpents; and George Washington chopping down cherry trees!

Baptist editors appeared about evenly divided over the wisdom of a child labor amendment, opposition being concentrated in the South. On the other hand, the *Congregationalist, Reformed Church Messenger, Lutheran, Universalist Leader, Christian-Evangelist, Christian Register, Homiletic Review,* and at least three Episcopal papers all sanctioned the regulation of child labor by the federal government.

Further, a host of denominational boards, ministerial associations, and local church groups, as well as many of the leading churchmen in the country, publicly recorded their endorsement of child labor amendments. However, rather than engage in further tedious listing, an examination might be made of several polls.

In 1935 the *Christian Herald* conducted a poll of Protestants and 3,458 stated approval of a child labor amendment while less than 600 were in opposition. In 1935 also a poll of some five thousand clergymen found 66.6 per cent saying they would actively campaign for the amendment. Finally, a survey of New England Methodists revealed over 90 per cent believed child labor should be abolished.

III

It is evident that the attitudes of American Protestantism on labor questions ran the gamut from supreme indifference—not to say hostility —to deep sympathy and concern. The stage has now been set for a more detailed analysis of the churches and labor in the succeeding chapters.

CHAPTER XV

The Condition and Status of the Worker: I

"Social conditions do not of themselves save souls but they do of themselves damn souls, if damnation is interpreted not as a legal status known to God alone but as a quality of life known to men only too well."—John C. Bennett

I

THE FEDERAL COUNCIL of the Churches of Christ in America had a magnificent record on labor questions. If ever the American worker had a friend, it was this great cooperative organization of American Protestantism. The thesis that the churches served simply to sanctify the status quo, that they ministered only to the upper classes, that their sole concern with the laboring man was to dull his sense of injustice with shots of spiritual opiates may be retained, but even a cursory examination of the record of the Federal Council demonstrates that such a thesis cannot be maintained.

Formed in 1908, from its inception the Council interested itself in economic justice. The "Social Ideals of the Churches"—more popularly called the "Social Creed of the Churches"—eloquently testifies to this fact. The first draft of this statement was formulated by the General Conference of the Methodist Episcopal Church early in 1908, before the Federal Council had been established. At the first quadrennial meeting of the Council at Philadelphia in December of the same year, the Methodist statement was borrowed, slightly changed, and adopted. In 1912 at the second quadrennium of the Council the statement was expanded and reaffirmed and became the famous "Social Creed of the Churches" which served American Protestantism until 1932. In that year, after much careful thought, preparation, and discussion, a new statement was adopted to meet modern conditions. The Social Creed had great influence. Almost all of the leading denominations by official action made the statement their own, in addition to such cooperative religious groups as the Y.M.C.A., Y.W.C.A., and the Home Missions Council.

It is not without significance that most of the points in both the original and revised statement dealt with labor: a living wage, a maximum six-day week, protection of working women, the elimination of child labor, safeguards against occupational injuries and disease, unemployment, accident, and old age insurance, and the right of labor to organize and bargain collectively.

These two statements served as the framework for further action on the part of the Council. In 1919, a year of great industrial unrest, the Council at a special meeting in Cleveland adopted four new resolutions. Included in these resolutions was an expression of sympathy for labor's desire for a better day and an equitable share in the profits of management and industry. This necessitated not only a guaranteed minimum wage, social insurance, and governmental control of unemployment, but also greater economic democracy through collective bargaining and the sharing of shop control and management by labor.

In that same year the Council's Commission on the Church and Social Service issued a statement on "The Church and Social Reconstruction." The report argued that a living wage was the first charge upon industry, taking precedence over dividends. It held that labor was justified in resisting the attempts of management to reduce wages to their pre-war level. It called for unemployment insurance and denounced brutality toward strikers. Women were to be accorded greater protection. Trade unions were endorsed, for a "deep cause of unrest in industry is the denial to labor of a fair share in industrial management. Controversies over wages and hours never go to the root of the industrial problem. Democracy must be applied to the government of industry as well as to the government of the nation, and as rapidly and as far as the workers shall become able and willing to accept such responsibility."[1]

A year later the Federal Council, in cooperation with the General War-Time Commission of the Churches, issued a volume on *The Church and Industrial Reconstruction,* which called for higher wages, shorter hours of work, safer conditions, the protection of women and children, and the right of labor to bargain collectively. Within a year the Council was deeply involved in the determined drive of management to break labor unions. Although management's campaign was disguised under such euphemistic titles as the "American Plan" and the "Open-Shop Program," the Council was not duped by these fine sounding names. "These terms," it said in conjunction with Catholic and Jewish agencies, "are now being frequently used to designate establishments that are definitely anti-union. Obviously a shop of this kind is not an 'open-shop' but a 'closed-shop'—closed against the members of labor unions. We feel impelled to call public attention to the fact that a very widespread im-

1. *Quadrennial Report of the Federal Council,* 1916-20, pp. 109-13.

pression exists that the present 'open-shop' campaign is . . . an attempt to destroy the organized labor movement."[2]

During the remainder of the twenties and throughout the thirties the Council continued to endorse reform legislation. Even more basic, labor's right to organize was vigorously upheld, for the Council believed that "when labor is denied the right of free choice of representatives and when employers refuse to deal with representatives so chosen, the spirit and purpose of justice and democracy are thwarted."[3]

The Council acted in other ways. Scarcely an issue of *Information Service* failed to carry an item on labor: reviews of Supreme Court decisions involving wages and hours, statistical summaries of wages in a given industry, accounts of conditions among share-croppers and farmers, exposures of labor spies and company police, sympathetic portraits of labor leaders and strikers, descriptions of industrial accidents, and endorsement of such congressional legislation as the Wagner Act, the Social Security Act, and the Fair Labor Standards Act. Only slightly less concern in all these matters was evidenced by the *Federal Council Bulletin*.

In addition, the Council issued an annual Labor Sunday Message, frequently quoted or summarized in the press and read from the pulpits of the land on the Sunday prior to Labor Day. These messages repeatedly called for better conditions of work and for the extension of democracy in industrial life. The Commission on the Church and Social Service held hundreds of industrial seminars with business and labor leaders, investigated factory and mill conditions, testified in favor of reform legislation before congressional committees, and arranged for union officials to speak from the pulpits in many cities. This commission augmented the spoken with the written word by printing and distributing thousands of pamphlets dealing with *The Wage Question, The Church's Appeal in Behalf of Labor, How the Churches Are Helping in Unemployment, Social Aspects of Agriculture Credit,* and other related topics. Council officer Cavert said in 1934: "The demand that the Church be impartial is always just: to ask that it be *neutral* is another matter. In the present situation, with labor's fundamental rights so widely denied, and at threatened cost of a thwarted recovery program, neutrality would be immoral. The churches now have an opportunity to register moral judgment in a crucial issue—and to win the right to influence and guide the labor movement of the future."[4]

In brief, the Federal Council advocated continuously from 1919 to 1939 just about every demand that labor itself was asking. When this

2. *Federal Council Bulletin*, Jan., 1921, p. 26.
3. *Biennial Report of the Federal Council*, 1934, p. 132.
4. *Federal Council Bulletin*, April, 1934, p. 5.

fact is coupled with the Council's support of many specific strikes, it becomes evident that here, at any rate, American Protestantism confounded the old cliché about religion, the masses, and opium.

II

The Methodist Episcopal Church, South, adopted as its own the "Social Creed of the Churches" and beginning in 1918 it was printed in the *Discipline*. Further, in 1922 the Episcopal Address, after noting several examples of the Christian spirit in industry, added: "But a comparative few of these instances of the benevolent use of power and opportunity are not enough. What the industrial classes are asking is not charity, not toleration, but the recognition of their right to a righteous compensation as the basis of a safe and intelligent family life and of themselves and their engagements as a necessary and honorable part of the great business life of our nation. We believe this claim to be just and worthy of respect on the part of all Christian Churches."[5] An adopted report to this Conference urged, in a rather vague fashion, the application of brotherly principles in industry.

At the next quadrennium the bishops upheld the right of all men and women to a living wage, limited hours, safer and cleaner conditions, a larger participation in the fruits of industry, opportunity for culture and development—in short, whatever makes for a richer, fuller life. In 1930 much of the Episcopal Address was devoted to conditions in southern mill towns. The bishops recognized that injustices did exist, held the matter was of intense concern to the churches, and affirmed human rights were above property rights. The Committee on Temperance and Social Service also requested greater industrial justice, although about the only specific point mentioned was the desirability of the six-day week. At the following quadrennium the Conference endorsed the revised "Social Creed" and the bishops averred that Christian principles must be applied to all aspects of industrial life. The last General Conference of Southern Methodism prior to unification said nothing specific about conditions of work, although a committee maintained that the economic system, with its abuses, was subject to serious questioning. Lastly, liberal Southern Methodists in 1934 formed an unofficial Council on a Christian Social Order, and this group did important work in the field of labor relations.

If the position of Southern Methodism on questions of labor was not such as to seriously disturb the business community, the same can hardly be said of Northern Methodists. As early as 1908 the Methodist

5. *Journal of the General Conference of the Methodist Episcopal Church, South,* 1922, p. 359.

Episcopal Church officially stood for a minimum living wage and the highest wage that each industry can afford, a maximum six-day week, protection of women and the abolition of child labor, and industrial safeguards. Additional statements on social security and collective bargaining were subsequently added before the First World War, and the creed containing these reforms was reaffirmed in 1920.

A year earlier, the Board of Bishops adopted a resolution which was issued as a Pastoral Letter to the eighteen thousand pastors of that church entitled "The Church and Social Reconstruction." The bishops called for the end of "selfish competition" and sought the extension of democracy into industrial life. They rejoiced in such "ameliorative measures" as better housing and various forms of social insurance, but they also recognized the need for an equitable wage which should have the right of way over rent, interest, and profits. Above all, the bishops believed that collective bargaining was an essential instrument in the attainment of industrial justice. In 1920 the bishops enjoined the churches to stand in unflinching, uncompromising denunciation of all economic injustice. And these injustices were specifically named. They were many. Four years later the General Conference called once again not merely for the physical conditions which would make for the Christianization of industry—for a living wage and for all possible safeguards for health and security—but also for the higher prerequisites for sound human existence, for the recognition of labor's right to organize, for the laborer's right to be heard through representatives of his own choosing, and for an increasing share of responsibility by labor in the control of industry.

The Episcopal Address of 1928 asked for the safeguarding of workers in hazardous industries, and for a wage capable of not merely prolonging existence but of supporting life. It does not satisfy the requirement, concluded the address, if there be given to the toiler today only so much as shall enable him to resume his toil tomorrow. In addition, the bishops upheld reasonable provisions for the days of illness and old age, and labor's right to organize was specifically recognized. The General Conference of 1928 again endorsed the "Social Creed of Methodism," and then proceeded to adopt and order printed into the *Discipline* a long statement containing a dozen specific reforms which should be accorded to labor.

In 1930 the bishops issued a letter which was so critical of the existing order and so friendly to labor that it might have been ghost written by "Mother" Bloor and John L. Lewis. The Methodist *Discipline* of 1932 carried many labor reforms and the 1932 General Conference branded the present economic order unchristian, unethical, and anti-social. To help remedy injustices, unemployment, accident, and old age insurance was endorsed. At the same convention the bishops charged that industrial practices of the past decades were responsible for the deplorable conditions of today. "Industry has as a rule," continued the bishops, "given labor a grudging, insufficient wage, keeping it down by child exploitation, by suppression of legitimate organizations, and by other expedients, while at the same time huge fortunes have been amassed for the favored owners of the resources of production. Today the burden is without conscience shifted to the worker who, after giving his labor for miserable financial results, is turned off to starve or beg. Thus, the machine, which might have been used to lift the load of poverty from the backs of all the people, has been used selfishly for the benefit of the few."[6] The General Conference of 1936 and the Uniting Conference of 1939 did not use the strong terms of the 1932 meeting, but they did continue to espouse such betterment of working conditions as Northern Methodism had stood for since 1908.

On scores of occasions Northern Methodist annual conferences echoed these outspoken sentiments friendly to labor. Further, much of the Methodist press was warmly pro-labor. *Zion's Herald,* for instance, in the twenties exposed brutal conditions of work, championed reform legislation, and, in spite of exceptions, generally gave moderate support to unions. During the thirties this support was intensified. It should be sufficient to note this Boston publication denounced "yellow dog" contracts and injunctions aimed at labor and upheld minimum wage laws. The passage of the Social Security Act encouraged the editors to believe that God was in His heaven, and the Wagner Act was termed a decisive step forward for human rights in the field of industrial relationships. The *Nashville Christian Advocate* was somewhat less sympathetic to labor, in the twenties following a policy that can best be described as neutral. Harsh working conditions were exposed, conservative unions praised, and the editors realized that the American farmer was in the grip of a severe depression not entirely of his own making. On the other hand, workingmen were sometimes chided for being lazy and unions were scored for their greed. In the thirties this paper advanced to a warmly sympathetic attitude toward labor. Industrial conditions were hit hard, but the strongest indictments of the American economy came in descriptions of Southern share-croppers. The Wagner Act was termed fair, balanced, intelligent, and judicial—an admirable and promising piece of legislation. The editors considered the Social Security Act the most far-reaching, significant, forward-looking, and just reform of the New Deal.

6. *Journal of the General Conference of the Methodist Episcopal Church,* 1932, pp. 173-74.

They believed the Fair Labor Standards Act worthy of the support of all those interested in economic justice.

The position of the *Northwestern Christian Advocate* on labor questions was about the same as the Nashville journal. During the twenties labor unions were occasionally criticized for their violence and greed. But unchristian conditions of work were also denounced and inequities in the economic order exposed. In the thirties the number and intensity of items on labor quickened. Conditions in mines and mills and among share-croppers and migratory workers were exposed. During the mid-thirties, when the question of labor's right to organize was being hotly debated, the editors somewhat smugly observed that to the church such a right was "old stuff." The Social Security Act was hailed as by far the most ambitious American project for attacking the evils of enforced idleness and destitution in old age. "How slowly," said the editors, "does any political party follow and with what tardy, limping step, the great assumption of our Master, that a man is worth considerably more than a sheep!"[7] When the wage and hour law was being debated before Congress, the editors said "we need to remind ourselves once more that the pagan idea of the devil take the hindmost is still openly defended— and by people classed for the purpose of the census, and otherwise, as 'Christian.' "[8] It was also maintained that without organization the worker was powerless, while through union membership he won dignity and a voice, and the proposition was advanced that a strong labor movement was the firmest bulwark against both communism and fascism. A fourth Methodist journal, the *New York Christian Advocate,* was at best only mildly pro-labor, while the *Arkansas Methodist* was rather clearly antagonistic to the urban worker.

Methodism also gave witness to its concern in the laboring man through two unofficial organizations. The Laymen's Religious Movement, formed in 1936, was friendly to labor, but more important was the Methodist Federation for Social Service. The Federation is open to many grave charges, but on the labor question its record was consistent, courageous, and, for the most part, wise. Throughout its entire history the Federation championed the eight-hour day, minimum wage laws, social security, safer conditions of work, and the right of labor to organize and bargain collectively. The Federation was happy to publicize conditions in the steel industry as brought forth in the Interchurch report, particularly since Bishop McConnell was chairman of the investigating committee. In 1920 the Federation warned that if the gains made in collective bargaining during the war were taken away from organized

7. Sept. 5, 1935, p. 779.
8. Dec. 2, 1937, p. 1107.

labor the consequences would be extremely serious. In its regular bulletins and in special leaflets the "open-shop" campaign was branded a declaration of war against trade unionism which, if successful, would mean for the workers long hours, low wages, and bad living conditions.

Throughout the twenties the Federation challenged the accepted thesis that the entire country was basking in golden prosperity. Time and again the troubled state of American farmers, miners, textile hands, and factory workers were unveiled. Numerous conferences, national and local, were held with business and labor leaders to the end that greater economic justice might be secured. The Federation investigated many strikes, almost invariably reporting that the grievances of the workers were real. Management's use of spies, company police, injunctions, black lists, and "yellow dog" contracts were all deprecated.

During the Depression Decade the Federation swung far to the Left. It repudiated capitalism, viewed the Russian experiment with an uncritical eye, cooperated with Communists, and termed the New Deal fascistic and palliative. Nevertheless, its concern for the workingman remained realistic. The right of labor to organize was, upheld. The C.I.O. was praised. The Wagner Act was termed a milestone in the progress of American democracy. The Social Security Act, although "full of fallacies and inadequacies," was deemed a step in the right direction, while the abuses of unemployment, low wages, industrial accidents, child labor, and the autocratic rule of management were exposed repeatedly.

Whatever the final evaluation of the Methodist Federation for Social Service may be, its concern for the workingman was genuine, and its contributions to industrial democracy real. Certainly the activities of this group helped gain for the Methodist Episcopal Church the reputation of being the laborer's friend. The Federation in part made it possible for the *New York Christian Advocate* to say that "the Christian Church is the most powerful friend of all the beneficent aims of labor. The teachings of the Church have laid the groundwork for every item of humane legislation which the labor leaders have ever promoted."[9]

If applied to certain elements in Methodism, particularly in the southern church, this statement is an exaggeration. But an examination of the record of the Methodist press, General Conferences, various local conferences, the Federation for Social Service, and leaders supports the conclusion that on the whole Methodists did indeed support labor in its legitimate demands.

9. July 25, 1929, p. 916.

III

The Southern Baptist Convention was not a member of the Federal Council of Churches and hence did not adhere to the "Social Creed of the Churches." It issued few statements on labor questions to make up for this omission. In 1921 the Commission on Social Service, it is true, expressed mild sympathy for the worker, but not a single other Southern Baptist Convention of the twenties saw fit to repeat even such an innocuous statement, and it was not until 1930 that Southern Baptists again spoke on the question of labor. In that year, however, Southern Baptists not only called for the application of Christianity to economic problems, but specifically endorsed a fair living wage, a work-week of not more than forty-nine and one-half hours, safer conditions, and the right of labor to organize and bargain collectively. Moreover, the Commission on Social Service quoted with approval and incorporated into its own report an important declaration made by the Georgia Baptist Convention. Included in this report were petitions for a shorter work-week, a decent living wage, the elimination of the "stretch-out" system, and the abolition of night work for women. In addition, the report recognized the inalienable right of labor to organize, to bargain collectively, and to be represented at the council table by representatives of its own choosing. The following year all of these reforms were again endorsed. Silence then prevailed on labor questions until 1938 when the Southern Baptist Convention adopted resolutions upholding labor's right to a living wage and to unionization.

The relative conservatism of Southern Baptists on labor questions is seen at the state and local level. Hugh A. Brimm, attempting to discover the attitude of Southern Baptists toward the system of farm tenancy, failed to find a single reference to the problem in twenty-six meetings of the Southern Baptist Convention or in 363 meetings of various state conventions. Further, only four very weak statements were discovered in some 1,120 district association meetings. "There was . . . no indication anywhere," Brimm concluded, "that a sense of responsibility was felt toward the economic and social conditions which produced a system with such deep needs as were found in farm tenancy. In relation to this problem Southern Baptists expressed no social consciousness."[10]   Brimm also studied twenty-seven district associations for the years 1925-35 to determine the awareness of Southern Baptists of the problem of migrant laborers. He concluded there was no indication whatsoever of concern. Typical reports on social problems at these district associations

---

10. Hugh A. Brimm, "The Social Consciousness of Southern Baptists in Relation to Some Regional Problems, 1910-1935" (unpublished Th.D. dissertation, Southern Baptist Theological Seminary, 1944), p. 71.

were confined to denouncing dancing, "mixed bathing," motion pictures, and booze. The migrant labor problem was also ignored by the Southern Baptist Convention, and only two vague references to it were found among 363 state convention meetings. The record regarding southern textile mills was somewhat better. Occasional district and state associations as well as the Southern Baptist Convention spoke on mill conditions. But these few exceptions only bring into sharper focus the general conservatism of Southern Baptists on labor questions.

This conservatism was also evident in the Southern Baptist press. For instance, under the appropriate heading of "Editorial Varieties," the editors of *Western Recorder* shamed into silence agitators for the eight-hour day with the penetrating observation that the blackbird works seventeen hours and feeds its young one hundred times a day—and blackbirds do not complain! The Virginia journal, *Religious Herald,* was somewhat more compassionate, occasionally passing judgment on conditions of work and endorsing such legislation as the Social Security Act. However, its tone was not such as seriously to disturb the business community.

For the most part, Southern Baptist papers, with the rather clear exception of the *Alabama Baptist,* believed prosperity the reward of righteous living and poverty the result of sloth and indolence. It was generally held that if the poor worked hard and the rich shared their wealth and if both classes drove bitterness from their hearts and trusted God, all would continue to be sunny in the economic life of the South.

Northern Baptists appeared more interested in bettering the lot of labor than their southern brethren. Even before America's entrance into the First World War the Northern Baptist Convention had endorsed the "Social Creed of the Churches" and had passed many strong resolutions on labor questions. Immediately following the war the Convention called for an equitable sharing of the profits of industry, and in 1920 this sentiment was repeated, for all partners in industry should share in the fruits and in the direction of their enterprise. Moreover, shorter hours, the six-day week, social insurance for the aged and the injured, and the protection of working women were demanded. Pamphlets were issued calling for a guaranteed living wage; after all, men were not mere units in production. In 1921 the report of the Social Service Committee reminded Baptists that "human values are at stake in every industrial situation. Human relations underlie all such questions as labor and capital, hours and wages, and these relations must ever be considered. . . . It is for us . . . to develop an active and discriminating conscience in the people which shall make them quick to feel the

inequalities and evils of our present system."[11]   To implement this statement Baptists sanctioned a living wage as the first moral claim upon
industry, reduction of hours of work and at least the six-day week,
protection of women, unemployment insurance, and public works and
labor exchanges to reduce unemployment.

These goals were repeated in 1922, and in that year also the Social
Service Committee reaffirmed its belief in labor's right to organize. The
following Convention expressed concern over the agrarian depression,
and resolutions were adopted endorsing higher wages, shorter hours,
suitable provision for the aged and injured, and labor's right to organize.
Support of all these reforms was given again in 1924 and 1928 and in a
modified form in 1927.

The 1930 Convention was not unaware of the blight of unemployment
that had fallen upon the land, and the 1931 Convention adopted a
resolution approving of any and all movements which look toward
better conditions for the working man and a more equitable distribution
of wealth.   The report of the Social Service Committee specifically
championed free employment agencies, public works, and unemployment
insurance as an indispensable part of sound social policy.   A 1932 resolution reaffirmed Baptist faith in the principle of human rights over
property rights, while in 1933 Baptists spoke on wages, hours, collective
bargaining, and social security. The Convention further regretted the
exploitation of personality which persisted in sweat-shops, coal fields,
and in many industrial centers where precedence was given to profits
over human worth as taught by Jesus.

Resolutions were adopted at the following Convention endorsing
labor's right to organize and bargain collectively. The economic system
was indicted as unchristian because it brought want and misery to millions and a great wealth to a few. In 1935 the report of the newly created
Committee on Christian Social Action spoke of undernourished, poorly
housed, thinly clad people. It found the economic system a failure and
called for fundamental changes including collective bargaining in industry, extensive aid to the farmers, and sickness, accident, and old-age
insurance. In 1937 Northern Baptists requested a living minimum wage
for every worker and a maximum income to be set by law. The last
Convention of the Depression Decade saw the adoption of an important
set of resolutions regarding working conditions, wages, hours, social
security, and the right of labor to organize.

The *Baptist,* official organ of the Northern Baptist Convention until
1930, echoed these friendly resolutions. America was reminded that

11. *Annual of the Northern Baptist Convention,* 1921, p. 203.

workers were not animals, that prosperity in the twenties was not shared by much of the laboring and farming community, and that

A community in which the laboring people may not, or cannot, organize and build up among themselves a constructive community program, is a community of slaves. The form of government which it invites, accepts and makes necessary is that of a plutocracy—a plutocracy whose center of control over its slave population resides in the power to hire and fire. The test of a free and democratic government is its success in shifting that power to organized labor.[12]

On the other hand, the attitude of the fundamentalist paper, *Watchman-Examiner,* can be ascertained when one remembers that in the teeth of the depression the editors were still finding the "most fruitful source of poverty" to be the "accursed liquor traffic."[13]

IV

Southern Presbyterians had little to say on labor questions. Indeed, until 1936 the General Assembly of the Presbyterian Church, U.S., was almost sphinx-like in its silence on this matter. In that year, however, the Permanent Committee on Moral and Social Welfare, in its second report to the General Assembly, spoke strongly. After noting the great inequalities in American society, the committee affirmed the supremacy of human rights over property rights, and urged wholesome conditions of work, fair wages, shorter hours, adequate security against illness, unemployment, and old age, and the application of democracy to the economic order. The following year this committee requested relief for the unemployed and presented with facts and figures a devastating picture of the millions of Americans who were living at a bare subsistence level. Share-cropping came in for harsh criticism, the report deploring the fact that attempts of the share-croppers to "secure better conditions of living have resulted in a widespread violation of civil rights and that in some sections there has developed a system of forced labor which amounts to peonage."[14]

What was the situation among Northern Presbyterians? Prior to the First World War they had voiced their concern with conditions of work and had scored the more flagrant industrial abuses. The General Assembly of 1919 voted approval of President Wilson's "courageous, wise and timely" utterance in defense of labor's right to organize. This Assembly instructed the Board of Home Missions to make a thorough study of the industrial situation and report its findings to the next meeting.

12. June 7, 1930, p. 741.
13. Dec. 13, 1934, p. 1305.
14. *Minutes of the General Assembly of the Presbyterian Church, U.S.,* 1937, p. 104.

The Reverend John McDowell, one-armed ex-coal miner who owed his disability to a mine accident, was secretary of the Board of Home Missions, and his report, adopted by the 1920 Assembly as the social creed of the denomination, vigorously indicted the industrial abuses of the day. Included among the reforms that Presbyterians "ought to declare for" were a living wage adequate to maintain the laborer and his family in health and honor, safer and cleaner conditions of work, the assumption by industry of the burdens entailed by accidents, disease, and death, shorter hours of work including the six-day week, and the right of wage earners to organize and bargain with management through their chosen representatives. The following year the Assembly endorsed the Saturday half-holiday, and in 1922 Presbyterians spoke again for higher wages, shorter hours, greater protection, and unionization.

Throughout the twenties and thirties John McDowell and others annually delivered a Labor Day Message, reflecting Presbyterian thought on this question, and the message was printed in the Presbyterian press and widely distributed in pamphlet form. These Labor Day Messages consistently and strongly repeated the belief of Presbyterians in a living wage, safe and healthful conditions of work, shorter hours, protection of women, and labor's right to organize and bargain collectively. Sometimes these messages were eloquent:

Let us . . . affirm again on this Labor Day that any social system and industrial system which grinds up men and women and children to make cheap goods, is an un-Christian system; that no social and industrial system can be Christian until it is so organized that every honest and willing worker can find work, and work so remunerative that he cannot only maintain his own working powers in health and efficiency, but shall also be able to give his wife and children a decent, healthy, joyous and honorable life; in other words, 'the abundant life' which Christ came to give to the world.[15]

In 1930 the General Assembly directed that a study be made of economic conditions, asked that individual congregations discuss thoroughly the question of old age security, and urged all employers to retain their workers and thus not add to the growing number of unemployed. The following year the Assembly adopted a report beseeching adequate wages and the protection of the worker from industrial conditions beyond his control. It was in 1932, however, that the General Assembly dealt most vigorously with labor questions. The adopted report of the Committee on Social and Industrial Relations of the Board of National Missions declared that the depression was not a mere incident but rather an indictment of the whole economic system. The report

15. John McDowell, *Industry and Social Justice* (n.p., 1928), a pamphlet.

then went on to present a set of ideals and objectives, adopted by the Assembly *seriatim,* invoking a living wage, better conditions and shorter hours of work, protection of the laborer in his old age and sickness, and the right of labor to unionize. These protections for labor were reaffirmed in 1933 and again in 1934 when a universal system of unemployment insurance was also requested. The delegates to the 1935 General Assembly repeated their belief in all of these reforms.

Once again in 1936 the Assembly expressed itself on these matters, being dissatisfied with any industrial order which provides no security against involuntary want of children, widows, the aged, and the victims of an era of machinery. In addition the delegates affirmed

the long-established position of our Church that employers and employees should have the right to organize for collective bargaining and social action. . . . The right of labor to organize is essential to prevent irresponsible autocracy in industry. It is also necessary to create an instrument for orderly economic change. In the present significant struggle for labor organization it is only fitting that Christian ministers make application of this principle, long accepted by the Church, to specific situations.[16]

The 1937 General Assembly supported the principle of collective bargaining, expressed gratification that progress toward an adequate program of social security was being made, urged the protection of workers against unemployment, indicated concern over share-croppers and tenant farmers, and attacked dangerous and unhealthy working conditions. In 1937 also the Labor Day Message termed the right of collective bargaining the very foundation of social justice and the basis of any sensible conduct of industrial affairs by management. A booklet published in that year by the Department of Social Education and Action asked for those manifold reforms which were needed to bring justice and security to the worker.

The 1938 General Assembly promulgated statements which should have satisfied even the most militant of labor leaders—statements on wages, hours, security, and the right of collective bargaining which Presbyterians had recognized since 1910. Once again in 1939 all of these industrial and agrarian reforms were endorsed, for the industrial life of the nation must be as democratic as its political life.

The Presbyterian press varied considerably in its attitudes toward labor. For example, the Kentucky publication, *Christian Observer,* carried almost nothing on this problem (or any other social issue, for that matter), while *Social Progress,* a journal of the Department of Social Education and Action, repeatedly crusaded for labor reforms, in-

16. *Minutes of the General Assembly of the Presbyterian Church, U.S.A.,* 1936, p. 155.

cluding endorsement of such specific legislation as the Wagner Act, Social Security Act, and Fair Labor Standards Act. The *Presbyterian Tribune,* this denomination's most liberal journal, did not come into existence until 1934, but in the remaining years of the Depression Decade it established a reputation as labor's ally. Labor spies were exposed, the disinherited befriended, and reform legislation endorsed. Above all, the organized labor movement was consistently defended not only because it raised the material standards of the common man, but also because of its spiritual contributions—the desire for essential justice, for a better life for the humblest which made the movement a great crusade for human justice. The editors were convinced that a strong and responsible workers' movement was necessary in a complex industrial economy if democracy was to be made real.

On the other hand, the record of the *United Presbyterian* on labor questions was both longer and darker. The poverty of great elements of America's population left this journal's news commentator, H. H. Marlin, unmoved: "Laziness, booze, improvidence, the habit of prodigality, a persistent blindness to the truth of the parable of the seven fat years followed by the seven lean years, have very much to do with the fact that 86 per cent of America's population is poor."[17] The rock-like conservatism of the *United Presbyterian* remained unshaken by the cataclysmic upheavals of the thirties. The Wagner Act and the National Labor Relations Board were damned. John L. Lewis was a megalomaniac. The C.I.O. was declared a menace which, if unchecked, would leave America at the mercy of a greedy oligarchy. Other Presbyterian journals ran the gamut from blatant hostility to open friendship toward labor, but on the whole the Presbyterian press was not an outstanding champion of the worker.

American Presbyterians, however, have in their Labor Temple one of the noblest efforts ever made by the churches to minister to the workingman. Located on the tough East Side of New York, the Labor Temple was founded in 1910 through the courageous and imaginative efforts of Charles Stelzle. Here was a place where the church could know the aspirations of the disinherited and where they in turn could discover the love of Christ. Here open forums were held, people studied, great men spoke and humble people listened. Here the homeless slept, labor unions held their meetings, radicals blew off steam, and the poor worshiped. The object of repeated attacks by conservatives, the Labor Temple carried on in the twenties and thirties bringing the facts of life to the church and the teaching of Christ to the disinherited.

Another Presbyterian organization which interested itself in the

17. Jan. 31, 1929, p. 2.

workingman, although less directly than the Labor Temple, was the small, unofficial, now defunct Presbyterian Fellowship for Social Action. The Fellowship paid particular attention to the labor question. Delegates were sent to union conventions, members lobbied for reform laws before the legislatures, strikes were given moral and material support, and studies were made of industrial problems. In 1938 the Fellowship arranged to have union leaders deliver a series of addresses in connection with the General Assembly. Posters advertising these speakers, however, were ordered removed by Dr. Lewis S. Mudge, Stated Clerk of the General Assembly.

Presbyterian interest in the labor question varied considerably. The Southern church evidenced little concern while, on the other hand, official pronouncements of the General Assembly of the Presbyterian Church, U.S.A., and to a much lesser extent, the Northern Presbyterian press, endorsed most of the major reforms designed to better labor's condition.

V

Congregationalists were pioneers in the Social Gospel movement and long before 1919 they had launched Christianizing expeditions into the jungle of industrial relations. Nor was the Congregational conscience completely deadened with the nation's return to "normalcy" after the First World War. The first post-war National Council recorded its support of a living wage and of conditions of work conducive to health and security. It further encouraged labor's organizing activities. In 1921 the Council called for greater brotherhood in industrial life, but made clear that in the contest between labor and capital, a total victory for either side would prove contrary to the spirit of Christ. A similar vague plea for economic justice was made by the 1923 Council. In that year the Commission on Social Service devoted its entire report to rural conditions, painting a gloomy picture of the general farm depression, and the Congregational Educational Society reissued the strong 1919 statement on labor.

The next National Council, meeting in 1925, adopted a far-reaching "Statement on Social Ideals"—one of the most important church pronouncements of the decade. The section on industry asserted that a Christian social order entailed the eight-hour day, six-day week, a minimum comfort wage, safe and sanitary working conditions, national employment bureaus, accident, sickness, unemployment, and old age insurance, and labor's right to organize and share in the management of industrial relations. In 1927 the report of the Commission on Social

Relations stated that unless workers are permitted to organize and bargain collectively it was useless to talk of freedom of contract.

Meeting in the deepening shadows of the depression, the 1931 General Council of the now united Congregational and Christian Churches voiced its endorsement of a living wage and forty-hour week, and protested the rise of injunctions, "yellow dog" contracts, and all similar efforts to deprive labor of its authority to organize. It was at the following General Council of 1934, meeting at Oberlin, Ohio, that the Congregational Christian Churches veered far to the Left and adopted the much discussed resolution repudiating the capitalist system. Rarely has a Protestant church leveled such extreme, unqualified charges against the American economic order. It was this Council, also, that brought into being the official Congregational Council for Social Action, and throughout the remainder of the Depression Decade most Congregational statements on labor came from this group.

Foreshadowing the work of the Council for Social Action was the Congregational Commission on Social Service, founded in 1913, known after 1927 as the Commission on Social Relations, and functioning as part of the Education Society. Arthur E. Holt, who looked like Washington and thought like Lincoln, brought in 1919 to the leadership of the Commission all the energy and grass-roots liberalism indigenous to the West from which he hailed. When Holt had served five years as secretary of the group and had succeeded to Graham Taylor's chair at the Chicago Theological Seminary in 1924, a young minister from Wichita, Kansas, Hubert C. Herring, came to assume responsibilities. Herring, with the notable aid of John Calder, expanded the range and usefulness of the Commission until its honorable retirement from the field in 1934.

Bearing witness to the memories of Josiah Strong, Washington Gladden, and other earlier Congregational prophets of social Christianity, this Commission did what it could to bring to a coupon-clipping, mahjong playing America the brutal facts of economic life as they were known to millions of workers even in the plush twenties. It held conferences and seminars with labor leaders and management, published and distributed books, pamphlets, and study courses dealing with social problems, sent out speakers to college campuses, investigated conditions of work, and gave moral and material aid to strikers. In addition, beginning in 1928, the Commission published a four-page monthly "bulletin of information and suggestion" entitled *Church and Society*. This journal ranged widely and critically over all the social problems confronting American society. Although three ladies, Hannah Hume Lee, Katherine Terrill, and Helen Grace Murray, were responsible for much of the material in the journal, its observations on unemployment, old age, textiles, coal mining, race relations, civil liberties, and kindred subjects were somewhat unlady-like in their candor. In issue after issue labor reforms were endorsed: higher wages, stronger unions, social security, and all the rest.

In 1934 this agency was replaced by the Congregational Council for Social Action. The Council's Rural Life Committee, headed by Ferry Platt, and after his untimely death in 1937, Shirley Green, and the Industrial Committee led by Frank W. McCulloch, performed yeoman work in the interests of the laboring man and farmer. Industrial seminars were held, unions helped in their campaigns for recognition, aid to strikers proffered, reform legislation espoused, conditions among share-croppers investigated, violations of civil liberties in industrial disputes exposed, and an experimental Rural Life Center established.

Above all, the Council sought to educate the American public in industrial and agrarian democracy through the publication of a semi-monthly journal, *Social Action,* the first thirty-two-page issue of which appeared in March 1935. Some issues were devoted entirely to the careful examination of one subject of social concern; others gave general material on a wide variety of problems. The contributors were distinguished: Charles A. Beard, Paul H. Douglas, Liston Pope, Harry W. Laidler, Nathaniel Peffer, Albert W. Palmer, James Myers, Benson Y. Landis, Holt, Herring, and others hardly less famous. The circulation was large for a religious journal of its type: about 800,000 copies were distributed by 1941. The coverage was broad: race relations, civil liberties, foreign affairs, news slanting by papers, the Constitution, the Insull Empire, and similar topics. But the majority of issues were devoted to labor spies, strikes, unions, labor legislation, conditions of work, share-cropping, and cooperatives. Although arguments on both sides were presented, the sympathies of the Council were clearly with the worker. "Steel and Men," "When Steel Organizes," "The Textile Primer," "Why Did the Auto Workers Strike?," "The Church and Labor Organizations," "Social Security in America," "Labor and Democracy," "Labor and the Local Church," "Uncle Sam and the Farmer," "Problems of Organized Labor," "Some Facts About Farming," and "Is This Why We Have Longs and Coughlins?" were some of the issues in which the workers and farmers were defended right down the line. In addition, readers were admonished to "DEFEND the dispossessed in their right to adequate relief and in the legitimate right to organize and strike" and to "DEMAND adequate social insurance for the unemployed and aged workers and farmers."[18] The CSA was not a lunatic-fringe organization. It did not

18. Inside cover of various issues of *Social Action.*

flirt with Moscow. But its support of labor was firm, militant, un-wavering, and unquestioned.

Congregationalism's sympathy with the workingman was also re-flected in the denominational journal, *Advance,* called prior to 1934 the *Congregationalist.* Heart-rending pictures of conditions among share-croppers, miners, textile operators, automobile workers, and migratory laborers appeared regularly. The editors believed human life was being subordinated to profits. Reform legislation such as the Wagner Act and Social Security Act were upheld. Injunctions, "yellow dog" contracts, labor spies, company police, company unions and other devices to prevent labor from organizing were denounced. This paper openly endorsed labor unions from the "open-shop" campaigns of management in the early twenties to the organizational drives of the C.I.O. in the late thirties.

In conclusion, there seems little doubt that Congregationalists, at least as their attitudes were expressed through their leaders, councils, agencies, and press, were sympathetic to the aims of labor.

VI

Long before 1919 the Protestant Episcopal Church had recorded its approval of labor reforms. In that strife-filled year, however, the General Convention merely mumbled a few bromides about Christian brotherhood in industrial relations. It was the Lambeth Conference of 1920, a world assembly of Anglican bishops, which gave outspoken ex-pression to the post-war economic ideals of the Protestant Episcopal Church. Although not mandatory upon its constituency, these pronounce-ments may be regarded as expressing the mind of the church. Workmen are not mere tools to be scrapped when they are no longer useful. The fact that men who are willing and able to work cannot find work is an offense to the conscience of Christianity. A living wage is the first charge upon industry for it is intolerable that industry should be organized upon the foundation of the misery and want of the laborer. Further, workers must have reasonable leisure, security against unemployment, and health-ful surroundings. This is the purpose of labor unions—the establish-ment of a fuller and better life for all.

The House of Bishops and the House of Deputies at the General Convention of 1922 concurred in reaffirming the important declarations made by the Lambeth Conference. Throughout the remainder of the twenties the General Conventions evidenced little interest in labor prob-lems, although it is true that official and unofficial Episcopal agencies were very active in these matters. The increasing gravity of the de-pression elicited statements on unemployment and social security at the 1931 meeting, and in 1933 the bishops issued a special Pastoral Letter on economic conditions. The 1934 General Convention went a long way toward meeting virtually all of the reforms that labor itself demanded. The bishops sanctioned the right of the worker to organize and bargain collectively and deemed unemployment and old age insurance vital. The Convention agreed with the bishops when it also endorsed social insurance against such modern industrial hazards as unemployment, illness, accident, and old age as being in accord with every principle of Christian brotherhood. Sweatshops and the exploitation of women in industry were censured. The Report of the Joint Committee of Ten on National and International Problems further recognized that unions were equitable. Later Episcopal General Conventions touched upon labor questions, but the high water mark of concern was reached at this 1934 meeting.

From time to time diocesan conventions and parishes expressed themselves favorably on labor reform. The record of the Episcopal press was fairly neutral, however. Neither the *American Church Monthly* nor *Living Church* devoted much space to labor affairs, in the rather infrequent references the latter being the more sympathetic. Greater interest was expressed by the *Churchman,* although this liberal journal was not as flagrantly pro-labor as might be expected. On the other hand, the *Southern Churchman,* during much of the period, was as friendly to the workingman as any church paper in the South.

The Protestant Episcopal Church, like most of the major denominations, gave witness to its concern in social problems through various official and unofficial agencies. One such organization was the Church Socialist League. Founded in 1911, this group stood for the abolition of the capitalist system with the obvious if theoretical betterment of labor this implied. Although never large—probably less than a hundred—the membership included such great names in the Protestant Episcopal Church as Bernard Iddings Bell, Bishop Paul Jones, and Bishop F. Spencer Spaulding. The group split over pacifism in the First World War. Mortally wounded by this fissure and by the climate of the Great Red Scare, the Church Socialist League made a final denunciation of capitalism in 1919 and then gradually staggered to its grave. By 1924 its pulse had stopped beating.

Much more significant was the Church Association for the Advancement of the Interests of Labor, although it too had passed the peak of its activities by 1919. Formed in 1887, the CAIL for a generation probably did more to bridge the gap between the churches and labor than any other single religious agency. Although an unofficial organization, it attracted the sympathetic support of the Protestant Episcopal Church and many Episcopal leaders flung themselves into the movement. One only need mention Bishops Huntington, Potter, Greer, Manning, Burch, Gilbert and the Reverends B. F. De Costa and W. D. P. Bliss. This group's work was magnificent. Without succumbing to the fanaticism and dogmatism of some later socio-religious organizations, CAIL unwaveringly strove to aid the laborer. It successfully lobbied for reform legislation, investigated and exposed brutal conditions of work, mediated strikes, cooperated with labor unions, published a warmly pro-labor journal, *Hammer and Pen,* channelized liberal sentiment in the General Conventions, and brought to American Protestantism an awareness of labor's disdain. By 1926 the Protestant Episcopal Church was officially prepared to minister to the workingman. CAIL had done its work well. It had lived long enough, but unlike King Lear, when it came to retire from the field, it had the honor and love of troops of friends.

The Church League for Industrial Democracy filled the gap in church-labor relations created by the dissolution of CAIL in 1926, and for the student of the twenties and thirties its activities are much more significant than those of its predecessor. Indeed, the older organization had passed the zenith of its influence by the beginning of the Prosperity Decade, the very moment when the CLID was born. The League's activities were many. In addition to its regular bulletin, the *Clipsheet,* it published numerous special pamphlets dealing with industrial problems. Social action units were formed to work at the local level; preaching teams canvassed the country spreading the Social Gospel according to Spofford; interseminary conferences were promoted to further work among young people; field investigators tested civil liberties in industrial disputes, joined the picket line, and engaged in protest demonstrations. The League investigated conditions of work, conducted experiments in industrial democracy, cooperated with labor unions, opened churches to union speakers, lobbied for reform legislation, and gave moral and material aid to strikers. Above all, perhaps, the League sought to influence the social thinking of the rank and file of Episcopalians, although these attempts sometimes resulted, as at the General Convention of 1937, in a grand donnybrook.

An examination of the pamphlets published by the League leaves no doubt as to its position. "Every advance that labor has made has been through the unions," declared Bishop Robert B. Gooden in a pamphlet entitled *The Church and Labor.* When a concern is unable to pay a living wage, affirmed a bulletin of 1922, it should be held bankrupt and either joined with a concern that can pay a living wage or be turned over to the government. In so far as the League's attitude toward labor is concerned, its position was very sympathetic.

Unlike the CAIL and the CLID, the Department of Christian Social Service was official. Formed by the action of the General Convention of 1919, as this Department developed its interests were organized under divisions with specialists as secretaries. In 1926 a Division on Industrial Relations was created, and the following year Spencer Miller was appointed Consultant on Industrial Relations. The Department's purpose was to study and report upon social and industrial conditions; to coordinate the attitudes of the various organizations existing in the church in the interest of social service; to cooperate with similar bodies in other communions; and to encourage sympathetic relations between capital and labor. As a responsible official agency of the church, the Department of Christian Social Service obviously could not be as flagrantly pro-labor in its attitude as unofficial groups. Nevertheless, under the leadership of such men as Charles N. Lathrop its position was far from evasive. In its reports to the Convention and in its special bulletins, the Department vigorously supported labor's demands, ranging from advocating social security to suggesting that goods bearing the union label be given preference over non-union material.

Although the membership of the Protestant Episcopal Church included precious few horny-handed laborers, this did not prevent Episcopalians from displaying some concern in labor questions. The worker might justly complain that resolutions of the General Convention were only mildly sympathetic toward him; this lament could hardly be leveled at the record of other official and unofficial Episcopal agencies.

VII

Disciples of Christ manifested some concern in labor matters. During the twenties most of these expressions were couched in generalities, although the Board of Temperance and Social Welfare under the excellent leadership of Alva W. Taylor did specifically demand reforms in regard to hours and conditions of work, wages, greater economic democracy, and security for the workers. The deepening of the depression caused the International Convention to express its concern over unemployment, and in 1932 this Convention favored social insurance against illness, accidents, want in old age, and unemployment. It also heard a report which condemned the low wages that made an "abundant life" impossible. In 1933 and in 1934 the Convention championed such measures as social security and higher wages. A resolution of 1935 called upon Disciples everywhere to oppose exploitation of the weak by the strong and to support such measures as shorter hours, higher wages, unemployment insurance, and greater old age security. In 1937 the Disciples recognized the right of labor to organize, upheld civil liberties in areas of industrial unrest, and affirmed that to Christianize an individual is to socialize him. The following year the Disciples passed resolutions dealing with social security. Further, they demanded a "just" wage which is more than a mere living wage but the highest wage that industry can afford. Labor unions were given an affirmative nod. Resolutions regarding most of these reforms were repeated in 1939.

The *Christian-Evangelist* reflected the position of the International Convention. During the twenties it was cool toward labor, but in the thirties this journal evolved to a strongly if sanely sympathetic position, which included endorsement of such New Deal legislation as the Wagner Act and the Social Security Act.

VIII

Although the Unitarian Churches represent the theological Left wing of Protestantism, their attitude on labor questions did not indicate a corresponding radicalism. This is not to say, however, that Unitarians can justly be called foes of the workingman. In 1919, for example, Unitarians stood for a living wage and for industrial democracy as a natural and proper corollary of political democracy. In 1920 the Unitarian Churches issued an official declaration on social questions which was widely hailed for its progressivism by such diverse authorities as Edward A. Ross, Walter Lippmann, and Thomas Nixon Carver. And well it might have been. This declaration called for social insurance against misfortune, accident, unemployment, illness, and old age. It defended labor's right to organize and bargain collectively. Shorter hours and better conditions of work were endorsed. Wages should be high enough to permit workers to live in comfort and health. The graduated income tax and inheritance tax were hailed as agents of economic democracy.

It was not until the depression that Unitarians again spoke vigorously on labor problems. In 1931 resolutions were passed by the Annual Conference urging more adequate relief for the unemployed, a public works program, social insurance covering unemployment, health, old age, and other forms of disability, and reduction of hours of labor. Not only so, wage cuts were termed socially unjust and specific conditions in soft coal fields were denounced, with the further recommendation that assistance be sent the miners. Throughout the remainder of the thirties most of the expressions on labor came from the Department of Social Relations. Although an official agency of Unitarians, its pronouncements did not necessarily represent the official position of the church. Under the leadership of Robert C. Dexter, the Department held discussion groups, aided strikers, and distributed pamphlets exposing soul-searing conditions among share-croppers and textile operators. This group also issued "A Program of Social Action" which was the source of much discussion among Unitarians. This program urged social security and minimum wage laws, a shorter work week and the unionization of labor. Further, it requested a fairer distribution of wealth through the use of progressive taxation, and advised greater governmental control and ownership of basic industries. Earlier the Department of Social and Public Service had worked for social justice within Unitarianism.

In addition to these official agencies, there was the unofficial Unitarian Fellowship for Social Justice. Formed in 1908, it had as its purpose the establishment of a fellowship for united action against all forms of social injustice, and to enable its members to sustain one another in the application of their religious ideals to the needs of the present day. Although apparently the Fellowship never swung as far to the Left as the Methodist Federation and some other socio-religious groups, it did attempt within the framework of capitalism to better labor's conditions.

The attitude of Unitarianism also found expression in the pages of the denominational journal, *Christian Register*. During the twenties this paper was very weak in its sympathy to labor. Occasionally, it is true, conditions in coal fields and cotton mills were exposed and labor's right to organize defended. The Depression Decade ushered in a more sympathetic attitude toward labor; indeed, an attitude that was almost completely uncritical of the workingman and his unions.

In spite of these later manifestations on the part of the *Christian Register*, it is probably fair to conclude that on the whole Unitarians were not as unqualified in their sympathy to labor as some other denominations.

IX

The United Lutheran Church was formed in 1918 by the merger of several synods. Although the most liberal of Lutheran groups—and the only one with any kind of affiliation with the Federal Council—it had very little to say on labor questions. An examination of the minutes of the Biennial Conventions of the United Lutheran Church in America revealed slight interest in economic matters. To be sure the reports of the Committee on Moral and Social Welfare occasionally touched on industrial issues—particularly in the thirties—but even these reports were so vague as to be almost meaningless. If labor and capital, admonished this committee, purged greed and hatred from their hearts, all would be well. The denominational journal, the *Lutheran*, was not blatantly hostile to labor. In truth, a number of editorials indicated that the workingman should be adequately paid and treated fairly with regard to hours and conditions of work. But that was about the extent of the encouragement given to labor.

X

The Reformed Church in the United States before 1919 had adopted the "Social Creed of the Churches" with its manifold labor reforms. At a special post-war meeting of the General Synod there was talk of the great silent revolution of the "underfed and overworked" who were emerging from the depths to demand recognition, justice, and human rights. In 1926 the General Synod adopted the 1925 Congregational statement on social justice which, it will be remembered, urged many labor reforms. A pronouncement of the Commission on Social Service adopted by the 1932 Synod termed unemployment the product of an unchristian economic order, built upon greed and ruthless competition. Compulsory unemployment, disability, and old age insurance were endorsed.

In 1934 this denomination merged with the Evangelical Synod of North America to form the Evangelical and Reformed Church. Before unification, however, the Evangelical Synod had issued some strong statements on labor matters. Not only did it endorse the "Social Creed of the Churches," but in 1921 the General Conference declared for a living wage, the six-day week, safer and healthier conditions of work, suitable provision for old age, the right of labor to organize and bargain collectively, and, in general, the championship of "personal against property values." In the late twenties the Conference again concerned itself with old age security, minimum wages, and the general status of labor. Labor was not just a commodity to be bought and sold. "Human need, human rights, and human welfare transcend property rights and profits on investments."[19]

A report to the 1936 Synod of the Evangelical and Reformed Church read:

No maudlin sympathy for the poor will do. It [the church] must see the poor as they really are, poor not only because they have nothing but because they pay so high a price for having nothing. It must recognize the liar in the political spell-binder who bemoans the lot of the rich and the middle class because a heavy tax-burden has fallen on them when the poor and unemployed whose wages have been taken from them are the real bearers of the tax-burden. They pay not only in dollars and cents, they pay in life and death.[20]

A second report to this Synod called for a living wage, shorter and safer conditions of work, social security, and the right of labor to organize. However, the *Reformed Church Messenger's* coverage of labor

19. *Reports and Minutes of the General Conference of the Evangelical Synod of North America,* 1929, p. 252.

20. *Acts and Proceedings of the General Synod of the Evangelical and Reformed Church,* 1936, p. 248.

questions was rather thin and can best be described as middle-of-the-road in attitude.

XI

From time to time other denominations spoke on labor problems. For instance, the United Brethren, Friends, and Universalists issued notable statements. But the time has now come to leave the denominational record and turn to an examination of certain undenominational papers, organizations, and agencies.

CHAPTER XVI

The Condition and Status of
the Worker: II

"Jesus was not crucified for saying, 'Consider the lilies of the field, how they grow'; what got Him into trouble was saying, 'Consider the thieves of the temple, how they steal.'"—Halford E. Luccock

I

THE PURPOSE of this chapter is to discover to what extent, if any, undenominational papers, organizations, and individual clergymen were concerned with the condition and status of the worker.

II

The *Christian Century,* edited by Charles Clayton Morrison in both decades, was America's leading undenominational journal. Save for a few months following the First World War when labor was charged with irresponsibility, its coverage of labor problems was very full and very sympathetic. This was equally true in the twenties as in the thirties. The labor policies of virtually every major industry fell under harsh criticism. The coal industry was said to be in a state of putrefaction; conditions were as black as the veins of coal. Mine accidents, low wages, chronic unemployment, harsh working and drab living conditions made up the stark facts of life as known by the average miner and his family. Textile hands—North and South—were scarcely better off. Steel-workers continued to suffer even after the end of the twelve-hour day. Judge Gary was an orthodox Christian, believed the editors, but Christ could never have discovered much of the Kingdom of God in one of his mills. Ford's alleged humanitarianism was bunk; his moral pretentions "preposterous." The high wages paid Ford workers, upon analysis, proved to be pretty much of a mirage. His famous short working week was undermined by a "speed-up" system which left his men broken physically. "The fact that Henry Ford has been accepted by the American people at his own evaluation," believed the editors, "is the best proof of the general incompetence of the American mind and conscience for the intricate problems of modern industrial society."[1] Low wages and lay-

1. Nov. 4, 1926, p. 1355.

offs in industry were of course condemned in the Depression Decade, but more significant is the fact that the *Century* condemned these evils in the "prosperous" twenties. Time and again it was shown that labor was not receiving a fair share of America's wealth; that poverty existed in the midst of plenty. Management's use of labor spies, black lists, "yellow dog" contracts, and other devices to break labor were excoriated.

Nor was the desperate plight of millions of tillers of the soil overlooked. Migratory workers, share-croppers, and tenant farmers obviously had a tough row to hoe. Their fate was depicted with sickening realism. The editors also realized the less clear fact that even independent farmers of the Middle West knew the meaning of the word "depression" long before 1929. And after the "crash" they were to know the meaning of the word despair.

Of great relevance is the fact that this journal looked with sympathy upon the organized labor movement. Indeed, when critical of unions it was generally because of their timidity and conservatism. The A.F. of L., for instance, was termed as exclusive, reactionary, super-patriotic, and as fearful of "radicals" as the most conservative elements of the business community. The editors believed that the labor movement was infinitely greater than an organized demand for better wages and shorter hours. It was a fine human movement to lift the toiling millions out of industrial slavery.

The only conclusion that can be drawn from the hundreds of editorials and articles on labor appearing in the *Christian Century* is that this important independent journal was a great and true champion of the workingman.

This conclusion applies with even greater force to the *World Tomorrow*. As a paper representing the view point of Christian socialism, it was inevitable that virtually every issue would agitate for greater economic justice.

Two other important independent journals, the *Christian Work* and the *Christian Herald,* compiled a sanely friendly record toward labor. Conditions of work were exposed, low wages condemned, the "open-shop" movement deplored, and collective bargaining upheld.

III

The National Religion and Labor Foundation was an important interfaith agency. The Foundation had as its objectives the application of Judeo-Christian faith to economic life, the increased cooperation of labor and the churches, the encouragement and support of organized and unorganized labor, the passage of constructive social legislation, cooperation with all democratic movements to build an economy of abundance and security, and the establishment of an economic system which would eliminate the evils of concentrated wealth and restore to the people the riches of the earth which "God in His Providence created for them."

The Foundation sought to achieve these objectives through a varied program. Seminars brought the facts of economic life to "naïve" clergymen. Peripatetic speakers and conferences carried the Foundation's ideals to local communities. Conditions of work in field and factory were investigated, labor and management encouraged to mediate their differences, and, when necessary, strikers were joined on the picket line by Foundation members and strengthened in their protests by Foundation contributions of food, clothing, and money. Branches were established at the grass roots level and its representatives lobbied before Congress and state legislatures for reform legislation. From time to time special pamphlets on economic matters were issued and a regular loan library made available to Foundation members the latest studies on economic questions.

In addition, the group published a monthly bulletin, *Economic Justice,* which carried much sane support of the legitimate demands of labor along with considerable Marxian nonsense. It cannot be stressed too strongly that this organization was militantly aggressive in its determination to aid labor. Certainly as long as it stuck to the road of straight labor reform and did not wander off into the bog of Marxian theory, it was a useful instrument for bringing organized religion and labor closer together.

A second religious organization seeking to preach the gospel to the poor, to heal the broken hearted and give sight to the blind, to set at liberty them that are bruised, and to preach the acceptable year of the Lord, was the Fellowship of Southern Churchmen. In the summer of 1934 a group of parsons, teachers, and labor leaders met at Monteagle, Tennessee to examine the "time of troubles" that had fallen upon the land. Coming from nearly every southern state, this company was determined to free their beloved South from her bondage of poverty and injustice through the redemptive gospel of Christ. Numbered among this little band were James Weldon Johnson, Franz Daniel, Gene Smathers, John Dillingham, Charles Webber, T. B. Cowan, A. L. De Jarnette, James Dombrowski, E. N. Shultz, Herbert King, J. H. Davis, Abram Nightingale, and Howard Kester.

In many respects Reinhold Niebuhr was the spiritual godfather of the Fellowship. He it was who helped the delegates to "delineate truth from fiction, fact from fancy." So eloquent were his exhortations that the group dubbed him "Judgment Day in britches." After two days of deliberation, the men organized themselves into the Conference of Younger Churchmen of the South. They met again in Chattanooga in December of 1934 and adopted a number of justice-seeking resolutions.

Feeling the need for a name which would adequately describe their commitments, the group hit upon the Fellowship of Southern Churchmen. They adopted a Statement of Principles, to be replaced, however, in 1939, which read in part:

2. We reject the idea that the labor of man should be bought and sold as a commodity, a pawn in the hands of exploiters, since it violates the rights of men and women to participate as responsible personalities in the organization of their economic life and moreover relegates them to a status practically identical with that of the machine in present society. In the belief that human values are more important than property values we seek to supplant an economic system motivated by profit with one motivated by service.[2]

Unlike some self-styled "friends of labor" who gave witness to their friendship only through cocktail-inspired platitudes about the "noble worker" and the "vicious capitalist," the members of this Fellowship worked at the grass roots level, often at the sacrifice of sweat and tears. De Jarnette, a Congregational minister, organized the unemployed and spoke frequently to various struggling labor groups. Cowan in Chattanooga fed the hungry, clothed the needy, and preached the love and wrath of God from pulpit, hall, and cockpit. "Buck" Kester roamed the southern states organizing farmers, the unemployed, and industrial workers, investigating lynchings and strikes, and writing and speaking in colleges and seminaries. Eugene Smathers, Presbyterian, created a model cooperative farm community on the Cumberland Plateau in East Tennessee. In Mississippi, Sam Franklin and Gene Cox, with the aid of Sherwood Eddy, built a cooperative farming experiment.

Of equal importance was the work done in southern classrooms. Here a great band of liberal teachers in seminaries stirred the youth of the South with the vision of a finer, fairer world.

But these men paid the price of their convictions. Cowan reported the annual Fellowship conference at his church cost him twenty-two subtractions from the rolls. Taylor's "radicalism," it is alleged, cost him his position at Vanderbilt. Others paid with tired muscles, taut nerves, money, and social prestige. Some were flogged.

The Fellowship worked in cooperation with the Southern Tenant Farmers' Union—a desperate and dangerous attempt to organize the disinherited whites and blacks of the southern soil. It is not without significance that fourteen of the Union's executive committee were ministers.

2. *Information Service*, Jan., 1938, p. 4.

It was five members of the Fellowship—Smathers, Cowan, De Jarnette, Sikes, and Kester—who founded the Friends of the Soil. This group proclaimed the sacred trinity of God, man, and the earth. Their purpose was to lead men to regard the earth as holy and to cultivate a reverence toward the soil, to strengthen and fortify the rural church, to declare a just relationship between man and man, to strive for a more abundant life for those who till the soil, to combat the monopoly of the land by the few at the expense of the many, to seek the preservation of the landed heritage, and to work for the realization of these goals through effective legislation, education, and the organization of local groups, especially through the churches.

The Fellowship of Southern Churchmen and its smaller offshoot, the Friends of the Soil, inspire the greatest respect. True, some of the members fell under the golden smog of extreme radicalism, but these gloomy aberrations must not obscure the truly prophetic character of the membership. Whether in cotton field or conference, pulpit or picket line, work camp or classroom, by word, pen, and deed, this tiny group of southern churchmen sought to bring the Kingdom of God to both blacks and whites in the South. Drawing inspiration from the Book of Jeremiah, the Fellowship and the Friends belong in that company of indigenous American protestants dating back to the Populists, the Regulators, and the followers of Shays.

Deeply but less directly concerned with labor questions was the Fellowship of Socialist Christians. Formed in 1931 and embracing such great names in American Protestantism as Reinhold Niebuhr, John C. Bennett, and Buell G. Gallagher, this group worked for the replacement of capitalism by a Socialist order. The Fellowship believed that the workers of the world, who suffer most from the injustices of the present system, have a peculiar mission to be the instruments and heralds of this new society. The Fellowship sought to associate itself with the cause of labor by protesting unjust labor conditions, joining or supporting labor unions, and financing labor churches. It aided strikers, shared speakerships with union leaders, and trained religious leaders in labor's cause.

Much the same observation can be made concerning the United Christian Council for Democracy. Formed in 1936, led by such men as Niebuhr, Ward, Kester, and Spofford, the UCCD was a federation of unofficial liberal church agencies. It too repudiated capitalism. It too cooperated with labor and backed its demands to the hilt.

The Fellowship of Reconciliation, formed in England during the First World War, was composed of men and women of many nations and races who recognized the unity of the world-wide family and who believed in an approach to life that substituted reconciliation and good will for retaliation and violence. In America, clergymen comprised much of the band's membership. The Fellowship was dedicated to the establishment of a social order which will suffer no individual or group to be exploited for the profit or pleasure of another, and which will assure to all the means of realizing the best possibilities of life. This being so, it did much in the field of labor: supporting remedial legislation, backing the attempts of labor to organize, and investigating conditions of work. In truth, Fellowship members frequently could be found on the picket line.

More militant was the Christian Social Action Movement, formed in 1932 and guided by such men as Paul Hutchinson, Gilbert Cox, Owen Greer, W. B. Waltmire, J. Sitt Wilson, Clarence Craig Tucker, and James M. Yard. The members were to aid labor in every possible way, including leadership in picketing and labor demonstrations.

An earlier group was the Fellowship for a Christian Social Order. Formed in 1922 and including most of the leading liberal ministers of the period, this group viewed the aims of labor with sympathy and gave workingmen support, albeit largely of a moral nature.

The Ministers' Union of America was organized in 1931 by a few liberal clergymen called together by the Reverend Edmund B. Chaffee. These men believed that the ministry needed an organization modeled on the lines of a trade union in order to carry on a more effective program of cooperation with organized labor. Although never large—only a hundred members or so coming mostly from the New York area—the Union made up in determination what it lacked in size. In strike situations its members joined the picket line, addressed meetings, and secured aid. On several occasions these picketing parsons were beaten and imprisoned. The Union officially engaged in labor parades and demonstrations, conducted a campaign to have the churches support the use of the union label, defended ministers persecuted for their radicalism, and sought to affiliate with the A.F. of L.

There emerged also in the teeth of the depression a new order in Cambridge, Massachusetts. Claiming their spirit was akin to that of St. Francis, the members placed themselves under vows of poverty and obedience, together with a rule entailing purity, but not necessarily celibacy. Their purpose was to lead strike lines in the "place of danger," thus shielding the workers while at the same time their religious habit protected their own heads. A second purpose was to preach radical religion as guest speakers in pulpits where the regular minister would not dare to do so.

IV

There remains the final, almost impossible task of assessing the attitudes of individual clergymen. Certainly many ministers were supremely indifferent to the plight of the workingman. There is no doubt that thousands of ministers ignored labor's legitimate grievances. This fact has been attested to by historians, sociologists, labor leaders, and churchmen themselves.

On the other hand, a rather prodigious number of churchmen attempted to aid the workingman. A few actually left the ministry to enter actively into labor work, some of them attaining important union posts. To cite a few examples, there were A. J. Muste, Paul Blanchard, Charles Webber, Francis Henson, A. A. Heist, Homer Martin, William Fincke, Harold Rotzel, Albert Coyle, Claude Williams, Howard Williams, Claude Nelson, and Cedric Long. The list could be extended, and when coupled with those churchmen who forsook the pulpit for active work in liberal politics, the number becomes quite formidable.

Also large in number were the statements friendly to labor coming from men who remained in the ministry. In 1927, for example, forty-one southern church leaders, including ten bishops, issued an "Appeal to Industrial Leaders of the South." It was a very vigorous indictment of southern working conditions, especially in textile mills. A storm of abuse was unleashed upon the heads of the churchmen, but they stuck by their guns. It was interesting to find Bishop James Cannon, Jr., favorite whipping-boy of the so-called liberal press, eloquently defending the "Appeal" and refusing to retreat an inch.

Southern churchmen also comprised over half the total membership of the Committee for the Defense of Southern Share Croppers, formed in 1934. Fosdick, Ward, Jerome Davis, and Alva W. Taylor were on the national committee of the Committee on Labor Injunctions, a group having as its purpose the protection of labor from sweeping court orders. In 1937 the American Association for Economic Freedom began its work to assist in the further democratization of American economic institutions. McConnell, Shipler, Herring, and James Myers comprised part of its officership.

In Denver, the Grace Community Church, directed first by George Lackland and A. A. Heist, was definitely orientated toward labor. It sponsored forums, conducted investigations, housed a labor school, and cooperated closely with unions. In 1934 Bishops Brewster, Gilbert, and McConnell and the Reverends Spofford, Niebuhr, and Cadman urged in a memorial to President Roosevelt the immediate and complete outlawing of company unions. The following year three hundred clergymen petitioned the United States Senate to investigate civil liberties violations in labor disputes. Seventeen churchmen in 1932 urged a study of the economic conditions facing American farmers.

The Brookwood Labor College, the League for Industrial Democracy, the International Labor Defense, the Labor Defense Council, the Worker's Defense League, the Social Security Association, the Conference for Progressive Labor Action, and the American Association for Labor Legislation were some of the many other groups designed to aid labor in which clergymen often played a significant role.

From time to time ministers opened their churches and offered their pulpits to union leaders. Here a group of ministers attended a union convention and there a similar group met to endorse reform legislation. Other churchmen wrote books and pamphlets, signed petitions, contributed funds, delivered sermons, all to the end that the workingman might receive a "square deal." Some parsons joined unions, helped in the organization of workers, and even entered the picket line.

To cite chapter and verse for all of these instances is not possible here. Nor would it be wise to attempt to list all the churchmen who actively sided with labor. Suffice it to say that a host of clergymen, many of them nationally famous, publicly associated themselves with the workingman in his fight for a more abundant life. An examination of several polls makes this point clearer.

A poll of some twenty thousand ministers in 1934 revealed 63 per cent favored and 13 per cent opposed (the rest being in doubt) a system of compulsory unemployment insurance under government supervision. Similarly, 54 per cent favored and 12 per cent opposed (the rest being in doubt) national unions instead of local company unions.

A year later 4,700 churchmen replied to a National Religion and Labor Foundation poll. About 67 per cent pledged themselves to publicly support old age pensions, unemployment insurance, and a child labor amendment. When asked if they would make the acquaintanceship of local labor leaders, 40 per cent replied in the affirmative. Similarly, 32 per cent would entertain union officials in their homes and 21 per cent would invite union leaders to speak in their churches. Twenty-six per cent promised to aid labor organize, and about half agreed to appear before labor boards in an effort to secure the full rights of labor in local situations. About 36 per cent would resist attempts to substitute company unions for "genuine" workers' unions. In every instance, however, a much smaller number had *already taken these steps!*

Earlier this organization sent a letter to sixty-six city and state church federations soliciting the names of individual pastors within their jurisdiction who had been active in making their religion meaningful in the field of labor. Twenty-one replies were received giving the names of ninety preachers who came within the requested category.

A poll of 32,580 Congregationalists found well over a majority favoring national labor unions. The *Christian Herald* discovered that of sixty thousand Protestants, almost 97 per cent favored the principle of pensions for the aged. It is a commentary on the reliability of polls that 93.5 per cent favored the *Townsend Plan!*

V

Before drawing any conclusions regarding the attitude of the churches toward labor it is necessary to examine the very important question of strikes. This will be the burden of the following chapters.

CHAPTER XVII

Post-War Strikes

"There is no right to strike against the public safety by anybody, any time, anywhere!"—Calvin Coolidge

I

MR. DOOLEY once observed that "among men, Hinnissy, wet eye manes dhry heart." This dictum is applicable to some churchmen. Certain it is that a number of clergymen who cried over unchristian conditions of work suddenly displayed remarkably dry hearts when labor struck in protest against the very conditions that in theory these ministers deplored. Perhaps this paradoxical attitude was inevitable. True, the churches preached the full life for all and adopted a remarkable number of resolutions favoring economic justice. But they also preached peace and good will among men. How then could they endorse strikes which were inevitably accompanied by hatred and perhaps violence and bloodshed? Did not strikes represent the very antithesis of all that Christ taught? Would the Carpenter of Nazareth have joined the picket line, mobbed "scabs," destroyed property, and shouted bloody hatred of the employers? Did not even the most peaceful of strikes mark the failure of Christian love to resolve disputes between man and man? Was not the only true solution to the workers' grievances in filling the hearts of all with a spirit of brotherhood and Christian charity, and not in coercion?

Labor, hardened by experience, believed that management would meet its demands only when faced with a strike or the threat of a strike. Here was labor's classic weapon and here, in the opinion of the workingman, was an acid test of the churches' claim to be labor's friend. Sweet reasonableness had to be buttressed with coercion to impress upon management the wisdom of fair wages, shorter hours, and other reforms. To be sure, the churches could not be expected to justify every strike. In many cases labor's requests were excessive and illegitimate. Some strikes were simply the result of jurisdictional war between rival unions and had nothing to do with the betterment of the rank and file worker. Often the employer simply could not pay higher wages if he was to survive the competition of other firms. In still other instances, strikes were incited and led by Communists with the sole purpose of disrupting production and inflaming class hatred.

But having made these admissions, if the churches sided with management in all strikes, then the workingman could justly charge American Protestantism with insincerity. It was not enough for the churches to endorse reforms if they then condemned labor for striking in order to make these reforms a reality. They could not emulate Bunyan's Mr. Facing-Both-Ways and still win labor's respect. And so an examination of the churches' attitude toward strikes is crucial to a true understanding of their attitude toward labor in general.

II

As it happened, the very year in which this study begins, 1919, was a year of intense labor unrest. If the Western Front was now quiet, the industrial front in America erupted in a succession of strikes so numerous, so vast in scope, and so bitter in their conduct as to dangerously threaten the whole process of national reconversion to peace. The fact is, the armistice brought war, not peace to the American labor scene. Labor was determined to maintain its wartime wages, particularly since the cost of living continued to soar. Management, on the other hand, naturally wanted to retreat to "normalcy," that is, 1914 wages.

Even more crucial was labor's conviction that since America had fought to save the world for democracy, more democracy in business was in order. This meant, of course, an extension of unionization and collective bargaining. Management countered with the charge that labor's idea of democracy meant only "mobocracy" and that, to put it bluntly, management should manage and workers should work. Complicating any honest and peaceful settlement of the legitimate differences between labor and management was the hysteria over communism. Why all this labor unrest? "Red" agitation! Who were these labor leaders? Wild-eyed Bolsheviks! Was labor underpaid and overworked? Russian propaganda! Samuel Gompers and most workers were as super-patriotic as a senator at a Fourth of July picnic during an election year, but fanatics threw enough bombs, management unleashed enough propaganda, and enough workers embraced radical doctrines to wreck any chance of labor's retaining the confidence of the public. It was in this atmosphere that labor launched 3,630 strikes involving over four million workers.

III

As Steel goes so goes the nation, and hence the most basic, dangerous, and far-reaching strike in post-war America occurred in that industry. The country is lost if the strikers win, moaned the editors of the *Presbyterian Banner*. Here was not simply a strike, but a revolt—a conflict "between the American employes and the foreigners who would unionize in order to enslave American citizens." These agitators deserve no sympathy. "It is astonishing how some men, who should know better," continued the editors, "confuse counsel by talking about constitutional rights and the freedom of speech."[1] The *Herald and Presbyter* expressed an almost identical opinion, while the Reverend H. H. Marlin suffered near-apoplexy at the work of the striking "Reds." Even the rather liberal *Continent* talked of "Reds" and liquor behind the strike. The *Presbyterian Advance* averred the steelworkers were handsomely paid and that the only reason they lived in squalor was in order to save their money and return to their native lands as "capitalists."

The *Alabama Baptist* accused foreign radicals of leading faithful American workers astray, and a Baptist leader spoke in this fashion:

This tribe cannot be satisfied even with better pay and shorter hours, and nothing less than the destruction of the American government will gratify their diabolical ambition. They are anarchists at heart and Bolshevists in practice. They have wrought ruin in their own land and are attempting to repeat in our land their destructive deviltry. They are enemies of God and man and short shift should be made of this Bolshevistic band. Our people are ever ready to listen sympathetically to the grievances of the honest American workman, but they will not listen to the ravings of the Bolshevistic beast.[2]

Even Methodists viewed the strike as through a glass darkly. Its revolutionary aim, believed the *Arkansas Methodist,* was to seize control of government as well as industry. One church leader cited the strike as an example of bolshevism, while the *Nashville Christian Advocate* painted a glowing picture of the happy conditions that prevailed in the mills, concluding that the strike was a grab for power on the part of "Reds."

A Congregational spokesman held the demands of the strikers excessive, and a Disciples leader declared that those who believed in the Constitution could not possibly support the strikers The *Lutheran* upheld Judge Gary's firm stand and counseled labor to practice self-denial, temperance, economy, and faithfulness. The *Reformed Church Messenger* termed the strike leaders "Reds" whose real object was revolution, while a Unitarian spokesman chided labor for following radical leaders. The *Christian Work* was almost completely sympathetic to management, conceding only one legitimate grievance to labor: the long hours of work. Even the *Christian Century* talked much about irresponsible, greedy unions and light-hearted, gay strikers. As editor Morrison saw it, labor could better afford to endure injustice with honor than to win an

1. Sept. 25, 1919, p. 3.
2. *Western Recorder,* Oct. 30, 1919, p. 8.

industrial paradise at the cost of its own moral character. Indeed, only a handful of expressions friendly to the strikers appeared in the religious press.

It has been noted already, however, that American Protestantism fully entered the steel controversy through the Commission of Inquiry of the Interchurch World Movement. Its findings were presented in two memorable volumes: *Report on the Steel Strike of 1919* and *Public Opinion and the Steel Strike*. The conclusions of these volumes may be summed up in one sentence: most of the grievances suffered by the workers were real, most of their demands just, and the strike failed only because management, using unscrupulous tactics, convinced the public that the strike was a bolshevist plot.

The second of these reports contained an interesting analysis of the attitude of the churches in Allegheny County, the heart of the Pittsburgh district, toward the strike. Although the secular press played up sermons hostile to the strikers, many Protestant clergymen in the area expressed sympathy toward them. A poll revealed that, in theory at any rate, a number of ministers believed that labor had just complaints and that it had the right to organize in the mills. The Pittsburgh Council of Churches initiated an investigation of the strike in the fall, but when the Interchurch Commission entered the scene the local group decided to cooperate rather than to conduct a separate study. On the whole, the Pittsburgh churches had a record that was certainly no more hostile toward the strikers than public opinion in the country generally.

It is not without significance, also, that the Social Service Commission of the Federal Council publicly appealed to the governor of Pennsylvania to restore the rights of free speech and assembly—rights that had been crushed as part of management's campaign to end the strike.

These exceptions coupled with the stand of a few groups such as the Methodist Federation for Social Service and of a few papers such as *World Tomorrow*—and the fact that many ministers were later to reverse their attitudes—cannot obscure the obvious conclusion that the churches during the Great Steel Strike of 1919 hardly ranked as labor's friend.

Although this was the most far-reaching strike of the post-war period, it was only one of several thousand. Early in 1919 the strike mania got off to an unfortunate start with the Seattle General Strike. The church press reflected the angry mood of the nation. The *Homiletic Review* spoke of the "cold-blooded criminality" of the strikers. "The overthrow of the Bolsheviki . . . in Seattle is a matter of profound thanksgiving," commented another journal.[3] The *Presbyterian Advance* believed it was more than a strike; it was attempted revolution. The strike

3. *Herald and Presbyter*, Feb. 19, 1919, p. 5.

was a grand lesson to the bolshevist, said one minister. "He shall know that true Americans are going to rule this land and not Russian madmen, and men whose sole aim is lust and loot."[4] That is the way to treat strikers—no more "mush and milk dealings," cried the *New Era Magazine*. A Presbyterian spokesman found at least one bright aspect to the whole affair. There was no violence, no rioting, no lives lost. "The reason—no saloons in Seattle, no liquor drunk during the crisis."[5] Truth to tell, with a few exceptions, there simply was not much support for the strike in church quarters.

Seven months and 2500 miles separated the Seattle General Strike from the Boston Police Strike, but the two had much in common. Both sent a thrill of horror through the nation; both placed a relatively obscure politician in the public spotlight. Not since the Tea Party days had Boston enjoyed so much excitement as when her policemen walked out on strike. There was some looting and rioting and forty men were arrested for shooting craps on the Common, but the newspapers exaggerated out of all proportion the extent of lawlessness. Harvard students promptly offered their services to the terrified (but hardly *that* terrified) populace. With somewhat less alacrity, Governor Calvin Coolidge, as William Allen White observed, looked at the traffic each way, sized up the speed and tensity of events before him, and finally made the pronouncement concerning strikes and public safety which was to place him in the vice-presidency.

American Protestantism, as all of the nation, appeared virtually united in its opposition to the strikers. The pulpits of Boston rang with angry outcries. The *Churchman* termed the strike an act of mutiny, and a second Episcopal journal echoed this sentiment. The Methodist press stood for law and order which, in this instance, meant opposition to the police. Shall the guardians of public order place class above community, wondered a Congregational leader. The *Presbyterian Advance* believed the strike "the nearest approach to Bolshevism which we have had in this country."[6] Other Presbyterian papers said much the same thing. A Disciples journal termed the situation in Boston civic treason. Immoral madness was the phrase used by the *Lutheran*. The United States, opined a Unitarian, has had a glimpse of the Huns and Vandals at work. Many church voices praised Coolidge for his firm (if belated) stand. "Boston is Armageddon for the nation," cried a Baptist editor.[7] Perhaps a Kentucky Baptist leader had the most interesting explanation for the strike: "The truth is . . . a majority of our policemen cannot be relied

4. *United Presbyterian*, Feb. 13, 1919, p. 8.
5. *Continent*, March 13, 1919, p. 297.   6. Sept. 18, 1919, p. 5.
7. *Watchman-Examiner*, Sept. 18, 1919, p. 1315.

upon either for their Americanism or their integrity. A large number of them are raw recruits from riotous Ireland, who love our liquor much better than our laws."[8]

Hard upon the heels of the Boston Police Strike came tension in the bituminous coal fields. In contrast to the Boston trouble, about a third of the church journals in the country sympathized with the miners and indicated that perhaps the strike was justified. Further, the Social Service Commission of the Federal Council, after a careful study of the strike, issued the following statement:

The miners unquestionably have a real grievance and yet they were powerless to make their demands effective save through a strike. If the strike cannot be tolerated because the strength of those who use it has become so great as to constitute a public peril, then the Government must find a way to secure its workers against exploitation, to guarantee an adequate hearing of demands, and to secure wages and hours of work that will make possible **an American** standard of living.[9]

These are some of the more important strikes of the post-war era. There were others. For instance, in 1920 the Denver tramway strike involved the loss of seven lives and engendered a wave of bitterness. In this instance the churches of Denver—Protestant, Catholic, and Jewish— played a crucial role. Representatives of forty churches met to discuss the strike and proceeded to elect a commission to further investigate the trouble. After ascertaining the grievances of the workers, the Denver churches invited the Federal Council and a Catholic agency to conduct a deeper probe. The following report, while not completely exonerating the strikers, passed harsh judgment on the company for its brutal labor policies and for its illegitimate methods of combating the strike. A storm of criticism was unleashed against the churches for interfering in "secular" matters, and several Denver clergymen were denounced by the governor. In many quarters, however, the report was praised for its fairness.

The 1919 Lawrence textile strike, a bloody, violent struggle, was also significant because of the role played by clergymen in its settlement. Three ministers, A. J. Muste, Harold L. Rotzel, and Cedric Long, showed up at the strike headquarters, and the gaunt, raw-boned "Fool-for-Christ" Muste was elected chairman of the strike committee. He won for the workers and thus began an association with labor unparalleled by that of any other cleric.

It was in this strike, also, that the State Conference of Congregational Churches of Massachusetts selected Dean Charles R. Brown of the Yale

8. *Western Recorder*, Oct. 2, 1919, p. 8.
9. *Federal Council Bulletin*, Jan., 1920, p. 14.

Divinity School to investigate conditions. His report, adopted by the conference after heated debate, vindicated the workers and severely criticized the mill owners. It was printed at the conference's expense and given wide circulation, and this perhaps explains why a number of church journals carried accounts of the strike very favorable to the workers. The Federal Council also issued a pamphlet on the strike.

Scores of other examples might be cited of the attitude of the churches toward strikes in the post-war period. On the whole, it is not a happy record. The churches in their insistence on peace probably liked to think of themselves as being neutral. But by failing to recognize that labor might, on occasion, be driven to the use of coercion, the churches played into the hands of management. And so in speaking of the years 1919-20, labor was probably justified in accusing the churches of failing to apply their manifestations of sympathy to specific strike situations.

CHAPTER XVIII

Prosperity Decade Strikes

"After God had finished the rattlesnake, the toad and the vampire, He had some awful substance left with which He made a SCAB."—Jack London

I

INDUSTRIAL conflict was much diminished during the Prosperity Decade, particularly after 1922. The annual average of strikes was only a small fraction of the immediate post-war years. By the end of the decade hardly more than 1 per cent of the aggregate labor force was involved in only eight hundred strikes annually.

Labor's docility is explainable. Annual earnings rose between 1921 and 1928 from an average of $1,171 to $1,405. In terms of actual purchasing power this meant a gain of more than 20 per cent. Company unions, company welfare plans, public antipathy, hostile courts, and the full dinner pail all combined to sap the strength of organized labor until by 1929 unions could claim a membership of only 3,440,000 in contrast to over 5,000,000 in 1920. And without adequate organization, strikes are doomed from the start. But there were important exceptions to the general prosperity of the workingman, and here occurred strikes almost unparalleled in their intensity and violence.

II

Trouble was the word for textiles even in the "decade of wonderful nonsense." Starting in the hard pressed mills of New England, unrest fanned southward to the Middle Atlantic states and finally by the end of the twenties the Southern Piedmont was aflame.

The year 1922 saw a series of textile strikes in New England. In one instance, the Manchester, New Hampshire, ministerial association met and appointed a strike committee. The association addressed an invitation to all parties concerned to meet for a conference, looking toward some possibility of arbitration. Although the offer was not accepted by management, the ministers proceeded to issue a statement calling for a fair settlement.

A strike in Lawrence, Massachusetts, in 1922 found several church leaders backing the strikers, notably the Reverend D. H. G. Gerrish, Methodist. Methodist and Congregational journals and church leaders, including Jerome Davis, placed themselves on labor's side in the strike. *Information Service* believed the real issue in these textile strikes was whether industry should pay a living wage or a starvation wage.

A year later, in Buffalo, New York, the Reverend Alfred S. Priddis addressed a group of five hundred striking clothing workers. He lauded their heroism, self-sacrifice, and idealism. "Necessity, common sense, justice and Christian teaching," he believed, "are on the side of those who fight for collective bargaining."[1] A strike of silk workers in Paterson, New Jersey, in 1925 brought the Reverend William Spofford of the Episcopal Church League for Industrial Democracy to the scene. In cooperation with two local pastors, Dr. Scudder and Dr. Hamilton, he successfully mediated the dispute.

The 1926 strike of textile workers in Passaic and the adjoining towns of Clifton, Garfield, and Lodi, New Jersey, involved over fifteen thousand workers and lasted a year. From many aspects it was one of the most crucial upheavals of the decade. The strike organizer, Albert Weisbord, was a Communist and he brought to the leadership of the strike all the fanaticism, efficiency, and violent tactics that his faith engendered. Another party man, Benjamin Gitlow, takes the credit for starting the affair in the first place.

The important role played by Communists in the strike, however, must not obscure the fact that only a small number of the workers themselves were Communists, and that low wages, long hours, night work for women, the "stretch-out" system, and labor spies actually existed. Here, as so often in recent history, the Communists capitalized on unjust conditions and provided leadership to disunited but genuinely dissatisfied workers. True, in championing the workers the Communist party had as its real goal the advancement of the party, but in the Passaic strike the Communists found themselves (inadvertently and temporarily) fighting the battle of industrial democracy.

What was the position of the churches toward the warfare in Passaic? Norman Thomas, ordained Presbyterian minister who forsook the pulpit to inherit Gene Debs's mantle as America's leading Socialist, told a group of Presbyterian ministers gathered in Passaic that the strike proved Protestant ministers were hypocrites who might mouth the Golden Rule but who were actually boot-licking lackies of labor-sweating employers. The accusation is a little unfair. Protestant parsons, who ministered to only a few of the strikers, most of whom were foreign-born from southern and eastern Europe, were not indifferent; they were bewildered and confused. Generally, they recognized that injustices existed in the mills, but their fear of the imported "Red" strike leaders

1. *Churchman*, July 14, 1923, p. 21.

was so great that they could not give wholehearted support to the workers.

For example, a local Methodist group called for the establishment of an American standard of living, but also condemned the importation of "un-American" labor leaders. The Reverend George H. Talbott, minister of the First Presbyterian Church of Passaic, and president of the local ministerial association, was deeply concerned. Hoping that the clergy might arbitrate the dispute, the Reverend Mr. Talbott listened to the arguments of both management and the strikers. He dug deeply, holding over 115 interviews. In the seventh week of the strike, Talbott and other clergymen met with Weisbord at strike headquarters. It was an unfortunate meeting. The naïveté of the parsons nettled Weisbord and his extreme radicalism angered the churchmen, so much so that Talbott walked out. The thirteen ministers who remained voted to approach the mill owners for a settlement, but their efforts were ignored by management. The Reverend Mr. Talbott made his position clear in a speech at the Y.M.C.A. in which he indicted the cruel labor policies of the mill owners. He concluded, however, with an equally severe criticism of those Communist leaders who had as their aim the overthrow of existing American institutions.

In the seventeenth week of the strike a group of ministers, mostly, however, priests of the workers' churches—Polish, Slavic, Hungarian, Russian, and Italian—endorsed the strikers' demands and sent a committee to Washington to press for a Senate investigation of conditions in Passaic. On the other hand, a short time later a petition was signed by leading citizens, including some churchmen, which demanded the elimination of the imported Communist agitators who were deluding the workers with false promises.

In the meantime, the Federal Council of Churches, under the prodding of the secretaries of the Board of National Missions of the Presbyterian Church, the Department of Social Relations of the Congregational Church, the Methodist Federation for Social Service, the Board of Social Service of the Diocese of New Jersey of the Protestant Episcopal Church, and the executive secretary of the Department of Social Service of the Protestant Episcopal Church, offered to help in any way possible toward mediation. Although the local ministerial association was cool to the proposal, a conference was held on July 23 under the auspices of the Federal Council, and out of it grew the decision to investigate the strike more thoroughly.

To repeat, most of the Protestant ministers of Passaic were confused and vainly attempted to remain neutral. Here and there individuals conceived of Christianity as revolutionary in character. One such minister was the Reverend Theodore Andrews of St. George's Episcopal Church. Another was the colorful preacher, William Simpson, who unexpectedly and quite suddenly stood up in a fashionable Presbyterian church and called the congregation to judgment for the shameful mill conditions. He was promptly ejected by the ushers. The Reverend Norman W. Pendleton, a Congregational minister, declared in a sermon that the action of the police toward the strikers was unnecessarily brutal, and that if any group of ministers or businessmen had been meted out such treatment there would have been something done. The Reverend John Haynes Holmes was active in upholding the civil liberties of the strikers. The Church League for Industrial Democracy, through its secretary, "Bill" Spofford, studied the situation and cast its lot with the strikers. The Methodist Federation for Social Service also gave moral and material aid to the workers.

A portion of the church press also sympathized with the strikers. The *Christian Century,* for instance, devoted an entire issue to the strike. Although the actual manuscript was prepared in its editorial office, the research had been conducted by Miss Winifred L. Chappell of the Methodist Federation. Considering the sympathies of both Miss Chappell and the magazine, it was inevitable that the study would be highly favorable to the strikers. The *Congregationalist* admitted that the workers had real grievances and flayed the brutality of the police. Episcopal, Presbyterian, and Baptist journals all related the frightful working conditions that brought on the strike and the cruel methods used to break it. *Zion's Herald* urged funds and clothing be sent to aid the families of the workers, and the *New York Christian Advocate* had this to say:

It is not a local matter that in Passaic, New Jersey, in the course of a textile strike, the local police have revived the old Russian outdoor sport of clubbing the people. The attack of the police on the strikers, who were assembled in orderly and legal fashion, clubbing them over the heads, running them down, turning water upon them, is a matter to which the whole country must pay attention. The police did not act as guardians of the law but as partisans of the employers. It is hard to see where the part that they played differed from that of the thugs, frequently hired by lawless employers to "beat up" strikers.[2]

The issues in the Passaic strike were so complex, involving as they did downtrodden workers, arbitrary employers, and militant Communists, that it is small wonder that the Protestant churches were not united in their attitudes. But they were not indifferent. And some clergymen, at least, kept their perspective and did not permit their detestation of communism to blind them to the real injustices suffered by the workers.

2. March 25, 1926, p. 358.

The Passaic strike, in some respects, was repeated in the New Bedford textile strike of 1928. Once again the rupture came because of a sudden and arbitrary wage cut which seemed the final straw to workers already surfeited with legitimate grievances. Once again a prolonged strike of thousands paralyzed not only a city, but also an area. And once again Weisbord and his Communist lieutenants came to the scene to capitalize on the unrest and to confuse issues and to win the workers away from the old-line conservative unions.

The New Bedford Council of Churches, under the leadership of its secretary, John M. Trout, faced the strike squarely. It called into the community for consultation representatives of the Federal Council and of denominational agencies. Conferences looking toward a peaceful compromise were held with management and labor. The New Bedford church group made large use of the press which published sermons and articles. It held public meetings. It first approached the state board of conciliation and arbitration, which later came into the community and held hearings. It continually urged arbitration. The New Bedford Council of Churches did not become partisans of the strikers; throughout its attitude was that of an active neutral seeking to save all belligerents from their own blindness and folly. The council attempted to deal with the fundamental questions involved in the strike and judge them in the light of deliverances by the churches on social and industrial issues and by fair interpretations of Christian principles.

One Methodist preacher refused to take his vacation while the town was in distress. An Episcopal parson turned down a call from another community because he did not wish to desert his congregation in their time of trouble. The Reverend F. W. Knickrehm drafted a statement in which the strike was termed an example of capitalism's failure to provide economic justice. The Reverend Linden H. White was offered a bribe to help break the strike. Indignantly refusing to become a "scab," he gave the story to the local press.

The "Social Creed of the Churches" was read from many pulpits, its application to the justice of the strike being obvious. The Reverend John Calder, a Federal Council representative, told a group of New Bedford ministers: "Your own dispute seems to me to be lacking in a quality of manners on the part of the employers which no weight of economic right can justify and which workers rightly resent. 'The Mills have spoken' is not an answer. It is a brusque assertion of a superiority complex of which employers must rid themselves."[3] A Unitarian minister termed the autocratic control of management over the lives of the workers a relic of an earlier, brutal stage of industry.

3. *Congregationalist*, June 28, 1928, p, 823.

Sympathy with the strikers, of course, was not universal. Two women organizers were ousted from the local Y.W.C.A. where they had been boarding. Some ministers remained aloof and unconcerned, one of them terming the wage cut unimportant as it was his experience that people in financial difficulties "economized on their church last of all."

The church press appeared concerned with New Bedford. The editors of *Zion's Herald* were not impressed with the charge that "outsiders in the pay of Moscow" were behind the unrest. "If half the tales," read the editorial, "that reiterate 'in the pay of Moscow' were true, the world today would be bankrupt. For not all the assets of all the nations of earth could possibly finance fifty per cent of the revolutionary enterprises attributed to Russia."[4] A second Methodist journal presented a deeply moving account of how the average textile worker's family suffered from low wages, and asked the reader if he, faced with such a condition, would not also strike. The Methodist Federation for Social Service devoted two issues of its *Bulletin* to defending the strikers. Two Congregational publications carried accounts of the dispute favorable to the workers. A Unitarian journal editorially supported the strike and also carried an article written by three New Bedford ministers which was equally sympathetic to the workers. *Information Service* devoted an entire issue to the event. Independent papers such as the *World Tomorrow* and the *Christian Century* leveled their sights on the mill owners. The strike, averred editor Morrison, is an example of "muddleheaded" industrial policy indicating that New Bedford was still in the "dark ages" of industrial despotism.

Passaic and New Bedford were tragic chapters in the history of American labor, but they were soon to be overshadowed by events in the southern textile industry. Gastonia! Marion! Elizabethton! The historian who speaks of a blissfully happy America in the Golden Twenties must first reckon with these names. It was in 1929 that the supposedly docile "lint-heads" of the Carolinas and Tennessee rose in revolt. For "revolt" is the only word to properly describe the textile strikes of that year as kidnappings, floggings, bombings, and murders engulfed mill village after mill village. Low wages, long hours, and the "stretch-out" system left the southern textile industry as primed for conflagration as a parched forest after a rain-free summer. The match was dropped when the workers attempted to organize—and at least some of the organizers were Communists. Before the strikes ended both management and labor paid heavily in blood and money. In the end the beaten strikers (those that lived), gutted and broken, returned to their machines on the owners'

4. Aug. 8, 1928, p. 1036.

terms while some of the leaders languished in prison or, as in the case of Fred Beal, fled to Russia.

The evidence is overwhelming that the local clergy were almost without exception unsympathetic to the strikes. Textile village parsons rarely found anything to criticize in mill conditions. Believing as they did, it was almost inevitable that they should view the strikes with hostility. Besides, strikes were accompanied by hate and violence and thus were doubly deplorable.

Liston Pope has said about all that needs to be said concerning Gastonia. There the issue of communism was strong and there the local churches clearly allied themselves with management. None of the local religious associations or organizations adopted any resolutions or engaged in any institutional action with regard to the strike. But the attitude was not simply one of quiescence. By their failure to protest conditions of work that caused the strike and by their willingness to condone police brutality to break the strike, the ministers placed themselves actively in management's camp. A Federal Council representative said the attitudes revealed by the Gastonia clergy were defensive, cold, unresponsive to a degree he had never met before in a group of ministers.

In Marion, North Carolina, and Elizabethton, Tennessee, although the strikes were led by conservative, anti-Communist labor leaders, the local clergy displayed the same temper. No resolutions were passed; no ministers publicly endorsed the strike. A terrible silence prevailed broken only by pro-management statements. Small wonder that the strikers considered the clergy their worst enemy.

Fortunately for the honor of American Protestantism, church groups outside the immediate strike towns displayed a keener sense of industrial justice. All the major denominations in North Carolina, save the Presbyterians and Lutherans, adopted pertinent resolutions concerning the Gastonia strike. Some of the statements were hard hitting. The mill owners were charged with brutal labor policies and with even more ruthless methods of strike breaking. The Synod of the Province of Sewanee of the Protestant Episcopal Church, the Mid-Southern Federation of Liberals, comprised of Unitarians, Universalists, and Congregationalists, the Georgia Baptist Convention, the Greensboro, North Carolina, ministerial association, the North Carolina Universalist Convention, are examples of other southern church groups who interested themselves in the strike. The National Board of the Y.M.C.A. also expressed concern.

The Federal Council of Churches lived up to its reputation for courage and justice by defending the strikers. James Myers, industrial secretary of the Council's Social Service Commission, probed the issues. Speaking at the funeral of a murdered striker, Myers brought a message of sympathy from nation-wide church forces and begged the workers to put aside thoughts of revenge. But he assured them that the churches' endorsed the right of labor to organize and said the mill conditions were inconsistent with a belief in a God of love. So desperate was the situation in the textile areas that the Federal Council, working with the Friends, issued a plea for food, clothing, and funds to succor the families of the workers.

Under the urging of a host of church groups, the Council's Research Department launched a thorough investigation of the strike and found, generally, in favor of the workers. Even before this the Council, in conjunction with Catholic and Jewish agencies, issued a statement condemning the violence employed by both sides. But its conclusion ripped the owners for overworking and underpaying their employees, and for denying them the right to organize. "Manufacturers who organize associations of their own and act collectively, often through paid representatives," read the report, "have no sound ethical basis for objecting to efforts of workers to organize for their own welfare and to act through representatives of their own choosing."[5]

The Church League for Industrial Democracy threw its lot with the strikers. The ubiquitous Spofford was on hand to give moral support and to distribute what meager aid his group could raise. Alva W. Taylor of the Board of Temperance and Social Welfare of the Disciples of Christ worked in raising help for the strikers. The Methodist Federation for Social Service did more than its share along this line. The Emergency Committee for Strikers Relief, formed at Passaic in 1926, entered the scene. Included in its membership were such figures as Niebuhr, McConnell, Chaffee, Holmes, and Melish. It has been noted that at this time a number of denominations passed resolutions calling for better conditions in textiles, although judgment was not passed on the merits of the strikes.

Nor was the church press silent. *Zion's Herald* in both editorials and articles presented stomach-churning accounts of the injustices suffered by the strikers, particularly since the courts invariably applied a double standard to acts of violence committed by the workers and to those committed against them. The New York and Nashville editions of the *Christian Advocate* related the events darkening southern textiles, and the Northwestern edition believed that if Christians remained silent in the face of such abuses the very stones would cry out.

Both the *Churchman* and the *Presbyterian Advance* carried pleas for aid for the embattled strikers. The organs of the Federal Council gave the strikes wide coverage. The *World Tomorrow* scored the abuses of

5. *Information Service*, Dec. 28, 1929.

the mills, as did the *Christian Century* on a half-dozen occasions. Both journals justified the strikes. The *Baptist* believed the strikes the result of "social incompetency"—a feudal capitalism, low wages, bad conditions, and unorganized labor. Robert C. Dexter, Unitarian leader, spoke bluntly in favor of the strikers. In general, these examples of church interest and sympathy helped to balance the record of indifference and hostility chalked by the local mill clergy.

The coal industry was not only sick in the twenties; it was in a state of putrefaction. The hard pressed operators sought to retain their profits at the expense of the workers. Taking a dim view of this sort of budget balancing, the miners fought back. Attempts to unionize new fields, especially in the South, were generally unsuccessful. Organizers met with the same reception given Pope at Second Manassas. And when non-union miners went out on strike they waited in vain for support from the beetle-browed president of the United Mine Workers, John L. Lewis. Truth to tell, Lewis was backed to the wall himself and emerged from the twenties with barely fifteen thousand followers. As in the case of textiles, the coal strikes were not pretty. One need only recall Herrin, Illinois, where in 1922 twenty "scabs" were massacred by desperate strikers. The throats of the wounded were slit; the bodies of the dead urinated upon.

The Federal Council of Churches was deeply concerned with the coal strikes. In the great strike of 1922 it urged President Harding and Congress to investigate the issues. It conducted a searching review itself and presented the findings in a special bulletin. While recognizing the complexity of the situation, the report was sympathetic to the demands of the striking miners. In 1928 the Federal Council, at the request of the Pittsburgh Council of Churches, launched an investigation of the coal strike in western Pennsylvania. Once again its findings were presented in a scholarly, dispassionate manner, but one that none the less clearly favored the strikers. The Pittsburgh group, incidentally, played an important role in connection with the strike, not only by calling for an impartial inquiry into its causes, but also by initiating relief work for the miners' families.

Further action was taken by the Council. It sent a representative to Colorado to help settle a coal strike there. It worked in cooperation with local churches in raising food, clothing, and money to succor the families of striking miners in many areas. It reported on the bituminous wage controversy of 1927. Louis Untermeyer tells of the miners who called upon God to fling them a handful of stars. The Federal Council concentrated on giving the miners aid of a more mundane sort.

From time to time other church groups concerned themselves with coal strikes. Perhaps the best example was the trouble in Colorado in 1927-28. Early in the strike the social service commission of the Colorado Methodists issued a pronouncement defending the miners' right to a living wage and to unionization. The abridgment of civil liberties was also protested. This pronouncement, termed by the *Rocky Mountain News* the "most sensible statement which has been issued," was sent to every newspaper in the state. The Weld County ministerial association raised an investigating committee which issued a strong condemnation of the low wages and violations of civil liberties suffered by the strikers. A group of Denver ministers published a statement setting forth the human values involved in the strike, and the Denver ministerial association called for the entrance of the Federal Council on the scene and defended the principle of unionization. Grace Community Church opened its door to a strike meeting. Students of the Iliff School of Theology interviewed the strikers and the Fellowship of Reconciliation rented the municipal auditorium as a means of giving wide publicity to the findings of the students. All in all, the Protestant churches were very active in the Colorado coal conflict of 1927-28.

Now and then ministers or church groups entered into other labor disputes in the coal fields. Sometimes the position taken was clear-cut. "Opposition to the right of labor to organize is foolish," declared a Baptist parson in West Virginia. "The day of industrial democracy is coming. Morning is here and the labor movement is responsible for it."[6] Sometimes the position taken was equivocal, the Lynds's reporting that the Middletown ministerial association sent a telegram to the miners' and operators' conference in Washington asking the delegates to invoke Divine Wisdom in deciding the questions before them.

The church press, judging from scores of editorials in many different journals, waxed hot and cold toward the striking miners. Some periodicals were sympathetic to the miners; some were not. Generally, as the decade deepened sympathy increased.

Railroads were still another area in American economic life in which there was considerable unrest. The striking railroad shopmen in 1922 received repeated support from the Federal Council's *Information Service*. Not only were the workers justified in striking in the first place, but the sweeping injunction issued by a federal judge to break the protest was termed unfair. In 1927 the Council, in cooperation with Catholic and Jewish agencies, investigated a railroad strike in western Maryland and reported in favor of the workers. However, the local churches did little

6. *West Virginia Federationist*, Jan. 22, 1925, clipping in files of ACLU (Vol. 297) in NYPL.

either in settling the dispute or in undertaking to make the issues plain to the public.

Undoubtedly the most interesting account of the impact of a railroad strike upon local churches appeared in an article in the *Christian Century*, July 31, 1924, written by Dr. Worth M. Tippy, Federal Council officer. Congregations, he observed, were torn apart by union and non-union factions. Ministers who sided with the strikers— and many of them did —found themselves hounded from the pulpit. Conversely, in strongly union congregations, pastors who attempted to remain neutral or who ministered to "scabs" were threatened with their lives. A large group of ministers who had gone through the storm held a post mortem.

It was the consensus of opinion in the discussion that the church must have a first concern for the rights of the workers and the welfare of their families, and that pastors of congregations made up of strikers should espouse their cause so far as they can conscientiously do so, but that they should keep the mind of Christ themselves and exert their influence for Christian methods in the conduct of a strike. Those who had gone through the fires of the conflict were convinced that the use of Christian methods strengthened rather than weakened the conduct of a strike. There was no difference of opinion that pastors should not become partisans of hatred, vituperation and violence. It was agreed also that pastors should insist upon their right and duty to minister to all their people, and that they should not allow men or families to be driven from the churches. In a strike where the right is clearly with the men, it was agreed that it is wrong for men to accept replacement positions, and that it is legitimate for the pastor to say as much; also to urge upon non-union workers the unfairness of accepting the benefits of labor organization without helping to pay the costs. The necessity of discovering a method of settling such disputes without industrial warfare aroused the deepest interest. It was realized by all the study groups that there is an advanced step to be taken by both labor and capital, which shall make them partners in industry by forms of industrial government, and that collective bargaining is not the final word in labor policy, although absolutely necessary at the present time.

Thus far the discussion has covered strikes in three specific industries: textiles, coal, and railroads. This survey of the churches' attitude toward labor unrest in the twenties can be concluded by noting clerical reaction to various miscellaneous strikes.

Here and there individual clergymen arbitrated strikes. Dr. Justin Wroe Nixon of Rochester, for instance, settled a strike of tile and marble workers in 1929. Mark A. Matthews, noted Presbyterian minister of Seattle, successfully brought management and labor together and thus averted a strike of laundry workers. Further south, in Los Angeles, the Reverend Edwin P. Ryland mediated numerous industrial conflicts. A taxi cab strike was concluded through the intervention of a committee of ministers led by Dr. Albert Day. In 1927 the New York Federation of Churches intervened on behalf of paper-box makers. During this violent dispute, churches were opened to mass meetings of strikers and Union Seminary students joined the picket line. Although the strike failed, a labor leader declared that the help of the church did more good than a thousand sermons or resolutions. The Reverend Jonathan C. Day, Presbyterian, told a group of strikers: "Fight for your rights. . . . Perhaps you don't give a damn about prayers," he continued. "Perhaps you are exploited by those who make long prayers. But don't forget the Lord's Prayer is a communistic prayer. The man who exploits his fellow men denies the vitality of the Christian creed."[7] In Philadelphia, Kenosha, and many other cities church groups investigated and mediated strikes.

The church press was not silent regarding other strikes, but the reader will be spared any further citations. Suffice it to say, in the twenties a rather significant element in American Protestantism backed labor in its use of coercion. At any rate, not all of the churchmen were as enslaved by the business community as historians of the Prosperity Decade have chosen to believe.

7. *Waterbury Republican*, July 16, 1920, clipping in files of ACLU (Vol. 143) in NYPL.

CHAPTER XIX

Depression Decade Strikes

"If you are hungry you are a red and if you tell your neighbor you are hungry that is criminal syndicalism."—An old Kentucky coal miner

I

THE DEPRESSION hit the laborer like a blow in the solar plexus. He doubled up in pain, gasping only a weak protest. Haunted by the specter of unemployment, he docilely clung to his job although his wages and conditions of work sunk to a pitiful level. The few strikes of 1930-33 were launched in bitter desperation rather than in hope, and for this very reason were characterized by unusual violence. By 1933 union membership had fallen to less than three million.

Section 7A of the National Industrial Recovery Act of that year appeared to offer new guarantees to labor. The workingman's hopes in this act were ill-founded. As management increasingly ignored or violated the codes, labor struck back with its classic weapon, the strike. In 1935 President Roosevelt, realizing that he could not count upon support from the business community, intensified his wooing of labor. Protected by the Wagner-Connery Act and a sympathetic National Labor Relations Board, unions swung aggressively into action. The emphasis now was on organization on the basis of industry rather than craft. Failure of the conservative A.F. of L. to break from its traditional belief in craft unions led to the rise of the militant Committee for Industrial Organization (later Congress of Industrial Organizations). Labor was successful. By 1939 union membership was over eight million.

Labor was often victorious in organizing industries not only because of a friendly federal government and an increasingly friendly public opinion, but also because management had been coerced by the strike. In 1937 alone there were 4,720 strikes engaging almost two million workers. It was a desperate fight. Unions were brutally efficient in keeping their members in line and in intimidating non-union workers. New techniques such as the sit-down strike more than matched management's labor spies, company police, black lists and arsenals—arsenals, as Senator La Follette disclosed, adequate for a small war.

Communists were even more successful in infiltrating labor's ranks in the thirties than they had been in the twenties. Although never large in relation to total union membership, their discipline and ability to seize key posts enhanced their power and made their presence a real danger. Undoubtedly in some strikes their influence was paramount. But the following pages are based on the premise that industrial unrest cannot be laid entirely at Moscow's door and that most of the strikes would have occurred even without the Communist catalyst.

II

The textile industry in the thirties remained in a troubled state. In 1931 unrest flared in Lawrence, Massachusetts. Students from Boston University School of Theology marched on the picket line. The New England Methodist Conference passed a resolution condemning the abridgment of civil liberties during the strike. Local ministers endorsed the strike from the pulpit and in the press. Church investigators were sent into the city. Editorials in the religious press sided with the workers. Said *Zion's Herald:*

In screaming headlines the newspapers of New England . . . announced, "Lawrence Strike Is Broken." Yes, but just what was "broken"? Was it not men who were broken? Cold and hungry, hopeless and forsaken, these workers, striving against a cut in wages already inadequate for proper comfort and self-development, finally had to surrender to the will of the mill owners. Self-respect was broken; ambition was broken; desire for self-improvement was broken; the spirit of self-sacrifice for wife and family was broken. Broken! What a terrible thing it is to break a fellow man even in the interests of profits and dividends![1]

Clerical endorsement of the strike, of course, was not unanimous. Three New England congregations protested the action of the Methodist conference and at least one local minister refused to take sides, saying his pulpit was not a "propaganda soapbox."

Early in the decade a mill strike occurred in Nazareth, Pennsylvania. The Federal Council of Churches and the Fellowship of Reconciliation sent in representatives to help reach a settlement. The attitude of the local clergy was as tough as whang-leather; only one agreed to cooperate with the investigators. Even that was more than could be said for the mill owners. Finally the Reverend Charles C. Webber, the Fellowship delegate, gave up in his mediation efforts and joined the picket line carrying a placard which read: "The United States government and the Churches stand for arbitration in industrial disputes. Why don't you?"[2] He was promptly arrested.

1. Nov. 18, 1931, p. 1444.   2. *Christian Century,* May 13, 1931, pp. 648-50.

In 1931 another textile strike broke out in Paterson, New Jersey. A. J. Muste, as usual, was on hand, a battle-scarred veteran of a hundred strikes. He was joined by Bradford Young and Spear Knebel, both active clergymen in the Protestant Episcopal Church, who were just beginning to win a reputation for this sort of thing. They were marching around the mill with the pickets like Israel about Jericho when they were arrested and politely escorted into patrol wagons.

In 1930 an unofficial Church Emergency Committee for the Relief of Textile Strikers was formed. Included in its membership were such important religious leaders as Bowie, Spofford, Herring, Tippy, and Alva W. Taylor. This group originally gave aid to the strikers in Danville, Virginia, but it continued on to lend support in other areas. The message accompanying the money, food, and clothing to the Danville strikers wished them success in their attempts to win collective bargaining rights. One strike in which this group was active took place in Allentown, Pennsylvania. Here also the ministerial association did a good job in mediating the strike, insisting, as their telegram to the governor stated, in the right of the workers to organize and bargain collectively.

In New York a committee composed of Fosdick, Bowie, Melish, Bishop Gilbert, and others was organized on behalf of striking garment workers. The Emergency Committee for Strikers Relief, formed, as has been noted, in 1926 and embracing such leaders as Niebuhr, Chaffee, Holmes, and Bishop McConnell, worked on in the thirties to bring aid to strikers, including those in textiles. In the middle thirties a group of ministers helped settle a New England textile strike. The Congregational Council for Social Action sided with the cotton mill workers in Pelzer, South Carolina. Los Angeles clergymen questioned striking garment workers on the picket line and worked for mediation. The Reverend Cameron Hall extended the hospitality of his New York church to striking clothing makers, and in Cleveland the Reverend Howard M. Wells, Presbyterian, protested the use of the national guard to break a strike of rayon workers. The Reverend Eliot White, Episcopal priest, exhorted New Jersey textile strikers to carry on even with the courts and the police against them. A group of Chattanooga churchmen, including T. B. Cowan, A. J. De Jarnette, and James Dombrowski, addressed a meeting of strikers at the Hardwick Woolen Mills and wished them success.

The most serious outburst in textiles occurred in 1934 when almost a half-million workers in twenty states walked out in protest against violations of the NRA codes. Church groups sent aid to the strikers. James Myers, Federal Council official, preached the funeral sermons for strikers killed in South Carolina and Georgia. The Council, in cooperation with Catholic and Jewish agencies, issued a strongly worded statement concerning the workers' grievances. An expression of sympathy was adopted by the National Council of Methodist Youth. Some church journals opposed the strike, and some hedged, but the majority seemed to give endorsement to the workers.

The coal industry suffered its share of unrest in the thirties. Once again elements in the churches showed concern. For instance, in 1933 the Federal Council issued a nation-wide appeal to all the denominations to respond with both funds and clothing for miners in Kentucky and West Virginia. A Congregational minister, the Reverend Allen Keedy, serving a summer pastorate in Harlan County, Kentucky, threw in his lot with the striking miners. Charged with "obstructing justice," he was jailed and eventually forced from the state. It is instructive if not inspiring to note that none of his middle class congregation visited him during his incarceration, and that, indeed, part of his flock instigated his imprisonment.

In like manner, a Union Seminary student, Arnold Johnson, who came into Harlan as the representative of the ACLU and the Fellowship of Reconciliation, was promptly jailed on the charge of "criminal syndicalism." Such also was the fate of the Reverend Frank Martin, Baptist parson of Kentucky, who had actively endorsed unions as the miners' only hope. Miss Winifred Chappell, of the Methodist Federation for Social Service, spent six weeks in West Virginia mining camps participating (as she put it) in the class struggle, frankly and without apology on the workers' side. In Illinois, the Reverend Douglas Anderson served as chairman of the Midwest Striking Miners Relief Fund, and a Chicago divinity school student was president of another fund. Several churchmen were counted among the members of the National Committee to Aid Striking Miners Fighting Starvation. Both the Methodist Federation for Social Service and the Church League for Industrial Democracy allied themselves with the miners.

Perhaps of greater significance is the fact that twenty-one New York ministers including Fosdick, McConnell, Buttrick, Sockman, Gilbert, and Chalmers petitioned Congress to investigate conditions in the coal fields of southeastern Kentucky. Nettled by this reflection on their honor, the authorities of Pineville, Kentucky, invited the clerics to come to their community and see the error of their accusations. A sub-committee, which consisted of C. Rankin Barnes, Cameron P. Hall, Spofford, and Niebuhr, did just that. However, these dubious dominies returned from their visit more firmly convinced than ever that civil liberties were dead in Harlan and Bell counties, and that the plight of the striking miners was desperate. The local churches in the coal fields, it was discovered, were about as friendly to the striking miners as a mongoose to a cobra.

Church press editors plied the pen and prayed to God to the end that the miners might know greater justice. The *Christian Leader* appealed for aid for the striking miners and averred that it was hard to realize that there was any place in the United States under Fascist government, but such was the case. Both the *World Tomorrow* and the *Christian Century* wielded a pick in support of the miners. "The time is past for any American employer to fight the collective bargaining rights of labor, and the coal operators must recognize it," declared a Disciples journal.[3] "All in all," believed a Methodist writer "nowhere in the entire world are liberty and freedom more dead today than in Harlan County, Kentucky."[4] Page, Spofford, and Herring used the church press to excoriate the operators. An Episcopal journal also rang the charges against the operators.

Unrest in the coal industry was matched in other areas. Labor's efforts to organize Steel were crushed in the great 1919 strike. It was not until the mid-thirties that conditions were favorable for another attempt, this time by the young, aggressive C.I.O. Reading the handwriting on the wall as boldly carved by the Wagner Act, NLRB findings, court decisions, F.D.R., and the general public, "Big Steel" led by the United States Steel Corporation dramatically capitulated without a fight on March 1, 1937.

Myron C. Taylor, chairman of the board of the United States Steel Corporation, displayed a sense of enlightened self-interest in marked contrast to the stubborn determination of "Tough Tom" Girdler, leader of "Little Steel"—Republic, Youngstown, Inland, and Bethlehem—to fight unionization to the death.

And indeed death stalked the battle to organize "Little Steel." One need remember only the "Memorial Day Massacre." On May 30, 1937, police fired on a group of pickets at the South Chicago shop of the Republic Steel Company. When the smoking guns were stilled, ten workers lay dead or dying; over a hundred writhed with wounds. Twenty-two Chicago policemen were also wounded, although fortunately none critically, and none had been hit by bullets.

The Reverend Chester Fiske, minister of the South Shore Community Congregational Church, was on the scene and took pictures of the clash. He was seized by the police, held nineteen hours, and his film confiscated. President Albert W. Palmer of the Chicago Theological Seminary spoke before a mass meeting of five thousand citizens at the Civic Opera House.

3. *Christian-Evangelist*, Oct. 5, 1933, p. 1269.
4. *Zion's Herald*, Aug. 2, 1939, p. 741.

Quietly, calmly, but with moving conviction he addressed himself to the dead strikers. He closed with these words: "You are dead because we of the community have failed not only in the training of our police, but in adjusting the deeper background tensions between labor and management in our industrial life. It is because we are so selfish, stupid and self-willed that we have not yet learned how to give labor a fair, recognized and democratic way in which to voice its grievances."[5]

The Chicago Church Federation passed a resolution which stated there was no apparent provocation for the use of extreme violence and gunfire by the police. It protested the denial of civil liberties, called for a thorough investigation, and demanded the prosecution of those responsible for the shootings. The Reverend W. B. Waltmire, Methodist, conducted a funeral service for the dead steelworkers. Recalling the death of a Nazarene carpenter at the hands of Roman soldiers, he cried: "Their sacrifice is not in vain as His was not in vain."[6] The industrial relations secretary of the Congregational Council for Social Action was an eyewitness to the clash and he testified before a Senate investigating committee on behalf of the workers. Typifying much church press opinion, the editors of the *Christian-Evangelist* maintained: "Bloody battle is not the way for labor to win, or be forced to win, collective bargaining."[7]

Interest in labor's attempt to organize Steel was not confined to the "Memorial Day Massacre." As early as 1936 the Federal Council's *Information Service* devoted an entire issue to the subject, and when "Big Steel" and labor peacefully came to terms the Council sent a telegram to both parties praising their agreement as a splendid example to all industry. Several weeks later over a hundred clergymen signed an appeal, drafted by James Myers, Federal Council official, urging the settlement of the steel strikes on the principle of labor's right to organize and be represented through spokesmen of its own choosing. Although the signers included Catholics and Jews, the great bulk were Protestants. It is significant that the appeal was widely and approvingly quoted in the church press.

Other examples might be cited. A group of Chicago ministers investigated the strike in the Fansteel Corporation in North Chicago and found in favor of the strikers. Earlier the Reverend Paul Cotton, Presbyterian, of Bethlehem, lost his pulpit because he joined pickets on the line and exposed what he considered the shoddy practices of the Bethlehem Steel Company. True, clerical denunciations of the strikers

5. *Northwestern Christian Advocate*, June 17, 1937, p. 577.
6. *Christian Century*, June 16, 1937, p. 777.
7. June 24, 1937, pp. 808-9.

were not entirely absent, but the average attitude seemed to be expressed in the words of the *Presbyterian Tribune:*

We cannot be so obtuse as not to recognize that the officials of the steel industry have gigantic problems with which to cope. We have no desire to direct any unfair criticism against them but we do believe that they will be ahead in the long run if they grant to their men the basic right of organization in organizations of their own choosing. We believe this is an elementary condition for justice and peace in industry.[8]

The attempts to organize the automobile industry and the resultant strikes were as basic and far-reaching as the organizational drives in Steel. The widespread adoption of the sit-down technique deprived labor of much public support that otherwise might have been forthcoming. How did the churches face up to the issues involved?

Left-of-center religious groups such as the Methodist Federation for Social Service, the Presbyterian Fellowship for Social Action, the National Religion and Labor Foundation, and the Fellowship of Socialist Christians readily embraced the aims of labor and justified the method of the sit-down strike. Said a spokesman for the Fellowship of Reconciliation:

Nothing is gained . . . by contending that when workers who have long worked in a plant, who have contributed skill, experience and labor to the prosperity of an industry, sit-down peacefully in a plant pending the adjustment of grievances, they are simply "trespassers" like the man who occupies another's home against the latter's will.

When people participate in, or condone, or fail earnestly to protest against, the gross inequalities in distribution of income which exists in our country, refusal of employers to recognize the right to organize, labor espionage, the use of gas and machine-guns against strikers, lynching, war and preparation for war and then suddenly become indignant about sit-down strikes, truth compels us to remind them of Jesus' saying about those who "strain at a gnat and swallow a camel."[9]

The less militant Congregational Council for Social Action vigorously sympathized with the efforts of the workers to organize, condemned management for its harsh labor policies, petitioned Congress to investigate the abridgment of civil liberties in the strike, and gave implied although unspoken approval of the sit-down method. On the other hand, the Presbyterian Department of Social Education and Action sent a telegram to President Roosevelt and Governor Murphy of Michigan calling upon them to uphold law and order in the automobile strikes. While favoring the workers' right to organize, this statement certainly implied disapproval

8. July 23, 1936, p. 4.   9. *Fellowship*, May, 1937, p. 6.

of the sit-down strikes. In a similar vein, the Federal Council issued a pronouncement flatly supporting labor's attempt to organize. However, it went on to say that when labor is denied this right then "illegal procedures almost inevitably result. The sit-in strike is manifestly a dangerous weapon. It can be employed in a wholly tyrannical way by a minority of workers. . . ."[10] The New York Methodist Conference also endorsed the Wagner Act and labor's organizing efforts, but refused by a vote of 92 to 57 to give approval to the sit-down method.

During the teeth of the General Motors strike the Michigan Conference for the Protection of Civil Rights called a special emergency meeting to protest the use of tear gas and bullets against the strikers. Speakers at the meeting included the Reverend Frederick G. Poole, executive secretary of the Board of Education of the Methodist Episcopal Church. The Reverend John H. Bollens, chairman of the group, believed "further bloodshed and violence, as that which occurred in the unprovoked attack of the Flint police upon peaceful picketers and sit-down strikers, faces the sharp scrutiny of state and national public opinion, aroused by the horror of this incident."[11] The Michigan State Council of Churches called a state-wide emergency ministers' conference to probe the issues. The Detroit Council of Churches expressed the belief that Governor Murphy had handled the situation "tolerantly and with understanding" and called for the greatest possible sympathy and dispatch in adjusting the strike. It will be remembered that Governor Murphy had refused to use troops to drive out the sit-down strikers. Many local pastors were active in bringing influence on civic authorities to work for a peaceful settlement. Included on the governor's committee of mediation was a Protestant clergyman, the Reverend Benjamin J. Bush, Presbyterian.

Earlier strikes in the industry saw clergymen playing prominent roles. For instance, in 1933 a strike in the Ford plant in Edgewater, New Jersey, was mediated by a group of ministers. Although acting as an impartial body and retaining contacts with both the workers and management, the clergymen did make clear their belief in collective bargaining, secured aid for the strikers' families, and held that if the strikers did choose to return to work they should not be penalized. In that year also a strike in the Briggs body plant was investigated by a fact-finding commission appointed by the governor consisting of three churchmen—a Protestant, a Catholic, and a Jew. From time to time such leaders of Protestant opinion as John Haynes Holmes and Reinhold Niebuhr spoke in defense of the sit-down strikes.

10. *New York Times,* Feb. 6, 1937, p. 2.
11. *New York Daily Worker,* Jan. 16, 1937, clipping in files of ACLU (Vol. 1019) in NYPL.

On the other hand, a commentator in the *United Presbyterian* peered at what was happening in Detroit and averred that if the sit-down strikes prevailed, Russian law would rule in America. A noted Southern Baptist believed sit-down strikers break the law and wantonly flout the duly constituted authorities. The *Presbyterian Banner* said the whole principle of property rights was at stake, and the distinguished Presbyterian, James E. Clarke, held sit-down strikes substituted anarchy for law. To the *Christian Leader* it was a clear case of right and wrong. Even many normally pro-labor journals and individuals were not at all sure about this new sit-down technique.

And this appeared to be the common attitude. The articulate element in American Protestantism clearly favored the principle of labor's right to organize the automobile industry. A significant minority—but still a minority—endorsed the sit-down strike method. But probably the bulk of Protestant church opinion felt that labor in using this new technique had gone too far.

Much the same conclusion can be drawn concerning the San Francisco General Strike of 1934. Regardless of the legitimate grievances of the longshoremen, when their protest was followed by sympathetic strikes in other industries and finally by a general strike, most clerical observers felt this was too much. True, a few West Coast Methodist and Episcopal bishops and clergymen evidenced sympathy with the strikers. True, some church journals took a similar position, but the body of church opinion, while recognizing the honest claims of the longshoremen, deplored the whole concept of a general strike. Rather than cite many examples, the following editorial seems to typify the churches' attitude:

In the case of the San Francisco strike, the aim of the real leaders was not revolution but a square deal in the method of hiring for the loading and unloading of ships. The demand was a just one that ought to have been met years ago. Since it was not so met and labor's right of collective bargaining was denied, organized labor resorted to its only weapon in such cases, the strike. But when that strike in a particular industry was followed by a general strike, it grew beyond the bounds of legitimate action and forced government to step in for the protection of the public. The fact that government was able to do so with the full support of the public, laboring people included, shows that the agitators who had hoped to take advantage of a turbulent situation . . . reckoned without the fact that Americans are by no means ready to give up the freedom for which their ancestors have fought. If the failure of the San Francisco general strike has brought this lesson home to irresponsible agitators it has served a valuable purpose.[12]

Thus far church opinion regarding strikes in specific industries has

12. *Living Church*, July 28, 1934, pp. 169-70.

been sketched. Now it is time to glance at Protestantism's attitudes in various random and generally less crucial strikes. For instance, an attempt to organize Brooklyn-Edison Company employees in 1930-31 found several churchmen active. Believing in the justice of the drive, the Reverends David Cory, Presbyterian, Bradford Young, Episcopalian, Eliot White, Episcopalian, and several Union Seminary students offered to distribute organizational literature among the workmen. Both Cory and White were knocked about by company "goons" before being rescued by a flying wedge of police. The former almost lost an eye, the latter in fact lost teeth. In 1933 a group of ministers, serving as a fact-finding committee in the strike of San Joaquin Valley cotton pickers, recommended the payment of higher wages. The following year the California State Federation of Churches passed a resolution condemning the violation of civil liberties during labor unrest in Imperial Valley. A group of clergymen upheld the right of Whitney Blake Company workers in Connecticut to organize. Every effort was made to bring the pressure of public opinion to bear on the situation. Students from Yale Divinity School were recruited for picket duty. New Haven ministers protested the abuses of management to civic officials. A group of church women invited the union organizers to present their case before them. The efforts were successful.

The exceedingly bitter strike in Consumers' Research was justified by an investigating committee headed by Reinhold Niebuhr. In 1935 the Brooklyn Church and Mission Federation charged the National Biscuit Company with trying to make use of the churches to break strikes. Churchmen joined the picket line about May's department store. Methodist minister Ward Rogers led a group of California migratory workers in a strike. He was beaten. In Gadsden, Alabama, three Protestant parsons investigated the flogging of C.I.O. organizers and pointed the finger of blame at management. Labor war in Portland in 1937 found several ministers attempting to mediate the dispute, although in this instance not entirely to the satisfaction of labor. Three clergymen, two of them Protestant, of Jamaica, Long Island, did an excellent piece of work as arbitrators in a newspaper strike. In 1938 Minneapolis ministers mediated a taxi cab strike. A strike of Maytag employees in Newton, Iowa, cost the Reverend E. A. Ramige his pulpit because he defended the workers—in contrast to the position of most of the town pastors. A strike in Maine found two clergymen on the workers' side.

These examples of church interest in strikes are intended to be indicative rather than exhaustive. In particular, no attempt has been made to trace all of the interventions in strike situations made by such groups as the Methodist Federation for Social Service, the Church

League for Industrial Democracy, the Congregational Council for Social Action, the Fellowship of Reconciliation, the Fellowship of Southern Churchmen, the National Religion and Labor Foundation, and others. It is only a slight exaggeration to say that there was not a man-sized strike in the thirties that did not see a representative from one of these groups on hand.

It remains only to note that virtually all of the denominations passed resolutions urging the settlement of industrial disputes by means of conciliation and arbitration, and that the majority of northern church journals and perhaps half of the southern church papers acknowledged labor's theoretical right to strike. In regard to the attitude of local clergymen in labor disputes, reference can be made to two studies.

In 1937 the National Conference of Jews and Christians conducted a survey in strike areas. The study revealed no completely consistent line of action on the part of local clergymen. Some parsons aided and others opposed the strikers. Generally, large city clerics were more active and outspoken than their small town brethren. But balancing exception against exception, the study concluded that the "large majority of opinion has been in favor of labor's efforts to win collective bargaining rights. The clergy has been generally on the side of labor, and in many places have used their influence on both factors, to bring about a peaceful settlement, without any publicity in recognition of their efforts."[13]

The results of a 1935 Religion and Labor Foundation poll of 4,700 parsons are interesting. Over 2,000 said they would support the legal and ethical right of labor to strike, picket and engage in mass demonstrations; less than 5 per cent had already done so. About 11 per cent said they would assist in recruiting pickets for the unions and about 8 per cent averred they would march on the picket line themselves; in both cases only about one per cent had already done so. Those who would offer aid to strikers numbered 1,598 and those who would open their church to strike meetings numbered 540. Over 3,000 promised that in case of an industrial dispute they would make an effort to get the facts and acquaint their people with them.

III

The time has now come to attempt to arrive at some conclusions concerning the attitude of the churches toward labor. An event occurred in 1926 which perhaps points up all that has been said thus far. The American Federation of Labor decided to hold its annual convention in Detroit. Following a common practice, the clergy extended invitations to the union leaders to share their pulpits, William Green, president of

13. *Presbyterian Tribune*, Aug. 19, 1937, p. 29.

the union, being asked to address the Detroit Young Men's Christian Association. The business community of Detroit, anxious to preserve their "open-shop" stronghold, applied pressure to force the cancellation of the speaking engagements. The churches succumbed. Some of the invitations were withdrawn. The Federal Council, national church groups, a host of prominent clergymen, including many of Detroit, and virtually the entire church press denounced this craven action. However, protests from the South were not as numerous as those from the North. There followed a desperate attempt to make amends. Invitations to labor leaders were once again extended. In fact, ultimately a number of churches opened their pulpits and more labor leaders spoke in the churches than had been planned originally. But it was too late. The harm had been done. American Protestantism had given further evidence of the fact that it did not "think much of labor."

Now, the conclusions that can be drawn from this incident apply to the broader picture. The churches had an honest desire to win the friendship of labor and cooperate with it. The Federal Council and most of the denominations at the national level were indeed sympathetic to labor. At the local level, however, this cooperation was often unrealized and, in fact, clergymen openly sided with management. There was, then, a gulf between denominational pronouncements and the actual application of these pronouncements. Further, churchmen of national fame tended to be more sympathetic to labor than the local clergy, and northern ministers were more sympathetic than southern parsons. And, lastly, Protestantism has usually been judged by its worst and most reactionary acts.

This final point deserves further comment. As one reviews the evidence presented in this section, labor's charge that it has been "betrayed" by the churches seems a little unfair. To be sure, in some communities, in some denominations, in regard to some parsons, the accusation must stand. But as an over-all judgment it does not jibe with the record.

William Green once asked what the church could do for labor. And almost invariably this has been labor's position. Rarely was the question raised, "What can labor do for the church?" Often labor used the church only if the church could secure for labor the physical ends it desired. It was indifferent to the church as a spiritual and moral force. There are interesting parallels between the attitude of the business community and the attitude of labor toward the church.

Bruce Barton, reflecting the business position, transformed Jesus into the image of a modern successful business executive. But was labor's picture of "Jesus the (union) Carpenter" any more appealing than Barton's? If the business view seems a little distorted, what can be said of labor's picture of Jesus as a sort of sublimated John L. Lewis and of Moses as the first walking delegate? If churchmen investigated a dispute and found in favor of labor, management of course charged the parsons to stick to their spiritual knitting. If, on the other hand, the decision was against labor, then labor immediately informed the ministers to avoid "secular" affairs that they knew nothing about.

Truth to tell, labor can be accused of practicing an inverted form of snobbery: the horny-handed workman refused to accept the extended hand of the parson because it lacked calluses. Labor indeed suffered grievous abuses and adopted the somewhat smug attitude that they were beyond the comprehension of corpulent clerics. But the average American parson lived an existence somewhat harsher than that of the village vicar in English novels. In many cases, his wages were no higher than those of the laborer. His hours of work were back-breaking and his conditions of work often intolerable. The personal experience of many ministers made them as aware of the brutal facts of economic life as any workingman.

What particularly galled churchmen—and this view was widely expressed—was that labor often left the initiative for a rapprochement between labor and the church entirely up to the church. Instance after instance occurred where a pastor befriended labor in the face of a conservative congregation and suffered expulsion for his pains. And where was the workingman? Did he join the church and come to the minister's support? No! For example, a Protestant church in Butte had a reputation for being friendly to labor. Seven ministers in twelve years had been forced out because of their pro-labor views. Here was a church that surely deserved the support of workingmen. Here was an opportunity for labor to join a church having a sympathetic minister, and by so joining labor could have liberalized the complexion of the congregation. Less than ten members of organized labor made the effort. Indeed, Butte had three ministers who never failed to support labor in its numerous struggles. And yet the combined, active membership of the churches of these three men totaled less than four hundred. Where were the eight thousand union men and women of Butte? "To the best of my knowledge," wrote one minister, "the church has not betrayed labor but labor has betrayed both churches and ministers where such churches and such men have taken the side of labor. It has stood off and scoffed while ministers have sacrificed position and personal welfare in behalf of an organization that does not support their budgets nor fill their church pews."[14]

The Protestant churches are mostly democratic institutions and re-

14. *Christian Century*, Sept. 9, 1931, p. 1113.

flect the views of their members. If workingmen wished to have the church take a more friendly position on certain issues, they might well have entered the church and caused their views to prevail.

This observation, of course, oversimplifies the situation and the solution in order to drive home a point. Nevertheless, there is substantial evidence to support the thesis that generally speaking American Protestantism did not betray labor.

Part IV

The Churches and Race Relations

CHAPTER XX

The Churches and Race Relations

"There is neither Jew nor Greek, there is neither bond nor free
. . . for ye are all one in Christ Jesus."—Galatians 3:28

I

THE DOGMATIST is never a very pleasant person. And yet, in all conscience, it must be confessed that the following pages rest upon the dogmatic assumption that the white Protestant American who supposes himself superior to his black, brown, yellow, or Semite neighbor solely because of the pigmentation of his neighbor's skin, the texture of his hair, or the shape of his nose is mistaken in his pride.

II

It would be difficult to find a more perfect example of what has been called the alluring yet ineluctable problem of human folly than the clause in the immigration act of 1924 which provided for the total exclusion of Japanese. By this measure some 250 Japanese were annually barred from entering the United States. In exchange for this dubious benefit, America gratuitously insulted a proud and sensitive people, seriously hindered Christian missions, strengthened the hand of anti-American militarists, and possibly laid a plank in the long road to Pearl Harbor.

Spokesmen for American Protestantism, particularly in the South, had long argued for stricter immigration laws. A considerable element viewed most of the provisions of the 1924 act favorably. But the evidence revealed very little support for the total exclusion of Japanese. On the contrary, most of the Protestant churches strongly protested against this action.

For instance, it is difficult to see how the Federal Council's position could have been more unmistakable. Its representatives appeared before Congress to argue against the bill. Every member of the Senate and House received a statement flaying the measure. When the act was passed, the Council's executive committee adopted a declaration placing this great cooperative agency squarely in opposition. This position was held again and again in the late twenties and thirties. The *Federal Council Bulletin* played upon the same theme, as did a special pamphlet entitled "Japan Wonders Why." In fact, so determined was the Council's fight that certain of its officers were accused of being in the pay of Japan.

Northern Methodists were also active. Their 1924 General Conference adopted a two-page resolution criticizing the exclusion act and mailed copies to every congressman. The Episcopal Address of 1928 termed the bill an "utter perversion" of both Christian and American standards. E. Stanley Jones then introduced a resolution to this effect. Criticism of the exclusion was repeated in the thirties. Northern Baptists lobbied to prevent the passage of the act, and when this failed issued a vigorous protest in 1924 and 1925. In these years also the Southern Baptist Convention called for the "righting of this great wrong." Further, Northern Presbyterians, Episcopalians, Unitarians, Congregationalists, Disciples, Christians, United Brethren, Reformed Presbyterians, and the Reformed Church all officially worked for the modification of the law to end a foolish and insulting measure.

The World Alliance for International Friendship through the Churches and the Church Peace Union begged Congress to reconsider, and every member of the House and Senate was petitioned. The National Study Conference on the Church and World Peace assumed this posture, as did the Y.M.C.A., the Y.W.C.A., and the World's Sunday School Association. The Ministerial Association of Los Angeles telegraphed its protest to Congress, and the American Baptist Foreign Mission Society and a Methodist missionary group also acted. Eighty-two Presbyterian and three hundred missionaries of all denominations in Japan deprecated the step as fatal to their work. They wrote of walking the streets alone to save Japanese Christians the embarrassment of being seen with an American. Dr. John R. Mott, great leader of world evangelism, cabled from Berlin to both the White House and the State Department in a futile effort to block the act. Another great leader, Dr. Robert E. Speer, also emphasized the fateful repercussions total exclusion would have in Japan.

Indeed, a list of the men who publicly opposed the exclusion measure would read like an honor roll of American Protestantism. Much the same could be said of the church press. Almost without exception, religious editors unleashed a torrent of criticism against Congress. Epitomizing the attitude of a score of church papers, the *Southern Churchmen* held, "It would be an intolerable blunder if Congress, through sheer callous bad manners should destroy the good will which the United States now possesses in the Orient, and rouse resentments which play straight into the hands of every militarist and jingo and loud inciter of possible war both in this country and in Japan."[1] All in all, it seems

1. May 17, 1924, pp. 5-6.

clear that the Protestant churches recognized folly when they saw it—and did not hesitate to say so.

III

One of the most baneful legacies bequeathed by the First World War was a heightened feeling of anti-Semitism. Hostility toward the Jew was not unknown in American history, but it was not until the twenties that this insidious form of infantilism reached organized proportions. Calvin's views concerning the depravity of man partially explain this rise of intolerance. There are other reasons. Lothrop Stoddard, Madison Grant, and other proponents of Nordic nonsense gave their scholarly sanction; America's most honored industrialist, Henry Ford, added his voice in condemnation of the Jew; Klan organs published much poisoned pap; conservatives strengthened their opposition to radical and labor groups by charging that Jews led these movements; Hitler's master race theories leaped the Atlantic; and during the depression competition for jobs fanned racial antagonisms.

The record of Protestantism is blemished. To begin with, there is the simple fact that the Ku Klux Klan was anti-Semitic. The Klan was comprised of Protestants, regardless of its unofficial nature and regardless of the fact that church groups, papers, and leaders disavowed its aims. Precisely the same thing can be said of the many anti-Semitic organizations spawned in the thirties. Donald S. Strong in his volume, *Organized Anti-Semitism in America,* lists 121 of these groups, and it is his belief that with the exception of Father Coughlin's followers, all of them were led and dominated by Protestants. Thus it was that thousands of Protestants joined groups that were hostile to the Jew. Unofficial as these organizations may have been, it is of little credit to the Protestant churches that so many of their members could worship Christ on Sunday and attend on, say, Monday an anti-Semitic meeting.

From time to time, also, there appeared in the church press signs of irritation with the Jew. It is not an injustice to say that both the *Lutheran* and the *American Church Monthly,* an Episcopal journal, were rather lacking in the spirit of brotherhood. The Jew was termed clannish, radical, ruthless. The persecutions in Germany were at least partially understandable. And why did he persist in rejecting Christ as his Redeemer? Southern Baptist papers were generally not hostile to the Jew, but now and then the old insinuations appeared. For instance, what can one say of an editorial entitled, "Jew Movies Urging Sex Vice"?[2] The Presbyterian press contained a few anti-Semitic items. It was pointed out that Hollywood, that den of iniquity, was dominated by Jews.

2. *Alabama Baptist,* July 24, 1924, p. 6.

Ford was praised for keeping his business out of the hands of Jews, a "performance of some proportions." Jews were chided for Sabbath desecration, stubborn refusal to recognize Christ as their Master, affinity for radical causes, and generally unattractive ways. Attempts were made to rationalize Hitler's persecutions on the ground that Jews had not been good German citizens. H. H. Marlin, weekly contributor to the *United Presbyterian,* wrote: "Where he [the Jew] predominates in a community he is said to be as a rule intolerable as a neighbor. He is offensive in his almost total lack of thoughfulness and consideration of the rights of others. His children are as a rule utterly lawless."[3] Mr. Marlin later expressed amazement that his readers could interpret his remarks as anti-Semitic! From time to time a few other denominational journals carried items unfavorable to the Jew, but they were infrequent. On the whole the record of American Protestantism was more honorable.

Immediately following the war a Committee on Goodwill between Jews and Christians was formed to consider methods of combating anti-Semitism. Dr. Alfred Williams Anthony, executive secretary of the Home Missions Council, was instrumental in the group's birth. Two years later, February 10, 1923, the Committee was adopted and formally authorized by the Administrative Committee of the Federal Council as a sub-committee of the Commission on International Justice and Goodwill. In this capacity it held conferences with groups of Jews and Christians, conducted forums to discover the cause and cure of prejudice, exchanged speakers and teachers in seminaries, issued pronouncements, and held inter-faith student meetings.

Out of this Federal Council agency there emerged as an independent group the National Conference of Jews and Christians, originally called the National Conference of Jews, Protestants, and Catholics, which in the thirties did important work in lessening misunderstanding. "When we lose the right to be different, we lose the right to be free," believed Charles Evans Hughes, one of the leaders of the movement.[4]

In the twenties other Protestant voices were raised to stem the tide of prejudice. A substantial element denounced the intolerance of the Klan. Many denominations passed resolutions deprecating racial hatred and upholding the rights of minorities, although often in these cases anti-Semitism was not specifically mentioned. The Committee on the Rights of Religious Minorities issued burning appeals. And the church press not infrequently carried editorials and articles aiming at brotherhood between Christians and Jews.

3. Aug. 2, 1928, p. 2.
4. Anson Phelps Stokes, *Church and State in the United States* (3 vols., New York, 1950), II, 462.

Rather than cite random examples from the church press, it might be well to pin point a particularly flagrant case of anti-Semitism and note the reaction to it. For seven years, from 1920 to 1927, Henry Ford's *Dearborn Independent* spewed ugly charges against the Jews, even printing the "Protocols of Zion." These documents were as slanderous to the Jewish people as they were spurious, and only a man who truly believed that "history is bunk" could accept their authenticity. Threatened with a law suit, Mr. Ford finally made a public apology in 1927, stating that he had been unaware of what appeared in his own paper.

The Federal Council and the Church Peace Union passed splendid resolutions protesting the Ford articles. Four independent journals, the *Christian Century, Christian Herald, Christian Work,* and *World Tomorrow,* spoke in unmeasured terms. The New York, Northwestern, and Nashville *Christian Advocates* and *Zion's Herald* all indicated that Methodism believed the "Protocols" pure "humbuggery." Their appearance in Ford's paper was no credit to his "bump of credulity." The *Baptist* repeatedly unmasked the spurious nature of Ford's charges. At least three Presbyterian journals condemned Ford in the strongest possible terms, the *Continent* terming the whole affair a "sorry exhibition of how much harm wealth can do in the hands of the ignorant and gullible."[5] The *Congregationalist* joined in the criticism of Ford, and a Disciples paper declared that "of all the absurd, ridiculous and utterly unfounded hoaxes which have been foisted upon the American people this attack of Ford upon the Jews will take the front rank."[6] The *Universalist Leader* spoke of the attack as being sinister and malevolent and the *Christian Leader* termed it one of the most monstrous performances in reputable journalism. The editors of the *Reformed Church Messenger* said: "Far be it for us to profess that we understand the workings of Henry Ford's mind. We have not been specializing on vacuums. We are unable to explain what is back of his propaganda."[7] Even the *Lutheran* contained a contributed article condemning Ford.

Anti-Semitism waxed rather than waned in the Depression Decade. Fortunately there was a corresponding increase in the number of Protestants who rose to the defense of the Jews, particularly as the unbelievably shocking reports from Nazi Germany rolled in. To relate in detail this counterattack against intolerance would require a small volume, and only a hint can be given of its extent.

To begin with, the Federal Council brought all its resources into play in an heroic attempt to stem the tide. Declarations, petitions, conferences,

5. Jan. 27, 1921, p. 89.
6. *Christian-Evangelist,* July 28, 1927, p. 1009.
7. Jan. 20, 1921, p. 4.

publications, special days of prayer were all utilized. The Council's position was unequivocal. "We declare," resolved the Biennial Session of 1939, "anti-Semitism to be a plain denial of the spirit of our Lord, who was Himself a Hebrew according to the flesh and who taught us that all men are brothers."[8]   Naturally, perhaps, the National Conference of Jews and Christians also extended its resources to the limit in the cause of tolerance. The Home Missions Council, Christian Endeavor, the Church Peace Union, the National Committee for Religion and Welfare Recovery, the Golden Rule Foundation, and the "Y's" all stood up to be counted.

Of significance too is the fact that the major denominations in national meeting, with only a few possible exceptions, spoke out against the cancerous growth of anti-Semitism. Regional and local church groups followed this course in instance after instance. Unofficial agencies such as the Methodist Federation for Social Service and the Church League for Industrial Democracy without exception recognized the menace of Jew-baiting. Literally thousands of ministers (and this is a matter of record) signed petitions branding anti-Semitism a sin. Many church leaders in pulpit, assembly, and press exposed the terrible thing. Numbered in this group were the greatest names of American Protestantism, and significantly here was one issue on which liberals and conservatives could agree. The church press carried much more information on the Jew in the thirties than in the preceding decade, and, with few exceptions, editors and contributors were in agreement that this evil must end.

On the whole and balancing exception against exception, the official record of the Protestant churches on the question of anti-Semitism was honorable. But the fact that millions of individual Protestants harbored this sin in their hearts darkens the judgment. If the God that Christians worship is just as well as merciful, American Protestants, rather than priding themselves on their tolerance, might well fall to their knees in penitence.

IV

"If the treatment of the Negro by the Christian church is called 'divine,'" wrote W. E. B. Du Bois, militant Negro leader, "this is an attack on the conception of God more blasphemous than any which the church has always been so ready and eager to punish."[9]   Du Bois is not noted for his temperance or objectivity, and if his opinion stood alone it could be discounted.*   But his harsh evaluation has been echoed by far

---

8. *Federal Council Bulletin*, Jan., 1939, p. 17.

9. *Christian Century*, Dec. 9, 1931, p. 1556.

* Substantial portions of this section were first published in *The Journal of Negro History*, XLI (July, 1956).

too many scholars—black and white—to be easily dismissed. There was in truth a vast gulf between the Christian creed and the actual deeds of Protestants.

In the first place, Protestant churches were segregated and segregating institutions. White Protestants, while they professed to worship a God who was no respecter of persons, did their worshipping in buildings where the color of skin and not the purity of heart was the entrance test. At the end of the Depression Decade there were approximately eight million Protestant Negroes in America. About seven and a half million were in separate Negro denominations. Of the remaining half million in predominately white denominations, about 99 per cent were in segregated congregations. Thus about one-tenth of one per cent of all Negro Protestants in the United States—eight thousand souls—actually gathered together with whites for worship.

This searing fact rests with the whites. It is true that most Negroes prefer to worship in their own churches. It is true that most Negroes probably would be reluctant to unite with whites even if the invitations were warmly extended. But why? Because they believe they would not be accepted as equals. There could hardly be a more devastating indictment of white Christian America. And what fate threatened white congregations that accepted Negroes? Often if the blacks were poorly treated, they left. If well treated, they were joined by others until the whites, being gradually outnumbered, started to leave. In time the church ended up just as it had started—a segregated institution only now with a congregation entirely black rather than white. Such were the bleak alternatives often facing even those ministers who wanted to do the right thing.

Now, if the churches were ordinary institutions they could be excused for bowing to society's pressures. So deeply ingrained is prejudice against the Negro that even with the best will in the world it has been difficult for labor unions, business groups, fraternal organizations, and even historical societies to break down the barriers. What man is so wise as to possess an easy and quick solution to the Negro problem?

But—and this is the point—Christian churches are not merely groups of individuals banded together for fraternal or cooperative purposes. They are not judged by frail human standards but by the uncompromising ideals of the Christian creed. However noble the aims of other institutions, only the churches claim a divine mandate to glorify Almighty God. Other groups may falter and equivocate, but the churches cannot excuse the gulf between their professions of faith and their practices of paganism. A segregated church *content in its segregation* cannot claim to speak for Christ.

Since segregation is such an irrefutable fact, there remains only the question of how many white Protestants were content with its existence. The evidence is very ugly. "Of all the groups devoted to social uplift," wrote a Negro leader, "I have least hope in the white Christian ministers."[10] This view is accepted wholly or in part by almost all students of race relations in the United States. Their findings are well known and it would serve no useful purpose to burden the narrative with quotations from a score of authorities. One or two important examples must suffice. Gunnar Myrdal, the author of the most exhaustive study of the Negro problem in America, wrote:

Southern whites usually succeed in keeping the Christian challenge of religious brotherhood off their minds. The observer feels that the very incompatibility between the uncompromising Christian creed, on the one hand, and the actual caste relations, on the other, is a reason why white ministers in the South keep so aloof from the race problem and why the white church in the South has generally played so inconsequential a part in changing race relations. It is also a reason why the white minister has been closely watched by his congregation so that he does not start to draw practical conclusions from Christian doctrine that would favor the improvement of race relations.[11]

Frank S. Loescher, author of what many consider to be the definitive study of the interracial principles, practices, and policies of the Protestant churches, believed that "Protestantism, by its policies and practices, far from helping to integrate the Negro in American life, is actually contributing to the segregation of Negro Americans."[12]

Myrdal and Loescher presented their findings in published studies which are well known. Narrower in scope but probing much deeper into the thought of a single denomination are three unpublished studies of Southern Baptists by George Kelsey, Hugh Brimm, and Foy Valentine. Together they represent a searching analysis of the racial attitudes of Southern Baptists as revealed in regional, state, and district association meetings and in the press. Southern Baptists, with rare exceptions, accepted and defended the racial caste system; they accorded priority to the prevailing cultural climate rather than to the commandments of Christ. Racial pride cut the heart out of the Christian ethic. It is enough to say that many Southern Baptists defended Negro segregation in the mid-twentieth century as fervently as they did Negro slavery in the mid-nineteenth.

Further, when an investigator sent out over three hundred letters of

10. *Ibid.*, April 16, 1925, p. 507.
11. Gunnar Myrdal, *An American Dilemma. The Negro Problem and Modern Democracy* (2 vols., New York, 1944), II, 868.
12. Loescher, *The Protestant Church and the Negro*, p. 15.

inquiry to people from one end of the South to the other asking for examples of particularly good practices in race relations, less than a dozen replies referred to any known instance of organized church action. "So little does the Christian church," sadly commented the writer, "exemplify any practice better than that of the world to which it conforms."[13]

These examples are from the findings of other students. Independent research also revealed instance after instance of the racial pride of white Protestants. A few illustrations must serve to drive this point home.

For example, a New England minister suggested to his congregation that they invite the members of a neighboring Negro church to a supper, whereupon the ladies of his flock served notice that they would not attend such an affair, much less help prepare the meal. Or to take a second example. The first national student-faculty conference of the Council of Christian Associations meeting in Detroit in 1931 was racked by the race issue. The hotel, reneging on its signed agreement, segregated the Negro delegates, refusing them access to the same facilities as the whites. The whites voted to remain at the hotel. The Negroes bolted the conference.

Indeed, segregation at church meetings was always a problem. William Joseph McGlothlin, president of the Southern Baptist Convention, refused to attend a banquet to be given in his honor by the Rochester, New York, Baptist Association, when he discovered that by unhappy chance the banquet chairman was Dr. James E. Rose, Negro moderator of the Rochester group. In 1928 Southern Presbyterians in General Assembly went on record in favor of interracial good will and understanding—*after carefully segregating the Negro delegates!*

Resolutions or reports on the Negro problem were not infrequent, but truth to tell they were not always conclusive. For instance, the *complete* statement of the Committee on Interracial Relationships to the Northern Baptist Convention in 1929 read:

The Committee on Interracial Relationships for the last few years has found nothing definite to do, and has had no appropriation for its work. During the last year it has, therefore, done no work and has no report to make, unless it should reiterate the very true and important principles which it has presented before. It is doubtful whether such repetition would be of value; the committee therefore begs leave to be excused from making a report.[14]

In 1929 the Reverend William S. Blackshear of St. Matthew's Protestant Episcopal Church, Brooklyn, informed the Negroes in his congrega-

13. Charles S. Johnson and Associates, *Into the Main Stream. A Survey of Best Practices in Race Relations in the South* (Chapel Hill, 1947), p. 282.
14. *Annual of the Northern Baptist Convention*, 1929, p. 153.

tion that they were not welcome. When, on the other hand, an Episcopal minister in New York insisted upon permitting Negroes to worship, his vestry, by a vote of seven to four, had the church closed "for repairs" and locked. Similarly, the pastor of the Bethel Evangelical Church in Detroit resigned when two Negroes were denied membership.

When the National Preaching Mission reached Atlanta, Georgia, in 1936, the local church authorities decided that the Negro member should be excluded from the proceedings. It is instructive that the Chinese member, Dr. T. Z. Koo, promptly left the caravan in protest. Five years earlier Atlanta had played host to a conference of world Methodism. There was no segregation of delegates. However, when an attempt was made to report on the color problem it was blocked by the chairman on the grounds that reports could not refer to "specific evils." Whereupon a delegate with a sense of consistency immediately offered a resolution to the effect that any and all references to the enforcement of prohibition be expunged from the record in order to fully comply with the chairman's ruling.

Of greater moment to American Methodism is the fact that the Negro question was a major factor in delaying unification until 1939. Scores of Southern Methodists, including such leaders as Bishops Candler and Ainsworth, made clear their reluctance to accept any merger that would bring them into familiar contact with Negroes. ("Shall we Negroize the Methodist Church," it was asked?) The relative tolerance of Northern Methodists toward "people of color" was repeatedly chided by southerners. And when unification was consummated, most Methodist Negroes were placed in a Central Jurisdiction, an arrangement believed by many to mark a retrogression in race relations.

It is not pleasant to view the position taken by some churchmen at the time of the savage race riots following the First World War. In some of these riots the churches remained shamefully silent. For instance, although the riots of East St. Louis, Illinois, Phillips County, Arkansas, and Tulsa, Oklahoma, took a frightful toll of life and property, the Southern Baptist Convention, the state conventions of Arkansas and Oklahoma, and the district conventions which convened soon after the riots remained silent. In other cases, Negro agitators were blamed and the whites excused for resorting to violence. This myopic explanation for the cruel bloodshed was held by several responsible church journals and by a number of individual clergymen, including even such leaders as Methodist Bishop Mouzon and Episcopal Bishop Thurston. And what could whites do to prevent race riots? "Let our Christian people," suggested a Southern Episcopal journal, always conscious of propriety, "set the example of never occupying a seat in the street car reserved for colored people, no matter how crowded that car may be. . . . When certain seats are set aside for colored people in the street cars, they should be guarded and reserved for that purpose just as scrupulously as are the seats kept for the white people."[15]

Elements of the church press provide a clear indication of Protestantism's acceptance of the racial status quo. Literally hundreds of editorials and articles, the great majority of them appearing in southern journals, reflected the myth that a peaceful and harmonious relationship existed between the races. There was no need to trouble oneself about the "race problem" for the simple reason that the problem was nonexistent. The black and the white each had his place in the scheme of things, and it was suggested that this plan was part of God's orderly design for the races. On the one hand, "darkies" should be content, law abiding, industrious, peaceful, and happy in their subordinate but not onerous status. On the other, it was the white man's duty to be patient, helpful, understanding, kindly but firm in his relations with his child-like, simple, and often mischievous colored wards. In a word, the black should be proper and the white paternalistic.

The "good" Negro, then, played the role assigned to him in ante-bellum days—a faithful, cheerful, banjo-plunking clown who could, on occasion, be made to work hard. If, however, the Negro displayed the traditional American virtues of independence, ambition, pride, aggressiveness, resourcefulness, he did not "know his place" and was getting "uppish." The severest strictures of the whites were reserved for such aggressive Negro leaders as Du Bois, and for "meddling Yankees" who did not "understand" the black man and who encouraged him in his ambitions. And apparently the ultimate ambition of all blacks was to marry a white woman. Every attempt to break the existing caste system was answered with the charge that it would lead to the "amalgamation of the races." Social equality—there was the enemy!

It is important to remember that the clerical proponents of the racial status quo were hardly ever vicious or brutal in their arguments. Only very rarely was the Negro referred to in hostile tones. And there is the rub! Except for a few "radical" Negroes, the black man was considered a rather humorous and child-like individual hardly worthy of serious thought. Nature and Nature's God had placed upon the earth the black and the white, the one to serve and the other to rule. This relationship was to endure forever and if there was such a thing as a "race problem" —which few admitted—it was unsolvable. Save for the deletion of the word slavery, there had been little change since Civil War days in the white man's arguments of superiority. Even those who recognized that

15. *Southern Churchman*, Aug. 9, 1919, p. 13.

all was not perfect fell somewhat short in their analysis of the problem. For instance, a Kentucky Baptist began his discussion of race relations by recalling his beloved "ebon mammy" who crooned over his cradle and then concluded that

the race problem of the South can be composed, if we shall show the spirit of Christian helpfulness to the children of the child race whom our ancestors bought from slave ships to do their farm work for them.

The Negro is no angel. His weaknesses, sins and foibles are known to all men. But he also has good points that many other races have not. He is a patriot. He loves the South. He loves his "white folks." He understands the Southern white. He has a genius for religion. He does not hate or retain malice. The mean things sometimes said about whites by Negro writers will be found nearly always to be written by Negroes with white blood in them.

The Negro is a thousand times better for the South than the white Bolshevists, Radical Socialists and Atheists that are a curse in some other sections of America. Let us be faithful to God and help the Southern Negro to work out to wholesome and worthy ends the strange destiny which has placed him here among us.[16]

There was enough evidence of a different nature, however, to permit the hope that the churches had not entirely forsaken their redemptive mission. Timid and faltering as these formal, organized institutions often were, it was nevertheless through them that the teachings of Christ were preserved, perpetuated, and disseminated. It is absurd to claim the churches were unspotted; it is blindness to ignore their positive role in American history. The American Dream is based upon Christian foundations and the active presence of Christian faith has given a quiet strength and sustaining courage to millions of unremembered men and women. And Christian teachings have inspired many of the great reform and humanitarian movements in the nation's past. Even those crusaders for justice who disavow formal religion must acknowledge their indebtedness to the spiritual foundations of society which alone make justice possible. In a sense, all those questing decency in human relations draw upon the faith proclaimed by the churches, however unfaithful the churches may be to their own ideals. The churches are democratic in their fundamental values and, as even so critical an observer as Myrdal realized, by their very *being* they served to lessen racial pride. Try as it may, the conscience of America cannot ignore the Christian creed.

This point is illustrated by an observer who sent out fifty questionnaires to young people asking if they had overcome their racial prejudice and the influence contributing to this change. His findings were reported in the *World Tomorrow* of February, 1928:

16. *Western Recorder*, Aug. 23, 1923, p. 11.

The connection between vital religion and social pioneering is realized when one reflects that practically all the leadership in inter-racial student activity in the South comes from those who are active in Christian organizations. Either the liberal without religious affiliation is absent from the scene or he does not dare to risk social disapproval. But the organized church can take little comfort from these conclusions. As an institution it seems to have directly influenced the recipients of the questionnaire very slightly. The work of the ministry, the services of the church, the Sunday School, and the Young People's Society were seldom if at all referred to. . . . It is the old story that has occurred so often through the ages, of pioneering to which the church has been indifferent or which it has even opposed, but for which it has been fundamentally responsible because of the gospel which it has taught and half believed.

In the second place, before judging the churches too harshly it is well to remember their charitable contributions. Thousands of Negroes owe their education or their health to schools and hospitals founded and supported by Protestant denominations. It is true that expenditures to succor the American Negro were not large in relation to total church budgets. It is true that sometimes the churches concentrated on bringing the gospel to the "heathen Chinese" or the native of "darkest Africa" to the neglect of America's own second class Negro citizens. And it is further true that charitable works are no substitute for justice, for the giving of alms from one's pocketbook does not excuse racial pride in one's heart. It is interesting to speculate on what proportion of the funds given by churchmen to aid the Negro was in the form of "conscience money." Having made these admissions, the fact still remains that the Protestant churches did important work in bettering the education and health of the Negro. This sort of charitable work is sometimes deprecated by sophisticated liberals, but it must be placed in the scales when weighing the churches' contributions to racial justice.

It is not irrelevant to observe also that the important Commission on Interracial Co-operation, while not the instrument of any particular denomination, was born and led by devout churchmen. It worked closely with church groups and over 25 per cent of its members were ministers. In a very real sense the Commission, as the Association of Southern Women for the Prevention of Lynching, represented the leading Christian forces in the South.

The churches directly worked for racial justice in addition, as has been noted, to combating lynching. The record of the Federal Council, for example, was honorable. In the tension-fraught year, 1919, the Administrative Committee issued a special statement urging justice for the Negro. Included in the eight-point appeal were protection from mob violence, opportunity to hold the same work on the same terms as other men, the sanctity of the Negro home, equal traveling, educational, and recreational facilities, political equality, and closer cooperation between the races. These demands were reiterated in the Council's statement on "The Church and Social Reconstruction." The 1924 meeting of the Council held that the "assumption of inherent racial superiority by dominant groups around the world is neither supported by science nor justified by ethics."[17] The removal of discriminations in housing, schools, travel, and industry was urged, in addition to the equal protection of the law and other reforms. Repeatedly in the thirties the Council spoke on the Negro issue, especially in regard to segregation at church meetings. Putting precept into practice, the Council refused to fix definitely upon Indianapolis for its 1932 quadrennium until assurance had been given that all the delegates would be received without discrimination in the matter of race and color.

The attitude of the Council was also reflected in its two journals. The *Federal Council Bulletin* carried hundreds of references to the Negro question, and at least a score of issues of *Information Service* were devoted to race relations. A contributor seemed to express the general tone of these items. The good Christian, he believed, should not be willing to stop with justice alone, "But justice is a good starting point and, if we follow the road honestly, we shall have quite enough to do for a while."[18]

In addition, a Commission on the Church and Race Relations (later the Department of Race Relations) was organized in 1921. It held hundreds of interracial conferences, sought the birth of local interracial committees, encouraged the exchange of pulpits, printed thousands of posters and pamphlets, sent out speakers, established a Race Relations Sunday (first observed in 1923) and a Brotherhood Month. At one time this group was headed by a Negro and seemed to rely on education to lessen friction between the races. For instance, in 1939 this group distributed exactly 10,320 educational posters and 82,349 pieces of other educational literature. The effectiveness of this activity is not made clear in the reports of the group.

Northern Methodism also assumed a relatively advanced position on the Negro question. It is fitting that this should be so for Methodism's interest in the Negro dated back to the first General Conference of 1784 when the question was asked: "What methods can we take to extirpate slavery?" The Episcopal Address to the 1920 General Conference pointed out that this is not a white man's world nor was the church a white man's church. Talk of "lesser breeds," inferior castes, and "white man's

17. *Quadrennial Report of the Federal Council of Churches,* 1920-24, p. 82.
18. *Federal Council Bulletin,* March, 1927, p. 16.

burdens" is not for Methodists. Four years later the bishops again spoke on the race question. The Conference also adopted a resolution introduced by E. Stanley Jones rejecting "as unchristian and untrue the idea that certain races are born to inherent and fixed superiority and rulership, while others are born to inherent and fixed inferiority and subordination. We stand for the life of open opportunity for all."[19] In 1926 when the Methodist Board of Bishops met in Washington, three Negro bishops, quite unknown to their white comrades, were excluded from a dinner given by the Washington Methodist Union. To assuage the wound, the bishops unanimously adopted a statement declaring that in the future they would not attend segregated meetings. The 1928 General Conference adopted a report reaffirming the oneness of humanity and calling for equal opportunity in religion, education, citizenship, and industry. In addition, a long statement on social ideals included a demand for the elimination of racial discrimination and for the equal rights of all. Bishop Robert E. Jones, a Negro, presided over a conference session, and the delegates adopted a resolution thanking Bishop Jones for his courtesy and skill.

The world service agencies of the Methodist Episcopal Church issued a New Year's message for 1931 which contained a strong statement on race relations. A more significant action took place at the 1932 General Conference. It was here that Northern Methodists adopted the following resolution introduced by Ernest Fremont Tittle:

WHEREAS, 'There cannot be Greek and Jew, circumcision and uncircumcision; barbarian, Scythian, bondman, freedman, but Christ is all and in all'; therefore, be it

RESOLVED, That the General Conference of the Methodist Episcopal Church shall hereafter meet only in cities where hotels, sufficient in number to accommodate its Delegates, shall in writing agree to meet the following conditions:

(1) No segregation of specific groups in room assignments.
(2) No discrimination against any Delegates in the use of hotel entrances, lobbies, elevators, dining rooms and other hotel services or facilities.
(3) Specific instruction of hotel employes by the hotel authorities regarding the interracial character of the Conference and the treatment of all Delegates with equal courtesy.[20]

The Committee on Entertainment took this resolution seriously and in 1936 informed each inviting city plainly of the conditions upon which invitations would be accepted. Columbus, Ohio, observed the agreement in both spirit and letter and the 1936 General Conference was unmarred

19. *Journal of the General Conference of the Methodist Episcopal Church*, 1924, p. 295.
20. *Ibid.*, 1932, pp. 259-60.

by segregation. At this meeting the bishops once again condemned racial intolerance.

From time to time Methodist conferences at the local level issued pronouncements on the Negro question. Certain it is that the Methodist Federation for Social Service assumed an unequivocal position regarding the sinfulness of racial pride. Encouraging too is the fact that the National Council of Methodist Youth adopted statements on race relations that could hardly have been stronger. The Epworth League also gave evidence of lessened prejudice among Methodist young people.

Southern Methodists were conscious of a Negro problem. In 1919 the Committee on Temperance and Social Service called for cooperation and helpfulness between the races and cautioned whites to accept the child-like infirmities of the Negro with tolerance. By 1922 the tone had become less patronizing. The Episcopal Address of that year observed the great strides made by Negroes since emancipation and asked that they be accorded justice "where their lawful rights are concerned." An adopted report to this Conference sought the solution to intolerance by the application of "Christian principles." In 1926 Southern Methodists held Christ's teachings concerning human brotherhood required equal justice and opportunity for all persons regardless of race or color.

In 1930 the bishops issued a strong condemnation of racial pride and pointed out specific disabilities which must be ended. Four years later the bishops again maintained that Negroes "deserve and should have equality before the law, social, civil, and industrial justice, equitable educational, community, and religious advantages, and a human chance at the finer spiritual realities of American life."[21] These sentiments were echoed in the adopted report of the Committee on Temperance and Social Service, with the additional provision that Negroes be guaranteed by law the equal protection to life, liberty, and property. The Conference as a whole adopted a social creed calling for justice, opportunity, and equal rights for all regardless of race. In 1938 the Episcopal Address indicted the white race for its unchristian and proud attitude toward the Negro and again noted the Negro's needs in the fields of housing, education, the courts and economic life.

The Uniting Conference of 1939 also demanded justice for the Negro. It is true that the place of Negro Methodists in the new merger was a compromise to white pride. So much so, indeed, that many white Methodists felt it was too high a price to pay for unification. Such was the attitude of Ernest Fremont Tittle, the New York East Conference, *Zion's Herald,* and the National Council of Methodist Youth, to mention

21. *Journal of the General Conference of the Methodist Episcopal Church, South,* 1934, p. 369.

a few examples of those who believed that the color line in Methodism should be completely erased. And yet it is significant that Charles S. Johnson, noted Negro leader, found in the compromise much that was good, believing it on the whole a "great step towards terminating sectionalism and racialism and bringing many Methodists together into one great church stream of all-American life."[22]

Southern Methodists in local conferences now and then championed tolerance. The unofficial Council on a Christian Social Order did important work in bettering race relations.

There remains only the task of assessing the attitude of the Methodist press toward the Negro. With the exception of the *Arkansas Methodist,* the record of those papers examined was excellent. *Zion's Herald,* published in Boston, was very advanced in its thinking on race relations. It carried scores of editorials and articles on the Negro, many of the contributed items being written by Negroes. From the race riots of 1919 to the unification compromise of 1939 this journal consistently and courageously championed the Negro. Nor was its tone paternalistic. Inherently the white was not superior to the black. The Negro deserved not merely kindness, but justice and equality—and equality that was not on a segregated basis.

Perhaps it is unfair to single out this Boston paper for special praise, because actually both the *New York* and the *Northwestern Christian Advocates* were almost as advanced. In countless items these journals sought to end the Negro's second class citizenship. They damned a segregated America and a segregated church.

Of great significance is that these views, somewhat modified, were accepted by the *Nashville Christian Advocate.* In the matter of race relations, this Methodist publication was clearly the most liberal of denominational church journals published in the South. Not only did it demand justice for the Negro, it did so without undue patronage and by specifically pinpointing the inequities suffered by the Negro. "The unavoidable fact is," maintained the editors, "racial prejudice and racial enmity are un-Christian—are now and ever will be."[23] Or witness this statement:

How often do we hear, "The Negro is all right in his place." As to that matter, the white man is all right in his place, but he is too frequently out of place. We are told that the Negro is inferior and will always remain so. Those who reiterate this seem to doubt it, since they feel impelled to resort to artificial pressure to "keep him down".... The fact is any person of one race is only superior to a member of any other race as he is *superior*.[24]

22. Johnson, *Into the Main Stream,* p. 294.
23. Feb. 28, 1936, p. 287.   24. Nov. 12, 1937, pp. 1444-45.

All in all, if Methodism be judged not by the uncompromising Christian ethic but by the prevailing attitude of white Americans, it need not be too ashamed of its record on race relations.

Northern Baptists were articulate on the Negro problem. In 1922 the Northern Baptist Convention adopted a resolution ruing unchristian discrimination, and favored legislation to remedy matters. The following Convention resolved to organize interracial committees at the local level. In 1925 the American Baptist Foreign Missionary Society held the most ominous sign on the world horizon was the apparent growth of race prejudice. In this year also the Convention believed America could not survive if racial lines continued to separate the nation into groups that misunderstood and despised one another. In 1926 the Committee on Interracial Relationships slashed at the "barbarous assumption of racial superiority" which caused whites to disdain and neglect their Negro neighbors. The Committee suggested that "so long as Negroes cannot get lodgings or food in some towns, and have in many places, North and South, inferior wages, housing, police protection, street lighting, and schools, and are treated by many professing Christians as the Jews treated the Samaritans; there is need of emphasizing the spirit of Christ in race relations."[25] Two years later this Committee reported to the Convention that the superiority of any one race was a shibboleth. Moreover, since racial antipathy is not inborn or innate, but inherited and communicated, all Christians should avoid by word and deed the passing on to the younger generations the racial hatreds of the past.

The opening year of the Depression Decade found the Northern Baptist Convention terming race prejudice the greatest hindrance to the establishment of the Kingdom of God on earth. This view was repeated in 1931 and 1934, with special reference to the desperate economic plight of the Negroes. In 1935 a resolution was adopted calling for equality in education, housing, and labor. Since race prejudice was unchristian the Convention also voted to hold future meetings in only those cities where accommodations would be available to all delegates regardless of race or color. The delegates to the next Convention promised to boycott restaurants and other establishments that discriminated against Negroes. America was guilty of flagrantly unchristian practices toward the Negro, believed Northern Baptists in 1937, and this view was repeated in 1938 and 1939. From time to time local Baptist groups took a strong stand against racial intolerance.

The Southern Baptist Convention was not silent on lynching, as has been noted, but aside from this there was little to indicate concern with the Negro problem. In 1920 and 1932 calls were issued for a more

25. *Annual of the Northern Baptist Convention*, 1926, pp. 168-69.

brotherly treatment of the Negro, but it was not until the report of the Home Missions Board in 1937 that Southern Baptists spoke with vigor. This report emphasized the infinite worth of personality, regardless of color. It flatly stated that the Negro was not divinely doomed to perpetual subordination. And it listed specific disabilities which must be removed in education, housing, the courts, and labor. The report concluded: "In making these suggestions it is recognized that our conventional attitudes toward other races, our assumption of superiority, our consequent arrogance and lack of consideration, the limitations of opportunity which we lay on those whom we count inferior, the petty humiliations which we visit upon them, constitute some of the greatest paradoxes of all times. For it is, or should be, assumed that Christians neither would nor could be guilty of such; but the facts are too well known to be denied."[26]   In 1939 the Southern Baptist Convention adopted a very vigorous resolution calling for the end of inequalities. Occasionally Baptist state and district conventions assumed an advanced position.

The Southern Baptist press was not noted for its tolerance on the race question. To be sure, a few excellent articles thundered for justice and now and then editorials pointed out the grievances suffered by Negroes. But these were exceptions. On the whole the Southern Baptist press appeared satisfied with the racial status quo. In the North, the *Baptist* had a particularly fine record. It pointed out the sinfulness of racial pride with Garrison-like bluntness.

To generalize, it can be said that Northern Baptists displayed a greater awareness of the unchristian nature of race relations in America than their southern brethren, but that toward the end of the thirties even Southern Baptists began to speak rather strongly.

Northern Presbyterians were not silent. In 1919 the General Assembly condemned mob violence and in 1920 the Standing Committee on Freedmen rather patronizingly urged the extension of a brotherly hand to the colored people. A resolution of 1922 called upon Presbyterians to aid the Negro in securing better education, health, housing, recreation, and all other necessities of a Christian community. The 1928 General Assembly adopted a strongly worded protest against racial intolerance.

In the Depression Decade almost every one of the General Assemblies discussed the Negro issue. A resolution of 1937 catches the spirit of these discussions:

We accept completely the ideal of the brotherhood of all races, as all are the children of God. We therefore call upon Christians everywhere to practice mutual good-will and coöperation among all racial groups, to eliminate every

26. *Annual of the Southern Baptist Convention*, 1937, pp. 271-72.

form of discrimination and to work actively for the recognition of the civil and religious rights of all minority groups. Conscious of our failures in the past to act upon this accepted principle, we urge that particularly in all conferences under the sanction of the church the utmost care be taken to avoid discrimination.[27]

From time to time presbyteries went on record in support of racial justice and, occasionally, in Omaha and Pittsburgh, for instance, a Negro was elected moderator of a presbytery. The Presbyterian Board of Christian Education, through special pamphlets and its regular journals, *Moral Welfare* and *Social Progress,* spoke strongly. It is difficult to see how its criticism of racial pride could have been more severe. Further, the unofficial Presbyterian Fellowship for Social Action fought to end racial disabilities.

Apparently Southern Presbyterians did not have a deep sense of guilt concerning the treatment of Negroes in America. The 1921 General Assembly requested justice and righteousness in race relations, but it did not speak again forcefully until 1936. The Assembly of that year, however, heard an effective presentation of the Negro's plight by the Committee on Moral and Social Welfare. Citing statistics, the report showed how the Negro suffered in education, health, politics, the courts, and economic life. This group again reported to the Assembly in 1937. It was perhaps the ablest presentation of the Negro's grievances ever read before a church conference in the South. It was specific and it was excellent. A few instances appeared in the church press of local groups of Southern Presbyterians taking a liberal stand on the race issue, but they were neither frequent nor very vigorous in expression.

What was the record of the Presbyterian press? The *Christian Observer,* published in Kentucky, confined itself almost exclusively to religious news and items on the Negro were rare. It did comment harshly on mob violence and from time to time pointed out examples of Negro progress, but there was little indication of real dissatisfaction with existing Negro-white relationships. On the other hand, the *Presbyterian Advance,* published in Nashville, assumed a quite liberal attitude toward the Negro. On the whole, this journal could be termed a strong defender of Negro rights even if it never urged full equality. Certainly its position was far ahead of average southern white opinion. It is significant also that the official monthly of Southern Presbyterians, *Program Builder,* carried a series of lessons for young people in which a more Christian treatment of the Negro was urged.

In the North, the *Presbyterian Tribune* was probably the most advanced on racial issues as it was on economic matters. And yet the

27. *Minutes of the General Assembly of the Presbyterian Church, U.S.A.,* 1937, p. 223.

record of such papers as the *Continent* and the *Presbyterian Banner* was quite good also. A half-dozen other Presbyterian journals were less vigorous in their arguments, but even they realized the Negro suffered injustices.

Speaking broadly, Northern Presbyterians could be cited as an influence for breaking down racial barriers, and Southern Presbyterians were perhaps a shade in advance of the general thinking of their section.

Congregationalists, historically the Negro's friend and geographically concentrated north of the Mason-Dixon Line, displayed dissatisfaction with existing race relations. In 1919 they pledged themselves to fight race prejudice and every means by which men rob our neighbor of his good name. They further claimed for the Negro equal rights before the law and the complete citizenship guaranteed by the Constitution, and called attention to the acute problems confronting the black in housing, industry, and education. The 1921 National Council urged Congregationalists to form local interracial committees and steps were taken to promote these groups. Twice again this Council spoke on the need for racial justice.

The famous social creed of Congregationalism, adopted in 1925, requested the elimination of racial discrimination. To augment this view a Commission on Inter-Racial Relations, with Albert W. Palmer as chairman, was established. This group promoted Race Relations Sunday, worked with the Federal Council, published a quarterly bulletin, sent forth speakers, and investigated specific cases of racial injustice. At the next Council, church groups were urged not to meet in any hotel or club that practiced segregation. The 1931 General Council of the now united Congregational and Christian Churches resolved not to meet in any city or any hotel that could not promise in advance equal treatment to all delegates. And in 1934 the General Conference spoke on specific abuses and stated that racial prejudice was rooted in a competitive economic order. The idea of Nordic superiority, the statement continued, is a rationalization growing out of the desire to keep other races in subjection.

In the meantime, the Commission on Social Relations, through seminars and its publication, *Church and Society,* attacked race prejudice in an outspoken fashion. The official Congregational Council for Social Action, founded in 1934, had a Committee on Race Relations as one of its four major departments. Although it worked for tolerance, it was probably the Council's weakest department and no great credit can be given to its activities. The *Congregationalist,* the denominational journal, did its bit in the cause of racial justice.

The Protestant Episcopal Church is one of the distinctly national churches. Although most of its congregations are all white or all Negro, it is not divided into racial branches. It frequently spoke on lynching and mob violence and forwarded race relations through the American Church Institute for Negroes, the authorized agency responsible to the General Convention. Having said this, it still remains true that only rarely did the General Convention indicate an interest in the Negro. This gap was compensated somewhat by the fact that unofficial agencies and the Episcopal press were generally advanced in their thinking on the Negro question, albeit the *Southern Churchman* supported a segregated society.

Without presenting the evidence in detail, it may be said that other denominations on occasion forwarded the cause of racial justice. The Disciples of Christ, for example, resolved not to meet in International Convention unless assurance was given that there would be no discrimination against Negro delegates. A special advance guard traveled to the city in question to confirm these arrangements. The United Lutheran Church, the Unitarians, and the Evangelical and Reformed Church spoke on the Negro question, as did other denominations.

Denominational journals, in varying degrees, urged racial justice. The *Reformed Church Messenger, Christian Register,* and *Universalist Leader* had excellent records, as did the *Christian-Evangelist* in the thirties. On the other hand, a Negro would probably rate the *Lutheran* as something less than a warm friend.

Several undenominational journals had enviable records. The *Christian Work* and the *Christian Herald* laid claim to racial enlightenment, while the *World Tomorrow* and the *Christian Century* displayed a sensitivity toward the Negro probably unmatched in any papers in the country, religious or secular. This is important, particularly in the case of the *Christian Century*. The most influential Protestant periodical in the country, it devoted scores of items to the race question. Without exception, these editorials and articles were characterized by courage, candor, and compassion.

Similar praise can be bestowed on a number of unofficial cooperative religious organizations. The Fellowship of Reconciliation and the Fellowship of Southern Churchmen provide happy examples of blacks and whites working together to further the cause of Christ, which meant, in part, the end of racial pride. It is to the credit of the whites in these organizations that they accepted the brotherhood of man, fully aware that in so doing they were inviting contempt and even physical violence from other whites. Other groups such as the Fellowship of Socialist Christians, although primarily concerned with economic matters, worked to better the lot of the Negro in America.

And what can be said of the record of individual churchmen? Many examples could be cited—albeit mostly from the North—of a minister bolting a conference or resigning a pastorate or signing a petition or preaching a sermon in the interest of racial justice.

V

To cite chapter and verse for these instances would not absolve American Protestantism of the charge that it all too often—in congregations, seminaries, church colleges, assemblies—accommodated itself to prejudice at the peril of its own soul. Christ must weep at the fraility of His church. And yet, as the years passed Protestantism came increasingly to the recognition that a segregated church *content in its segregation* was wrong. And as the years passed, also, the gulf between Christ's ideal of brotherhood and men's practices narrowed.

Certainly the magnificent showing made by the Protestant churches on desegregation in the forties and fifties drew strength from the precedents established in the twenties and more especially in the thirties. The churches have led in shattering racial pride in America, and although much remains to be done, there abides the hope that the churches will continue to send forth crusaders for racial justice.

Part V

The Churches and War and Peace

CHAPTER XXI

War and Peace in a Peaceful Decade

"And he shall judge among the nations, and shall rebuke many people: and they shall beat their swords into plowshares, and their spears into pruninghooks: nation shall not lift up sword against nation, neither shall they learn war any more."

—Isaiah 3:4

I

WITH THE exception of a handful of pacifist clergymen, many of whom were also Socialists, American Protestantism gave its blessing to the war effort in 1917-18.* Preachers presented arms with the rest of the nation. This is neither surprising nor blameworthy. The churches, for the most part, did not urge intervention, but once war came they accepted the justice of the struggle. Wilsonian idealism clothed the appeal to the sword in the mantle of a holy crusade. In the course of the fighting it was inevitable that some ministers would succumb to wartime hysteria and view the Germans not merely as an enemy to be defeated but as "mad dogs" and "damnable criminals." Love of country, then, was sometimes combined with hatred of the "Hun."[1]

However, the attitude of the Protestant churches is not quite as reprehensible as some commentators—including churchmen themselves—later insisted. It is possible to admire the pacifists who refused to support the war without indicting, as Ray H. Abrams does in his study, *Preachers Present Arms,* all those churchmen who believed their duty lay in another direction. A pacifist between wars is like a prohibitionist between drinks, argued Episcopal Bishop Paul Jones. Logically appealing, this aphorism has little relevance to the large number of clerics who hated war and labored for peace in time of peace, but who accepted the gage of battle once it had been thrown down.

II

As American Protestantism believed the war just, so it believed the Treaty of Versailles fair. Germany, the aggressor, had lost, and she must

---

* Substantial portions of this chapter first appeared in *The Historian,* XIX (Nov., 1956).

1. Asked to renew his subscription, an Episcopal rector complained to a church paper editor: "A little insertion from 1914 to 1918 of German Monstrosity, and a christian [sic] mans [sic] clear duty would have done no harm." G. R. Van De Water to Silas McBee, Jan. 29, 1919, McBee *papers.*

pay her debt to civilization. "History holds no record of peace-making," averred a Presbyterian spokesman, "more significant of Christian influences."[2] A Disciples journal found no prejudice, revenge, or hatred in the peace and felt the terms to Germany would stand the acid test of the teachings of Jesus. An Episcopal paper viewed the treaty as the charter of a new civilization, comparable to the Magna Charta and the Declaration of Independence.

There were some leading ministers who refused to call the treaty a "Christian peace," but who nevertheless defended its essential fairness. If the terms were severe, they were no harsher than Germany deserved. The *Universalist Leader* growled editorially: "There will be general satisfaction with the severity of the terms to Germany, and she deserves just what she is getting. Taking her own announced purpose of what she would do with her enemies when she had beaten them, her maudlin whine of 'drastic terms,' appears nothing less than craven. She pleads for justice, but the world is not brutal enough to give it to her!"[3] After all, maintained another church spokesman, the treaty was not designed to be a "source of joy to the German people. It was not prepared for their pleasure, but as an expression of justice. It is not a reward of merit, but a verdict for a guilty nation, and is to be accepted by it as a court sentence is accepted by a prisoner at the bar."[4]

Within ten or fifteen years clerical criticism of the Treaty of Versailles became as common and as fashionable as denunciations of liquor, but in 1919 and 1920 only a very small minority of churchmen found the peace unjust. And this minority was composed almost entirely of Left of center ministers such as John Haynes Holmes and liberal journals such as the *World Tomorrow*. Speaking for some secular as well as clerical liberals, Holmes termed the treaty a "flat betrayal of the hopes and ideals with which America sincerely entered into the War."[5] In addition, by late 1919 the influential *Christian Century,* originally an advocate of a tough peace, called the terms "punitive, vindictive, terrorizing. They look to the impossible end of permanently maiming Germany. They are not redemptive, and they are therefore not Christian."[6]

Nevertheless, in the immediate post-war period, criticism of the Treaty of Versailles in church quarters was the exception rather than the rule. The revisionists add this fact to their long list of charges against the churches: not only did the churches support an unjust and bloody war, they also endorsed an unholy and vindictive peace. If and when the final verdict is in, however, the treaty may be judged less harsh and those who supported it less cruel than the revisionists believed.

2. *New Era Magazine,* Aug., 1919, p. 423.   3. May 24, 1919, pp 480-81.
4. *Herald and Presbyter,* May 14, 1919, p. 6.
5. *World Tomorrow,* June, 1919, p. 169.   6. Sept. 18, 1919, p. 6.

To American Protestantism the most significant aspect of the treaty was unquestionably the League of Nations. It appealed to the idealism of the churches and gave the hope that the war had not been fought in vain. Perhaps dimly aware that the war had been something less than a noble crusade of righteousness against evil, churchmen embraced the League as if to prove to themselves that their motives had been pure. Whatever the motivation, the major Protestant churches gave overwhelming endorsement to the League.

For example, the Federal Council cabled Wilson at Paris hailing the League as the "political expression of the Kingdom of God on earth."[7] To make certain that the President got the point, a committee of five sailed to Paris to convey the message in person. At a special meeting in Cleveland in 1919, at Baltimore in 1919, and at the regular quadrennial meeting of 1920 this great cooperative body endorsed the League. The Council did more than resolve. A Sunday was set aside for special prayer and supplication. Protestants were urged to make their wishes felt in the Senate. Speakers toured the country and local church committees were established to stimulate sentiment in favor of the League. A flood of pamphlets was unleashed, one series going to over one hundred thousand ministers. The *Federal Council Bulletin* was brought into play. The United States Senate and President-elect Harding were informed of the moral and religious principles underlying the League. As the intensity of the fight in the Senate became clear, the Council insisted upon ratification "with such reservations only as are necessary to safeguard the constitution of the United States and which shall not substantially alter the character of the Covenant, and shall not require its submission to the allies and Germany, and shall not in any way hinder the full and equal participation on the part of the United States in all the activities of the League."[8]

Closely cooperating with the Federal Council were the Church Peace Union and the World Alliance for International Friendship Through the Churches. Both groups, now that the fighting had ceased, once again labored for a warless world. A good starting point was a League of Nations. And so these peace agencies threw all of their resources into the fight for ratification. Pamphlets were issued, the Senate petitioned, speakers sent forth, meetings held, all to the end that America might not turn its back on the world. "The issue is squarely joined," believed Henry A. Atkinson, of the Church Peace Union. "The Church must lift its voice, must cry aloud and spare none. Those who are against a League of Nations are for war."[9] Mr. Atkinson put the matter a little

7. *Report of Special Meeting of the Federal Council of Churches*, 1919, p. 9.
8. *Federal Council Bulletin*, Jan., 1920, p. 9.   9. *Ibid.*, March, 1919, p. 42.

strongly. More to the point is that 14,450 clergymen, representing virtually every denomination, affixed their signatures to a monster petition urging the Senate to ratify the League without amendments or such reservations as would require resubmission of the treaty to the peace conference. In late 1919 a canvass revealed that 17,309 clergymen—Protestant, Catholic, and Jewish—favored the League without drastic changes, while only 805—mostly Irish Catholic priests—recorded their opposition. Further, the Church Peace Union and the World Alliance for International Friendship organized, in conjunction with the League to Enforce Peace, a Committee on the Churches and the Moral Aims of the War. This agency sent out speakers, held institutes for ministers, published literature, and in general organized religious leadership in support of the League. Over 33,000 ministers and 700,000 laymen attended meetings sponsored by the committee.

Denominational pronouncements supporting the League were very numerous. Northern Methodists in 1916 called upon the United States to take the lead in the establishment of a league or federation of nations, and in 1919 the bishops of the Methodist Episcopal Church urged acceptance of Wilson's plan. The bishops repeated their plea for a "real and effective" League at the General Conference of 1920. The Conference greeted the utterance warmly and ordered the message transmitted to the President and the Senate. Earlier the Board of Foreign Missions expressed approval of the League. At least twenty-nine annual conferences in the North alone endorsed the League either with or without reservations, but by 1920 the number had dropped to seven. Further, Bishop Edwin Holt Hughes stated that he did not know of a single minister in the Methodist Episcopal Church who opposed the adoption of the League. This was at least a slight exaggeration inasmuch as he made this statement in reply to a minister who obviously opposed the League.

The first post-war General Conference of Southern Methodism did not meet until 1922, and hence the Conference did not speak on the merits of the Treaty of Versailles. However, such leaders as Bishop John M. Moore were on record favorably.

In 1919 the Northern Baptist Convention adopted a resolution asking that Baptists use their "utmost influence" to secure the ratification of the treaty. This plea was repeated by the Social Service Committee in 1920 and the Convention as a whole condemned the Senate for "leaving the world in chaos, ignoring the plainly indicated desire and will of the people, and forfeiting our conceded leadership in world reconstruction."[10] Many state and local Baptist groups in the North also backed the League.

10. *Annual of the Northern Baptist Convention*, 1920, p. 227.

Although the Southern Baptist Convention did not officially speak, such leaders as Convention President E. Y. Mullins were on record. In addition, Dr. George W. Truett, perhaps the South's most distinguished minister, delivered an eloquent address from the east steps of the Capitol in defense of the League.

The 1919 General Assembly of Northern Presbyterians strongly resolved in favor of the League, and the 1920 Assembly by specific decision termed the Senate's rejection of the League the "most profound and shameful humiliation ever suffered in all their [the American people's] history. The prestige and moral leadership of our beloved country has been trampled under foot, our lofty idealism and proud championship of the rights of small nations has been virtually labeled hypocrisy, and the astounding fiasco has made us the laughing stock and derision of the world."[11] The General Assembly of the United Presbyterian Church was on record, and an observer after a tour of the Middle West found Presbyterian parsons vigorously promoting the League.

Episcopalians, in General Convention in 1919, endorsed the League through resolutions by the House of Bishops and the House of Deputies. These resolutions, restrained in wording, were passed on to the Senate. Diocese conventions spoke, as did the bishops of Pittsburgh, Connecticut, Florida, Vermont, Albany, Michigan, North Carolina, Erie, Maine, and Spokane. Thundered the Bishop of Maine: "For the honor of our country . . . , for the victory of reason over barbarism, for the cause of Christ and His suffering members, and for the doctrine of love which He taught, let us raise our voices for the acceptance of the League of Nations."[12] Further, the Lambeth Conference, representing the entire Anglican communion, termed the League the most promising step towards the ideal of the family of nations ever projected.

Congregationalists in 1917 recognized the necessity of an international federation, and when Wilson presented the country with the League, they endorsed it. The National Council of 1919 favored the League, forwarded its views to the Senate, urged that the resolution be read in the pulpits of the land, and gave the statement wide publicity. The record shows that local Congregational groups acted. The Hampden, Massachusetts, Congregational ministers, for example, informed Senator Henry Cabot Lodge of their displeasure at his stand.

Other denominations evidenced approval. The American Unitarian Association held that the "full results of the war cannot be obtained except through an effective League of Nations such as that proposed by

11. *Minutes of the General Assembly of the Presbyterian Church, U.S.A.*, 1920, pp. 207-8.

12. *Southern Churchman*, July 5, 1919, p. 5.

the Paris Conference."[13]   The General Synod of the Reformed Church in the United States favored the "speedy ratification of the Treaty of Peace and participation in a League of Nations, being thoroughly convinced that some form of international covenant which seeks to prevent war is a moral necessity."[14]   The United Lutheran Church recorded its support of the League, and the secretary of the Evangelical Lutheran Synod of North America believed that the great majority of the ministers of his church favored it.   The Church of the Brethren also gave its approval.

The attitude of a few church journals was less enthusiastic.   The liberal *World Tomorrow,* indeed, rejoiced in the Senate's rejection of the League, for this kept the United States "from a close partnership with the unholy Alliance which has brought to devasted Europe not peace but new wars."[15]   The *Christian Century* saw the League as the one saving feature of the Treaty of Versailles.   Since there was no hope of changing the Treaty by rejecting it, the only thing to do was to accept it and trust to God and the League to preserve peace in the future.

The remainder of the church press appeared virtually unanimous in its support of the League.   A few journals kept their enthusiasm in check, but the great majority accepted the League with an alacrity and warmth equal to their acceptance of prohibition.   The independent *Christian Work,* edited by Frederick Lynch, who had long been an ardent advocate of peace and official in peace organizations, viewed the fight over the League as a holy crusade.   In literally scores of editorials and articles this journal attacked anti-League individuals with all the zeal of a fundamentalist on the trail of a modernist.   A second independent paper, the *Christian Herald,* exhibited only slightly less fervor, while the *Homiletic Review* termed the League an "International Magna Carta."

The Methodist press did its part.   The *New York Christian Advocate,* commenting on the defeat of the League, suggested that America change its motto from "In God We Trust" to "Ourselves Alone."   The *Northwestern Christian Advocate* termed the League the "most profoundly significant document ever penned by man,"[16] and suggested it was "destined to more profoundly affect the course of human history than any one act since the sacrifice of Christ."[17]   "Blind fatuity," "blatant selfishness," and "partisan narrowness" were some of the terms used by the *Nashville Christian Advocate* against opponents of the League.

13. *Annual Report of the American Unitarian Association,* 1918-19, p. 85.

14. *Acts and Proceedings of the General Synod of the Reformed Church in the United States,* 1920, p. 124.

15. Dec., 1919, p. 327.   16. Feb. 19, 1919, p. 197.

17. Feb. 5, 1919, p. 147.

Zion's Herald and the *Methodist Review* added their support, and the *Arkansas Methodist* was proud to announce that one of its pro-League editorials had been printed in the *Congressional Record*.

At least six Presbyterian papers gave the League zealous backing and one, the *Presbyterian Banner,* displayed luke-warm approval. Similarly, at least five Baptist journals supported the League. The *Living Church,* an Episcopal publication, commented when the League went down in defeat: "This is the day of America's shame before the world and at the bar of history."[18] The *Southern Churchman* believed the "objections and criticisms of the League of Nations proceeding from the Senate chamber and certain newspapers may be ascribed to narrow-minded partisanship, to sheer selfishness or to moral cowardice, but they will have their evil effect."[19] The *Congregationalist* gave its approval, while the *Christian-Evangelist,* a Disciples paper published in St. Louis, displayed a devotion to the League unsurpassed by any church paper in the land. Almost as partisan were the *Reformed Church Messenger* and the Unitarian organ, the *Christian Register.* "We are in the relentless hands of men," declared the latter journal in reference to the Senate, "of that shameful breed who dare to cover their dark and stupid works with the garment of patriotism."[20] The *Universalist Leader* gave generously of itself in defense of the League, while the *Lutheran* evidenced approval in a more cautious fashion.

It remains only to observe that the leaders of American Protestantism were virtually unanimous in their endorsement of the League. Harry Emerson Fosdick, Robert Speer, S. Parkes Cadman, Peter Ainslie, Charles Jefferson, Shailer Mathews, Worth Tippy, William Brown, Graham Taylor, Charles Macfarland, William Merrill, George Truett, E. Y. Mullins, Bishop Brent—to mention a few of the greater names— were all on record. In short, the Protestant churches seemed to agree with Joseph Fort Newton's estimate of the League: "It is the noblest achievement so far in the history of statesmanship."[21]

It is commonly believed that with the rejection of the League that the United States turned its back on the world and retreated into a shell of selfish isolation. Whatever truth this thesis may have for America as a whole, it does not jibe with the attitude of the Protestant churches. In the decade of the twenties Protestantism evidenced a great interest in and concern for America's relations with other countries.

This conclusion is illustrated, in the first place, by the fact that the churches did not completely push the League out of their thoughts. The

18. March 27, 1920, p. 701.   19. June 28, 1919, p. 4.
20. March 18, 1920, p. 274.
21. *Reformed Church Messenger,* Oct. 16, 1919, p. 8.

Federal Council believed that, with proper reservations, the United States should join that body. In any event, America's relations with the League should be full, open, and friendly. The League was praised in special bulletins, and at the end of the decade Council officer Cavert held that its accomplishments made an impressive list.

The 1924 and 1928 General Conferences of Northern Methodism urged participation in the League. Now and then this position was taken by various annual conferences and agencies. The Committee on Temperance and Social Service of Southern Methodism, in 1922 and 1926, expressed approval of the League. Indeed, a student of Methodism believes that in the twenties official Methodism used every available means to strengthen the desire for participation.

The Southern Baptist Convention suggested cooperation with the League and the Northern Baptist Convention supported membership in that body. The General Convention of the Protestant Episcopal Church spoke kindly of it. Congregationalists in National Council and at the state level assumed this position, as did groups of Presbyterians. The Commission on International Friendship of the General Synod of the Reformed Church in the United States suggested American adherence, and the American Unitarian Association upheld the wisdom of this course. A referendum of Disciples ministers in 1925 found 80 per cent favoring the League, as did well over 50 per cent of the ministers of Philadelphia. The list of church groups favoring American cooperation with or membership in (and the distinction was not always made clear) the League could be extended: the Church Peace Union, the World Alliance for International Friendship Through the Churches, the National Study Conference on the Church and World Peace—representing twenty-eight denominations—the Y.W.C.A., the Christian Church, the Moravians, the Christian Endeavor, and others.

While the churches continued to support the League as an instrument for world peace, on the whole they placed greater hope in the Permanent Court for International Justice. After much controversy, the Senate of the United States finally voted qualified adherence to the Court in 1926. However, one of the reservations attached to American entrance was unacceptable to the other members, and the whole problem of America and the Court was carried over to the thirties. It seems clear that, as in the case of the League, the reluctance of the Senate to enter the Court was not shared by the major Protestant churches.

The 1924 and 1928 General Conference of Northern Methodism, through Episcopal Addresses, committee reports, and resolutions, gave "hearty endorsement" to American entry—and this conviction was transmitted to the Senate in blunt language. The General Conference of

Southern Methodism adopted a report to this effect, and many annual conferences and local Methodist groups were on record. Almost every annual meeting of the Northern Baptist Convention brought forth a resolution favoring American adherence. The Southern Baptist Convention spoke on the matter once, as did local groups. The Presbyterian Church, U.S.A., in General Assembly and presbyteries, repeatedly recorded the hope that America might enter the Court. This was also the position of the United Presbyterian Church, the Protestant Episcopal Church, the Congregationalists, the Reformed Church in the United States, the Evangelical Synod of North America, the American Unitarian Association, the Disciples of Christ, and the Universalists.

The Federal Council, the Church Peace Union, and the World Alliance for International Friendship Through the Churches cooperated in conducting a great campaign to secure American entrance into the Court. Gatherings of clergymen and public mass meetings were held in sixty strategic cities. A document defending and explaining the Court was mailed to seventy thousand pastors. Church representatives met with Secretary of State Hughes, President Harding, and President Coolidge on four different occasions. Petitions signed by thousands of churchmen were presented to the government. A World Court Sunday and a World Court Week were set aside to advance American adherence, at which time hundreds of meetings were held, tens of thousands (according to the *Federal Council Bulletin*) of sermons were preached on the subject, and a very large number of resolutions were passed and petitions signed by churchmen. Every senator was personally button-holed in his office by a church representative. Bishop Charles H. Brent, vice-chairman of the Federal Council's Commission on International Justice and Goodwill, testified before a hearing of the Senate Foreign Relations Committee. In addition, many other church groups recorded themselves in favor of the World Court, as did the church press in scores of editorials and articles.

Although the League of Nations and the World Court received the support of much of American Protestantism, greater enthusiasm was probably engendered by the Pact of Paris. This agreement was signed at Paris by representatives of the United States and fourteen other powers on August 27, 1928, and approved by the Senate on January 15, 1929. The signatories agreed to renounce war as an instrument of national policy. As interpreted, however, defensive wars were still permitted. Elements in the churches had long advocated the outlawry of war, and the Pact of Paris was received with great warmth.

The 1928 General Conference of Northern Methodism heralded the negotiations leading to the Pact. And well it might, for Northern Methodism had been extremely active in the movement to renounce war. A host of local conferences had supported the idea. The Methodist World Peace Commission circulated a petition and secured ninety thousand signatures urging ratification of the Kellogg-Briand Pact. As early as 1924 the General Conference, in a detailed maneuver, checked the attitude of every candidate for the Senate and the House of Representatives toward outlawry of war and ordered the information announced to each individual congregation. The political threat in this action was obvious. The bishops of the Methodist Episcopal Church, South, praised the agreement, and the General Conference of Southern Methodism was informed that the "declaration in the Briand-Kellogg Treaty is shot through with the light that shone in Bethlehem. The inspiration is the man of Galilee."[22]

The Northern Baptist Convention and the Southern Baptist Convention greeted the renunciation proposal with lavish praise, as did the General Assemblies of Northern and Southern Presbyterianism. The General Convention of the Protestant Episcopal Church and the National Council of Congregationalism rejoiced in this step toward world peace. Unitarians expressed their approval in a resolution, and the Pact was endorsed by the Reformed Church in the United States and the Evangelical Synod of North America. The Pact received further backing from the Reformed Presbyterian Church, the Reformed Church in America, the Disciples of Christ, the Christian Church, Christian Endeavor, and the Y.W.C.A.

The Federal Council of Churches advocated the renunciation of war as early as 1921 and conducted a vigorous campaign to secure the adoption of the Pact of Paris. Many resolutions to this effect were passed by the Council. The Council's regular organs and special pamphlets publicized the idea. Representatives of the Council presented to the White House on December 17, 1928, a memorial signed by 185,333 members of some thirty communions expressing the "earnest hope" that the Senate would ratify the agreement. Congress too was petitioned. A four-week study course explaining the Pact was distributed to the churches. A special Sunday was set aside to mobilize support for the agreement. The day following the Senate's approval of the Pact the Council sent telegrams to all the secretaries of state and city councils of churches throughout the United States saying: "Let church bells be rung, songs sung, prayers of thanksgiving be offered and petitions for help from God that our nation may ever follow the spirit and meaning of the

22. *Journal of the General Conference of the Methodist Episcopal Church, South,* 1930, p. 305.

Pact."[23] As the Council believed, the Pact opened a new era in human history—an era free from war, an era glorious with the happiness and prosperity of brotherly humanity.

Scores of local and state church groups toiled in behalf of the Pact. Church delegations called on Secretary of State Kellogg bearing petitions signed by hundreds of prominent churchmen. The National Committee on the Churches and World Peace meeting in 1929—and now representing thirty-five communions—welcomed the Pact. And the World Alliance for International Friendship Through the Churches believed the agreement marked "a great step forward in human history—one of the greatest steps ever taken, perhaps the greatest governments have ever taken."[24]

This view was widely echoed. Charles Clayton Morrison, editor of the *Christian Century,* long had championed outlawry rather than the League or the World Court, and with the signing of the Pact of Paris he exulted: "Today international war was banished from civilization."[25] The moderator of the Presbyterian Church, U.S.A., believed, "Surely the rosy dawn of a new peace consciousness is at hand."[26] Here, affirmed Walter Van Kirk, is the most "stupendous step yet taken by the great powers to put war under the ban of law."[27] The agreement, asserted S. Parkes Cadman, is an epoch-making event in the spiritual and moral life of mankind. It "will remove at one sweep the awful fear of war which hangs today like a pall over all nations and fills them with terror," opined a Baptist spokesman.[28] *"Te deum laudamus,"* sang the *Northwestern Christian Advocate,*[29] reflecting the view of at least a dozen church papers.

Not all of American Protestantism, of course, held such high hopes. A number of church press editors, while not opposing the Pact, warned of its limitations. A few voices put their criticism in stronger terms. The editor of *Living Church,* for example, believed it a "futile gesture, a jumble of high-sounding but meaningless words."[30] And, as might be expected, Protestantism's supreme realist, Reinhold Niebuhr, was very skeptical of this outlawry of war business.

The Protestant churches sought to preserve world peace through American participation in the League of Nations, the World Court, and the Pact of Paris. They also believed, however, that permanent peace

23. *Federal Council Bulletin,* Feb., 1929, p. 24.

24. *World Alliance for International Friendship Through the Churches News Letter,* Jan. 29, 1929.

25. Sept. 6, 1928, p. 1070.

26. *Presbyterian Magazine,* Nov., 1928, p. 563.

27. *Zion's Herald,* Nov. 14, 1928, p. 1461.   28. *Baptist,* March 17, 1928, p. 339.

29. Aug. 30, 1928, p. 875.   30. Aug. 11, 1928, p. 484.

was impossible so long as nations prepared for war. Hence the cause of disarmament was very close to the hearts of the churches, and they encouraged every international conference looking to the reduction of weapons of war.

The most signal gathering of this type in the twenties was the Washington Conference. Accepting the invitation of the United States, nine nations met at Washington on November 12, 1921. There resulted certain agreements regarding the Pacific and the Far East. Further, limitations were set on the construction of capital ships and aircraft carriers.

Every major denomination concerned itself with the Washington Conference. They passed resolutions urging the United States to take the initiative in calling a disarmament meeting, and these views were transmitted to the proper authorities. The results of the Conference were hailed with great rejoicing and the Senate of the United States was petitioned to approve the Conference treaties. At every stage of the event—from the initial invitation to the final ratification—the churches were very active.

Church journals, apparently without a single exception, threw their support behind the meeting. They stirred up sentiment for summoning the Conference in the first instance, called upon the delegates to act without fear or hesitation, and backed the ratification of the agreements. The interest of some of the journals was perfunctory; many others, however, devoted literally tens of thousands of words to the proceedings and looked upon the meeting as a divinely inspired step to world peace. Subscribers were repeatedly urged to "generate in this country an atmosphere that shall be surcharged with disarmament sentiment";[31] they were petitioned to "make the air electric with international unselfishness."[32] One paper believed the Conference marked the "longest step on the road to peace that has been taken since civilization began."[33] The *Presbyterian Advance* declared: "It left a record of the application of Christian principles to international problems such as was never before accomplished by the human race."[34] The outcome of the Conference, held another editor, would determine "the course of human history for a hundred years to come."[35] The highest accolade was given by the *Northwestern Christian Advocate* when it ranked the Washington Conference with Prohibition as the two greatest victories achieved by Christianity in the past fifty years.

31. *Presbyterian Banner*, Sept. 8, 1921, p. 5.
32. *Continent*, Sept. 29, 1921, p. 1081.
33. *New York Christian Advocate*, Feb. 16, 1922, p. 185.
34. Feb. 14, 1922, p. 3.
35. *Federal Council Bulletin*, Oct.-Nov., 1921, p. 111.

The churches acted in still other ways. The Federal Council, in cooperation with Catholic and Jewish agencies, issued an appeal to 120,000 preachers to observe June 5, 1921, as Reduction of Armament Sunday. As a result of the call, thousands of sermons were preached on the subject. There was held in Chicago, May 17-19, 1921, a great conference on disarmament under the sponsorship of the World Alliance for International Friendship Through the Churches. Representatives from twenty denominations were in attendance and they pledged themselves to work for armament reduction. The Church Peace Union polled the ministers of the land and on June 22, 1921, President Harding was presented with a petition bearing the signatures of 20,503 clergymen urging America to take the initiative in calling an international disarmament meeting. Once the Conference had been called, church sentiment was mobilized behind it. The Federal Council set aside Sunday, November 6, 1921, as a day of prayer for the delegates meeting in Washington. Mass demonstrations and union services were held throughout the country. Numerous pamphlets—some totaling 170,000 and 300,000 copies —were distributed among the churches. Letters, telegrams, and petitions poured into Washington signed by 13,878,671 names. Council officer Charles Macfarland attended all the sessions of the Conference and was largely responsible for the fact that they were opened with prayer. The moderators and presiding officers of the various denominations united, for the first time in American history, in a joint appeal to the nation on a great public issue. They demanded effective armament reduction and outlined a program including special church services on the opening day of the Conference, special meetings in every major city to study the disarmament problem, emphasis on armament reduction on Thanksgiving Day, and the coordination of local activities. Several denominational agencies whipped up support for disarmament in parallel campaigns. The *Christian Herald* conducted its own program.

When the Washington Conference adjourned there still remained the task of getting the treaties ratified by the Senate. The churches kept the pressure on. The Church Peace Union mailed letters to 120,000 clergymen urging them to make their will felt in Washington, and a petition was signed by 16,185 ministers and presented to the Senate urging that body to ratify the treaties. The Federal Council, individual denominations, and local church groups bombarded the Senate also. Perhaps Lord Riddell of the British delegation was not simply being polite when he stated that all this church pressure had great influence on the Conference deliberations.

The United States participated in naval disarmament conferences at Geneva in 1927 and at London in 1930, the first being an utter failure and the second a very limited success. In both instances, however, the churches showed great interest and once again resolutions were passed, sermons preached, special Sundays of prayer set aside, petitions signed, meetings held, and pamphlets issued. The enthusiasm was by no means as great as in 1921-22, and yet there is considerable evidence to indicate that the Protestant churches favored American participation in these international conferences and hoped that they would result in significant naval reductions.

It would be erroneous to assume that the churches supported American disarmament only if and when the other nations agreed to reciprocate. On the contrary, strong elements argued for cutting military expenditures to the bone regardless of the position taken by other countries. If necessary, the United States should "go it alone" and set an example to the rest of the world.

The evidence supporting this conclusion is overwhelming. Most of the major denominations repeatedly urged drastic reduction of armaments and opposed anything that hinted of "militarism." A clear majority of the major denominations resolved against compulsory military training in public schools or in tax-supported or land grant colleges. When the War Department proposed a "Mobilization Day" for September 12, 1924 to test the nation's preparedness for war, a growl of protest sprang from a score of church journals and agencies. The test was indefinitely postponed. The churches also opposed a proposed cruiser building program in 1928. The Federal Council mailed to 75,000 ministers a leaflet damning the bill; resolutions were passed and sermons preached and editorials written. The result was a flood of protests to Congress. In addition, the churches overwhelmingly supported the rights of conscientious objectors. A minority element was so obsessed with a hatred of war that it advocated complete abolition of the armed forces of the United States and even suggested that the churches withdraw their chaplains.

It is true that a few clerical voices, especially in the South, objected to stripping America of her military shield. Here and there a sermon was preached or an editorial written in defense of adequate military preparation. Nevertheless, the conclusion is rather inescapable that the vocal element in the major Protestant denominations was in substantial opposition to any but token military preparations on the part of the United States.

The intense interest of the churches in international cooperation and disarmament is explainable only in terms of the powerful anti-war sentiment that swept through the churches in the post-Versailles years. A shudder of revulsion seemed to seize organized religion as it remembered the horrors of the First World War. A guilt neurosis haunted the clergy and virtually without exception those ministers who vowed never again to support war based their pledge on their experiences in 1917-18.

The disillusionment suffered by the churches was, of course, shared by American society in general. Novelists, playwrights, and journalists deluged the country with anti-war material, and their views were to be given scholarly sanction by revisionist historians. The disillusionment of the churches, however, did not take the form of resurgent isolationism. Popular opinion to the contrary, the churches believed that America must participate in world affairs, for the only way to keep America out of war was to keep war out of the world. And so it was that the expressions of Protestant opinion in the twenties unquestionably carried as many references to war and peace as to any other single issue. Individuals, papers, denominations when isolated offer exceptions to this statement, but taking the major groups as a whole, war and peace loomed as large as either prohibition or the fundamentalist-modernist controversy. Those readers familiar with recent religious history in the United States will recognize that this conclusion could not be put in stronger terms.

Hundreds of anti-war resolutions were passed at the national, state, and local level. These resolutions "excommunicated," "outlawed," "repudiated," "denounced," and "deplored" war. Obviously, of course, these terms are open to varying interpretation. Everyone "deplores" war and such a resolution is almost meaningless. On the other hand, many of the resolutions were couched in terms that verged on a position of outright pacifism. Hundreds of ministers, including many of the most distinguished in the land, vowed that it was their conviction never again to sanction or support war. Again, it is impossible to interpret precisely the meaning of such declarations. But for some it was tantamount to accepting the pacifist position. Many of the leading peace groups were church dominated. The Church Peace Union and the World Alliance for International Friendship Through the Churches are illustrations in point. Further, the Federal Council's Commission on International Justice and Goodwill was a very powerful group, and many of the major denominations established committees on international relations. The National Council for Prevention of War was a near-church peace lobby headed by Frederick J. Libby, an ordained Congregational minister converted to the Quaker position. The Fellowship of Reconciliation was religiously oriented and led by churchmen. Then there were the historic peace churches such as the Friends and the Brethren. In short, it is only a slight exaggeration to say that almost all of the organized peace groups in the country were affiliated with the churches or led and membered by churchmen.

It would require a volume to cite all the anti-war statements coming from Protestant church sources in the years 1919-29. They are virtually unanimous, however, in declaring a faith that war should be wiped from the face of the earth, and that the surest way to accomplish this goal was through American cooperation with the other nations of the world. The churches threw themselves into the peace crusade with high hopes and noble zeal, and for a glorious moment in the Golden Twenties it seemed in truth that war had been outlawed, not only in a legal sense, but in the hearts of men as well.

Now, many commentators, including "realistic" clergymen, looking back upon the twenties from the vantage point of the Second World War, have chided the churches for their participation in this naïve "peace crusade." It is easy to smile at the wistful simplicity of the Pact of Paris. It is fashionable to deplore the disarmament attempts of the Washington Conference.

Although this chiding is not entirely ill-founded, nevertheless there is much that can be said in defense of the churches' record in the twenties. They recognized the high necessity of international cooperation, supporting such agencies as the League and the World Court. They faced the implications of an armament race with no forseeable termination and explored the possibilities of disarmament. Had there been no Washington Conference it does not follow that preparedness preparations in the thirties would have been any more adequate. The Pact of Paris placed the conscience of the world on record and its violations by the dictators strengthened the moral and legal case of the democracies. The churches made a noble effort toward permanent peace in the twenties, and because the effort failed it does not mean that the attempt was ill-considered.

In truth, the real failure came in the thirties when a program designed for a decade of peace was applied to a decade of war. It was one thing to endorse disarmament in 1921 and quite another to pursue disarmament in 1939. The Pact of Paris was in itself not unwise; the folly came in believing it sufficient to halt Hitler. The churches in the twenties worked for international cooperation, but the Depression Decade showed that adherance to the principle of collective security involved the risk and perhaps the ultimate payment of the high price of war. In the twenties the churches sought peace and justice in the world. The thirties showed that in an age of aggression it might be necessary to sacrifice peace to attain justice.

The real failure of the churches in the Prosperity Decade is twofold. They did not forsee that the twentieth century could produce the irrational brutality of Nazi Germany and—as events proved—Soviet Russia. Nor did they assess the priority Christians would one day be forced to accord to the ideal of justice on the one hand and on the other the war that might be necessary to insure that justice.

CHAPTER XXII

War and Peace in a Warring Decade

"No man is an Iland, intire of itselfe; every man is a peece of the Continent . . . any man's death diminishes me, because I am involved in Mankind; And therefore never send to know for whom the bell tolls; it tolls for thee."—John Donne

I

HIGH NOON for the peacemakers came for a brief moment in the late twenties; then ominous clouds of war suddenly shadowed the scene and by 1939 the dark night of total war had descended upon Europe and Asia. Two years later peace passed below the horizon in the Western hemisphere also.*

History affords no sadder tale than the impact of events in Manchuria, China, Ethiopia, Spain, the Rhineland, Munich, and finally Poland upon the followers of the Prince of Peace in America. The high hopes of the twenties were shattered by the demoniac happenings of the thirties. Churchmen cried "peace, peace" even as the paddy fields of Asia and the rivers of Spain ran crimson with blood. It was no longer merely a theoretical question of "outlawing" war; it was a question of how to face war that actually existed in much of the world. Should America disarm with predatory powers on the march? Should America continue to cooperate with other nations in seeking peace when such cooperation carried the threat of involvement in war. Should America refuse to fight with her own security threatened? Terrible modern war may be, but were the alternatives of victory by Nazi Germany and Imperial Japan any less fearsome? Should America take refuge in storm cellar neutrality, ride out the struggle, and keep her hands unstained by blood? And if she followed this course, could white hands cloak a conscience stricken by the fate of conquered peoples in Asia and Europe?

The response of the major Protestant churches to the breakdown of peace in the Depression Decade was pathetically confused, halting, divided, and uncertain. It is a heartbreaking record of alternating deep despair and naïve optimism, of timid vacillation and blind dogmatism. Some elements of Protestantism followed the plumb line of pacifism straight and true to Pearl Harbor and beyond. Other churchmen began the

* Substantial portions of this chapter first appeared in *The Social Studies*, XLVIII (April, 1957).

thirties with a vow never to support war, but as the tortuous decade deepened and the menace of the dictators became apparent, they forsook consistency and saw that there were evils even worse than war. An important group originally believed in world cooperation, but as the wall of collective security crumpled they retreated to a position of isolationism. Then there were those who had always taken a pragmatic view toward war and thus did not have to answer to their conscience when, on pragmatic considerations alone, they adhered either to isolation or collective security. And still others changed their position from event to event and almost month to month, now denouncing war and now urging sanctions against aggressors, now opposing adequate military preparations for the United States and now warning Germany or Japan to halt on the threat of war.

The impact of war on the Protestant churches was as divisive as the fundamentalist-modernist controversy. The editorial staffs of religious journals were split asunder, unofficial groups such as the Fellowship of Reconciliation and official agencies such as the Congregational Council for Social Action were badly divided, individual congregations broke with their pastors, entire denominations were rocked, and even peace groups such as the Church Peace Union and the World Alliance for International Friendship Through the Churches offered contradictory counsel. To put it bluntly, confusion over war and peace seemed more starkly extreme in the Protestant churches than in American society as a whole—and this is a damning comparison.

Until the mid-thirties, however, the churches followed much the same policy as they had in the twenties, and there was no great amount of doubt and confusion. They still believed that international cooperation was the key to peace. This point cannot be stressed too strongly. From the conclusion of the First World War to about 1935 the churches appeared overwhelmingly opposed to any course of isolation and selfish nationalism. The record is replete with resolutions, editorials, sermons, and utterances urging the United States to shun jingo nonsense and to enter fully and freely in world cooperation.

Thus it was that a significant element in the churches during the thirties continued to favor American entrance into the League of Nations. Enthusiasm for the League was not at fever pitch, but at least the churches had not entirely given up hope for the League early in the decade.

The evidence regarding the World Court is clearer. Almost every major denomination continued to support American adherence to the Court, the church press overwhelmingly favored the court, as did many unofficial church groups and famous clergymen. In January 1935 the

Senate refused to take this step, partially due to the opposition of Father Charles Coughlin, Will Rogers, and the Hearst papers. Clerical criticism of the Senate was extremely outspoken. "We have to swallow the galling fact," declared one church journal, "that the foreign policies of the United States are practically dictated by a sensational priest, a stuttering comedian and a cynical newspaper man."[1]

A third illustration of the willingness of the churches to cooperate in world affairs lies in their attitude toward the war debts owed to the United States by European countries. In contrast to what appeared to be the general attitude in America, some of the churches gracefully accepted proposals to scale down or suspend payments. This was the position of the Federal Council of Churches, several denominations, unofficial religious groups, many church papers, and a number of ministers. The sources of major denominational opinion reveal little opposition to the moratorium declared by President Hoover.

The churches also continued to advocate cooperation in disarmament. The final, futile gesture in this direction was the World Disarmament Conference, meeting in Geneva, February 2, 1932. With what appeared to be a virtually united voice, American Protestantism gave warm approval to the meeting and advocated drastic reduction in armaments. Once again resolutions were passed, days of prayer set side, sermons preached, pamphlets distributed, and editorials written in support of the conference. The effort was of no avail. While the delegates conferred, Japan was on the march in Asia.

It was the seizure of Manchuria by Japan in 1931 which first cracked the wall of collective security laboriously built in the twenties. War was no longer in the realm of theory. For many pacifist clergymen the haunting questions occurred: How can aggressor nations be halted without the use of force? Are there evils even worse than war?

And yet such was the horror of war that the sources of Protestant opinion reveal only a very few voices urging the use of military coercion against Japan. Indeed, probably less than a majority of church opinion favored even the use of economic sanctions, although included in this group was the Federal Council of Churches. Such was the passion for peace, when Japan invaded Manchuria the churches would not support either military coercion or an economic boycott to bring Japan to her senses. Even Reinhold Niebuhr, the great exponent of coercion, opposed an economic boycott. The churches would agree to no pressure stronger than Secretary of State Stimson's nonrecognition doctrine. And some churchmen felt that even nonrecognition was too warlike a gesture.

Even as the wall of collective security crumbled the churches cried out

1. *Christian Leader*, Feb. 9, 1935, p. 164.

against war and preparations for war. It may be that the present writer has lost his perspective through working so long in the sources of Protestant opinion. It may be that the anti-war people were more articulate than their non-pacifist brethren and pushed through resolutions, wrote editorials, signed petitions, organized, and preached sermons that distorted the true sentiment of the churches. And yet, a truly tremendous surge of anti-war sentiment swept through the churches in the thirties, and especially in the first half of the decade. The evidence supporting this assertion is mountainous. Material coming from the churches on war and peace equaled that on economic matters or any other problem facing American society.

The most important factor making for this revulsion to war—aside from the example and ethics of Christ—was disillusionment over the First World War. When asked why they assumed an anti-war position churchmen almost invariably cited their experiences in 1917-18. Not only the war itself but the Treaty of Versailles as well was branded a ghastly mistake. German aggression was repeatedly blamed on the excesses of the peace terms of 1919. In addition to the personal experiences of churchmen, there were the alleged disclosures brought forth by the Nye Committee, the writings of the revisionist historians, and the publication of that influential volume, *Preachers Present Arms*. Important also in the growth of the anti-war spirit was the example of Gandhi in India. Again almost invariably, when questioned as to the practicability of non-resistance, churchmen pointed to Ghandi. And of course back of it all was the growing awareness of the complete terror of modern war.

Whatever the motivation, the churches were swept by an anti-war spirit. Thousands of resolutions were passed by denominations in national, state, and local convention, by ministerial associations, church federations, young peoples' societies, official and unofficial agencies, and individual congregations. These resolutions were not always vague and meaningless. Many of them amounted to a flat repudiation of war, a refusal to endorse, support, or participate in armed conflict, unless—and this stipulation was often added—the United States itself was invaded.

Without exception the major denominations made provision for those in their fellowship who would not take up arms under any circumstances. The government was requested to give conscientious objectors the same exemption from military training and military service as granted to the members of the Society of Friends. When in 1931 the Supreme Court denied the application for naturalization of Douglas Clyde Macintosh because he would not give a definite pledge in advance to fight in any war in which the United States should engage, a thunder of protest came from the churches. The fate of Macintosh was of intense concern to American Protestantism.

Considering the extent of anti-war sentiment, it is not surprising to find the churches in violent opposition to any build up of the military or naval strength of the United States. Again the illustrations supporting this assertion numbers not simply in the scores but in the hundreds. Stories of the profits made by munitions makers and Wall Street bankers in the First World War increased opposition to preparedness, as did the disclosures of the Nye Committee. Through sermons, resolutions, petitions, editorials, mass meetings, pamphlets, and every medium of expression, the churches made clear their opposition to military training, increased appropriations for the army and navy, naval maneuvers in the Pacific, fortification of American Pacific possessions, private manufacturing of armaments, and, in general, any preparations for war.

It is not unreasonable that the churches should take this position in the early thirties when, perhaps, the menace of aggressor nations was not yet crystal clear. But it is difficult to understand—with the handwriting on the wall—how important churchmen could still oppose defensive preparations as late as 1938 and 1939. When, in 1939, Congress refused to vote appropriations for the strengthening of Guam, America's leading Protestant journal, the *Christian Century,* heralded the rejection as a sign of national sanity. And the Federal Council of Churches in 1938 termed American appropriations for the army and navy unwarranted by any evidence thus far presented.

Of greater curiosity is the fact that church journals or denominational resolutions often began with vigorous condemnations of aggressor nations and ended with equally vigorous opposition to American military expenditures. And what comment can be made on the following case? *Radical Religion,* edited by that strong critic of pacifism, Reinhold Niebuhr, repudiated pacifism and called for a strong stand against aggressor nations. And yet in 1938 it termed the defense budget of the United States the worst piece of militarism in modern history. Niebuhr's journal further asserted that America's naval program was the most unjustified piece of military expansion in a world full of such madness.

It is difficult to say just what proportion of American Protestantism assumed an anti-war position. Whatever the exact figure, the number was large. Polls do not always provide a precise measurement, but the cumulative impact of the following is not without interest.

In 1931, 19,372 clergymen responded to a questionnaire sent out by Kirby Page and associates. A total of 12,076 persons, or 62 per cent, expressed the opinion that the churches should go on record as refusing to sanction or support any future war or participate as an armed combatant.

The number who regarded the distinction between "defensive" and "aggressive" war sufficiently valid to justify their sanctioning or participating in a future war of "defense" was 8,316 or 43 per cent. Only 45 per cent said they would serve as an official army chaplain in wartime. Over 80 per cent favored a substantial reduction in armaments, even if the United States had to go it alone. And 87 per cent opposed military training in schools and colleges.[2]

In 1934, 20,870 clergymen (including Lutherans, Southern Baptists, and Southern Methodists) responded to a second poll conducted by Mr. Page. A total of 13,977 clergymen, or 67 per cent, believed the churches should go on record as refusing to sanction or support any future war. Of greater significance, 12,904 ministers, or 62 per cent, stated that it was their present purpose not to sanction any future war or participate as an armed combatant. Some 41 per cent would not serve as an official chaplain on active duty in wartime. An overwhelming majority favored reduction of armaments.

In 1936 Bishop James C. Baker, Methodist Episcopal Church, and associates, received replies to a questionnaire from 12,854 Protestant and Jewish clergymen. Of this number, 7,237, or 56 per cent, stated that it was their purpose not to sanction any future war or participate as an armed combatant. Only 36 per cent favored the use of armed force against nations proclaimed aggressors by the League of Nations. It is to the point to inquire just how many clergymen in any war are required to "participate as an armed combatant."

A poll conducted by the Congregational Council for Social Action in 1935 is revealing. Laymen as well as ministers participated. Some 6 per cent would fight in any war declared by the United States. About 4 per cent would bear arms or support any war declared by the United States against an internationally recognized aggressor. Thirty-three per cent would support a war in which United States territory had been invaded. Some 24,667, or 15 per cent, adopted the strict pacifist position of refusing to fight at all, regardless of the nature of the war. That is, about 48 per cent would not fight at all or only in a war in which the territory of the United States was invaded.

In 1937 the Disciples of Christ conducted a poll of its members, 14,000 replying. Only 2,270 stated their willingness to bear arms or otherwise support any war in which the United States might engage. However, 8,774 were willing to fight if the United States were invaded. Some

2. After examining the returns, a manufacturing journal predicted that should war come there would emerge a brand new national sport: "gunning for clergymen." This questionnaire was not sent to Jews, Catholics, Lutherans, Southern Baptists, or Southern Methodists. This fact is, of course, important.

3,069 assumed an absolute pacifist position and refused to fight in any war, while another 3,191 were undecided about this question.

In 1936 the Northern Baptist Convention conducted a poll of its members. Less than 2 per cent would fight in any and all wars declared by the United States. Over 42 per cent would bear arms, however, if the United States were invaded. About 26.62 per cent said they would refuse service under any conditions.

One thousand churchmen replied in 1937 to a poll conducted by the Oxford Conference on Church and State and there was an almost even balance between those who believed in the pacifist position and those who did not.

Slightly over 50 per cent of the ministers who responded to a poll conducted by Reverend Allan Knight Chalmers in 1935 assumed an outright pacifist position. A poll conducted by the *Christian Herald* in that year also revealed a significant number who would not support any war, offensive or defensive.

The irrationality of war was sometimes matched by the irrationality of the peacemakers; and pacifists sometimes displayed an intolerance as great as that which they themselves endured. For example, Ethiopia was condemned because it did not meet the Italian invasion with brotherly love and passive resistance. The *Christian Century* termed Albert Einstein's defection from absolute pacifism (after his experiences in Nazi Germany) an unworthy deed indicating the scientist was not made of stern stuff. One minister, writing in the *Christian Register,* urged the workers of the world to simultaneously call a great general strike as the only way to prevent war—war, obviously, being caused by imperialistic Fascist powers. A Methodist leader, writing in *Epworth Herald,* a magazine for young folks, urged youth not simply to plead conscientious objections and go to jail, but to enter the army and industry and then sabotage war preparations and any war effort. While less treasonable, the Federal Council's solution for war was not always realistic. For example, when trouble erupted in the Far East, the Council issued a series of little booklets with such folksy titles as "Uncle Joe's Solution of the Japan-China Struggle." (Uncle Joe suggested more love.) The distinguished Disciples of Christ leader, Dr. Peter Ainslie, in a sermon in Washington's First Congregational Church, declared that "There is no more justification for being a chaplain in the Army or Navy than there is for being a chaplain in a speakeasy!"[3] Unhappily, Col. Julian E. Yates, chief of the U.S. Army Chaplains, was in the audience. Whatever may be said of Dr. Ainslie's tact, his position concerning the chaplaincy was echoed by thousands of ministers.

3. *Time,* April 28, 1930, p. 26.

These curious instances must not obscure the fact that for tens of thousands of devout Protestants repudiation of war was a thoughtful, sincere, and consecrated act. And on occasions far too numerous to mention here, solemn bands of church folk vowed never to bear arms in any war whatsoever. On May 2, 1935, for instance, in Riverside Church, New York, 254 ministers and rabbis, clad in their robes of office, repeated the following pledge in an atmosphere of hushed reverence:

In loyalty to God I believe that the way of true religion cannot be reconciled with the way of war. In loyalty to my country I support its adoption of the Kellogg-Briand Pact which renounces war. In the spirit of true patriotism and with deep personal conviction, I therefore renounce war and never will I support another.[4]

Three years later, 149 of this distinguished group, along with new churchmen, convened again in the church of Dr. Allan Knight Chalmers, chairman of the Ministers Peace Committee, and repeated their pledge. From this hard core of nationally famous clergymen there emerged the "Covenant of Peace Group," which secured signatures to a beautiful pledge of absolute pacifism. By 1939 over one thousand ministers had signed this promise not to participate in, sanction, or support war. By 1941, nineteen hundred ministers had signed the pledge. Scores of similar vows were taken by tens of thousands of religious people throughout the country. Typical of more restrained and temperate utterances was the declaration taken by the Young Men's Club of the Broadway Tabernacle Church, New York:

I have quietly considered what I would do if my nation should again be drawn into war.

I am not taking a pledge, because I do not know what I would do when the heat of the war mood is upon the country. But in a mood of calm consideration I do today declare that I cannot reconcile the way of Christ with the practice of war.

I do therefore set down my name to be kept in the record of my Church, so that it will be for me a reminder if war should come; and will be a solemn declaration to those who hold to this conviction in time of war that I believe them to be right; and I do desire with my whole mind and heart that I shall be among those who keep to this belief.

I set down my name to make concrete my present thought upon the question of war, and declare my purpose to think and talk with others about it, that my belief in the Way of Christ shall become operative in this and in other questions which now confuse our thought and action.[5]

Even Reinhold Niebuhr could declare as late as 1935: "I do not intend

4. *Fellowship*, June, 1935, p. 15.
5. *Federal Council Bulletin*, March, 1933, p. 10.

to participate in any war now in prospect. I take this position not on strictly pacifistic grounds, for I am not an absolutist, but simply because I can see no good coming out of any of the wars confronting us. The position of Russia on the one hand and of Germany on the other hand in any of these wars would not effect my decision."[6]

Church or church affiliated peace groups mushroomed. A Disciples of Christ Peace Fellowship was organized in 1935, and in 1939 an Episcopal Pacifist Fellowship was born. The greatest effort of the peacemakers in the thirties, the huge Emergency Peace Campaign, found the overwhelming percentage of its leadership, personnel, and support in the ranks of the clergy. Then there were the church peace groups or those drawing great support from the churches: World Peace Fellowship of Christian Endeavor, World Peaceways, World Peace Foundation, World Alliance for International Friendship Through the Churches, National Council for Prevention of War, the "Y's", World Peace Commission of the Methodist Episcopal Church, Fellowship of Reconciliation, Department of International Justice and Good Will of the Federal Council, Committee on Women's Work of the Foreign Missions Conference, Committee on Militarism in Education, Church Peace Union, Carnegie Endowment for International Peace, War Resisters League, and a number of denominational agencies concerned with international affairs. In 1934 Paul Hutchinson, noted Methodist and future editor of the *Christian Century,* declared that approximately twenty million members of the Protestant churches had declared officially their intention to oppose all wars. If denominational resolutions are taken to represent the declaration of the members, this statement is not too exaggerated. Certain it is that the prominence of those churchmen who adopted a pacifist or near-pacifist position cannot be denied. Such a list reads like a *Who's Who* of American Protestantism.

A considerable element within American Protestantism, in its great desire for friendly international relations, favored the extension of diplomatic recognition to Soviet Russia. Such an element may have been a minority, but it was nonetheless vocal.[7] The General Council of Congregational Churches adopted a resolution urging this action. Part of Unitarianism favored it. Several unofficial religious groups recorded their support of this step. Over a dozen leading church journals approved recognition. A host of individual ministers went on record to this effect. For instance, 430 ministers in New York State alone signed a petition urging recognition. Harry Emerson Fosdick, Samuel Parkes

6. *Fellowship,* Oct., 1935, p. 13.

7. A clear distinction must be made between the position of the Roman Catholic Church and that of the Protestant churches. Historians make a crucial error in noting Catholic hostility to recognition and then equating it with all American church opinion.

Cadman, Bishop Francis J. McConnell, Henry Sloane Coffin, Reinhold Niebuhr, Bishop G. Bromley Oxnam, Ernest Fremont Tittle, Burris Jenkins, and Henry P. Van Dusen are only a few of the distinguished Protestant leaders who publicly supported the diplomatic recognition of Soviet Russia.

Although anti-war sentiment continued to be very powerful throughout the entire decade, the crest was reached by the mid-thirties. The unity of the peacemakers broke on the rocks of Ethiopia, Spain, Munich, China, and Poland. From about 1935 on the churches split badly on the issue of foreign policy. Those who hewed to the line of pacifism lost their international outlook and took refuge in storm cellar neutrality. Originally very strong in their support of international cooperation, they retreated to a position indistinguishable from that of the isolationists. It was a strange alliance, because pacifism and isolationism are poles apart. And yet by 1940 such pacifists as Fosdick, Tittle, and C. C. Morrison found themselves in the camp of the America Firsters.

On the other hand, many of the peacemakers placed common sense above consistency and recognized that the triumph of dictators would be a fate worse than war. And increasingly as the decade deepened churchmen forsook pacifism for collective security. They accepted the revision of American neutrality legislation, urged sanctions against aggressor nations and aid to those attacked, and finally evidenced a willingness to risk war to prevent the victory of Germany and Japan.

The rupture between the pacifists—most of whom were now also isolationists—and the believers in collective security was bitter and confused. The Federal Council had leaders in both camps, but these two elements managed to hold together in rather stable equilibrium. The clash in the Fellowship of Reconciliation was divisive. A stormy debate racked Northern Presbyterians when pacifists attempted to secure a rewording of the Confession of Faith. Some church journals followed the practice of printing two sets of editorials on foreign policy to reflect the divided view of the editorial board. J. A. MacCallum resigned as editor of the *Presbyterian Tribune* because he believed in collective security and the directors of the paper did not. Leaders in the Congregational Council for Social Action resigned over this same dispute. The Methodist Federation for Social Service could not seem to be able to make up its mind. Church peace groups, including the Church Peace Union and the World Alliance for International Friendship Through the Churches, faced this division. Everywhere confusion and mistrust increased as the peacemakers split into two camps.

The growing spirit of isolationism and peace at any price is reflected in many ways. To begin with, it appears clear that a majority of church opinion favored the neutrality acts of 1935, 1936, and 1937. This legislation was hailed in church quarters as a safeguard against the United States being sucked into foreign wars by munition makers and bankers, for by the mid-thirties it was believed that economic factors almost alone had brought America into the First World War. The encouragement this neutrality legislation gave to aggressor nations was considered worth the price. By 1939 an important element in the churches still opposed any modification of the neutrality laws.

The proposed Ludlow amendment to the Constitution, making a declaration of war dependent upon a referendum, was also widely supported by the churches. However, endorsement was far from unanimous.

It seems clear that some churchmen opposed the use of economic sanctions against aggressor nations. Indeed, a rather surprising amount of material appeared in the sources of Protestant opinion defending—or rather rationalizing—the aggressions of Japan, Germany, and Italy. They were "have-not" nations, it was argued, only attempting to catch up with the richer countries. Germany had not been fairly treated in the Treaty of Versailles. There was precious little difference between the imperialism of England and France and that of Japan and Germany, save that the latter nations entered the game late. Besides, the hands of the United States were not clean and Americans should judge not that they be judged. Complicating the picture, of course, was Communist Russia. The argument was sometimes used—although not often—that Germany represented a bulwark against the expansion of communism. Even the Munich agreement was greeted as an honorable alternative to war. In short, as the thirties deepened more and more Protestants retreated to a position of isolationism.

Even as isolationist sentiment grew, the ranks of the pacifists thinned. War appeared less evil as the dictators stepped up their march of aggression. Bishop William Manning, Bishop James Cannon, Coffin, Niebuhr, Ward, and Christian F. Reisner were only a few of the diverse group that defended the position of collective security. The invasions of China and Ethiopia were important in showing churchmen that power as well as prayer were needed to preserve peace. Events in Spain had an even greater impact on the thinking of the Protestant churches, and important elements labored to amend the neutrality acts to permit materials of war to flow to the Loyalists, just as some churchmen had called for economic sanctions against Japan and Italy. And then came Munich which further depleted the ranks of pacifism. By 1939 a large and growing number of church people had joined the adherents of collective security.

Although the supporters of collective security grew in strength and number, the outbreak of total war in Europe in September 1939 found the churches almost unanimous in the belief that the United States should stay out. Only a very small group believed America should come to the immediate aid of the Allies. The crucial years of 1940 and 1941 are not part of the present story. It is sufficient to note that as the threat of Hitler increased, as England stood alone after the fall of France, church support of all aid short of war increased. And with Pearl Harbor the Protestant churches accepted the war as an "unnecessary necessity"—to use the words of the *Christian Century*. When the showdown came, only about twelve thousand of the once huge number of pacifists stuck by their figurative guns.

It is easy to condemn the Protestant peacemakers for their naïveté, inconsistency, and hypocrisy. The churches, as *Fortune* magazine bitterly complained in January, 1940, did not speak in a clear, strong voice of leadership to the people of America. Their counsel was confused, halting, and timid.

And yet, there is much that is honorable in the record of the Protestant churches. Until the mid-thirties they worked for peace through international cooperation and shunned a policy of jingoism and isolationism. After about 1935, it is true, the churches evidenced doubt and confusion, as they split between isolationism and collective security. As the lengthened shadow of their people, the Protestant churches were unable to take a clear, consistent, united stand on the coming of the Second World War.

The short term verdict of history—or rather, more accurately, of many historians—is that clerical pacifism debilitated the moral conscience of America and gave encouragement to the dictators. By insisting upon peace at any price, ministers blinded themselves to the enormity of the crimes of the dictators, risked the destruction of Western Europe, and cut their nation off from the democracies. Many churchmen overestimated the economic motivations for war, underestimated the demoniac element in man, minimized the necessity of coercion in international relations, and placed the pleasures of peace over the demands of justice. These accusations may be just.

But there is another side to the coin. Harry Emerson Fosdick, Charles Clayton Morrison, and Ernest Fremont Tittle may have been mistaken, but the present writer, for one, is unwilling to pass judgment on men of this character and say they were wrong.

CHAPTER XXIII

Conclusion

"[Americans] know, and are content that all the world should know, the worst as well as the best of themselves. They have a boundless faith in free inquiry and full discussion."
—James Bryce

I

PERHAPS the greatest proof that the churches are inspired institutions is that they have withstood so much bad writing, and this theory will assume irrefutable proportions unless this study is promptly brought to a halt. And so at long last the slow freight will pull into the station with a few conclusions riding the caboose.

II

What moral relevance did the Protestant churches have for America and the world in the second and third decades of the twentieth century? The answer depended in large measure on the churches' awareness of the tension between man's disorder and God's design. A church that is fully at home in society, a church that completely accommodates itself to its environment, a church that embraces prevailing standards and values has nothing important to say.

On the whole and with important exceptions, American Protestantism recognized this tension. The churches continued their historical tradition of deep concern with the structure and functioning of society. As in the past, they noted how far existing society fell short of divine standards. They sought to re-order America in accordance, as they saw it, with the will of God.

But it is terribly difficult to discern God's will. The temptation is great to equate human progress with divine blueprints; to cloak finite tactics in the justifying mantle of transcendent strategy. How often did the churches lay claim to interpretating the mind of Christ as they pursued their crusades of prohibition, pacifism, Christian socialism, and all the rest?

Misguided as these crusades may have been, their very existence pointed up the gulf between things as they were and things as they ought to be. Wisely or unwisely, they represented attempts on the part of the churches to face up to terrible evils.

More baneful was the fact that a large element in the churches appeared quite content with the status quo, and in the twenties in particular among some churchmen there was a complacent unawareness of any grave social wrongs; a smug assurance that America had solved the central problems of civilization and was rapidly evolving toward the establishment of an earthly Kingdom of God.

This optimism of the twenties gave way before the shattering events of the thirties: total war and total depression. In the thirties also the neo-orthodoxs under the leadership of Niebuhr provided a theological underpinning to social action which the earlier Social Gospel had pretty much lacked. Thus the social attitudes of the Depression Decade were characterized by pessimism, realism, an emphasis on the sinfulness of man and the judgment of God, and the cry, "Let the Church be the Church!"

And yet the evidence does not permit too sharp a distinction between the social attitudes of the churches in the twenties and in the thirties. It is conventional among historians to speak of the death of the old Social Gospel in the thirties and to pretend that there was no continuity between the two decades. Assuredly there was a difference in theological orientation, but on the practical level of action there remained basic similarities. The thread of social concern ran back to colonial times and forward into the forties and fifties. It would be hard to distinguish between the records of some Social Gospel champions and some neo-orthodox adherents in the realm of politics, economics, civil liberties, and race relations, however much their basic theological premises differed.

Nor is it quite fair to disparage, as almost all commentators have done, the old, idealistic, "naïve," Social Gospelites and to say the "realistic" neo-orthodoxs drove them from the field in utter route. After all, many "naïve" old-fashioned followers of the Social Gospel were willing to accept the New Deal and a purged and curbed capitalism while many of the "realistic" disciples of Niebuhr generally pushed for socialism. It is interesting to compare a "liberal" church journal such as *Advance* and Niebuhr's *Radical Religion,* and then ask the question which paper probed closer to the heart of the matter.

In brief, in both the twenties and the thirties American Protestantism continued its tradition of activism. The churches displayed great concern in the major public issues facing society. To be sure, this concern was greater in the latter decade, but it was by no means absent in the immediate post-Versailles years.

In these pages the churches have been studied as human institutions existing in a cultural environment which they influenced and in turn were influenced by, not as supra-historical bodies floating in some spiritual vacuum. This being the frame of reference, it is only fair that the record of the churches be stated in human terms. After all, to survive religion must be institutionalized, and as institutions the churches are as subject to the pressures and mores of society as any other agencies. And just because this treasure of religion is perpetuated in earthen vessels, compromise and corruption is inevitable. This is the tragedy of religion: institutionalized it becomes corrupt; without the churches it dies.

In casting up the balance sheet, then, the record of the churches should be examined not in absolute terms of divine perfection, but rather by the finite standards of the society in which they moved and had their being.

To begin with, the social record of the churches was influenced by the exigencies of time and geography. The southern churches, whatever the denomination, almost invariably evidenced a less liberal attitude than their northern brethren, and they spoke less frequently and in a muted key on social issues. Much of the moral fervor of southern Protestants was expended on personal sins, the fundamentalist churches with their emphasis on personal salvation, were strongest in the South, and the southern churches had inherited an individualistic and conservative tradition from slavery days. This does not mean that the attitudes of Yankee Protestants were always correct. In particular, the southern churches appeared more realistic in their approach to war, in their assessment of socialism, and in their awareness of the demoniac element in man. Neither does this mean that social Christianity was completely dead below the Mason-Dixon line, as many historians have assumed. As this inquiry has demonstrated, there always was a prophetic minority group of Southern churchmen to challenge the righteousness of the social order, and in the thirties this critical spirit gained strength in official church circles.

Time joined with geography in partially determining the social record of American Protestantism. The churches in their social attitudes reflected the temper of the twenties and thirties, and there often was a perceptible shift in these attitudes as the nation moved from a period of prosperity to one of depression. The churches did suffer from smugness in the Prosperity Decade; they did move to the Left after 1929. But care should be exercised not to overstress the conservatism of the earlier period. If there was little questioning of capitalism as a system, there was considerable concern with the condition of the laboring man. Moreover, civil liberties, foreign policy, and, to a lesser extent, race relations, aroused much attention. It is only natural that economic matters should move to the forefront of concern in the thirties.

While the churches did attempt to solve the major problems confronting American society in the years 1919-39, they did not always approach these matters from the same direction or with the same degree of intensity. Indeed, this inquiry emphasizes the vast sweep of Protestant opinion on virtually every major social issue. This opinion ran the gamut from hidebound conservatism through moderate liberalism to lunatic radicalism. A few churchmen appeared washed in the blood of the Marxian lamb and a few embraced Fascist notions, while the great majority stood closer to the vital center. On the whole, however, the extent of advanced—or to the Left of center—sentiment seems considerably greater than is generally realized. The evidence makes untenable the assumption that the churches are almost invariably the bulwarks of reaction.

It seems apparent also that theological conservatives tended to be conservative in their social attitudes, while the opposite holds true for liberals. This conclusion often has been questioned and pronounced fallacious by acute observers. True, Unitarians provide a partial exception. True, the neo-orthodoxs were often quite radical politically and in a sense their theology was conservative. But taking the period 1919-39 as a whole and balancing exception against exception, it seems clear that there existed a definite correlation between theological and political liberalism and between theological and political conservatism.

Curiously enough, no such correlation is apparent between the class composition of a denomination and its social attitudes. That is, the Protestant Episcopal Church draws heavily from the upper and upper middle classes while the Southern Baptists draw equally heavily from the lower and lower middle classes. And yet, Episcopalians displayed a more marked liberalism on social issues than Southern Baptists. A similar analogy could be drawn between Presbyterians and Lutherans, always remembering that the Southern wing of any given denomination lagged behind its Northern counterpart.

Another concluding observation is the gulf between pronouncement and action. The churches often permitted their words to outrun their deeds. Fine sounding utterances somehow never materialized in action. The old parson who termed denominational resolutions the most harmless form of amusement ever devised by the human mind was issuing more than a pleasantry. There was indeed a division between precept and practice. Such a gap is partially inevitable and will appear in the record of any institution, but it was widened also because church leaders frequently were ahead of laymen in their social attitudes.

An additional weakness in the record of the churches lies in the fact that their two greatest crusades—to abolish liquor and war—ended in failure. It is possible to acknowledge the justice of these crusades, but it is difficult always to condone the strategy employed in their conduct.

Indeed, a serious weakness in the social program of the churches was that too often it was not a program at all, but simply an indictment. And so it was that while the churches diagnosed the sickness of society with penetration and candor, the cures prescribed were all too frequently sketchy, superficial, unrealistic, optimistic, and as ill-directed as a leaky hose.

Regarding this matter, the churches faced a dilemma. If they advanced a vague program couched in generalities they were accused of evasiveness and sentimentalism. If their program was spelled out and contained concrete and specific points of action, they were accused of wading into deep technical waters better left to economists, sociologists, political scientists, and other professionals. In the fifties the trend is for the churches to set forth "norms of behavior" and let the experts work out the program of implementation. It is questionable whether this "new" trend is really new or if it is indeed advisable. Calling for a "Christian social order" is a rather meaningless gesture unless it is accompanied by a blueprint for action. For instance, is it really enough to demand "justice" in race relations without a commitment as to how this justice can be realized?

In the preface the reader was warned that in this inquiry he would find few bold theories or sweeping generalizations. It is to be hoped, however, that a few fresh facts and conclusions emerge in these pages.

For instance, in the section on civil liberties an attempt was made to show that the churches displayed an intense concern in this vital area. They had an excellent official record regarding lynching, however much this record fell short at the local level. They criticized such "patriotic" organizations as the Klan, Black Legion, Silver Shirts, Daughters of the American Revolution, and American Legion, and such "patriotic" individuals as Hague, Coughlin, and Long. While Protestants gave their support to the baneful anti-evolution movement, many leading ministers, church journals, and assemblies defended the principles of academic freedom. On the whole, such *causes célèbres* as Sacco and Vanzetti, Tom Mooney, and the Scottsboro boys found the churches sympathetic. And an element of American Protestantism went the last mile and upheld the civil liberties of Communists. In fine, the churches need not apologize for their record in this field in the twenties and thirties. And it is equally clear that this heritage was preserved in the early fifties as American Protestantism took its forthright stand against McCarthyism.

The record regarding labor is not unspotted. At the local level especially the churches often ignored the worker's plight. On the other hand, there is a tremendous amount of evidence indicating sympathy with labor. Truth to tell, the churches backed labor in most of its legitimate demands and made a sincere effort to achieve a rapprochement.

The record is less happy concerning race relations. Surely the churches must share the responsibility for the perpetuation of discrimination in the land of the free. Just as certainly, however, the churches in the fifties led in the crusade for racial justice, and there were important precedents established in the twenties and thirties upon which to draw.

Although peace was not preserved and although pacifism appeared to have little relevance in an age of Hitler and Stalin, the attitudes of Protestantism toward war and peace were not totally damning. An element of the churches, especially after 1935, embraced isolationism, but generally the churches sought international cooperation. They recognized that the only way to keep the United States out of war was to keep war out of the world. It is not without significance that after the Second World War the churches gave strong endorsement to the United Nations. Nor is it a matter of indifference that just as much of Protestantism supported disarmament endeavors in the twenties, so they encouraged international control of weapons in the age of H-bombs. Further, in a very real sense the ecumenical movement within world Protestantism was a counterpart to world political cooperation.

Lastly, one need not be too cynical about the efforts of the churches to achieve a society which approximated a divine ideal. Because the world at mid-century fell terribly short of this absolute mark, it does not follow that the effort should not have been made in the first instance. Every generation must fight the good fight in its own way and in its own day, and count itself lucky if it has inched forward almost imperceptibly toward a more just social order. At mid-century the churches know they cannot except perfection within history. They know too that corrupt man can do little without the forgiving grace of a sovereign King.

But these truths must not paralyze the social conscience of American Protestantism. It is just possible that America is a little finer because of the activities of the churches. If a righteous God condemns the churches for their abysmal deviations from absolute standards, a fallible historian can yet find much in the social attitudes of the Protestant churches of America, 1919-39, that is hopeful and charitable.

Bibliography

THE SOURCES FOR A STUDY of the Protestant churches in modern America are abundant. In an effort to keep this bibliography within reasonable bounds, almost all material not specifically concerned with the churches or written by churchmen or published by church groups will be omitted.

PRIMARY SOURCES

1. GOVERNMENT DOCUMENTS

Printed government documents were utilized sparingly. The census volumes for 1926 and 1936, published in 1929 and 1941 respectively, contain useful information for background purposes. The published records of the Special House Committee on Un-American Activities and of the House Committee on Un-American Activities for the years 1938 to 1952 were of some aid in determining the association of churchmen with organizations said to be Fascist or Communist dominated. The Committee has prepared a *Cumulative Index to Publications of the Committee on Un-American Activities* (Washington, D. C., 1953), which cites the title and date of each report and hearing. It also contains the names of approximately thirty-eight thousand individuals and when and where they are mentioned in the House records. This material was examined in the office of the Committee. I am indebted to the Committee for providing me with a desk and for granting me free and convenient access to its published records.

2. OFFICIAL DENOMINATIONAL RECORDS

Official denominational records were essential to this study. They contain the reports and recommendations of denominational agencies to the national governing bodies, convention speeches, episcopal addresses, and resolutions. The frequency of these national meetings varied from denomination to denomination: annual, biennial, triennial, and quadrennial. This fact is important in weighing the number of pronouncements issued by a church.

American Unitarian Association, *Annual Report of the American Unitarian Association,* 1919-39, inclusive.
Congregational Churches, *Minutes of the National Council of Congregational Churches,* 1919, 1921, 1923, 1925, 1927, 1929.

Congregational Christian Churches, *Minutes of the General Council of Congregational Christian Churches*, 1931, 1934, 1936, 1938.

Evangelical and Reformed Church, *Acts and Proceedings of the General Synod of the Evangelical and Reformed Church*, 1934, 1936, 1938.

Evangelical Synod of North America, *Reports and Minutes of the General Conference of the Evangelical Synod of North America*, 1921, 1925, 1929, 1933.

Evangelical Synod of North America, *Report of the Extraordinary General Conference of the Evangelical Synod of North America*, 1927.

Methodist Episcopal Church, *Journal of the General Conference of the Methodist Episcopal Church*, 1920, 1924, 1928, 1932, 1936.

Methodist Episcopal Church, South, *Journal of the General Conference of the Methodist Episcopal Church, South*, 1922, 1926, 1930, 1934, 1938.

Northern Baptist Convention, *Annual of the Northern Baptist Convention*, 1919-39, inclusive.

Presbyterian Church, U.S., *Minutes of the General Assembly of the Presbyterian Church, U.S.*, 1919-39, inclusive.

Presbyterian Church, U.S.A., *Minutes of the General Assembly of the Presbyterian Church, U.S.A.*, 1919-39, inclusive.

Protestant Episcopal Church, *Journal of the General Convention of the Protestant Episcopal Church*, 1919, 1922, 1925, 1928, 1931, 1934, 1937.

Reformed Church in the United States, *Acts and Proceedings of the General Synod of the Reformed Church in the United States*, 1920, 1923, 1926, 1929, 1932.

Reformed Church in the United States, *Minutes of Second Special Meeting of the Reformed Church in the United States*, 1919.

Southern Baptist Convention, *Annual of the Southern Baptist Convention*, 1919-39, inclusive.

United Lutheran Church in America, *Minutes of the Biennial Convention of the United Lutheran Church in America*, 1920, 1922, 1924, 1926, 1928, 1930, 1932, 1934, 1936, 1938.

In addition to the above records, some of the denominations published helpful yearbooks. More important than the denominational yearbooks were the following reference works and compilations of pronouncements.

Burton, Charles Emerson (comp.). *The National Council Digest*. New York, 1930. Contains a useful compilation of the major pronouncements of the National Council of Congregational Churches, 1781-1930.

Commission on Christian Social Action of the Evangelical and Reformed Church, *Social Pronouncements of the Evangelical and Reformed Church, 1934-1947*. Cleveland, n.d.

Department of the Church and Economic Life of the Federal Council of Churches, *Pronouncements on Religion and Economic Life*. New York, 1947.

Department of Research of the International Council of Religious Education,

Social Pronouncements by Religious Bodies Affiliated with and Related to the International Council of Religious Education, 1930-1939. Research Bulletin No. 16. Chicago, 1939.

Department of Social Education and Action of the Presbyterian Board of Christian Education, *Deliverances of the General Assembly of the Presbyterian Church in the United States of America, 1910-1945, on the issues of Social and Moral Welfare.* Philadelphia, 1945.

Graham, David Warner (comp.). *Resolutions on Social Action.* Crozer Theological Seminary, Chester, Pennsylvania, 1935. Contains a compilation of pronouncements for the years 1932-34.

Johnson, F. Ernest (ed.). *The Social Work of the Churches.* New York, 1930. Contains a useful compilation of the social pronouncements of the major American church bodies, 1908-30.

Yearbook of American Churches. First published in 1916, issued under the direction of various editors, and under the auspices of the Federal Council of Churches and then of the National Council of Churches.

3. Federal Council of the Churches of Christ in America Records

The records of the Federal Council, then American Protestantism's greatest interdenominational, cooperative agency, are now at the New York headquarters of the National Council of Churches. These records included *many* special studies, pamphlets, and bulletins. However, only the more basic official reports can be cited here.

Biennial Report of the Federal Council of the Churches of Christ in America, 1934, 1936, 1938.

Quadrennial Report of the Federal Council of the Churches of Christ in America, 1916-20, 1920-24, 1924-28, 1928-32.

Report of Special Meeting of the Federal Council of the Churches of Christ in America, 1919.

4. The Religious Press

An examination of the religious press was essential to this study. As a rough estimate, perhaps as much as 65 per cent of the material contained in these pages came from church journals. This source was important for editorials, contributed articles, sermon reprints, news items, book reviews, correspondence from subscribers, and special polls and symposiums which the papers themselves conducted. The mortality rate for church papers was very high, and while the dates given after each citation are for those years actually consulted, they usually indicate the life span of the paper. Since some journals changed over the years from weeklies to bi-weeklies to monthlies and then, perhaps, back again, references to periodicity will be to that practice followed by the paper over the longest span of time.*

* Of the several discussions of the church press—number, circulation, importance, and

METHODIST

Arkansas Methodist, 1919-39. A Southern Methodist weekly.

Methodist Review, 1919-31. A Northern Methodist bi-monthly.

Nashville Christian Advocate, 1919-39. A Southern Methodist weekly.

New York Christian Advocate, 1919-39. A Northern Methodist weekly. This is the New York edition of the *Christian Advocate*. Actually the words "New York" were not part of the official title, but for the sake of clarity and simplicity it has been cited throughout this study as the *New York Christian Advocate* rather than the *Christian Advocate*, New York edition. This statement also applies to the Nashville edition, cited above.

Northwestern Christian Advocate, 1919-39. A Northern Methodist weekly.

Social Service Bulletin, 1919-39. A monthly organ of the Methodist Federation for Social Service. In 1933 it took the title *Social Questions Bulletin*.

Zion's Herald, 1919-39. A Northern Methodist weekly.

BAPTIST

Alabama Baptist, 1919-39. A Southern Baptist weekly.

Baptist, 1920-32. A Northern Baptist weekly.

Chronicle, 1938-53. A Baptist historical journal.

Crozer Quarterly, 1924-39. A Crozer Theological Seminary quarterly.

Religious Herald, 1919-39. A Southern Baptist weekly.

Review and Expositor, 1919-32. A Southern Baptist Theological Seminary quarterly.

Watchman-Examiner, 1919-39. A Northern Baptist weekly.

Western Recorder, 1919-39. A Southern Baptist weekly.

PRESBYTERIAN

Christian Observer, 1919-39. A Southern Presbyterian weekly.

Continent, 1919-26. A Northern Presbyterian weekly.

Herald and Presbyter, 1919-25. A Northern Presbyterian weekly.

Journal of the Presbyterian Historical Society, 1919-53. A quarterly.

Moral Welfare, 1920-39. A Northern Presbyterian monthly. In 1934 it took the title *Social Progress*. No issues were published in 1938.

New Era Magazine, 1919-21. A Northern Presbyterian monthly.

Presbyterian, 1928-39. A Northern Presbyterian weekly.

Presbyterian Advance, 1919-34. A Northern Presbyterian weekly published, however, in Nashville and with a Southern readership until 1926 when it took over the subscription list of the *Continent* and became more national in scope.

Presbyterian Banner, 1919-37. A Northern Presbyterian weekly.

Presbyterian Magazine, 1921-33. A Northern Presbyterian monthly.

Presbyterian Tribune, 1934-39. A Northern Presbyterian bi-weekly.

caliber—see Alfred McClung Lee, "The Church Press and Public Relations of Religious Bodies," *The Annals* of the American Academy of Political and Social Science, Vol. 256 (March, 1948), 120-31.

Princeton Theological Review, 1919-29. A quarterly.
United Presbyterian, 1919-39. A United Presbyterian weekly.

PROTESTANT EPISCOPAL

American Church Monthly, 1919-39. A Protestant Episcopal monthly. In 1938 the word "New" was added to the title.
Churchman, 1919-39. A Protestant Episcopal weekly.
Historical Magazine of the Protestant Episcopal Church, 1932-53. A quarterly.
Living Church, 1919-39. A Protestant Episcopal weekly.
Southern Churchman, 1919-39. A Protestant Episcopal weekly.

CONGREGATIONAL

Church and Society, 1928-34. A Congregational monthly.
Congregationalist, 1919-39. A Congregational weekly. The title of this journal varied prior to 1934. In that year it took the title *Advance*.
Social Action, 1935-39. A monthly organ of the Council for Social Action.

LUTHERAN

Lutheran, 1919-39. A United Lutheran Church weekly.
Lutheran Church Quarterly, 1928-39. A quarterly organ of the Lutheran Theological Seminary at Gettysburg and the Lutheran Theological Seminary at Mount Airy.
Lutheran Quarterly, 1919-27. A quarterly organ of the Lutheran Theological Seminary at Gettysburg.

DISCIPLES

Christian-Evangelist, 1919-39. A Disciples of Christ weekly.

UNITARIAN

Christian Register, 1919-39. A Unitarian weekly.

UNIVERSALIST

Universalist Leader, 1919-39. A Universalist weekly. In 1926 it took the title *Christian Leader*.

REFORMED

Reformed Church Messenger, 1919-39. A Reformed Church in the United States weekly. In 1936 it took the title *Messenger* and became the organ of the Evangelical and Reformed Church.

MISCELLANEOUS

Bibliotheca Sacra, 1919-36. A theological quarterly.
Christendom, 1935-39. An undenominational weekly.
Christian Century, 1919-39. An undenominational weekly.
Christian Herald, 1919-39. An undenominational weekly.
Christian Work, 1919-26. An undenominational weekly.

Economic Justice, 1932-39. A monthly organ of the National Religion and Labor Foundation.

Federal Council Bulletin, 1919-39. A monthly organ of the Federal Council.

Fellowship, 1935-39. A monthly organ of the Fellowship of Reconciliation.

Harvard Theological Review, 1919-39. A quarterly.

Homiletic Review, 1919-32. An undenominational monthly.

Information Service, 1921-39. A weekly organ of the Federal Council.

Journal of Religion, 1921-39. A monthly organ of the Divinity Faculty of the University of Chicago.

News Letter of the World Alliance for International Friendship Through the Churches, isolated issues. Varied between weekly, bi-weekly, and monthly.

Prophetic Religion, isolated issues. A quarterly organ of the Fellowship of Southern Churchmen.

Protestant Digest, 1938-39. An undenominational monthly.

Radical Religion, 1936-39. A quarterly organ of the Fellowship of Socialist Christians.

Religion in Life, 1932-39. An undenominational quarterly.

Religious Digest, 1936-39. An undenominational monthly.

Review of Religion, 1936-39. An undenominational bi-monthly.

World Tomorrow, 1919-34. A monthly organ unofficially reflecting the point of view of the Fellowship of Reconciliation.

5. MISCELLANEOUS REPORTS, TRACTS, PAMPHLETS, LEAFLETS, AND STUDIES ISSUED BY CHURCH GROUPS

Denominational and interdenominational agencies printed a large amount of material in pamphlet and leaflet form. This material included minutes and reports of meetings, statements of principles, special studies of social problems, reprints of addresses, study outlines, descriptions of a group's activities, reports of investigations into strikes, lynchings, working conditions, and the like. Unfortunately, as church librarians are the first to admit, little effort has been made systematically to collect and preserve this material. Nevertheless, several hundred of these items were examined in the course of this study and they proved to be a rather important source.

6. SOCIALIST PARTY RECORDS

The records of the Socialist party at Duke University were of some aid in determining the extent of clerical sympathy for socialism.

7. AMERICAN CIVIL LIBERTIES UNION RECORDS

The New York office of the American Civil Libetries Union contains bulletins, reports, news releases, and special studies published by the Union. From time to time information dealing with churchmen or church groups appeared in this material. In addition, the New York

Public Library possessed the bound scrapbooks of the ACLU. Volumes 40 to 2,147 cover the years 1919-39. Approximately half of these volumes contain the correspondence of the Union. They were not examined. The remainder contain clippings from newspapers all over the country. Chapters IX through XIII of this study, and to a lesser extent other chapters, were materially enriched by the information gained from these scrapbooks. I am indebted to the Union for permitting me to examine the files in its office and for requesting the New York Public Library to grant me unrestricted access to the scrapbooks. Further, the bulletins of the various defense committees of Sacco and Vanzetti, Tom Mooney, the Scottsboro boys and others were helpful. The ACLU scrapbooks are now at Princeton University.

8. THE SECULAR PRESS

The secular press contained considerable material on the Protestant churches. On the whole, however, this proved to be a disappointing source. Most of the articles dealt with the *status* of religion in America, and not with the *attitudes* of the churches toward a particular social issue. It is not unfair to say that, on the whole, the Protestant churches received a "poor press." However, generally this source was important for gaining a feeling of the "temper of the times."

American Magazine, 1919-39.

American Mercury, 1924-39.

American Review of Reviews, 1919-37.

The Annals of the American Academy of Political and Social Science, 1919-39, 1948.

Atlantic Monthly, 1919-39.

Century, 1919-30.

Current History, 1919-39.

Current Opinion, 1919-25.

Fortune, January, 1940.

Forum, 1919-39. In 1930 it took the title *Forum and Century.*

Harper's Monthly, 1919-39.

Independent, 1919-28.

Literary Digest, 1919-38.

Nation, 1919-39.

New Republic, 1919-39.

New York Times, 1919-21, 1933-39.

North American Review, 1919-39.

Outlook, 1919-35. In 1928 it took the title *Outlook and Independent.* In 1932 it took the title *New Outlook.*

Scribner's Magazine, 1919-30.

Survey, 1919-39. Title changes to *Survey Graphic* and *Survey Midmonthly.*

Time, 1923-39.
World's Work, 1919-32.
Yale Review, 1919-39.

9. SERMON COLLECTIONS

The religious press frequently reprinted sermons. In addition, the following sermon collections were examined.

Black, Harold Garnet. *The Way Out: Twelve Christian Leaders of Southern California Speak to a World in Chaos.* Chicago, 1939.
Bonnell, J. Southerland. *Fifth Avenue Sermons.* New York, 1936.
Bowie, Walter Russell. *The Renewing Gospel.* New York, 1935.
Brown, Charles R. *Finding Ourselves.* New York, 1935.
Chalmers, Allan Knight. *Give Me Another Chance.* New York, 1936.
Chrisman, Lewis H. *The Message of the American Pulpit.* New York, 1930.
Davis, Ozora. *Preaching the Social Gospel.* New York, 1922.
Elmore, Carl. *The Inexhaustible Christ.* New York, 1935.
Fisher, Frederick B. *Can I Know God?* New York, 1934.
Fiske, Charles. *The Confessions of a Puzzled Parson and Other Pleas for Reality.* New York, 1928.
Fosdick, Harry Emerson. *Adventurous Religion.* New York, 1926.
———. *Christianity and Progress.* New York, 1922.
———. *The Hope of the World: Twenty-five Sermons on Christianity Today.* New York, 1933.
Holt, Ivan Lee. *The Return of Spring to Man's Soul.* New York, 1934.
Horton, Douglas. *Taking a City.* New York, 1934.
Jefferson, Charles E. *Like a Trumpet.* New York, 1934.
Jenny, Ray Freeman. *Speaking Boldly.* New York, 1935.
Krumbine, Miles H. (ed.). *American Lutheran Preaching: Twenty-five Sermons by Ministers of the United Lutheran Church.* New York, 1935.
Lawson, James Gilchrist (comp.). *Great Sermons on World Peace.* New York, 1937.
Lichliter, McIlyar Hamilton. *A Pillar of Stones.* New York, 1936.
Macartney, Clarence Edward. *Sermons from Life.* Nashville, 1933.
Matlock, Charles R. (ed.). *The Cumberland Presbyterian Pulpit.* Nashville, 1930.
McCall, Oswald W. S. *The Gods of Men.* New York, 1934.
Merrill, Boynton. *Arrows of Light.* New York, 1935.
Merrill, William Pierson. *We See Jesus.* New York, 1934.
Morrison, Charles Clayton. (ed.). *The American Pulpit.* New York, 1925.
Nabers, Charles Haddon (ed.). *The Southern Presbyterian Pulpit.* New York, 1928.
Newton, Joseph Fort (ed.). *Best Sermons 1924.* New York, 1924.
——— (ed.). *Best Sermons 1925.* New York, 1925.
——— (ed.). *Best Sermons 1926.* New York, 1926.
——— (ed.). *Best Sermons Book Four.* New York, 1927.

Nicely, Harold Elliott. *What Religion Does to Men.* New York, 1936.

Oxnam, G. Bromley (ed.). *Preaching and the Social Crisis.* New York, 1933.

Pierce, Ralph Milton (ed.). *Preachers and Preaching in Detroit.* New York, 1926.

Rice, M. S. *Hearing the Unheard.* New York, 1935.

———. *The Man With the Hope.* New York, 1939.

Searle, Robert Wyckoff and Frederick A. Bowers (ed.). *Contemporary Religious Thinking: Seventeen Sermons on the Church's Responsibility in the Period Just Ahead.* New York, 1933.

Speers, Theodore Cuyler. *The Power of the Commonplace.* New York, 1933.

Stewart, George Craig. *The Victory of Faith.* New York, 1935.

Tittle, Ernest Fremont. *Christians in an Unchristian Society.* New York, 1939.

———. *The Foolishness of Preaching and Other Sermons.* New York, 1937.

———. *A Way of Life.* New York, 1935.

Truett, George W. *"Follow Thou Me."* New York, 1932.

Vance, James I. *"Forbid Him Not."* New York, 1925.

———. *Worship God!* New York, 1932.

10. Unpublished Papers of Churchmen

Only a handful of unpublished papers were examined. As time passes and more of these papers become available, this source should grow in importance. The following are all located in the Southern Historical Collection, University of North Carolina.

James Atkins Papers.

Robah Fidus Bumpas Papers.

Henry L. Canfield Papers.

Allen H. Godbey Papers.

Silas McBee Papers.

Joseph Rennie Papers.

11. Autobiographies

Many church leaders active in the twenties and thirties have not yet written their autobiographies. On the whole, those who have taken pen in hand were not as informative as might be hoped.

Babson, Roger W. *Actions and Reactions: An Autobiography.* New York, 1935.

Barton, William E. *The Autobiography of William E. Barton.* Indianapolis, 1932.

Boaz, Hiram Abiff. *Eighty-Four Golden Years.* Nashville, 1951.

Brown, Charles Reynolds. *My Own Yesterdays.* New York, 1931.

Brown, William Adams. *A Teacher and His Times: A Story of Two Worlds.* New York, 1940.

Cannon, James, Jr. *Bishop Cannon's Own Story: Life As I Have Seen It.* Richard L. Watson, Jr. (ed.). Durham, 1955.

Du Bose, Horace Mellard. *Through Two Generations: A Study in Retrospect.* New York, 1934.

Fosdick, Harry Emerson. *The Living of These Days.* New York, 1956.

Gordon, George A. *My Education and Religion: An Autobiography.* Boston, 1925.

Gwaltney, L. L. *Forty of the Twentieth or the First Forty Years of the Twentieth Century.* Birmingham, 1940.

Hughes, Edwin Holt. *I Was Made a Minister.* New York, 1943.

Jenkins, Burris. *Where My Caravan Has Rested.* Chicago, 1939.

Leete, Frederick DeLand. *Adventures of a Traveling Preacher.* Boston, 1952.

Macfarland, Charles Stedman. *Across the Years.* New York, 1936.

Mathews, Shailer. *New Faith for Old.* New York, 1936.

McConnell, Francis J. *By the Way: An Autobiography.* New York, 1952.

Moore, John M. *Life and I.* Nashville, 1948.

Newton, Joseph Fort. *River of Years.* Philadelphia, 1946.

Niebuhr, Reinhold. *Leaves from the Notebook of a Tamed Cynic.* Chicago, 1929.

Potter, Charles Francis. *The Preacher and I: An Autobiography.* New York, 1951.

Sampey, John R. *Memoirs of John R. Sampey.* Nashville, 1947.

Scudder, Vida Dutton. *On Journey.* New York. 1937.

Smith, Fred B. *I Remember.* New York, 1936.

Stelzle, Charles. *A Son of the Bowery.* New York, 1926.

Taylor, Graham. *Pioneering on Social Frontiers.* Chicago, 1930.

12. Books Written by Churchmen Dealing with Social Issues

Babson, Roger W. *Religion and Business.* New York, 1920.

Barker, John Marshall. *The Social Gospel and the New Era.* New York, 1919.

Barton, Bruce. *The Book Nobody Knows.* Indianapolis, 1926.

———. *The Man Nobody Knows.* Indianapolis, 1924.

Bennett, John C. *Social Salvation.* New York, 1935.

Biederwolf, William Edward. *Awake, O America.* Grand Rapids, 1937.

Bowen, Trevor. *Divine White Right.* New York, 1934.

Brown, Charles Reynolds. *The Gospel for Main Street.* New York, 1930.

Brown, William Adams. *Church and State in Contemporary America.* New York, 1936.

———. *The Church in America.* New York, 1922.

Brown, William Montgomery. *Communism and Christianity Analyzed and Contrasted from the Marxian and Darwinian Points of View.* Galion, Ohio, 1920.

Cadman, S. Parkes. *Christianity and the State.* New York, 1924.

Cavert, Samuel McCrea and Henry Pitney Van Dusen (eds.). *The Church Through Half a Century: Essays in Honor of William Adams Brown.* New York, 1936.

Chaffee, Edmund B. *The Protestant Churches and the Industrial Crisis.* New York, 1933.

Coffin, Henry Sloane. *Religion Yesterday and Today.* Nashville, 1940.

The Committee on the War and the Religious Outlook. *The Church and Industrial Reconstruction.* New York, 1920.

Davis, Jerome. *Capitalism and its Culture.* New York, 1935.

—— (ed.). *Business and the Church.* New York, 1926.

—— (ed.). *Christianity and Social Adventuring.* New York, 1927.

—— (ed.). *Labor Speaks for Itself on Religion.* New York, 1929.

Dieffenbach, Albert C. *Religious Liberty: The Great American Illusion.* New York, 1927.

Douglass, H. Paul and Edmund deS. Brunner. *The Protestant Church as a Social Institution.* New York, 1935.

Eddy, Sherwood. *Religion and Social Justice.* New York, 1927.

——. *Revolutionary Christianity.* Chicago, 1939.

——. *Russia Today: What Can We Learn From It?* New York, 1934.

Gabriel, Ralph H. (ed.). *Christianity and Modern Thought.* New Haven, 1924.

Goddard, Alvin C. *Toward World Comradeship.* New York, 1932.

Harkness, Georgia. *The Resources of Religion.* New York, 1936.

Herring, Hubert C. *And So to War.* New Haven, 1938.

——. *The Church and Social Relations.* Boston, 1926.

High, Stanley. *The Church in Politics.* New York, 1930.

Holmes, John Haynes. *Rethinking Religion.* New York, 1938.

Holt, Arthur E. *This Nation Under God.* Chicago, 1939.

Holt, Ivan Lee. *The Search for a New Strategy in Protestantism.* Nashville, 1936.

Hough, Lynn Harold. *The Church and Civilization.* New York, 1935.

—— (ed.). *Whither Christianity.* New York, 1929.

Hutchinson, Paul. *The Ordeal of Western Religion.* Boston, 1933.

——. *World Revolution and Religion.* New York, 1931.

Johnson, F. Ernest. *The Church and Society.* New York, 1935.

——. *The Social Gospel Re-Examined.* New York, 1940.

Jones, E. Stanley. *The Choice Before Us.* New York, 1937.

——. *Christ's Alternative to Communism.* New York, 1935.

Leiper, Henry Smith. *Christ's Way and the World's Way in Church, State and Society.* New York, 1936.

Luccock, Halford E. *American Mirror: Social, Ethical and Religious Aspects of American Literature, 1930-1940.* New York, 1940.

——. *Christian Faith and Economic Change.* New York, 1936.

——. *Contemporary American Literature and Religion.* Chicago 1934.

—— and Francis Brentano (eds.). *The Questing Spirit: Religion in the Literature of Our Time.* New York, 1947.

McConnell, Francis J. *The Christian Ideal and Social Control.* Chicago, 1932.

——. *Christianity and Coercion.* Nashville, 1933.

——. *Democratic Christianity.* New York, 1919.

——. *Human Needs and World Christianity.* New York, 1929.

Macfarland, Charles S. *The Christian Faith in a Day of Crisis.* New York, 1939.

——. *Contemporary Christian Thought.* New York, 1936.

——. *Trends of Christian Thinking.* New York, 1937.

Macintosh, Douglas Clyde. *Social Religion.* New York, 1939.

MacLeod, Malcolm James. *The Challenge of the Changing.* New York, 1930.

Mathews, Shailer. *Christianity and the Social Process.* New York, 1934.

Morrison, Charles Clayton. *The Outlawry of War.* Chicago, 1927.

——. *The Social Gospel and the Christian Cultus.* New York, 1933.

Myers, James. *Religion Lends a Hand.* New York, 1929.

Niebuhr, H. Richard. *The Kingdom of God in America.* Chicago, 1937.

——. *The Social Sources of Denominationalism.* New York, 1929.

——, Wilhelm Pauck, and Francis P. Miller. *The Church Against the World.* Chicago, 1935.

Niebuhr, Reinhold. *Beyond Tragedy.* New York, 1938.

——. *The Contribution of Religion to Social Work.* New York, 1932.

——. *Does Civilization Need Religion?* New York, 1927.

——. *An Interpretation of Christian Ethics.* New York, 1935.

——. *Moral Man and Immoral Society.* New York, 1932.

——. *Reflections on the End of an Era.* New York, 1934.

—— (ed.). *This Ministry. The Contributions of Henry Sloane Coffin.* New York, 1945.

Nixon, Justin Wroe. *The Moral Crisis in Christianity.* New York, 1931.

Oldham, J. H. *Christianity and the Race Problem.* New York, 1924.

Page, Kirby. *Individualism and Socialism.* New York, 1933.

——. *Living Creatively.* New York, 1932.

——. *Living Triumphantly.* New York, 1934.

——. *War: Its Causes, Consequences and Cure.* New York, 1923.

Poteat, Edwin McNeill, Jr. *The Social Manifesto of Jesus.* New York, 1937.

Rall, Harris Franklin (ed.). *Christianity To-Day.* Nashville, 1928.

—— (ed.). *Religion and Public Affairs.* New York, 1937.

Read, Ralph H. (ed.). *The Younger Churchmen Look at the Church.* New York, 1935.

Schroeder, John C. *The Task of Religion.* New York, 1936.

Smith, Rembert Gilman. *Moscow Over Methodism.* St. Louis, 1936.

——. *Politics in a Protestant Church.* Atlanta, 1930.

Speer, Robert E. *The New Opportunity of the Church.* New York, 1919.

Spinka, Matthew. *Christianity Confronts Communism.* New York, 1936.
Taylor, Alva W. *Christianity and Industry in America.* New York, 1933.
Van Dusen, Henry P. *God in These Times.* New York, 1935.
────── and others. *Church and State in the Modern World.* New York, 1937.
Visser 't Hooft, W. A. and J. H. Oldham. *The Church and Its Function in Society.* Chicago, 1937.
Ward, Harry F. *In Place of Profit: Social Incentives in the Soviet Union.* New York, 1933.
──────. *The New Social Order.* New York, 1919.
──────. *Our Economic Morality and the Ethic of Jesus.* New York, 1929.

SECONDARY WORKS

1. Unpublished Theses and Dissertations

A number of candidates for regular and advanced degrees have labored in the vineyard of recent church history. These studies vary widely in excellence. Collectively, they provide a full record of denominational resolutions in several fields. Several probed deeply the thought of individual churchmen, denominations, or agencies. A few were based upon extensive examination of the press of one denomination. Several investigated thoroughly one area of social concern. Those studies which I found most helpful, *although not necessarily the best written or the most useful for other students,* will be starred. A few of the works cited did not deal primarily with the churches.*

Althouse, John N. "The Social Consciousness of Methodism." Unpublished M.Th. thesis, Crozer Theological Seminary, 1939.
Atwood, Jesse Howell. "The Attitude of Negro Ministers of the Major Denominations in Chicago Toward Racial Division in American Protestantism." Unpublished Ph.D. dissertation, University of Chicago, 1930.
Balls, Ernest George. "The Function of the Church in Relation to the Economic Order." Unpublished M.S.Th. thesis, Union Theological Seminary, 1939.
Baker, George Claude, Jr. "The Relations of American Methodism to Social and Political Movements." Unpublished M.Th. thesis, Union Theological Seminary, 1936.
Barnhart, Kenneth Edwin. "The Evolution of the Social Consciousness in Methodism." Unpublished Ph.D. dissertation, University of Chicago, 1924.
*Battenhouse, Paul F. "Theology in the Social Gospel, 1918-1946." Unpublished Ph.D. dissertation, Yale University, 1950.
Bergendoff, Conrad L. "The Protestant Churches and American Foreign

* Neils H. Sonne (ed.), *A Bibliography of Post-Graduate Masters' Theses in Religion* (American Theological Library Association, 1951), is a useful guide, as is *Doctoral Dissertations in the Field of Religion, 1940-1952* (supplement to Vol. XVIII of the *Review of Religion,* Columbia University Press, 1954).

Relations Since 1914." Unpublished M.A. thesis, University of Chicago, 1948.

Binkley, Olin T. "The Anti-Evolution Movement in Relation to Public Education in the United States." Unpublished Ph.D. dissertation, Yale University, 1933.

Bowers, Robert Edwin. "The American Peace Movement, 1933-1941." Unpublished Ph.D. dissertation, University of Wisconsin, 1949.

*Brimm, Hugh A. "The Social Consciousness of Southern Baptists in Relation to Some Regional Problems, 1910-1935." Unpublished Th.D. dissertation, Southern Baptist Theological Seminary, 1944.

Brunner, Hans Henry. "Coercive Power: A Study in American Protestant Ethics Between the Opening of the Twentieth Century and the Second World War." Unpublished Th.D. dissertation, Union Theological Seminary, 1947.

Bryant, Richard Whitney. "Christian Critiques of the Conception of Human Nature in Capitalism and Communism." Unpublished B.D. thesis, McCormick Theological Seminary, 1945.

Bulkley, Robert DeGroff. "An Analysis of Certain Contemporary Critiques of Christian Social Liberalism." Unpublished B.D. thesis, Presbyterian [now McCormick] Theological Seminary, 1936.

*Carter, Paul A. "The Decline and Revival of the Social Gospel: Social and Political Liberalism in American Protestant Churches, 1920-1940." Ph.D. dissertation, Columbia University, 1954. This study was published in 1956.

Carwithen, E. Franklin. "The Attitudes of the Methodist Episcopal Church Toward Peace and War." Unpublished S.Th.D. dissertation, Temple University, 1944.

Davidson, James Robert, Jr. "Some Effects of Liberal Theology on Attitudes Toward War and Peace." Unpublished M.Th. thesis, Union Theological Seminary, 1947.

De Vinney, James Marion. "The Attitude of the Methodist Episcopal Church Toward War From 1910 to 1927." Unpublished M.A. thesis, Northwestern University, 1928.

Escott, N. Ellsworth. "The Christian Minister: Protagonist of Social Justice." Unpublished M.Th. thesis, Oberlin Graduate School of Theology, 1937.

*Furniss, Norman F. "The Fundamentalist Controversy, 1918-1931." Ph.D. dissertation, Yale University, 1950. This study was published in 1954.

Gesler, Albert Urban. "Official Pronouncements of the United Lutheran Church in America Relating to Certain Moral and Social Problems." Unpublished Ph.D. dissertation, University of Pittsburgh, 1941.

Gray, L. Jack. "A Study of Protestant Preaching in the United States, 1920-1929." Unpublished Th.D. dissertation, Southern Baptist Theological Seminary, 1948.

Haas, Emma Elizabeth. "The Attitude of the Churches in the World War and the Present European War." Unpublished M.A. thesis, University of Chicago, 1942.

Hovey, Amos Arnold. "A History of the Religious Phase of the American Movement for International Peace to the Year 1914." Unpublished Ph.D. dissertation, University of Chicago, 1930.

*Huber, Milton John. "A History of the Methodist Federation for Social Action." Unpublished Ph.D. dissertation, Boston University, 1949.

Johnson, Charles Kenneth. "The Social Gospel Since 1914." Unpublished M.Th. thesis, Union Theological Seminary, 1936.

Kearns, Francis Emner. "Changing Social Emphases in the Methodist Episcopal Church." Unpublished Ph.D. dissertation, University of Pittsburgh, 1939.

*Kelsey, George D. "The Social Thought of Contemporary Southern Baptists." Unpublished Ph.D. dissertation, Yale University, 1946.

Kendall, William Aaron. "The Christian Ethics of Harry Frederick Ward." Unpublished M.Th. thesis, University of Southern California, 1944.

Kieffer, Martin. "The Attitudes and Practices of the Major American Protestant Denominations Toward the Negro Problem." Unpublished M.S.Th., Union Theological Seminary, 1947.

Knott, Maurice F. "Some Attitudes in American Protestantism Toward Economic Problems, 1928-1936." Unpublished B.D. thesis, University of Chicago, 1943.

Lam, Elizabeth Paxton. "The Attitude of the Presbyterian Church Toward World Peace." Unpublished M.A. thesis, University of Chicago, 1930.

*Larson, Roger Marshall. "Trends in the Economic Pronouncements of the Major American Church Bodies, 1908-1948." Unpublished Ph.D. dissertation, University of Southern California, 1950.

Lichtenberger, Arthur C. "The Relation of the Episcopal Church to Social Problems in America Since the Civil War." Unpublished M.A. [?] thesis, Cambridge Episcopal Theological School, 1925.

Locke, Harvey James. "A History and Critical Interpretation of the Social Gospel of Northern Baptist in the United States." Unpublished Ph.D. dissertation, University of Chicago, 1930.

McCelland, Robert Crawford. "The Soviet Union in American Opinion, 1933-1942." Unpublished Ph.D. dissertation, University of West Virginia, 1950.

Martin, B. Joseph. "The History of the Attitudes of the Methodist Church in the United States of America Toward Recreation." Unpublished Ph.D. dissertation, University of Southern California, 1944.

*Meyer, Donald Burton. "The Protestant Social Liberals in America, 1919-1941." Unpublished Ph.D. dissertation, Harvard University, 1953.

Minto, Robert Macfee. "The Churches and the Prohibition Issue in America." Unpublished M.S.Th. thesis, Union Theological Seminary, 1933.

Moyer, George S. "Attitude of the United States Toward the Recognition of Soviet Russia." Unpublished Ph.D. dissertation, University of Pennsylvania, 1926.

Murray, Robert Keith. "The Great Red Scare of 1919-1920." Ph.D. dissertation, Ohio State University, 1949. This study was published in 1955.

*Pangborn, Cyrus Ransom. "Free Churches and Social Change: A Critical Study of the Council for Social Action of the Congregational Christian Churches of the United States." Unpublished Ph.D. dissertation, Columbia University, 1951.

Parrott, John Henry. "The Preaching of Social Christianity in the United States in the Twentieth Century." Unpublished Th.D. dissertation, Southern Baptist Theological Seminary, 1950.

Pratt, Charles McCready. "The Social Teaching of the Presbyterian Churches in the Light of Their Background and Early Foreground." Unpublished M.Th. thesis, Union Theological Seminary of Richmond, Virginia, 1940.

Prosser, Donald N. "The Contribution of Certain Religious Bodies to World Peace." Unpublished M.Th. thesis, University of Southern California, 1940.

Shaw, James Patterson. "A Study of the Pronouncements on Social Issues by the Presbytery of Ohio and Its Successor the Presbytery of Pittsburgh." Unpublished M.S.Th. thesis, Western Theological Seminary of Pittsburgh, 1940.

*Shelton, Arthur Edwin. "The Methodist Church and Industrial Workers in the Southern Soft Coal Fields." Unpublished Th.D. dissertation, Boston University, 1950.

Smith, Kenneth Jackson. "John Haynes Holmes: Opponent of War." Unpublished B.D. thesis, Meadville Theological School, 1949.

Stiernotte, Alfred. "The Place of Marxism in Religious Thought." Unpublished B.D. thesis, Meadville Theological School, 1944.

Story, Delaine E. "The Contribution of Northern Baptists to Social Christianity—National Period." Unpublished M.Th. thesis, Crozer Theological Seminary, 1938.

Stuart, John M. "The Presbyterian Church and Labor, 1900-1945." Unpublished M.A. [?] thesis, Princeton Theological Seminary, 1946.

*Valentine, Foy Dan. "A Historical Study of Southern Baptists and Race Relations, 1917-1947." Unpublished Th.D. dissertation, Southwestern Baptist Theological Seminary, 1949.

*Voss, Carl Hermann. "The Rise of Social Consciousness in the Congregational Churches." Unpublished Ph.D. dissertation, University of Pittsburgh, 1942.

Walker, Edgar Allen. "Changing Emphases of the Presbyterian Church, U.S.A., on Social Problems." Unpublished Ph.D. dissertation, University of Pittsburgh, 1940.

Walters, Sumner. "Social Ethics in the History of the American Episcopal Church with Reference to Its Relations with the Colored Race." Unpublished M.S.Th. thesis, Pacific School of Religion, 1938.

Weatherly, Owen. "A Comparative Study of the Social Ethics of Walter Rauschenbusch and Reinhold Niebuhr." Unpublished M.A. thesis, University of Chicago, 1950.

Wesener, Paul. "Efforts for World Peace Since 1918." Unpublished M.S.Th. thesis, Hartford Theological Seminary, 1933.

*Williams, Hillman T. "The Methodist Episcopal Church and Industrial Reconstruction, 1908-1939." Unpublished S.Th.D. dissertation, Temple University, 1945.

Williams, John Paul. "Social Adjustment in Methodism." Columbia University Contributions to Education No. 765, Teachers College, 1938.

2. BIOGRAPHIES

Dabney, Virginius. *Dry Messiah: The Life of Bishop Cannon.* New York, 1949.

Dana, H. E. *Lee Rutland Scarborough: A Life of Service.* Nashville, 1942.

Davies, D. R. *Reinhold Niebuhr: Prophet From America.* New York, 1948.

Dempsey, Elam Franklin. *Life of Bishop Dickey: Bishop of the Methodist Episcopal Church, South.* Nashville, 1937.

Fisher, Welthy Honsinger. *Frederick Bohn Fisher: World Citizen.* New York, 1941.

Gill, Everett A. *A. T. Robertson: A Biography.* New York, 1943.

Hamlin, Fred S. *S. Parkes Cadman: Pioneer Radio Minister.* New York 1930.

Idleman, Finis S. *Peter Ainslie: Ambassador of Good Will.* Chicago, 1941.

James, Powhatan. *George W. Truett.* New York, 1939.

Jones, Edgar De Witt. *American Preachers Today.* Indianapolis, 1933.

———. *The Royalty of the Pulpit.* New York, 1951.

Kegley, Charles W., and Robert W. Bretall (eds.). *Reinhold Niebuhr: His Religious, Social, and Political Thought.* New York, 1956.

Leete, Frederick De Land. *Methodist Bishops: Personal Notes and Bibliography with Quotations from Unpublished Writings and Reminiscences.* Nashville, 1948.

Mann, A. Chester [Philip Roberts]. *The Life of John McDowell: Servant of God, Friend of Man.* Philadelphia, 1938.

Mathews, Basil. *John R. Mott: World Citizen.* New York, 1934.

Pierce, Alfred M. *Giant Against the Sky: The Life of Bishop Warren Akin Candler.* New York, 1948.

Robbins, Howard Chandler. *Charles Lewis Slattery.* New York, 1931.

Zabriskie, Alexander C. *Bishop Brent: Crusader for Christian Unity.* Philadelphia, 1948.

3. DENOMINATIONAL HISTORIES AND HISTORIES OF RELIGION IN AMERICA

Addison, James Thayer. *The Episcopal Church in the United States, 1798-1931.* New York, 1951.

Atkins, Gaius Glenn. *Religion in Our Times.* New York, 1932.

——— and Frederick L. Fagley. *History of American Congregationalism.* Boston, 1942.

Bach, Marcus. *They Have Found a Faith.* Indianapolis, 1946.

Barnes, William Wright. *The Southern Baptist Convention, 1845-1953.* Nashville, 1954.

Bass, Archer B. *Protestantism in the United States.* New York, 1929.

Clark, Elmer T. *The Small Sects in America.* Rev. ed., New York, 1949.

Douglass, H. Paul, "Religion" in Harold E. Stearns (ed.). *America Now: An Inquiry into Civilization in the United States.* New York, 1938.

———. *The St. Louis Church Survey.* New York, 1924.

Drummond, Andrew Landale. *Story of American Protestantism.* Edinburgh, Scotland, 1949.

Ferm, Vergilius (ed.). *Religion in the Twentieth Century.* New York, 1948.

Fosdick, Harry Emerson. "Recent Gains in Religion" in Kirby Page (ed.). *Recent Gains in American Civilization.* New York, 1928.

Fry, C. Luther. "Changes in Religious Organizations," *Recent Social Trends in the United States: Report of the President's Research Committee.* One vol. ed., New York, 1933.

Garrison, Winfred Ernest. *The March of Faith.* New York, 1933.

——— and Alfred T. De Grott. *The Disciples of Christ: A History.* St. Louis, 1948.

Hanzsche, William Thomson. *The Presbyterians: The Story of a Staunch and Sturdy People.* Philadelphia, 1934.

Hopkins, C. Howard. *History of the Y.M.C.A. in North America.* New York, 1951.

Hutchison, John A. *We Are Not Divided: A Critical and Historical Study of the Federal Council of the Churches of Christ in America.* New York, 1941.

Kinsheloe, Samuel C. *Research Memorandum on Religion in the Depression. Bulletin No. 33.* Social Science Research Council, New York, 1937.

Latourette, Kenneth Scott. *Advance Through Storm,* Vol. VII in *A History of the Expansion of Christianity.* New York, 1945.

Luccock, Halford E. and Paul Hutchinson. *The Story of Methodism.* New York, 1926.

Manross, William Wilson. *A History of the American Episcopal Church.* New York, 1950.

Matheny, E. Stacy. *American Devotion.* 4th ed., Columbus, Ohio, 1943.

Mead, Frank S. *See Those Banners Go: The Story of the Protestant Churches in America.* Indianapolis, 1936.

Nash, Arnold S. (ed.). *Protestant Thought in the Twentieth Century.* New York, 1951.

Nichols, James Hastings. *Democracy and the Churches.* Philadelphia, 1951.

Poteat, Edwin McNeill, Jr. "Religion in the South" in W. T. Couch (ed.). *Culture in the South.* Chapel Hill, 1934.

Robertson, Archie. *That Old-Time Religion.* Boston, 1950.

Rowe, Henry Kalloch. *The History of Religion in the United States.* New York, 1924.

Schneider, Herbert Wallace. *Religion in 20th Century America.* Cambridge, 1952.

Smeltzer, Wallace Guy. *Methodism on the Headwaters of the Ohio.* Nashville, 1951.

Smith, Gerald Birney (ed.). *Religious Thought in the Last Quarter-Century.* Chicago, 1927.

Sperry, Willard L. *Religion in America.* Cambridge, 1946.

Spinka, Matthew (ed.). *A History of Illinois Congregational and Christian Churches.* Chicago, 1944.

Stokes, Anson Phelps. *Church and State in the United States.* 3 vols., New York, 1950.

Sweet, William Warren. *Methodism in American History.* Rev. ed., New York, 1953.

———. *The Story of Religion in America.* Rev. ed., New York, 1939.

Torbet, Robert G. *A History of the Baptists.* Chicago, 1950.

Wentz, Abdel Ross. *A Basic History of Lutheranism in America.* Philadelphia, 1955.

Williams, J. Paul. *What Americans Believe and How They Worship.* New York, 1952.

Yinger, J. Milton. *Religion in the Struggle for Power.* Durham, North Carolina, 1946.

4. Studies of the Churches and Specific Issues

Abrams, Ray A. *Preachers Present Arms.* New York, 1933.

Bowman, Rufus D. *The Church of the Brethren and War, 1708-1941.* Elgin, Illinois, 1944.

Carter, Paul A. *The Decline and Revival of the Social Gospel: Social and Political Liberalism in American Protestant Churches, 1920-1940.* Ithaca, New York, 1956.

Cole, Stewart G. *The History of Fundamentalism.* New York, 1931.

Ebersole, Luke Eugene. *Church Lobbying in the Nation's Capitol.* New York, 1951.

Furniss, Norman F. *The Fundamentalist Controversy, 1918-1931.* New Haven, 1954.

Graebner, Theodore. *The Business Man and the Church: An Economic Study.* Clinton, South Carolina, 1942.

Hughley, J. Neal. *Trends in Protestant Social Idealism.* New York, 1948.

Loescher, Frank S. *The Protestant Church and the Negro.* New York, 1948.

Macfarland, Charles S. *Pioneers for Peace Through Religion Based on the Records of the Church Peace Union (Founded by Andrew Carnegie) 1914-1945.* New York, 1946.

Mays, Benjamin Elijah, and Joseph William Nicholson. *The Negro's Church.* New York, 1933.

Miller, Spencer, Jr., and Joseph F. Fletcher. *The Church and Industry.* New York, 1930.

Pope, Liston. *Millhands and Preachers.* New Haven, 1942.

Roy, Ralph Lord. *Apostles of Discord.* Boston, 1953.
Van Kirk, Walter W. *Religion Renounces War.* Chicago, 1934.
Williams, Michael. *The Shadow of the Pope.* New York, 1932.

5. Works Dealing with American Society in the Prosperity and Depression Decades

A number of items—in book, article, and pamphlet form—not specifically devoted to the churches were examined. These included not only general histories of the twenties and thirties, but also special studies dealing with such topics as strikes, lynching, academic freedom, race relations, the election of 1928, the Klan, the New Deal, foreign policy, and the like. To list these titles here would extend the bibliography beyond reasonable lengths.

Index

Abbott, Lyman, 44, 191
Abolition. *See* slavery
Abrams, Ray H., *Preachers Present Arms,* 317, 336
Academic freedom, 154-68
Addams, Jane, 146, 193
Advance, 80-81, 121, 149, 167, 238, 346. See also *Congregationalist*
Ainslie, Peter, 145, 323, 339
Ainsworth, William N., 300
Alabama Baptist, 39, 56, 74, 142, 167, 180, 229, 257, 293
Aldrich, Duane B., 23
Alexander, George, 190
Alexander, Gross W., 174
Allen, Devere, 90
Allentown ministerial association, 276
American Anti-False Science League, 160
American Association for Economic Freedom, 252
American Association for Labor Legislation, 253
American Association of Conservative Colleges, 156
American Baptist, 57
American Church Monthly, 84, 239, 293
American Civil Liberties Union, 165, 277
American Colonization Society, 8
American League Against War and Fascism, 70
American League for Peace and Democracy, 83
American Legion, 147-48, 180-81, 198, 349
American Mercury, 35
American Revolution, 4-5
American Scotttsboro Defense Committee, 179
American Unitarian Association. *See* Unitarian
Anderson, Douglas, 277
Anderson, William F., 145, 171
Anglican Church, 4-5
Anthony, Alfred Williams, 294
Anti-Semitism, 293-96
Appleby, A. B., 146

Arkansas Methodist, 19, 54, 72, 140, 157, 215, 219, 226, 257, 307, 322
Ashworth, Robert, 74, 147, 197
Association of Southern Women for the Prevention of Lynching, 303
Atkinson, Henry A., 319
Atteberry, E. Raymond, 181

Babson, Roger, on financial value of churches, 24, 26; on cure for depression, 117; mentioned, 17
Baer, George, 12
Bailey, John T., 23
Baker, James C., 213, 338
Baldwin, Roger, 97
Baptist, 27, 39-40, 44, 55, 74, 141, 164, 173, 177-78, 180, 195, 214, 230-31, 270, 295, 309
Baptist Advance, 57
Baptist and Commoner, 57
Baptist and Reflector, 56, 157
Baptist Bible Union, 157
Baptist Courier, 57, 142, 157
Baptist Message, 57
Baptist Messenger, 57
Baptist New Mexican, 57
Baptist, Northern Convention, on capitalism, 36-37, 73-74; on Russia, 44n; opposes Smith, 54-55; protests lynching, 134; and secret societies, 143; and loyalty oaths, 166; upholds civil liberties, 199; on labor, 218, 229-31; opposes oriental exclusion, 292; on race relations, 299, 308; supports League, 320, 324; and World Court, 325; and Pact of Paris, 326; members polled on war, 339
Baptist Observer, 56
Baptist Record, of Iowa, 57
Baptist Record, of Mississippi, 57
Baptist, Southern Convention, on Russia, 44n; opposes Smith, 55; on social justice, 74; on causes of depression, 116; censors socialism, 118, 122; and lynching, 132, 134; and secret societies, 143-44; and evolution, 158; upholds free speech, 189;

on labor, 218, 228-29; opposes oriental exclusion, 292; on race relations, 300, 308-9; on League, 321, 324; on World Court, 325; on Pact of Paris, 326

Baptists, in early wars, 4-7; on slavery, 8; oppose Smith, 55; praise New Deal, 74; oppose regimentation, 122; on Darwinism, 158; uphold academic freedom, 165, 167; defend Mooney, 175; on labor, 228; on strikes, 268; on segregation, 299

Barclay, Wade C., 102

Barnes, C. Rankin, 277

Barnes, Roswell P., 93

Barstrow, Robbins W., 174

Barth, Karl, 63

Barton, Bruce, *The Man Nobody Knows*, 26; criticized, 34; mentioned, 17, 38, 285

Bates, Ruby, 179

Batten, Samuel Zane, 44

Beal, Fred, 71, 204, 268

Beane, Roy H., 34

Beard, Charles A., 237

Beecher, Henry Ward, on sermons, 3; opposes war, 5; and slavery, 9; councils workingmen, 11

Beecher, Lyman, 5, 9, 11

Bell, Bernard Iddings, 44, 124, 239

Bell, Daniel, 110

Bell, William, 174

Benezet, Anthony, 9

Bennett, John C., member of PFSA, 77; and FSC, 93, 250; on New Deal, 122

Berger, Victor, 188

Bible Crusaders of America, 156-57

Bible Institute of Los Angeles, 158

Bible League of North America, 156

Biblical Recorder, 57

Bigelow, E. Victor, *Mistakes of the Interchurch Steel Report*, 212

Bigelow, Herbert, 45

Bimba, Anthony, 159

Birkhead, L. M., 153

Black Legion, 150-51, 349

Blackshear, William S., 299-300

Blake, B. B., 160

Blake, Edgar, 41, 124, 197

Blanchard, Paul, 252

Bliss, William D. P., 13, 240

Bollens, John, 86, 281

Boston Federation of Churches, 182

Boston University School of Theology, 170, 275

Bowie, Walter Russell, condemns Klan, 144; and American Legion, 148; defends Scottsboro boys, 179; aids strikers, 276

Bradford, William, 6

Bradley, Dwight, 79-80

Brent, Charles H., 182, 323, 325

Brethren, Church of the, 135, 322, 331

Brewster, Benjamin, 174, 282

Brightman, Edgar S., 102

Brimm, Hugh A., "The Social Consciousness of Southern Baptists in Relation to Some Regional Problems, 1910-1935," 132, 228-29, 298

Brooklyn Church and Mission Federation, 283

Brooks, R. W., 175

Brookwood Labor College, 253

Browder, Earl, 96, 109, 196

Brown, Charles R., defends social Christianity, 34; voted outstanding, 45n; upholds civil liberties, 190; on strikes, 260-61

Brown, Hugh Elmer, 80

Brown, William Adams, 323

Brown, William Montgomery, 42

Brummitt, Dan B., 73n, 102

Brunner, Emil, 63

Bryan, William Jennings, 155-56

Bryan Bible Belt League, 156

Budenz, Louis, 79, 204

Buehrer, Edwin T., 95

Burch, Charles S., 240

Burritt, Elihu, 6

Burt, Roy, 102

Bush, Benjamin J., 281

Bushnell, Horace, 5, 13

Business community, churches praise, 22-27

Buttrick, George, 277

Cadman, S. Parkes, on promiscuity, 20; on church promotion, 22; voted outstanding, 45n; president of Federal Council, 46; defends Bowie, 148; opposes loyalty oaths, 167; defends Scottsboro boys, 179; and free speech, 191, 196; protests company unions, 252; supports League, 323; and Pact of Paris, 327; and recognition of Russia, 342

Calder, John, 236

California State Federation of Churches, 175, 283

Callahan, Patrick K., 52

Candler, Warren A., eschews politics, 53; opposes socialism, 118; on academic freedom, 165; on segregation, 300

Cannon, James M., Jr., protests mill conditions, 50, 252; opposes Smith, 53; supports collective security, 343

Capitalism, and Protestantism, 204-6; defended, 17-30, 113-27 *passim;* criticized, 31-47, 63-112 *passim*

Carnegie Endowment for International Peace, 341

Carstensen, G. A., 187

Cartwright, Peter, 5

Carver, Thomas Nixon, 242

Cavert, Samuel McCrea, Federal Council officer, 46; praises New Deal, 88; opposes lynching, 136; defends Sacco and Vanzetti, 171; and labor, 222

Central Christian Advocate, 41

Central Conference of American Rabbis, 181, 215-16

Centralia affair, 180-82, 187-88

Chaffee, Edmund B., as editor, 77; member of PFSA, 77; on industrial crisis, 79; defends Sacco and Vanzetti, 171; opposes war, 191; supports strikes, 269, 276

Chalmers, Allan Knight, helps found CSA, 80; member of NRLF, 92; writes Roosevelt, 102; defends Scottsboro boys, 179; on mining conditions, 277; leads pacifists, 339-40

Channing, William Ellery, 5, 9

Chappell, Winifred, 79, 265, 277

Chase, Harry W., 161

Chicago Church Federation, 182, 279

Chicago Theological Seminary, 170

Child labor, 216-19

Chrisman, Lewis, *The Message of the Modern Pulpit,* 164

Christian Century, 32-35, 39, 41n, 43, 45, 58, 61, 64, 73, 91, 119-21, 138, 149, 156n, 162, 167, 172, 177, 179, 192, 194-95, 213, 219, 246-47, 257-58, 265, 267, 270, 272, 278, 295, 312, 314, 318, 322, 327, 337, 339, 344

Christian Church, 324, 326

Christian Education Movement, 29

Christian Endeavor Movement, supports Hoover, 120; protests anti-Semitism, 296; supports League, 324; and Pact of Paris, 326

Christian-Evangelist, 39, 58, 84, 149, 152, 167, 173, 177, 214, 219, 242, 278-79, 295, 312, 323

Christian Herald, 27, 39, 58, 139, 195, 219, 247, 254, 312, 322, 329, 339

Christian Index, 56

Christian Leader, 39, 58, 149, 152, 167, 173, 177, 195-97, 278, 282, 295. See also *Universalist Leader*

Christian Observer, 58, 117, 157, 233, 310

Christian Register, 34, 39, 43, 58, 64, 85, 121, 141, 172, 177, 179, 192, 195, 197, 214, 219, 243, 312, 323, 339

Christian Social Action Movement, 97-98, 251

Christian Work, 32, 39, 139, 162, 172, 187, 192, 213, 247, 257, 295, 312, 322

Christians, 292

Church and Society, 79, 236, 311

Church Association for the Advancement of the Interests of Labor. *See* Protestant Episcopal Church

Church construction, 25-26

Church Emergency Committee for the Relief of Textile Strikers, 276

Church League for Industrial Democracy. *See* Protestant Episcopal Church

Church Peace Union, combats anti-Semitism, 295-96; supports League, 319-20, 324; and World Court, 325; and disarmament, 329, 331; divides over policy, 334, 342; mentioned, 341

Church Socialist League. *See* Protestant Episcopal Church

Churchman, 39, 43, 83, 121, 141, 149, 167, 172, 177, 180, 193-95, 214, 239, 259, 269

Civil War, 7

Clarke, E. Y., 156

Clarke, James E., 282

Clinchy, Russell J., 80

Clipsheet, 240

Coal miners, and Methodist Church, 208-10

Cobleigh, Rolfe, 28

Cochran, William F., 95

Coe, Albert Buckner, 80, 198

Coe, George A., 191

Coffin, Henry Sloane, on materialism, 25; voted outstanding, 45n; eschews politics, 57n; defends Union students, 136; and Bowie, 148; president of Union, 168; defends Sacco and Vanzetti, 171; and Mooney, 176; upholds civil liberties, 190-92; approves recognition of Russia, 342; supports collective security, 343

Commission on Interracial Co-operation, 303

Committee for the Defense of Southern Share Croppers, 252

Committee on Goodwill between Jews and Christians, 294

Committee on Labor Injunctions, 252

Committee on Militarism in Education, 341

Committee on the Churches and the Moral Aims of the War, 320

Committee on the Rights of Religious Minorities, 294

Committee on the War and the Religious

Outlook, *The Church and Industrial Reconstruction,* 35-36

Commonwealth College, 106

Communists, cooperation with, 70, 83, 90, 93, 96, 98, 104n, 106, 109-12; opposed, 91, 105, 118-19; and Scottsboro boys, 178; and civil liberties, 184-200; and labor unions, 203-4; and strikes, 263-70, 275; mentioned, 349. *See also* Russia

Conference for Progressive Labor Action, 253

Conference of Younger Churchmen, 99

Congregational (Congregational Christian) Churches, in early wars, 4-6; challenge economic injustice, 37; oppose Smith, 58; criticize capitalism, 77-81; oppose lynching, 134-35; and masked societies, 143; uphold academic freedom, 165; defend Mooney, 175; and Scottsboro boys, 178-79; investigate Centralia affair, 181; uphold free speech, 189; on labor, 235-38; oppose oriental exclusion, 292; on race relations, 311; support League, 321, 324; and World Court, 325; and Pact of Paris, 326

(Congregational) Council for Social Action, description of activities, 78-81, 237-38; opposes loyalty oaths, 166-67; defends Scottsboro boys, 179; protests syndicalism law, 198; supports strikers, 276, 279-80, 284; on race relations, 311; divides over foreign policy, 334, 342; conducts poll, 338

Congregationalist, 39, 43, 58, 81, 163, 172, 177, 179, 195, 214, 219, 238, 265, 295, 311, 323. See also *Advance*

Congregationalists, on slavery, 9; defend capitalism, 78; criticize capitalism, 79; polled, 81, 254, 338; oppose loyalty oaths, 166; on Scottsboro boys, 178; on Centralia affair, 181; on child labor, 218; investigate strike, 260-61; support League, 331

Conrad, Arcturus, 159

Conscientious objectors. *See* Pacifism

Continent, 27, 32, 39, 140, 163-64, 187, 193, 215, 257, 295, 311, 328

Conwell, Russell H., 45n

Cook, Philip, 145

Cooke, Richard J., 187

Coolidge, Calvin, admired by churchmen, 27-28; and police strike, 259

Cory, David Munroe, 102, 283

Cotton, Paul, 279

Coughlin, Charles E., 149-50, 293, 335, 359

Council for Social Reconstruction, 86, 95

Council of Christian Associations, 299

Council on a Christian Social Order, 71, 223, 301

Cowan, T. B., 248-50, 276

Cox, Gene, 249

Cox, Gilbert, 98, 251

Coyle, Albert, 252

Crane, Frank, 26

Crowther, James, 181

Daniel, Franz, 248

Darlington, Henry, 136, 168

Darnell, Warren E., 197

Daughters of the American Revolution, 146-47, 349

Davis, J. H., 248

Davis, Jerome, on Russia, 42; member of NRLF, 91-93; writes Roosevelt, 102; defends Mooney, 174; opposes injunctions, 252; supports strikers, 263

Day, Albert, 273

Day, Jonathan C., 273

Debs, Eugene, 186, 263

De Costa, B. F., 240

Defenders of Science vs. Speculation of California, 157, 160

Defenders of the Christian Faith, 157

De Jarnette, A. L., member of FSC, 248-49; and FOS, 250; aids strikers, 276

Denny, Collins, 53

Denver ministerial association, 271

Depression, effect on churches, 63; severity minimized, 113-27

Detroit Council of Churches, 281

Devine, Edward T., 215

Dewey, Thomas E., 121

Dexter, Robert C., Unitarian leader, 84-85, 242; supports strikers, 270

Dieffenbach, Albert C., 85, 141

Dietrich, John H., 160

Diffendorfer, R. E., 120

Dilling, Elizabeth, 110, 198

Dillingham, John, 248

Disarmament, 317-44 *passim*

Disciples of Christ, urge industrial democracy, 38; criticize capitalism, 84; oppose lynching, 135; and loyalty oaths, 166; defend Scottsboro boys, 179; uphold free speech, 193; on labor, 218, 241-42; oppose oriental exclusion, 292; on race relations, 312; support League, 324; and World Court, 325; and Pact of Paris, 326; polled on war, 338-39

Disciples of Christ Peace Fellowship, 341

Disillusionment, post-war, of churchmen, 21, 330-31

Dombrowski, James, 248, 276

Donnelly, Thomas, 52
Douglas, Paul H., 90, 237
Du Bois, W. E. B., 296, 301
Du Bose, Horace M., 53, 53n
Dueling, churches oppose, 10
Dukes, Hubert, 181
Durkee, Stanley, 179
Dwight, Timothy, 5

Easley, Ralph, 124
Eastman, Fred, 165
Economic Justice, 92-93, 248
Eddy, Sherwood, on Russia, 42; member of
    FCSO, 46; and LIPA, 102; condemns
    Klan, 146; on evolution, 165; defends
    Sacco and Vanzetti, 171; and Mooney,
    174-75; supports farming experiment, 249
Edwards, Jonathan, 106
Einstein, Albert, 339
Elections, of 1924, 28, 45; of 1928, 45, 48-
    62; of 1932, 119-121; of 1936, 121; of
    1944, 121-22
Emergency Committee for Strikers Relief,
    269, 276
Emergency Peace Campaign, 341
Emerson, Ralph Waldo, 5
Empey, Guy, 186
Episcopal. *See* Protestant Episcopal
Epworth Herald, 177, 339
Evangelical and Reformed Church, on cap-
    italism, 86; condemns lynching, 135; on
    labor, 218, 244; on race relations, 312
Evangelical Synod of North America, up-
    holds human rights, 38; on capitalism,
    86; on labor, 218, 244; supports World
    Court, 325; and Pact of Paris, 326
Evangelical Theological College, 158
Evolutionary theories, and academic free-
    dom, 154-65

Fascist organizations, 150-53
Faunce, William H. P., 165
Federal Council Bulletin, 38-39, 88, 135,
    139, 179, 222, 291, 304, 319, 325, 328
Federal Council of Churches, criticized, 29,
    148; defends YWCA, 32; on social order,
    35; aids Russians, 40; leaders of, 46; on
    economic order, 88-89; on child labor,
    114, 217; condemns lynching, 132, 135-
    36; and Klan, 143; and Black Legion,
    151; and loyalty oaths, 166; defends
    Scottsboro boys, 178; investigates Cen-
    tralia affair, 181; defends conscientious
    objectors, 182; upholds free speech, 190,
    199; on labor, 220-23, 279; investigates
    strikes, 258, 260-61, 264, 266, 268-72;

275-77, 281; defends union leaders, 285;
    opposes oriental exclusion, 291-92; com-
    bats anti-Semitism, 294-96; on race rela-
    tions, 302-04; supports League, 319, 324;
    and World Court, 325; and Pact of
    Paris, 326-27; encourages disarmament,
    329-31, 337; on Manchurian invasion,
    335; on war debts, 335; on foreign policy,
    339, 342; mentioned, 31, 341
Fellowship for a Christian Social Order, 46,
    251
Fellowship of Reconciliation, absorbs FCSO,
    46; description of activities, 96-97, 250-
    51; defends Scottsboro boys, 179; on
    socialism, 190; aids strikers, 271, 275,
    277, 280, 284; on race relations, 312;
    splits over coercion, 334, 342; mentioned,
    331, 341
Fellowship of Socialist Christians, description
    of activities, 93-95; on labor, 250; on
    strikes, 280; on race relations, 312
Fellowship of Southern Churchmen, descrip-
    tion of activities, 95-96, 248-50; on race
    relations, 312
Ferguson, Miriam A., 156, 161
Fey, Harold E., 102
Fincke, William, 252
Finney, Charles G., 5
Fish, Hamilton, Jr., 104, 198
Fisher, Frederick Bohn, 120, 174, 211-12
Fiske, Charles, 21, 124
Fiske, Chester, 278
Florida Baptist Witness, 57
Flynn, John T., 110
Ford, Henry, 24, 27, 246, 293-96
Foreign Missions Conference, 341
Foreign policy, 1919-1929, 317-32; 1930-
    1939, 333-44
Fortune, 344
Fosdick, Harry Emerson, defends YWCA,
    32; on social Christianity, 33-34; criticizes
    materialism, 35; voted outstanding, 45n;
    sketch of views, 103-4; condemns Klan,
    144-45; and DAR, 147; defends Bowie,
    148; on evolutionary theories, 156, 164;
    defends Mooney, 174, 176; and Scotts-
    boro boys, 179; upholds civil liberties,
    190, 197; aids workers, 252, 276-77; sup-
    ports League, 323; approves recognition
    of Russia, 341; on pacifism, 342, 344;
    mentioned, 25, 106
Foster, William Z., 96, 204
Franklin, Sam, 249
Friends, Society of. *See* Quakers
Friends of Democracy, 153
Friends of the Soil, 250

Frye, G. Shubert, 77
Fulcher, George S., 145
Fuller, A. T., 170
Fundamentalism, 20-21, 154-65

Galatsky, William, 98
Gallagher, Buell G., 80, 93
Gandhi, Mohandas K., 336
Garrison, William Lloyd, 9
Garrison, Winfred, 64
Gary, Elbert, 24, 26, 212, 215, 257
General War-Time Commission of the Churches, 182
Geneva Naval Disarmament Conference, 329-30
Gerrish, D. H. G., 262
Gerson, Simon W., 197
Gilbert, Charles K., defends Mooney, 174; and Scottsboro boys, 179; member of CAIL, 240; protests company unions, 252; aids strikers, 276; and miners, 277
Gilkey, Charles W., 45n, 171, 174
Gilkey, James Gordon, 34
Gilroy, William E., 81
Gitlow, Benjamin, 109, 204, 263
Gladden, George Washington, 13, 44, 236
Golden Rule Foundation, 296
Gompers, Samuel, 256
Gooden, Robert B., 240
Goodsell, Fred B., 80
Gordon, George A., 45n, 171
Gordon School of Theology, 158
Goslin, Omar, 160
Grace Community Church, 252, 271
Graham, Billy, 127
Grant, Madison, 293
Grant, Percy Stickney, 191
Gray, Arthur D., 175
Greater Boston Federation of Churches, 170
Green, Shirley, 237
Green, William, 284-85
Greensboro ministerial association, 268
Greer, Owen, 98, 124-25, 251
Gresham, Paul, 117
Grimké, Angelina, 9
Grimké, Sarah, 9
Gwaltney, L. L., 74

Haessler, Carl, 98
Hague, Frank, 149, 349
Hahn, Herman J., resigns from FOR, 97; enters politics, 102; defends Mooney, 176; upholds free speech, 196
Hall, Arthur C., 191
Hall, Cameron, 276-77
Hall, P. B., 34

Hammer and Pen, 240
Hampton, William J., 27
Hardin, Floyd, 191
Harding, Warren G., admired by churchmen, 27; and scandals, 46n
Hart, Merwin K., 124
Hartman, Lewis, O., 41, 72-73, 174
Harvey, George U., 197
Haynes, George E., 179
Heist, A. A., 174, 252
Helfenstein, Edward T., 171
Helm, Wilbur, 125
Henschen, Henry S., 125
Henson, Francis A., 92-93, 252
Herald and Presbyter, 18n, 41n, 140, 188, 257
Herald of Gospel Liberty, 173
Herring, Hubert C., member of CSA, 79-81; supports Roosevelt, 81; condemns Klan, 146; defends Sacco and Vanzetti, 171; and Mooney, 174, 176; and Scottsboro boys, 179; leader of Congregational social action, 236-37; member of AAEF, 252; aids strikers, 276, 278
Herron, George D., 13, 44
Hicks, Granville, 197
High, Stanley, on Russia, 42; on Communists, 110; on evolution, 165; defends Mooney, 174
Hill, E. P., 186
Hillis, Newell Dwight, 46n
Hogue, Richard W., 45, 83
Holmes, John Haynes, as pastor, 44; writes Roosevelt, 102; sketch of views, 105-6; on evolution, 165; defends Sacco and Vanzetti, 171; and Mooney, 174, 176-77; and Scottsboro boys, 179; opposes war, 191; upholds free speech, 198; supports strikers, 265, 269, 276, 281; on Treaty of Versailles, 318
Holt, Arthur E., 79-81, 236-37
Holt, Ivan Lee, 118
Home-Church-State Protective Association, 160
Home Missions Council, 220, 294, 296
Homiletic Review, 214, 219, 258, 322
Hood, George A., 92
Hoover, J. Edgar, 109
Hoover, Herbert, as Secretary of Commerce, 28; as candidate in 1928, 48-62 *passim*; supported in 1932, 96, 114, 120-22; as President, 63-127 *passim*
Hopkins, Samuel, 9
Hought, Lynn Harold, voted outstanding, 46n; supports Hoover, 120; condemns

Klan, 145; and DAR, 147; on evolution, 164; defends Mooney, 174

House Committee on Un-American Activities, 90, 111n, 198-99

Hughes, Charles Evans, 294, 325

Hughes, Edwin Holt, voted outstanding, 46n; opposes socialism, 118; condemns Klan, 145-46; supports League, 320

Hunter, Allan A., 174

Huntington, Frederic Dan, 240

Huston, Arthur, 181

Hutchinson, Paul, on profit motive, 64; supports Thomas, 102; on evolution, 165; defends Mooney, 174; member of CSAM, 251; on pacifism, 341

Ickes, Harold, 51

Iliff School of Theology, 271

Industrial Workers of the World, 180-82, 187

Industry, 211

Information Service, 38-39, 88, 135, 139, 172, 177, 179, 222, 263, 267, 271, 279, 304

Inman, Samuel Guy, 197

Interchurch World Movement, 36, 190, 211-15, 258

Interdenominational Fundamentalists, 157

International Labor Defense, 253

Interreligious Committee for Justice for Thomas J. Mooney, 174

Iron Age, 211

Isaacs, Stanley M., 197

Jackson, Donald L., 104n, 110

Jefferson, Charles E., voted outstanding, 46n; condemns Klan, 146; on evolution, 164; upholds free speech, 191; supports League, 323

Jenkins, Burris, 26, 342

Jenks, Jeremiah, 212

Jenny, Ray Freeman, 77

Jernagin, William H., 175

Johnson, Arnold, 79, 92, 277

Johnson, Charles S., 299, 307

Johnson, F. Ernest, Federal Council official, 46; discounts resolutions, 113; upholds free speech, 190-91; on steel strike, 212, 215

Johnson, James Weldon, 248

Johnson, Joseph, 164

Johnson, M. G., 45

Jones, Ashby, 146

Jones, David, 5

Jones, E. Stanley, 144, 292, 305

Jones, John Paul, 77

Jones, Paul, loses official status, 44; defends Sacco and Vanzetti, 171; opposes war, 191, 317; member of CSL, 239

Jones, Robert E., 305

Juvinall, A. V., 98

Keedy, Allen, 277

Kellogg, Frank, 327

Kelsey, George, 298

Kester, Howard, 248-50

King, Henry Churchill, 164

King, Herbert, 248

King, William P., 72

Kingdom, Frank, 102

Kingdom of God, Kingdom of Heaven, establishment in history, 3, 6, 13, 35, 64, 107, 154-55, 308, 346

Kirkpatrick, Blane, 124-25

Koo, T. Z., 300

Kornfeder, Joseph Zack, 109

Knebel, Spear, 276

Knickrehm, F. W., 266

Knudsen, Carl, 80

Ku Klux Klan, influence in election of 1928, 49-50, 62; attitude of churches toward, 137-46; and anti-Semitism, 293; mentioned, 60, 111, 349

Kundred, A. L., 159

Labor, 203-287 *passim*

Labor, 211

Lackland, George, 252

Ladd, William, 6

La Follette, Robert, 28, 45

La Follette, Robert., Jr., 274

Laidler, Harry W., 237

Lambeth Conference, 37, 238, 321

Landis, Benson Y., 237

Landon, Alfred M., 96, 121

Lapp, John A., 92

Laski, Harold J., 40

Lathrop, Charles N., 197, 241

Lathrop, John Howland, 171, 197-98

Lawrence, William, 164, 167, 171

Laws, Curtis, 142, 156

Layman's Religious Movement. *See* Methodist

Laymen, less socially conscious than clergy, 115

League for Independent Political Action, 102

League for Industrial Democracy, 253

League of Nations, 319-24, 334

League to Enforce Peace, 320

Lee, Hannah Hume, 236

Leete, Frederick, 146

Leinbach, Paul S., 86

Lemke, William, 96

Leonard, Adna, 124
Leslie, Kenneth, 90
Lewis, John L., 234, 270
Libby, Frederick, 331
Liberal theology, tenets of, 13
Lippmann, Walter, 35, 242
Literary Digest, 122
Living Church, 58n, 83-84, 141, 149, 167, 180, 239, 282, 323, 327
Lodge, Henry Cabot, 321
Loescher, Frank S., 298
London Naval Disarmament Conference, 329-30
Long, Cedric, 252, 260
Long, Huey, 150, 349
Los Angeles Church Federation, 175
Los Angeles Ministerial Association, 292
Lovejoy, Elijah, 9
Lowell, James Russell, 5-6
Loyalty oaths, 165-68
Luccock, Halford L., on Barton, 34; as editor, 73n; supports Thomas, 102; on evolution, 164-65; defends Sacco and Vanzetti, 171
Ludlow Amendment, 343
Lusk Committee, 189, 192
Lutheran, 58, 87, 141, 163, 214, 219, 243, 257, 259, 293, 295, 312, 323
Lutheran, United Church, on depression, 87; on labor, 243; on race relations, 312; supports League, 322
Lutherans, and early wars, 5
Lynch, Frederick, 322
Lynching, 10, 131-36

MacCabe, C. C., 25
McCall, Oswald W. S., 176
MacCallum, J. A., 342
McClure, James, 164
McConnell, Francis J., president of Federal Council, 46; voted outstanding, 46n; president of MFSS, 69; member of NRLF, 92; supports Thomas, 102; sketch of views, 104; condemns Klan, 145; and DAR, 147; defends Bowie, 148; on evolution, 164-65; defends Sacco and Vanzetti, 171; and Mooney, 174, 176; upholds civil liberties, 198; on strikes, 211, 226, 269, 276; on labor, 252, 277; supports recognition of Russia, 342; mentioned, 106
McCulloch, Frank W., 237
McDowell, John, 76, 191, 232
McDowell, William F., 46n
Macfarland, Charles S., Federal Council official, 46; defends Sacco and Vanzetti,

171; upholds free speech, 191; supports League, 323; and disarmament, 329
McGiffert, Charles S., 191
McGlothlin, William Joseph, 299
McGowan, R. A., 215
McGuire, U. M., 74, 102, 142
Machen, J. Gresham, 123, 156
Macintosh, Douglas Clyde, 336-37
Macleod, Alexander, 5
McMichael, Jack, 111n
McMurray, W. F., 145
Manning, William, opposes socialism, 118, 187; on CLID, 124, 240; defends academic freedom, 164; on collective security, 343
Manufacturers' Record, 211
Marlin, H. H., 234, 257, 294
Marsh, Daniel, 120
Marshall, Charles C., 60
Martin, Frank, 277
Martin, George A., 33
Martin, Homer, 252
Martin, T. T., 161
Massee, Jasper, 159
Masters, Victor I., 156-57
Materialism, of churches, 17-30, 34-35
Mather, Cotton, 9, 159
Mather, Increase, 159
Mathews, Shailer, defends YWCA, 32; on capitalism, 118; on evolution, 165; supports League, 323
Matthews, J. B., 97, 104n, 109
Matthews, Mark A., 46n, 272
Melhorn, Nathan, 87
Melish, John Howard, opposes loyalty oaths, 167; defends Sacco and Vanzetti, 171; and Scottsboro boys, 179; upholds free speech, 191; on Gerson, 198-99; aids strikers, 269, 276
Mellon, Andrew, 26, 28
"Memorial Day Massacre," 278-79
Mennonites, 4
Merriam, Charles W., 80
Merrill, William P., defends YWCA, 32; voted outstanding, 46n; upholds civil liberties, 190-91; supports League, 323
Messenger, 167, 195. See also *Reformed Church Messenger*
(Methodist) Conference of Methodist Laymen, 125
Methodist Episcopal Church, on economic justice, 36, 220; on Russia, 40-41; opposes Smith, 53-54; criticizes capitalism, 65-71; condemns lynching, 133-34; and secret societies, 144; on labor, 189, 208-10, 217-18, 223-27; upholds free speech,

190; opposes oriental exclusion, 292; on race relations, 300, 304-7; supports League, 320, 324; and World Court, 324; and Pact of Paris, 325-26

Methodist Episcopal Church, South, opposes Smith, 53-54; seeks social justice, 71; condemns lynching, 134; and masked societies, 144; on academic freedom, 165; on labor, 218, 223; on race relations, 306; supports League, 324; and World Court, 325; and Pact of Paris, 326

(Methodist) Epworth League, 306

Methodist Federation for Social Service, defends YWCA, 32; description of activities, 36, 68-71, 95; criticized, 42, 124-25; supports La Follette, 45; opposes loyalty oaths, 166; defends Sacco and Vanzetti, 170; and Mooney, 175; and Scottsboro boys, 179; on Centralia affair, 181; on political prisoners, 182; upholds civil liberties, 189; on labor, 226-27, 277; supports strikers, 258, 264-65, 267, 269, 280, 283; on anti-Semitism, 296; on race relations, 306; on foreign policy, 342

(Methodist) Laymen's Religious Movement, 69, 226

Methodist League Against Communism, Fascism, and Unpatriotic Pacifism, 124

(Methodist) National Council of Methodist Youth, criticizes capitalism, 68; defends Scottsboro boys, 178; and Communists, 197; aids strikers, 277; on race relations, 306

Methodist Protestant Church, 118

Methodist Recorder, 54

Methodist Review, 323

Methodists, and early wars, 4-7; on slavery, 8; on civil liberties, 32, 144, 166, 170, 175-76, 181-82, 197; on capitalism, 36, 66-68, 102, 113-14; on strikes, 271, 275, 281; on race relations, 292, 306

Metropolitan Association, 157

Mexican War, 5-6

Michigan Conference for the Protection of Civil Rights, 281

Michigan State Council of Churches, 281

Middletown ministerial association, 271

Mid-Southern Federation of Liberals, 268

Midwest Striking Miners Relief Fund, 277

Millar, A. C., 157

Miller, Spencer, 82, 241

Mills, Ernest Lyman, 40

Milton, George Fort, 52

Ministers Peace Committee, 340

Ministers' Union of America, 251

Missionaries, oppose oriental exclusion, 292

Missionary Voice, 54

Mollegen, Albert T., 175

Moody, David W., 77

Moody Bible Institute, 146

Mooney, Thomas J., and Billings, Warren K., 173-78

Moore, John M., opposes Smith, 53; on child labor amendment, 114-15; on evolution, 165; supports League, 320

Moral Welfare, 58, 310. See also *Social Progress*

Moravians, 324

Morgan, G. Campbell, 46n

Morrison, Charles Clayton, as editor, 39, 91, 108n, 246, 257, 327; supports Hoover, 58; supports Roosevelt, 121; criticizes Long, 150; and Silver Shirts, 152; defends Mooney, 174; and Scottsboro boys, 179; and Strachey, 197; on pacifism, 342, 344

Mott, John R., 292

Mouzon, Edwin D., 53, 145, 300

Mudge, Lewis S., 22, 235

Muhlenberg, Henry Augustus, 5

Mullins, E. Y., 156, 165, 323-24

Murray, Helen G., 198, 236

Murray, John G., 165

Muste, A. J., embraces trade unionism, 44; member of LIPA, 102; opposes war, 191; supports strikers, 211, 260, 276; leaves ministry, 252

Myers, James, Federal Council official, 46; opposes twelve-hour day, 215; member of CSA, 237; and AAEF, 252; aids strikers, 268-69, 276, 279

Myrdal, Gunnar, 298, 302

Myskens, John, 22

Nashville *Christian Advocate,* 19, 39, 41, 54, 72, 117, 140, 148, 163, 167, 173, 180, 194, 198, 225, 257, 269, 295, 307, 322

Nation, 211

National Association for the Promotion of Holiness, 157

National Association of Manufacturers, 211

National Bible Institute, 158

National Catholic Welfare Council, 181

National Church Committee on Mooney and Billings, 174

National Committee for Religion and Welfare Recovery, 296

National Committee on the Churches and World Peace, 327

National Committee to Aid Striking Miners Fighting Starvation, 277

National Conference of Christian Ministers and Laymen, 125
National Conference of Jews and Christians, 284, 294, 296
National Council for Prevention of War, 331, 341
National Federal Evangelical Committee, 157
National Founders' Association, 211
National Mooney-Billings Committee, 174
National Preaching Mission, 300
National Reform Association, 157
National Religion and Labor Foundation, description of activities, 91-93, 247-48; conducts poll, 102, 111, 253; defends Mooney, 175; on strikes, 280, 284
National Study Conference on the Church and World Peace, 292, 324
Negroes, 296-313. *See also* Lynching
Nelson, Claude, 252
Neo-orthodoxy, 21, 63-64, 97
Neutrality Acts, 343
New Bedford Council of Churches, 266
New Deal, generally supported, 63-112 *passim;* generally opposed, 113-27 *passim*
New Era Magazine, 259
New Republic, 35
New York Call, 211
New York *Christian Advocate,* 32, 41, 43, 54, 73, 139-40, 163, 172, 180, 188, 213, 226-27, 265, 269, 295, 307, 322, 328
New York Daily Worker, 104
New York Federation of Churches, 273
New York Tom Mooney Committee, 175
Newton, Joseph Fort, 46n, 191, 323
Nicholas, Elmer, 103
Niebuhr, Reinhold, on materialism, 35; member of FCSO, 46; on election of 1928, 51; on critical spirit within churches, 64; as editor, 90; member of FSC, 93-94, 250; member of UCCD, 95, 250; on non-violence, 97; member of CYC, 97; writes Roosevelt, 102; sketch of views, 106-9; defends Mooney, 174; and Gerson, 198; addresses churchmen, 248; on labor, 252, 277; aids strikers, 269, 276-77, 281, 283; on Pact of Paris, 327; on Manchurian invasion, 335; on armaments, 337; approves recognition of Russia, 342; supports collective security, 343; mentioned, 66, 346
Nightingale, Abram, 248
Nixon, Justin Wroe, 198, 272
Norris, George W., 51
Norris, J. Frank, 123, 155
North, Frank Mason, president of Federal Council, 46; helps found MFSS, 69; supports Hoover, 120; upholds civil liberties, 190; mentioned, 44
North Carolina Christian Advocate, 140
North Carolina Universalist Convention, 268
Northwestern Christian Advocate, 32-33, 41, 54, 73, 115n, 139, 152, 163, 167, 172-73, 177, 180, 187, 194, 213, 226, 269, 295, 307, 322, 327-28
Nuelsen, John L., 40
Nye Committee, 336-37

Ogburn, William, 52
Olds, Marshall, *Analysis of the Interchurch World Movement Report on the Steel Strike,* 212
Oriental exclusion, 291-93
Our American Dreyfus Case: A Challenge to California Justice, 174
Our Economic Life in the Light of Christian Ideals, 89
Owen, Robert Dale, 11
Owenby, Richard, 165
Oxford Conference on Church and State, 339
Oxnam, G. Bromley, 42, 104n, 342

Pacific Christian Advocate, 140
Pacifism, 4, 6-8, 44, 182-83, 330-32, 336-44
Pact of Paris, 325-27
Paddock, Robert L., 179
Page, Kirby, member of FCSO, 46; addresses NCMY, 60; on socialism, 64; as editor, 90; conducts poll, 101-2, 111, 337-38; sketch of views, 104-5; defends Mooney, 174; aids miners, 278; mentioned, 66, 106
Paine, Thomas, 11
Palmer, A. Mitchell, 186, 191
Palmer, Albert W., defends Mooney, 174; on CSA, 237; on steel strike, 278-79; on race relations, 311
Parker, Theodore, 5, 9, 13, 44
Parsons, Edward L., 82
Patton, Carl S., 164
Peabody, Endicott, 197
Peay, Austin, 156
Peel, Roy, 52
Peffer, Nathaniel, 237
Pelley, William Dudley, 151-52
Pendleton, Norman W., 265
People's Institute of Applied Religion, 106
Permanent Court for International Justice, 324-25
Philadelphia School of the Bible, 158
Philbrick, Herbert, 109

Pitt, Robert H., 56, 164
Pittsburgh Christian Advocate, 54
Pittsburgh Council of Churches, 258
Pittsburgh Ministerial Association, 32
Platt,, Ferry, 237
Poling, Daniel A., 58, 110
Poole, Frederick, 281
Pope, Liston, *Millhands and Preachers*, 206-8; 268
Porter, Paul, 90n
Poteat, Edwin McNeil, 146, 165
Poteat, Edwin McNeil, Jr., 122
Poteat, William Louis, 161
Potter, Henry Codman, 240
Pound, Roscoe, 146
Presbyterian, 157-58, 177-78
Presbyterian Advance, 39, 57, 77, 118, 163, 177, 180, 187, 193, 214, 257-59, 269, 310, 328
Presbyterian Banner, 43-44, 140, 163, 180, 215, 256-57, 282, 311, 323, 328
Presbyterian Church in the United States, opposes Smith, 57-58; on depression, 77; condemns lynching, 77; and mob violence, 144; on labor, 217, 231; on race relations, 299, 310; praises Pact of Paris, 326
Presbyterian Church in the United States of America, on smoking, 19-20; on church publicity, 22; urges economic justice, 37; opposes Smith, 57-58; criticizes capitalism, 75-77; condemns lynching, 133; and mob violence, 144; on evolution, 158; on Scottsboro boys, 178; upholds civil liberties, 199; on labor, 217, 231-35, 280; opposes oriental exclusion, 292; on race relations, 309-10; supports League, 321; and World Court, 325; and Pact of Paris, 326; divides over pacifism, 342
Presbyterian Fellowship for Social Action, description of activities, 77; on labor, 235, 280; on race relations, 310
Presbyterian Labor Temple, 234-35
Presbyterian Tribune, 77, 121, 149, 167, 177, 180, 234, 280, 310, 342
Presbyterians, and early wars, 4-7; on slavery, 8; criticize capitalism, 76; oppose loyalty oaths, 166; defend Scottsboro boys, 178; uphold free speech, 189, 196-97; oppose oriental exclusion, 292
Price, Orlo J., 198
Priddis, Alfred S., 263
Program Builder, 310
Prohibition, supported by churches, 18-19; issue in the election of 1928, 48-62 *passim*; issue in the election of 1932, 119-20

(Protestant Episcopal) American Church Institute for Negroes, 312
Protestant Episcopal Church, on social justice, 38; criticizes capitalism, 82-84; on CLID, 124; condemns lynching, 135; and secret societies, 143; on pacifism, 182; upholds free speech, 190; on labor, 218, 238-41; opposes oriental exclusion, 292; on race relations, 311-12; supports League, 321; and World Court, 325; and Pact of Paris, 326
(Protestant Episcopal) Church Association for the Advancement of the Interests of Labor, 38, 239-40
(Protestant Episcopal) Church Laymen's Association, 124
(Protestant Episcopal) Church League for Industrial Democracy, description of activities, 38, 82-84; supports La Follette, 45; criticized, 124; defends Scottsboro boys, 179; and political prisoners, 182; upholds civil liberties, 190; supports strikers, 263-65, 269, 277, 283-84; combats anti-Semitism, 296; mentioned, 95, 240
(Protestant Episcopal) Church Socialist League, 38, 190, 239
(Protestant) Episcopal Peace Fellowship, 341
(Protestant) Episcopal Theological School of Cambridge, 170
Protestant Episcopalians, and early wars, 5; uphold academic freedom, 165; on Sacco and Vanzetti, 170; on strikes, 268

Quakers, and war, 4-7, 331, 336; oppose slavery, 9; aid Russians, 40; on labor, 245, 269
Quarterly Review, 54

Race Relations, 9-10, 291-313
Radical Religion, 94, 337, 346
Rall, Harris F., 102, 164
Ramige, E. A., 283
Raskob, John J., 51
Raulston, John T., 156
Rauschenbusch, Walter, 3, 13, 44
Rauschenbusch Fellowship of Baptists, 74, 95
Reese, Frederick, 165
Reform movements, in nineteenth century, 10-11
Reformed Church in America, 218, 326
Reformed Church in the United States, and social justice, 38, 86; condemns lynching, 135; on labor, 244; opposes oriental exclusion, 292; supports League, 322, 324;

and World Court, 325; and Pact of Paris, 326

Reformed Church Leader, 141

Reformed Church Messenger, 39, 58, 60, 86-87, 123, 149, 152-53, 163, 173, 179, 187, 192-93, 214, 219, 244-45, 257, 295, 312, 323. See also *Messenger*

Reformed Presbyterian Church, 326

Reformed Presbyterians, 292

Reisner, Christian F., 23, 118, 343

Reissig, Herman F., 95

Religious Herald, 56, 74, 142, 164, 229

Religious Liberty Association, 157

Resolutions, unrepresentative nature of, 113-15

Rice, Merton S., 46n

Richards, C. K., 98

Riley, William Bell, 160-61

Robbins, Howard Chandler, 174, 176, 190

Robertson, H. M., 205

Rockefeller, Jr., John D., 25

Rocky Mountain News, 271

Rogers, Ward, 283

Roman Catholic Church, in Mexico, 6; in Caribbean and Pacific, 7; on Russia, 41, 341n; issue in election of 1928, 48-62 *passim;* on Father Coughlin, 149; co-operates in Centralia investigation, 181; and fascism, 195; cooperates in steel investigation, 215-16

Roosevelt, Franklin D., in election of 1932, 96, 119-21; in election of 1936, 91, 96, 121; in election of 1944, 121-22; mentioned, 63-127, 333-44 *passim*

Rose, James E., 299

Rotzel, Harold L., 252, 260

Roundy, Rodney W., 144

Roy, Ralph Lord, *Apostles of Discord,* 110, 153

Russia, 29, 40-44, 64-65, 70-71, 73-75, 77, 79, 81, 83-85, 104-5, 109-12, 118-19, 127, 341-42

Rustin, John, 175

Ryan, John A., 59

Ryland, Edwin P., 272

Sabbatarian movement, 10

Saco, Nicola, and Vanzetti, Bartolomeo, 169-73, 348

Sanford, L. C., 171, 176

Sansbury, Marvin O., 181

Sayre, John Nevin, 44, 174, 191

Scandals, in Harding administration, 46, 49

Scarlett, William, 171, 179

Schermerhorn, William David, 146

School-Bag Gospel League, 157

Schroeder, John C., 80

Scopes, John, trial of, 157n; mentioned, 154-168 *passim*

Scottsboro boys, 178-80, 349

Scottsboro Defense Committee, 179

Scudder, Vida, 83

Searle, Robert W., 102, 145, 179

Sears, John W., 103

Segregation. See Negroes

Shannon, Frederick F., 46n

Shelton, Arthur E., "The Methodist Church and Industrial Workers in the Southern Soft Coal Fields," 208-10

Shelton, Willard E., 84

Shepard, Sheldon, 175

Sherrill, Henry Knox, 167

Shipler, Guy Emery, 83, 174, 252

Shorter, Fred, 181

Shuler, Robert, 156, 160

Shultz, E. N., 248

Silver Shirt Legion of America, 151-53, 349

Simons, George Albert, 187

Simpson, William, 265

Slavery, 8-9

Smathers, Eugene, 248-50

Smith, Alfred E., 48-62 *passim*

Smith, Fred B., 174

Smith, Gerald Birney, 165

Smith, Gerald L. K., 150-52

Smith, Gerrit, 9

Smith, Hay Watson, 162

Smith, Henry Leiper, 197

Smith, Rembert Gilman, 124

Smith, William Austin, 44, 190-91

Social Action, 81, 237

"Social Creed of the Churches," 31-32, 35, 71, 89, 217, 220, 244, 266

Social Progress, 233-34, 310. See also *Moral Welfare*

Social Security Association, 253

Social Service (Questions) Bulletin, 70, 213

Socialism, opposed by churches, 17-30, 113-27 *passim;* interest in increases, 63-112 *passim*

Socialist Ministers' Fellowship, 98-99

Sockman, Ralph W., Methodist leader, 66; supports Hoover, 120; condemns Klan, 144; defends Bowie, 148; upholds civil liberties, 190-91; supports miners, 277

Sommerlotte, John, 86

Southern Baptist Trumpet, 57

Southern Churchman, 58n, 84, 141, 180, 193-94, 214, 239, 292, 300-1, 312, 323

Southern Tenant Farmers' Union, 106, 249-50

Spanish-American War, 7

Spaulding, F. Spencer, 239
Speer, Robert E., president of Federal Council, 46; voted outstanding, 46n; opposes oriental exclusion, 292; supports League, 323
Speers, Guthrie, 118
Spencer, Harry, 98
Sperry, Willard L., 171
Spofford, William B., leader of CLID, 83, 124; member of UCCD, 95, 250; defends Gerson, 198; protests company unions, 252; aids strikers, 263, 265, 269, 276-78
Stelzle, Charles, 44, 234
Stewardship, doctrine of, 12, 206
Stiles, Ezra, 9
Stires, Ernest M., 148
Stoddard, Lothrop, 293
Stone, John Timothy, 46n
Stone, Warren S., 204
Storey, Harold S., 191
Strachey, John, 197
Straton, John Roach, 145, 155-56, 160
Strikes, 1919-1920, 255-61; 1921-1929, 262-73; 1930-39, 274-87
Strong, Donald S., *Organized Anti-Semitism in America*, 151, 293
Strong, Josiah, 13, 44, 236
Strong, Sidney, 191
Sunday, William A., 46n, 186
Supreme Kingdom, 157
Swan, Alfred W., 80

Talbot, Nell, 52
Talbott, George H., 264
Tappan, Arthur, 9
Tappan, Lewis, 9
Tawney, R. H., 205
Taylor, Alva W., on Russia, 42; defends Mooney, 174; Disciples leader, 241; member of FSC, 249; aids strikers, 212, 252, 269, 276
Taylor, Graham, defends Sacco and Vanzetti, 171; supports League, 323; mentioned, 44, 236
Terrill, Katherine, 237
Textile workers, in Gastonia, 206-8
Thirkield, W. P., 145, 165
Thomas, Norman, enters politics, 44; in 1928 election, 45, 51, 58; in 1932 election, 91, 96, 99, 102-4, 119n, 120n; in 1936 election, 96; opposes war, 191; on strike, 263; mentioned, 184
Thoreau, Henry David, 5
Thrope, George L., 160
Thurston, Theodore P., 300

Tippy, Worth M., Federal Council official, 46; on Sacco and Vanzetti, 171; upholds free speech, 191; on strikes, 272, 276; supports League, 323
Tittle, Ernest Fremont, voted outstanding, 46n; urges non-violence, 98; supports Thomas, 102; on evolution, 164; opposes segregation, 305-6; favors recognition of Russia, 342; and pacifism, 342, 344
Toccoa Falls Institute, 158
Treaty of Versailles, 317-18
Troeltsch, Ernst, 204
Truett, George W., 46n, 321, 323
Trout, John M., 266
Tucker, Clarence Craig, 98, 251
Tucker, Irwin St. John, 191
Tucker, Robert J., 102

Union Theological Seminary, students of, 136, 170, 273
Unitarian, American Association, on social justice, 38, 84; opposes loyalty oaths, 166; on Sacco and Vanzetti, 170; on Scottsboro boys, 179; on political prisoners, 182; on labor, 218, 242-43; opposes oriental exclusion, 292; on race relations, 312; supports League, 321-22, 324; and World Court, 325; and Pact of Paris, 326
Unitarian Fellowship for Social Justice, on social order, 38; description of activities, 85, 243; opposes loyalty oaths, 167; defends Scottsboro boys, 179; and political prisoners, 189
Unitarian Laymen's League, 165
Unitarians, and early wars, 5-7; critical of capitalism, 85; condemn lynching, 135; oppose loyalty oaths, 167; and Sacco and Vanzetti, 170
United Brethren in Christ, urge economic justice, 38; condemn lynching, 135; on labor, 218, 245; oppose oriental exclusion, 292
United Christian Council for Democracy, 95, 250
United Presbyterian Church of North America, 321, 325
United Presbyterian, 28-29, 58, 193, 215, 234, 282, 294
Universalist Leader, 39, 141, 163, 192, 214, 219, 295, 312, 318, 323. See also *Christian Leader*
Universalists, urge economic justice, 38; defend Scottsboro boys, 179; on labor, 218, 245; support World Court, 328
Uphaus, Willard E., 92-93

Urmy, Ralph B., 145

Vance, James I., 46n
Van Dusen, Henry P., 342
Van Dyke, Henry, 57n, 164
Van Kirk, Walter, 327
Valentine, Foy, 298
Velde, Harold, 110
Victorious Life Testimony, 157
Villard, Oswald Garrison, 79
Vogler, Theodore K., 181
Vorse, Mary Heaton, 210

Wall Street Journal, 211
Walsh, Thomas J., 54, 56, 60, 211
Waltmire, W. B., member of CSAM, 98, 251; member of SMF, 98; defends Mooney, 175; on steel strike, 279
War, 4-8, 317-344
War Resisters League, 341
Ward, Harry F., on Russia, 42; leader of MFSS, 69; on Communism, 70-71; defends Sacco and Vanzetti, 171; and Mooney, 174; opposes war, 191; defends Strachey, 197; and Gerson, 198; member of UCCD, 250; supports collective security, 343; mentioned, 66
Washington Conference, 328-29
Watchman-Examiner, 55, 74, 117, 142, 149, 157, 173, 231, 259
Wayland, Francis, 9
Webb, Walter P., 205
Webber, Charles, member of UCCD, 95; member of FSC, 248; leaves ministry, 252; mediates strike, 275
Webber, E. F., 151
Weber, Max, 204
Weisbord, Albert, 263-64
Welch, Herbert, 69
Weld, Theodore Dwight, 9
Weld County ministerial association, 271
Wells, Howard M., 276
Wesley, John, 4, 69
Wesleyan Christian Advocate, 54, 140
Western Christian Advocate, 54, 140
Western Recorder, 27, 56, 74, 142, 157, 187, 229
Whitaker, Robert, enters politics, 102; defends Mooney, 176; opposes war, 191; and civil liberties, 198
White, Eliot, 276, 283
White, Herbert Judson, 187
White, Linden, 266
White, Walter, 179
White, William Allen, 147, 259
Willard, Lawson, 198

Willebrant, Mable Walker, 53n
Williams, Albert Rhys, 191
Williams, Charles D., 44, 83, 192
Williams, Claude, 106, 252
Williams, David Rhys, 176, 198
Williams, Howard, 102, 252
Williams, Michael, 59-60
Williams, Roger, 11, 187
Willkie, Wendell, 91
Wilson, Clarence True, 120n
Wilson, Frank T., 93
Wilson, J. Sitt, 98, 102, 251
Wilson, Lawrence, 198
Wilson, Luther B., 145
Wilson, Woodrow, 186, 231, 319-20
Winrod, Gerald, 152, 156, 160
Winrod's Flying Defenders, 156
Winsborough, W. C., 145
Winthrop, John, 3, 6
Wise, Stephen S., 92
Witness, 83
Woelfkin, Cornelius, 165, 192
Wolf, Horace, 215
Woodcock, Charles Edward, 191-92
Woolever, Harry Earl, 117-18
Woolley, Mary E., 146
Woolman, John, 9
Woltman, Frederick, 110
Word and Way, 56-57, 142, 157
Workers' Defense League, 253
World Alliance for International Friendship Through the Churches, 292, 319, 327, 329, 331, 334, 341-42
World Christian Fundamentals Association, 156
World Court, 334-35
World Disarmament Conference, 335
World Peace Fellowship of Christian Endeavor, 341
World Peace Foundation, 341
World Peaceways, 341
World's Sunday School Association, 292
World Tomorrow, 39, 43, 58, 90-91, 119, 139, 171-72, 177, 179, 192, 247, 258, 267, 269-70, 278, 295, 302-3, 312, 318, 322
Wright, Francis, 11

Yard, James M., member of CSAM, 98, 251; member of FSM, 98; supports Thomas, 102
Yates, Julian, 339
Young, Bradford, resigns from FOR, 97; defends Gerson, 198; aids strikers, 276, 283
Young, S. Edward, 191

Young Men's Christian Association, critical of capitalism, 90; defends Scottsboro boys, 179; adopts "Social Creed," 220; on strikes, 268; on union leaders, 285; opposes oriental exclusion, 292; combats anti-Semitism, 296; on peace, 341

Young Women's Christian Association, under attack, 31; critical of capitalism, 90; on child labor, 218; adopts "Social Creed," 220; on strikes, 267; opposes oriental exclusion, 292; combats anti-Semitism, 296; supports League, 324; and Pact of Paris, 326; and peace, 341

Zion's Herald, 35, 39, 40-41, 54, 69, 72-73, 121, 140, 149, 167, 172, 177, 194, 196, 199, 213, 225, 265, 267, 269, 275, 295, 306-7, 323